WORDS MADE FLESH

STUDIES IN RELIGION AND CULTURE
John D. Barbour and Gary L. Ebersole, Editors

Words Made Flesh

Formations of the Postsecular in British Romanticism

SEAN DEMPSEY

UNIVERSITY OF VIRGINIA PRESS
Charlottesville and London

University of Virginia Press
© 2022 by the Rector and Visitors of the University of Virginia
All rights reserved

First published 2022

9 8 7 6 5 4 3 2 1

Library of Congress Cataloging-in-Publication Data

Names: Dempsey, Sean, author.
Title: Words made flesh : formations of the postsecular in British Romanticism / Sean Dempsey.
Description: Charlottesville : University of Virginia Press, 2022. | Series: Studies in religion and culture | Includes bibliographical references and index.
Identifiers: LCCN 2022010760 (print) | LCCN 2022010761 (ebook) | ISBN 9780813948119 (hardcover) | ISBN 9780813948126 (paperback) | ISBN 9780813948133 (ebook)
Subjects: LCSH: Self in literature. | Civilization, Secular, in literature. | English literature—18th century—History and criticism. | Great Britain—Intellectual life—18th century. | Romanticism—Great Britain.
Classification: LCC PR448.S35 D46 2022 (print) | LCC PR448.S35 (ebook) | DDC 820.9/353—dc23/eng/20220406
LC record available at https://lccn.loc.gov/2022010760
LC ebook record available at https://lccn.loc.gov/2022010761

Cover art: Jerusalem: The Emanation of the Giant Albion, plate 76, William Blake. (Yale Center for British Art, Paul Mellon Collection, B1992.8.1[76])

For Lisa, Iris, and Ada

The eye it cannot chuse but see,
We cannot bid the ear be still;
Our bodies feel, where'er they be,
Against, or with our will.
—WILLIAM WORDSWORTH, "Expostulation and Reply"

CONTENTS

List of Abbreviations	xi
Introduction: Postsecular Formations	1

Part I. Approaches to the Postsecular

1. Theorizing the Postsecular	35

Part II. Mediating the Postsecular

2. Poetic Faith	87
3. Coleridge's Parable of Modernity	110
4. "To See as a God Sees": Keats and Cinematic Subjectivity	142

Part III. Anthropology of the Postsecular

5. "Awful Doubt": Shelley's Tragic Skepticism	181
6. "Open-Hearted": *Persuasion* and the Cultivation of Good Humor	217
Coda: Postsecular Romanticism	235
Acknowledgments	239
Notes	243
Bibliography	285
Index	313

* ABBREVIATIONS *

AR   Coleridge, Samuel Taylor. *Aids to Reflection.* Edited by John B. Beer. Princeton, NJ: Princeton University Press, 1993.

BL   Coleridge, Samuel Taylor. *Biographia Literaria, or, Biographical Sketches of My Literary Life and Opinions.* Edited by James Engell and Walter Jackson Bate. Princeton, NJ: Princeton University Press, 1983.

CL   Coleridge, Samuel Taylor. *Collected Letters.* Edited by Earl Leslie Griggs. Oxford: Clarendon, 1956.

CPP   Coleridge, Samuel Taylor. *Coleridge's Poetry and Prose: Authoritative Texts, Criticism.* Edited by Nicholas Halmi, Paul Magnuson, and Raimonda Modiano. New York: Norton, 2004.

CIS   Coleridge, Samuel Taylor. "Confessions of an Inquiring Spirit." In *Shorter Works and Fragments.* Edited by H. J. Jackson and J. R. de J. Jackson. Princeton, NJ: Princeton University Press, 1995.

CW   Coleridge, Samuel Taylor. *The Collected Works of Samuel Taylor Coleridge.* Princeton, NJ: Princeton University Press, 1969.

F   Keats, John. "The Fall of Hyperion: A Dream." In *John Keats: Complete Poems.* Edited by Jack Stillinger. Cambridge: Belknap Press of Harvard University Press, 1991.

H   Keats, John. "Hyperion: A Fragment." In *John Keats: Complete Poems.* Edited by Jack Stillinger. Cambridge: Belknap Press of Harvard University Press, 1991.

LJK   Keats, John. *The Letters of John Keats, 1814–1821.* Edited by Hyder Edward Rollins. 2 vols. Cambridge: Harvard University Press, 1958.

P   Wordsworth, William. *The Prelude, 1799, 1805, 1850*. Edited by Jonathan Wordsworth, M. H. Abrams, and Stephen Gill. New York: Norton, 1979. Citations are from the 1805 version unless otherwise noted.

PS   Austen, Jane. *Persuasion*. Edited by Janet M. Todd and Antje Blank. In *The Cambridge Edition of the Works of Jane Austen*. Cambridge: Cambridge University Press, 2006.

S   Shelley, Percy Bysshe. *Shelley's Poetry and Prose: Authoritative Texts, Criticism*. Edited by Donald H. Reiman and Neil Fraistat. New York: Norton, 2002.

T   Hume, David. *A Treatise of Human Nature*. Edited by David Fate Norton and Mary J. Norton. New York: Oxford University Press, 2007. All references to Hume's *Treatise* are cited as book number, section number, chapter number, and paragraph number.

WPP   Wordsworth, William. *Wordsworth's Poetry and Prose: Authoritative Texts, Criticism*. Edited by Nicholas Halmi. New York: Norton, 2014.

WORDS MADE FLESH

* INTRODUCTION *
# Postsecular Formations

In a sonnet written in the opening years of the nineteenth century, William Wordsworth laments that the "world is too much with us." He found the world's proximity to be "too much" in part because he felt the economics of "getting and spending" had disordered our relation to nature and to the traditional attachments of the heart. Because of this "we are out of tune" and the world "moves us not." In response to the deadening proximity of the modern economic world, Wordsworth cries out in the sonnet's final sestet:

> —Great God! I'd rather be
> A Pagan suckled in a creed outworn;
> So might I, standing on this pleasant lea,
> Have glimpses that would make me less forlorn;
> Have sight of Proteus coming from the sea;
> Or hear old Triton blow his wreathed horn. (9–14)

Wordsworth laments the loss of a sense of connection and intimacy with the world around him. He would rather suckle in a "creed outworn" because doing so might offer glimpses of an enchanted world, one that would make him less forlorn than the naked and heartless modern industrial society developing around him.

Although Wordsworth's use of "outworn" can, and has been, read as worn out, as in used up and outdated, outworn can also be read in the sense of a garment outworn (i.e., worn out in public). A "creed outworn" then does not necessarily mean a used up and outdated creed, the abandonment of which would be a mark of maturity. Rather, a creed outworn could mean an embodied performance of a felt convergence that we put on in public in order to become who we are. From this perspective, what a creed outworn offers is a way of seeing, which affects not only what we see but how we see ourselves, because the particular posture of attention one puts on makes all the difference in how the world is viewed and how we are viewed in it.

"The World Is Too Much with Us" tells us something of what it means to live in a secular age, where conceptions of belief shift, as Colin Jager has shown, from the word's original sense of a "passionate longing and relationship," which provided "a certain posture or orientation," to a sense of belief as a concept or construct that resides in one's thinking.[1] The reasons why this shift occurs are overdetermined.[2] Nevertheless, Philip Fisher suggests one consequence of this shift is that within modernity a "new geography of the self" is established as the sentiments rather than the passions become the basis for self-understanding.[3] The passions "favor a narrow band of concern," and "my world" only consists of what concerns me most directly (218). However, the passionate longing and orienting relationships that make up "my world" become problematic when "the world" is too much with us. Confronted with "the world" of getting and spending, of politics, media, and markets, "my world" can seem like nothing more than "a back-formation from the real world, that prior world which is objective and shared" (248). Secular modernity is predicated upon "the structure of a dispassionate world—the world, as we could call it, in contrast to my world, or your world" (246).

A secular age is often felt to be unhooked from the ordered cosmos, and there is a general sense that the relation of sacramentality, whereby the divine is made materially manifest in the world, has been broken. Disenchantment disturbs our experience of ourselves and our orientation in the world because it "disqualifies the dimension of emphatic experience in which sentient embodiment, the felt fact of aliveness" is registered.[4] Within secularity, a dissociation of sensibility sets in as the orienting significance of sensory encounters within everyday life is no longer felt as frequently or vibrantly as it once did, as older sacramental orderings of the world break down or at least become far less compelling and as individuals feel themselves becoming more and more alienated from the natural and social worlds around them.[5]

Nevertheless, within modernity, "the arts have become the bearers of our now delegitimated capacity for significant sensory encounter."[6] As Eric Santner has suggested, part of the value of art lies in its presentation of "emphatic experience," because it is through such experience that we feel ourselves remaining "grounded in the sentience we share with the animal kingdom," thereby reassuring ourselves that we "are not Fichtean idealists whose conceptual schemes spin freely in a frictionless universe positing but never touching the 'not I.'"[7] It is through emphatic experience that we are in touch with the world around us. One task of the arts is to rescue embodied experience from the sense of alienation that paradoxically is too often experienced in a world that is too much with us.

Romanticism provides a useful field guide to the new geography of the self ushered in by secular modernity, and studying some of the essential documents of Romanticism can clarify the parameters of secularity while pointing toward potential postsecular futures. If secularism presupposes a particular set of habits and practices, or what Saba Mahmood has called "affective commitments," then a postsecular approach should seek to explore embodied practices and dispositions that do not necessarily conform to the conceptual coordinates and biopolitics of the European Enlightenment.[8] Jürgen Habermas claims that what makes a postsecular society different from a secular one is that it has undergone a "change in consciousness" about its own secularity.[9] To be postsecular is to participate in a situation where the familiar narratives of secularization are increasingly challenged. To be postsecular is to give up seeing the secular simply as an uncovering of what has been there all along and to recognize instead that with secularity comes the establishment of a new worldview or framework. The secular is not simply what is left over after the subtraction stories of secularization have run their course. Furthermore, secularity offers a framework that does not necessarily provide the only or even the best guide for how to live one's life.

Secularization has often been understood as the process whereby a generic rational religion or a generic reason was extracted from the Judeo-Christian traditions and made to underwrite a public sphere of rational debate, while all confessional religious and denominational disputes were sequestered to a private realm. The problem with this reading of secularization is the underlying assumption that there is some universal conception of rational religion, justice, human rights, or natural disposition at the root of human experience that everyone can agree on. It is precisely the desire to reveal this naked truth about ourselves that motivates those cultural critics who seek to strip away and unmask all ideologies, religious or otherwise. Increasingly this reading of secularization seems naïve. A postsecular perspective, in contrast, may be better equipped to recognize the value of those sentimental procedures whereby one's view of the world is achieved only after initial sense impressions are processed by, and mediated through, some form of sensibility.[10] If one can alter that sensibility, then one's worldview and even one's perceptual view of the world will differ.

A key interest of *Words Made Flesh* is in disclosing the ways in which central documents of British Romanticism, particularly those by Samuel Taylor Coleridge, John Keats, Percy Shelley, and Jane Austen, are invested in opening and altering channels of affective experience that are both infrasensible and suprasensible: both beneath and beyond the sensibly buffered subjectivity that is often felt to be the default experience of everyday life in a secular age. Part of the power and pleasure of Romantic writing is in how it generates works that can disarticulate and rearticulate normative ways of seeing. By doing so these works call attention to how the postures of attention we typically occupy can be altered. It is the posture of attention that one decides to take that ultimately determines what is legible in any given partition of the sensible. By approaching Romanticism in this way, *Words Made Flesh* argues that a model of a mediated soul emerges within Romanticism, which has broad applicability not only for understanding the work of Romanticism but also for clarifying more generally what it means to study literature and religion in a postsecular age.

Secularity, Second Nature, and the Soul

Before exploring further what I mean by a mediated soul, and how Romanticism more generally can help us move toward an understanding of the postsecular, I want to first acknowledge the foundational influence Charles Taylor's *A Secular Age* (2007) has had on subsequent thinkers within secular and postsecular studies. Taylor defines the secular in three basic ways: (1) in terms of public spaces or spheres that "have been allegedly emptied of God, or of any reference to ultimate reality"; (2) as the decline of religious practice and belief; and (3) as a shift in the "whole context of understanding in which our moral, spiritual or religious experience and search takes place."[11] His book offers a detailed and compelling argument for how the phenomenological experience of subjectivity for both the believer and the nonbeliever shifts radically during the course of the last five centuries: from a porous to a buffered sense of self. For a porous self, "the source of its most powerful and important emotions are outside the 'mind'; or better put, the very notion that there is a clear boundary, allowing us to define an inner base area, grounded in which we can disengage from the rest, has no sense" (38). The premodern world is filled with porous selves who experience their environment as teeming with "charged" objects, extrahuman powers, as well as political and religious dynamics that could affect human beings in deep and sustaining ways. However, in this earlier dispensation there was no easy defense against such influences precisely because the boundary between inside and outside was so porous. The formation of the buffered self within modernity lifts human experience up out of this fearful exposure to charged forces that can potentially control or harm us and into a mind-centered view of the world in which ideally the individual has sufficient agency to master the meaning of his or her surroundings.[12]

It is this buffered self, with its clear border between inside and outside, that Taylor sees as providing the basis for modern subjectivity. A radical reflexivity develops, which recognizes a boundary between inside and outside, so that the things outside don't necessarily affect the real "me" residing behind the buffer of my self-enclosure. Nevertheless, although there are clear advantages to this new constitution of subjectivity, modern agency comes at the cost of a feeling of alienation (as well as a tendency toward exploitation), and so within modernity there is a nostalgia for a sense of lost porousness. In this way, feelings of porousness become a potential source of pleasure rather than fear. The buffered self may even require occasions when a sense of porousness is brought into play and where for a moment at least there is the pleasurable oscillation of losing and finding oneself. One challenge for the buffered self, therefore, is discovering new or recovering old avenues of access to the feeling of fullness previously enjoyed by the porous self (at least potentially and perhaps only by the privileged few).

Taylor in effect treats secularization as a functional problem. During the process of secularization a blockage or break occurs in the channels of access to a feeling of fullness—to the spontaneous overflow of powerful feelings traditionally regulated through religious ritual and praxis. Secularization is seen as the process in which "we have moved from a world in which the place of fullness was understood as unproblematically outside of or 'beyond' human life, to a conflicted age in which this construal is challenged by others which place it (in a wide range of different ways) 'within' human life."[13] Prior to secularization God's presence in the world was a given. However, with the shift toward notions of nature as an immanent and rational domain, and through the transformation of the social, economic, and political organization of society, there is a challenge within modernity to traditional avenues of access to "the place of fullness." The question becomes how one should best respond to this investiture crisis experienced in secularity.

Although the overall argument of *A Secular Age* remains compelling, one way *Words Made Flesh* differs from Taylor's account is by demonstrating how postsecular subjectivity is better understood as being neither porous nor buffered but as instead incorporating two layers: the layer of the actual or material body and the layer of a habitual body that has become second nature. One implication of my approach is that the shift Taylor sees within modernity from a porous to a buffered form of subjectivity was always already a matter of habits and their alteration. Here I am influenced by the work of the French phenomenologist Maurice Merleau-Ponty and his interpreters. Merleau-Ponty calls this mediating form of sensibility, which is informed by habit, the "body schema." The body schema I put on or adopt makes up that part of myself at the core of my being that does not think to think of itself, that part of myself that has become second nature. It consists of "a flexible, plastic, systemic form of distributed agency" and "involves an extraintentional operation carried out prior to or outside of intentional awareness."[14] The body schema taps into what William Connolly calls the infrasensible: those thought-imbued intensities (or sentiments) moving beneath and through consciousness and reflective judgment.[15] Our grammar of assent is embodied and preformed through the postures of attention our body schemas put on.

If one can alter these underlying sensibilities, or body schemas, which have become second nature, then one's worldview and even one's perceptual view of the world will look different. Such alteration can occur through the acquisition and interruption of habits, because it is through habits that "the body both gains new significations, new meanings, and restructures its world and itself."[16] Since it is through our body that we inhabit the world, Merleau-Ponty suggests that to change our habits is to appropriate "fresh instruments" with which to express "our power of dilating our being-in-the-world."[17] Habits are significant politically, religiously, and poetically because "only at the depth of habit is radical change effected, where unconscious strata of culture are built into social routines as bodily disposition."[18] Habit is lodged in the "body as mediator of a world," and changes in habits result in the rearrangement and renewal of one's body schema, which is itself the "law of [the body's] constitution."[19] Poets are the "unacknowledged legislators of the world," as Percy Shelley puts it at the end of "A Defense of Poetry," precisely to the extent they can amend or revise this constitution.

In *Bodies in Code* (2006), Mark Hansen suggestively argues that the disclosive power of the body schema is an "essentially technical power," one that cannot simply be "dissociated from or thought independently of its concrete technical support" and that in the end, "emerges only through the technology that makes it possible in the first place."[20] To illustrate this point he recalls Merleau-Ponty's discussion of the blind man's stick, which offers a clear example of how a body schema can be profoundly altered by technology. For the blind man, habit could do the work of reason because his stick "ceased to be an object for him, and is no longer perceived for itself: its point has become an area of sensitivity, extending the scope and active radius of touch, and providing a parallel to sight." In this way, "to get used to a hat, a car or a stick is to be transplanted into them, or conversely, to convert them into the bulk of our own body."[21] For the blind man, his stick functions as a technical or mediating element that can seamlessly integrate with and thus extend the constitution of his body schema. Once the use of such a prosthesis is incorporated into bodily habit, then it is no longer an object that needs to be thought about but becomes instead an extension of how the blind man's potentiality is realized.

The blind man's stick is a technological extension of the blind man's body schema, which profoundly affects his ability to inhabit the environment he finds himself in. Other forms of mediation can function in similar ways, which is one reason why my book is so interested in what happens when words are made flesh. Part of the value of both religion and literature is that they provide opportunities for participants to engage in "new technical environments," which, as Hansen argues, "afford nothing less than an opportunity to suspend habitual causal patterns and, subsequently, to forge new patterns through the medium of embodiment."[22] Literature is one medium through which these more involved forms of sensibility can be modeled, staged, and performed. The disruption of habitual cause and effect couplings and the introduction of new patterns of becoming is made possible by the way an experimental poetics affects the medium of embodiment. Attentive readers are those who can engage with the "the sequence of particulars that enter this dance," and this act of giving an account reorients their postures of attention by giving a greater sense of agency over the forms of embodiment in which they participate.[23] How and why this should be the case are questions this book seeks to address.

Merleau-Ponty's work also helps clarify what I mean by a mediated soul. He argues that there are three orders of signification to the life-world (*Lebenswelt*) we inhabit: the physical, the living, and the mental. Each of these orders or aspects function as different dimensions of being, different forms of embodiment. The first order is the domain of "physiochemistry," which consists of the physical dimension in which the body is best understood as a "mass of chemical components in interaction."[24] The second order is that of the "animality" of living bodies, which "persist as living bodies in a constant state of dynamic interaction with their environment."[25] The third order is the human order, which generates the mind, the social, and culture. Each of these orders is a manifestation of a relationship of "founding" (*Fundierung*), wherein the higher order is founded upon the lower order so that the lower grounds or acts as a "pedestal" for the higher but in such a way that the lower "cannot disappear without resulting in the abolition of the 'founded' elements" (15). Such a founding is thus a kind of double relationship that holds together two elements: "both a kind of transcendence, a difference between the orders, and a fundamental relation between them" (14). Transcendence here does not mean a leaving behind but a taking up in a new way—a "recentering ... around a new pole."[26] In this way, "the higher reveals the meaning of the lower as the 'soul' of the 'body' of the lower."[27] For Merleau-Ponty, each sublimation (*Aufhebung*) of the previous order "is soul with respect to the preceding one, body with respect to the following one. . . . The body is the acquired dialectical soil upon which a higher 'formation' is accomplished, and the soul is the meaning which is then established."[28]

In Merleau-Ponty's model, the human mind, or soul, "'retakes' or 'recaptures' the corporeal existence of previous orders and uses them for a symbolic order."[29] Here we are very close to Wordsworth's description in the last stanza of *The Prelude*, which suggests how Wordsworth and his fellow "Prophets of Nature," can teach us how "the mind of man becomes / A thousand times more beautiful than the earth / On which he dwells, above this frame of things [. . .] In beauty exalted, as it is itself / Of substance and of fabric more divine."[30] Clearly, Merleau-Ponty's phenomenology offers insight into what Wordsworth means here and in his more general efforts to find "lodged" within certain peak experiences of Nature, "The soul, the imagination of the whole" (*P*, 13:64–65). Nevertheless, thinking about Romanticism more generally can help us take Merleau-Ponty's model one step further. In addition to the three orders of corporeality that Merleau-Ponty emphasizes—the physiochemical, the animal, and the mental—I add a fourth, the mediated.

One reason for doing so is suggested by Ralf Haekel, at the end of his book *The Soul in British Romanticism* (2014), but in order to make sense of this suggestion his work first needs to be situated within a broader context. Throughout his book, Haekel argues that the philosophic, scientific, and cultural shifts in understanding about what is meant by the soul taking place around 1800 contribute to the emergence of Romanticism as a form of literature "based on the author as originator and sole source of the text's meaning."[31] His book extends and builds upon previous overviews of the shifting concepts and theories of the soul from their Greek and Hebrew origins onwards, including works such as Paul MacDonald's *History of the Concept of Mind,* James Crabbe's edited collection *From Soul to Self,* John Yolton's *Thinking Matter,* and Raymond Martin and John Barresi's *The Rise and Fall of Soul and Self.*[32] Although I will not retrace the genealogies of soul outlined in these previous books, I do want to briefly highlight a few of the metaphoric schemas that have oriented various notions of the soul throughout history, since these underlying "metaphors we live by" will return in a variety of guises throughout this book.[33]

The two most influential figures in these genealogies are Plato and Aristotle. For Plato, the soul is tied more to the realm of ideas than to the material world, and this is why he has Socrates state in the *Phaedo,* "The soul is like the divine and the body like the mortal" (80a). Plato suggests that through the soul it becomes possible to achieve anamnesis or the remembrance of one's immortal existence before birth, an idea that Wordsworth takes up in his "Ode: Intimations of Immortality." For my purposes, however, the aspect of Plato's conception of the soul most resonate for my current argument is his description of the soul as a chariot in the *Phaedrus.* Here, he delineates a tripartite model of the soul: "We will liken the soul to the composite nature of a pair of winged horses and a charioteer. Now the horses and charioteers of the gods are all good and of good descent, but those of other races are mixed; and first the charioteer of the human soul drives a pair, and secondly one of the horses is noble and of noble breed, but the other quite the opposite in breed and character. Therefore in our case the driving is necessarily difficult and troublesome" (*Phaedrus* 246a-b). This idea that the soul takes the form of a vehicular consciousness, which moves by both tapping into and reigning in the driving forces of both reason and the passions, provides a model that will reappear repeatedly under various guises in the pages ahead.

In contrast to Plato, Aristotle was much more of a materialist and claimed the soul could not be separated from the body. Rather than being the link to the ideal or the divine, for Aristotle the soul is the actuality (*entelecheia*) of the body's potentiality. Not unlike Merleau-Ponty's model, Aristotle distinguished between various enfolding functions or faculties of the soul, which account for the different categories of living beings. So whereas plants have a nutritive faculty and animals have both a vegetative and a sensitive soul, human beings have both of these while also adding a rational soul with the capacity for thought. As Haekel notes, this notion of the rational soul "is particularly important, because in the eighteenth and early nineteenth centuries the soul is gradually reduced to this faculty alone."[34]

In addition to these two foundational views of the soul, I want to highlight two other conceptions that developed out of these earlier models. The first is a formulation from Marsilio Ficino, an Italian scholar, Catholic priest, and influential reviver of Neoplatonism within the early Italian renaissance. In *Platonic Theology* (1482), Ficino describes the soul as playing a central role in the mediation between the material world and a transcendent and idealized world. He understands the soul to be a mirror that serves as the mediating link between as above and so below, so that "between the things that are purely eternal and those that are purely temporal is soul, a bond as it were linking the two."[35] As we shall see, Coleridge will take up this notion of the soul as a medium for reflection and he'll identify the soul itself as an organ of spiritual or supersensuous perception. In his view, it is through this reflective capacity that the soul possesses the ability to modify and become one with ideas, thereby connecting itself to both the natural and supernatural worlds.

Another model of the soul that will have particular relevance for my argument descends more clearly from the Aristotelian line. This is the notion of the soul as a sensorium, which emerges out of the work of the Cambridge Platonist Henry More but is subsequently developed by a range of thinkers. Erasmus Darwin, for instance, uses the term when he tries to understand how simple and complex ideas are produced in the mind in response to sense experience. Although Darwin is working within the tradition of British empiricism and is developing a materialist psychology, in the course of his analysis of what happens when we try to make sense of sense experience, he shifts from a purely mechanistic account to one that accepts the significance of what he calls the "sensorium," a word that for him "is designed to express not only the medullary part of the brain, spinal marrow, nerves, organs of sense, and of the muscle; but also at the same time that living principle, or spirit of animation, which resides throughout the body."[36] I return to this idea of the sensorium in discussions of James Chandler's *An Archaeology of Sympathy* (2013) later in this introduction and again in chapter 1, but in anticipation I'll note here that this idea of the soul as a sensorium or spirit of animation was taken up by writers like Laurence Sterne to help explain how the novel could emerge as a medium in which a vehicular consciousness could be taken on a sentimental journey.

Nevertheless, whatever value these previous models of the soul may hold, through Enlightenment critique during the long eighteenth century, the idea that the soul had an immortal aspect that went to heaven was challenged, and a mechanistic and narrowed view of life began to become dominant. In James Engell's reading, as the soul was "stripped of its function as the vehicle of immortality and the object of doctrinal judgment—then mind and soul merge, or at least overlap, as a total concept of the individual self or psyche."[37] Countless authors throughout the eighteenth century continued to be interested in the soul as an object of psychological, emotional, religious, and moral analysis, but the domain of the soul became increasingly limited and for many was primarily connected with the idea of the imagination. Although changing notions of a vital force or "soul" were a key concern bridging eighteenth-century philosophy and science, the concept of the soul was no longer understood in purely theological terms and now potentially included and overlapped with "whatever is meant by mind, spirit, life, self, self-consciousness, and identity."[38] Of course, etymologically this overlap makes sense since the English term "soul" is used to translate the Greek term *psychê*, as well as the Latin terms *animus* and *anima*, and for Greek philosophy *psychê* originally meant something along the lines of "human life-perception-force."[39] Nevertheless, Roy Porter suggests that it is these developments that ultimately lead to the "death of the soul" within modern discourse, that are foundational for "our contemporary Western secular sense of identity."[40]

Significantly, however, and as Haekel's book highlights, Romanticism emerges during this key moment of transition in part as a result of the realization that "a self needs a narrative and a medium to come into existence at all." In other words, the soul does not exist "on the basis of God's creation but it is the result of a narrative formation."[41] Both body and language can thus be understood as alternative "forms of media which refer to the immaterial soul and at the same time are radically distinct from and even opposed to it" (176). Moreover, Haekel suggests that within Romanticism one finds "traces of the transition of the soul from the human to the textual body" (132). It is this transition that forms the basis of the mediated soul.

In his own analysis, Haekel finds a paradox in this transformation of the notion of a soul "from an anthropological to a medial phenomenon," which is rooted in the fact that the soul can be "contained in the medium of poetry only through its very absence" (214). One consequence of this paradox is that whenever the soul becomes the focus of a poem, the form of the poem is itself affected or troped, resulting in a tendency toward literary self-reflexivity.[42] Poems concerned with the soul, in other words, tend to become poems about poetry, ultimately referring "not to the speaker but to the poem itself, its artificiality and materiality."[43] In Haekel's reading, within literary history, this emphasis on reflexivity, artificiality, and materiality, ultimately results in literary modernism, which should be understood not as "the opposite of Romanticism but rather its logical consequence and part of the Romantic project as it negotiates, transforms, appropriates and eventually abandons the classical concept of the soul" (215).

Although Haekel's suggestions as to what emerges out of the paradox or irony at the heart of Romantic self-reflexivity are compelling, in a sense my own book starts where his ends by suggesting that there is a different and potentially more postsecular path out of Romanticism and its realization that "the medial condition of the soul, its reliance on a material carrier, is the very prerequisite of its coming into existence in the first place" (198). One way of conceptualizing this path forward is by looking backward because, as Haekel points out in his book's last chapter, Eric Havelock, in *Preface to Plato* (1963), argued that "the origin of the soul as the definition of individual selfhood is the consequence of the invention of writing" (199). Havelock bases his theory, in part, on the tenth book of *The Republic*, the book in which Plato banishes the poets from his ideal state. What Plato is banishing is specifically the rhapsode or oral poet, the one whose "mind necessarily merges with what he is to remember." Such poets represented a system of orality "in which an autonomous self with an individual psyche could not exist" (199). The rhapsode must be banished in order to make room for writing, the medial technology that enables what Havelock calls the "separation of the knower from the known."[44] In the rhapsodic model of Greek culture the "over-all body of experience ... is incorporated in a rhythmic narrative or set of narratives" which are memorized and subject to recall (199). According to Havelock, "the doctrine of the autonomous psyche is the counterpart of the rejection of the oral culture." The psyche which "slowly asserts itself in independence of the poetic performance and the poetised tradition had to be the reflective, thoughtful, critical psyche, or it could be nothing" (200). It is only by breaking the spell of oral repetition that the soul has a room of its own from which to develop and become an autonomous agency.

Havelock argues that in this way the doctrine of the autonomous psyche is the counterpart of the rejection of the oral culture. The mind or soul can become the basis for personal identity "only by externalizing its contents." [45] Thus the immaterial soul as the essence of selfhood always depends on the prosthesis of a material medium, although the body that it relies on may be at least as much the virtual body of written language as it is the human body or the processes of memory. It is this notion of the mediated soul, which according to Havelock was always already there within the earliest conceptions of the soul within Greek philosophy, that I want to add to the three aspects of corporeality delineated in Merleau-Ponty's phenomenology.[46]

Cinematic Empiricism and the Mediated Soul

If the Enlightenment is the effort to think in the clear light of reason, then Romanticism deals with the problematic (and at times triumphant) return of the infrasensible, which includes those affects, intensities, and body schemas previously channeled and shaped by religious praxis. Romanticism functions as a form of sentimental enlightenment, one that attempts to overturn overly rationalist understandings of the relationship between mind and body and recognizes that the reordering of affects must accompany rational enlightenment if it is not to become monstrous. A (Romantic) *poiesis* that experiments with sentiments and sympathy is still significant for our current moment, because if we are to face the numerous ecological, political, and ethical crises we are currently confronting, then we will need to extend our networks of regard not only across the spectrum of people now living but also intergenerationally and beyond the human.

Romanticism can affect our sense of self because it participates in new technical environments that, as Hansen suggested, "afford nothing less than an opportunity to suspend habitual causal patterns and, subsequently, to forge new patterns through the medium of embodiment." [47] Through poetry new forms of sensibility can be modeled, staged, and performed. Attentive readers are those who can engage with this sequence of particulars, and this act of giving an account orients their postures of attention and can offer a greater sense of agency over the forms of embodiment in which they participate. One of the benefits of poetry, literature, Scripture, and print technology more generally, is that, as Henri Bergson suggests, through these mediums "habits of mind acquired by individuals in the course of centuries can have become hereditary, modifying nature and giving a new mentality to the species."[48] In this way the signifying stress of previous postures of attention, or body schemas, can be broadcast widely and find fertile ground in those willing to put on its fictions. This is advantageous because such a "fiction, if its image is vivid and insistent, may indeed masquerade as perception and in that way prevent or modify action" (109).

Such "structures of feeling," to invoke Raymond Williams's familiar phrase, are embedded in and transmit a specific matrix of "particular linkages, particular emphases and suppressions, and in what are often its most recognizable forms, particular deep staring-points and conclusions."[49] Postures of attention can be transferred through the medium of poetry each time a certain force, disposition, rhythm, ratio of motion to rest, morphic resonance, or structure of feeling is successfully rebroadcast from a signal source and received by a receptive other. This book is interested in exploring both how these processes of mediation and embodiment work and in delineating what becomes possible once we better understand how words can be made flesh.

Although Romanticism has often been read as being best understood in the wake of the German Idealism of Kant, Fichte, Schelling, and Hegel, a number of scholars have recognized that both the foundations and implications of British Romanticism become clearer when the philosophic traditions surrounding British empiricism are emphasized over those of German Idealism.[50] A crucial difference between the two models is that unlike the German Idealism that influenced critics like M. H. Abrams, which presented a bifurcated "system of subject and object, ego and non-ego, the human mind or consciousness and its transactions with nature,"[51] the empiricist English ground I advocate for is based on an idea of the self that is always already implicated in a system or network of affects. This is one key way my reading of Romanticism diverges from Haekel's account in *The Soul in British Romanticism*. Although I agree with his overall analysis that "between 1800 and 1820 there occurs a paradigm shift within the system of literature—a transition from a proposed immediacy of poetry to a keen awareness of its medial condition," I diverge from his emphasis on reading Romanticism as primarily a form of literature "based on the author as originator and sole source of the text's meaning."[52]

One clear indication of this divergence is to notice our relative positions to David Hume. For Haekel, Hume effectively deconstructs the eighteenth-century notion of selfhood, dissociating what had appeared to be a sensibility constructed from continuous impressions into a stream of discrete and transient sensations. As Hume puts it, "If any impression gives rise to the idea of self, that impression must continue invariably the same, through the whole course of our lives; since self is supposed to exist after that manner. But there is no impression constant and invariable. Pain and pleasure, grief and joy, passions and sensations succeed each other, and never all exist at the same time. It cannot therefore be from any of these impressions, or from any other, that the idea of self is derived; and consequently there is no such idea" (T, 1.4.6.2). For understandable reasons, in Haekel's reading, this deconstruction of identity is at odds with the notion of the individual soul as an autonomous authority. Nevertheless, I find Hume to be a central figure in my project of understanding what it means to have a mediated soul.

Rather than defining the central problem of Romanticism as being rooted in a skeptical separation of subject and object, wherein an autonomous yet isolated buffered subjectivity is positioned in contrast to an other whose judgment must be faced, the form of empiricism I explore, which is rooted in the work of Hume and his interpreters, suggests that "beneath the self who acts and speaks, who learns and remembers, beneath the self to whom one might have otherwise ascribed the sole capacity to contract a habit swarms a multitude of contractile powers, a whole field of contemplative selves."[53] One of Hume's interpreters, Gilles Deleuze, claims that we can speak of our self only in "virtue of these thousands of little witnesses which contemplate within us."[54] We are "not in the world, we become with the world; we become by contemplating it."[55] As I will describe more fully in the next chapter, what the cinematic empiricism I find in Hume and his interpreters clarifies is how a mediated or contemplative soul is formed when our imagination contracts the series of punctual impressions of the world we are exposed to and strings or weaves these impressions together into a montage or (cinematic) film.[56]

By drawing upon resources from affect theory and media studies, as well as upon a model of cinematic subjectivity that can be developed out of the work of Hume and his interpreters, *Words Made Flesh* details how Romantic thinkers and writers provide both formal and conceptual resources that can help us move beyond the political and ethical limits of the buffered subjectivities that Taylor and others have found to be so dominant within a secular age. By approaching Romanticism in this way, I diverge from an old but still commonly told story that Romanticism emerged from an epistemological crisis, which resulted after Hume pushed empiricism to a skeptical "shipwreck," and after Immanuel Kant had established that there was no direct access to things in themselves and all that we actually possessed were ideas about these things. The Romantic response to this crisis, according to M. H. Abrams and many other critics, was to attempt to "join together the 'subject' and 'object' that modern intellection had put asunder."[57] Or conversely, what Romanticism had to come to realize was, as Paul de Man would have it, that they had to accept the "painful knowledge" that there was no way to heal or transcend this fundamental breach.[58] My sense of Romanticism suggests a different trajectory.

The mediated or contemplative soul, as I understand it, has a quality not of being one with all things but of being a particular thing—an intimate aspect of self that is in some way folded over and made personal. Deleuze suggests that the "contemplative soul" is what "has folds and is full of folds."[59] The soul is folded in the sense that is formed when a single surface is folded into two layers: the layer of the actual body and the layer of a body of habits that have become second nature. If the soul is an "organ with a contractile power," then "a soul must be attributed to the heart, to the muscles, nerves and cells, but a contemplative soul [is one] whose entire function is to contract a habit."[60] Such soulful contraction is needed because as Hume suggests all appearances are "broken appearances" (*T*, 1.4.2.36): discontinuous, separate, and interrupted. One's sense of identity is "rooted in movements of assemblage, recollection, projection, splicing, editing, and the like."[61] Images and atomistic sense perceptions do not bind themselves, and so the faculty of the imagination is needed to draw upon causality, contiguity, habit, and resemblance in order to "artifice strategies of composition in the face of ontological discontinuity" (2). One's sense of self "comes into existence only as the result of a laborious stitching together of disparate parts," and such acts of religion affect and are affected by how we see ourselves oriented in the world.[62] Depending upon the posture of attention one's contemplative soul adopts, things cohere in a certain way.

That these issues have something to do with the status and understanding of religious praxis within secularity becomes more evident when we recall that the word "religion" can itself be traced back to etymological roots that may mean either to bind again (*re-ligare*) or to reread (*re-legere*).[63] I will return to what I mean by religion later in this introduction, but here I should note how my understanding has been influenced by Mark C. Taylor's suggestion in *After God* (2007) that for our complex modern world a new interpretive framework for religion is needed where "the divine is not elsewhere but is the emergent creativity that figures, disfigures, and refigures the infinite fabric of life."[64] Émile Durkheim similarly saw religion as "first and foremost a system of ideas by means of which individuals imagine the society of which they are members and the obscure yet intimate relations they have with it." Thus, he understood religion not primarily as a means of representing or mapping the natural or supernatural world, because if this were all religion comprised, it would be "barely more than a fabric of errors."[65] Rather, religion is a dynamic process by which relationships between individuals, society, and the world are mediated and woven together.

The mediated soul initially comes into being as a loose assemblage of "perpetual formation and becoming, a bundle of multiplicities and little coalescings," which is contracted through habit.[66] Habits serve as the bedrock of social formations because, as Marcel Mauss argued, they are "physio-psycho-sociological assemblages of series of actions."[67] They provide a way of organizing "lived regularities, moments of cohesion and repetition, in a universe in which nothing truly repeats."[68] Habit serves as "an anchor, the rock to which the possibilities of personal identity and freedom are tethered, the condition under which learning is possible, the creation of a direction, a 'second nature,' an identity" (219). Through habit words are made flesh. The way one's sensibility is ultimately contracted and projected provides the "essential quickness, the vital sensorium that supplies the soul's moving vehicle."[69]

How such thinking is compatible with, and clarifying for, our understanding of Romanticism is made evident by noticing how closely this talk of a mediated soul resonates with what John Keats describes in his "vale of Soul-making" letter, a letter I will return to in more detail at the beginning of chapter 4. As Keats states toward the end of that letter: "I began by seeing how man was formed by circumstances—and what are circumstances?—but touchstones of his heart?—and what are touchstones?—but proovings of his heart?—and what are proovings of his heart but fortifiers or alterers of his nature? And what is his altered nature but his soul?" (*LJK*, 2:103).

Wordsworth's short lyric "A Slumber Did My Spirit Seal" helps further clarify what it means to be a mediated or contemplative soul. Here is the poem in its entirety:

> A slumber did my spirit seal,
> I had no human fears:
> She seem'd a thing that could not feel
> The touch of earthly years.
>
> No motion has she now, no force
> She neither hears nor sees
> Rolled round in earth's diurnal course
> With rocks, and stones, and trees.

Although admittedly this is one of those poems that seems to encrypt different secrets depending on one's current critical preoccupations, here I read the poem as a commentary on the composition and decomposition of the soul as an element.[70] Clearly the poem is about a death and about what happens when an individual identity or soul decomposes and becomes "rolled round" with the one life in all things, and yet the poem is also about how an individual soul is composed: "A slumber did *my* spirit seal." To seal is to join things together so as to prevent them from coming apart. The lyric speaker's spirit or soul was joined together or composed by witnessing the decomposition of another person's identity. Being affected by the death of another, in other words, gives form to the lyric speaker's spirit or soul.[71] The contemplative soul may be an element within a universe that rolls through all things, but although this uni-verse may be ontologically one, it should also be considered formally diverse. The universe may be one continuous cosmological fabric, but it is folded in myriad ways, and these folds form a whole host of contemplative souls.

In order to better understand what is meant by a soul made from folds, it is helpful to recall the influential distinction Friedrich Schiller makes between the naïve and the sentimental. To be naïve is to simply and directly experience the world before us, but to be sentimental is to possess the capacity and tendency to reflect upon and potentially alter the cognitive and affective impulses (or sentiments) that make up and inform how our world is being viewed and experienced. When we are naïve, the status of our soul is in question because the experience of the world is simple and direct. It is only with the development of sentimentality or some other form of sensibility that experience is folded over upon itself, enabling, in Mark Hansen's words, "an expanded model of perception rooted in the lineages of causal efficacy that stand behind and, in a sense, give body to any act of sense perception."[72]

The basic structure of how this works can clearly be seen in "Tintern Abbey." In the poem, Wordsworth has returned to the area of the abbey after five long years. He sees the same place again and realizes that although it is more or less similar he has changed a great deal. Where once was a "thoughtless youth" (91) passionately haunted by the crashing of a waterfall's "sounding cataract" (77), there now stands a man who must content himself with the "still, sad music of humanity" (92), the "joy / Of elevated thoughts" (95–96), and "a sense sublime / Of something far more deeply interfused" (96–97). Whereas the naïve youth reveled in immediacy, for Schiller, the sentimental poet is the one who "*reflects* on the impression the objects make upon him, and only on the basis of that reflection is emotion founded, into which he is transported and into which he transports us."[73] Overall, the poem can be considered sentimental because it is a "verse reflection that works through both its redoubled mental image and its associated ambivalence in finding poetic resolution."[74] But, as Noel Jackson notes, it is this folding or redoubling of the mental image that also enables Wordsworth to attempt to access a "visionary power accompanied by the suspension or momentary dimming of the physical senses."[75] It is by staging such moments of suspended animation that one can be "laid asleep / In body, and become a living soul" (*WPP*, "Tintern Abbey," 46–47).

The mediated or contemplative soul can be considered a form of consciousness that is sufficiently detached from the "glad animal movements" (76) of immediate experience, so that it can make connections backward and forward in time and is thus able to "retrace the long path of developments from the present back into the deepest night of the past" and speculate about the furthest reaches of the future.[76] The soul is that aspect or fold of our self that holds time enveloped within it, and it is this capacity that enables the human mind to become mobile and achieve vehicular consciousness.

The idea of a trainable human sensorium capable of achieving vehicular consciousness can be traced back to the response of the English latitudinarians to the "new philosophy" of Descartes, Hobbes, and Spinoza. As James

Chandler details in his book *An Archaeology of Sympathy*, the word "sensorium" was conceived by the Cambridge Platonist Henry More in the late 1640s, and by the 1650s More developed his idea of the sensorium in order to salvage key Christian tenets—such as the immortality of the soul—from materialist critique. More was willing to concede to the new mechanistic materialism that the soul was distinct from the body but nevertheless argued that the soul was "housed or 'carried' in a highly subtilized form of matter that registered perceptual vibration and effected locomotion."[77] The sensorium was a "subtilized body" that served as the soul's "vehicle," and More believed it could survive the death of the gross body. Leaving aside for the moment whether such survival is possible, Chandler argues that it is this subtilized body of "perceptual vibration and effected locomotion" that Romantic poetry, in particular, tries to affect through its use of "a subtler language of sentiment within the language of thrills, terrors, and tears, and of various political appropriations, in the wake of the French Revolution."[78]

Conceptions of the soul advanced by More and other Cambridge Platonists, or latitudinarians, were later taken up by the Earl of Shaftesbury and Francis Hutcheson, two key contributors to moral sense theory, and then developed further by Hume and Adam Smith, who associated these ideas of the soul with the figure of the virtualized spectator. As Chandler has traced, "from the eighteenth century forward, the discourse of sentiments would be closely connected to the discourse on the soul." In fact, the first known appearance of the term "sentimental" in English appears in the use of the phrase "sentimental soul" in 1743.[79] When I use the term "mediated soul," it is this network of associated concepts and categories that I have in mind, a network that includes the virtualized spectator, the sentimental soul, the sensorium, and vehicular consciousness. Regardless of which term is used, what is being referred to is an assemblage of perpetual formation and becoming, which is contracted through habit, and held together by sentiments, or, to use a more contemporary vocabulary, by affect.

Sara Ahmed argues that affect is "what sticks, or what sustains or preserves the connection between ideas, values, and objects."[80] We tend to "underdescribe the work of emotions, which involve forms of intensity, bodily orientation, and direction."[81] Although earlier critics influenced by deconstruction or new historicism may have found affect to be merely epiphenomenal to figure or ideology, in recent years critics have begun rehabilitating notions of affect by examining how literature articulates a variety of emotional states.[82]

If affect constitutes the links between bodies and power, then it is essential to ask, along with David Collings, how we can "recover a philosophically nuanced understanding of affect for romantic studies."[83] Affects and emotions are not "after-thoughts" but shape how bodies are moved by the worlds they inhabit. Before we are affected, as Ahmed notes, "Before something happens that creates an impression on the skin, things are already in place that incline us to be affected in some ways more than others."[84] How does this "already in place" establish itself? How does it change or evolve over time (personally, socially, transhistorically)? How can it be altered, abolished, or transformed? These are some of the key questions addressed throughout this book.

Literature can assist in both figuring and disfiguring the "already in place" of one's mediated soul, because literature's value lies, at least in part, in its capacity to carry and transmit the charge of nondiscursive truths through "the affectivity of a text as a material body."[85] Romantic poetry can be considered a form of what Jane Bennett calls micropolitics, which is made up of those "bodily disciplines through which ethical sensibilities and social relations are formed and reformed."[86] Like exercise, meditation, sex, activism, and eating, poetry is ethical if we consider ethics not as a set of doctrines but rather as "a complex set of relays between moral contents, aesthetic-affective styles, and public moods." Thus we should affirm "what Romantic thinkers . . . had long noted: if a set of moral principles is actually to be lived out, the right mood or landscape of affect has to be in place" (xii). Literature plays a role in the cultivation of our landscapes of affect, and understanding how and why literature can function in this way requires "paying attention to the textual dimension of the forms that envelop us and our bodies as a physical reality—something that can catalyze inner feelings without matters of representation necessarily being involved."[87] It is due to its capacity for reordering our sensibilities and sympathies that aesthetics participates in ethics.

One of the blind spots of secularism is its failure to fully thematize what Connolly calls the "infrasensible register" or the role of those "affects and dispositions operating below the threshold of consciousness."[88] A postsecular approach should recognize how not only religious cultures but aesthetic and political cultures as well function through processes of investiture (and divestiture). Saba Mahmood claims that one of the assumptions generally made by secularists is that religion is simply a set of propositions or "beliefs to which the individual gives assent."[89] Religion, however, is not merely a different way of thinking but is rather an alternative manner of being—it offers both a different way of attending to the world and a different form of embodiment.

Religion is one of those arts of the self, and literature is another, that is key to legislating new ways of being in the world because, as Connolly puts it, "To change an intersubjective ethos significantly is to modify the instinctive subjectivities and intersubjectivities in which it is set."[90] New patterns of behavior can be tailored through the modification of those infrasensible energies that are "too multiple, finely meshed, and fast to be captured entirely in the coarse nets of explicit identity, conscious representation, and public appearance" (181). Many of the key documents of Romantic writing can be understood as experimental attempts to access and retune this vibrant dimension of infrasensible energy in the hopes that by doing so it becomes possible to project virtual effects into the actual world of conscious thinking and judgment. The value of learning to attend to the affectivity of a text as a material body is that doing so can help cultivate a sensibility better suited to bearing witness to the vibrant materialities that flow through and around us.

Method

Before proceeding to a description of what is covered in the book's chapters, I want to step back for a moment and situate the argument of *Words Made Flesh* more generally. Ultimately, I am interested in asking not only "What does secularism feel like?" but also "What does it feel like to be postsecular?"[91] In order to answer such questions, my project draws from a variety of critical, philosophic, and disciplinary traditions with a particular emphasis on secular and postsecular studies, media studies, affect theory, empiricism, phenomenology, and religious studies. Although there have been many fine monographs in recent years that carefully concentrate on individual aspects of the issues explored in *Words Made Flesh*—including work on Romanticism and the secular, media studies, affect, empiricism, wonder, the soul, biopolitics, embodied cognition, attention, and sympathy—my book argues that to properly think the postsecular requires the recognition of a "situated void" that lies at the crossroads of previous work.[92] Thus there is an integrative and interdisciplinary emphasis to this book, one that respects and seeks to build upon the clarity and focus of previous scholarship while at the same time recognizing that to think the postsecular properly will require the integration of resources from many different kinds of scholarly conversation. By engaging in such acts of interdisciplinary integration, *Words Made Flesh* draws attention toward potential new constellations of scholarship.

The critical mood in which this work is conducted is rarely engaged in a "hermeneutics of suspicion." Acknowledging the postcritical turn suggested by Rita Felski and others, more often my argument participates in a "hermeneutics of restoration"—one wherein ideally "the reader luxuriates in the fullness of language rather than lamenting its poverty" and one where the experience of textual encounter "is infused with moments of wonder, reverence, exaltation, hope, epiphany, or joy."[93] Engagement in such postures of attention often necessitates a degree of "negative capability" because the efficacy attributed to a work of art is "recoverable only through a learned submission to its myriad textual prompts."[94] Interpretation should "be a matter of dispossession rather than possession, of exposing ourselves to a text as well as imposing ourselves on a text."[95]

To attend to texts in this way requires a participatory form of reading that often involves an effort at reading for *Stimmung*. Significantly, the German word *Stimmung* variously refers to attunement, mood, or affective experience ("an inner feeling so private it cannot be precisely circumscribed,") and climate ("something objective that surrounds people and exercises a physical influence").[96] The German Romantic poet Novalis wrote that "the word 'mood' [*Stimmung*] pertains to the musical relations of the soul—The acoustics of the soul is still an obscure, yet perhaps vitally important domain. Harmonious—and disharmonious vibrations."[97] In order to harmonize with such music, Hans Gumbrecht claims that "reading for Stimmung cannot mean 'deciphering' atmospheres and moods, for they have no fixed signification." Nor can reading for Stimmung simply "mean reconstructing or analyzing their historical or cultural genesis." Such reading should instead be a means of "discovering sources of energy in artifacts and giving oneself over to them affectively and bodily—yielding to them and gesturing toward them."[98]

The argument of *Words Made Flesh* tends to proceed through an immanent criticism, which Walter Benjamin described as "one which is not concerned with judging, and whose center of gravity lies not in the evaluation of the single work but in demonstrating its relations to all other works and, ultimately, to the idea of art."[99] My approach contrasts with the traditions of criticism stemming from deconstruction, culture studies, and new historicism, which tend to read texts within a paradigm of representation and are most often concerned with the capacity of texts to connect with some context—some discourse, power structure, or event outside of the text. These sorts of contextual approaches are of course useful in their own right, but the value of reading for Stimmung is that it means attending to and speculating through those forms of mediation that can make "intense moments of aesthetic experience feel as if they are in the orbit of knowing."[100]

This way of proceeding diverges widely from the injunction found in Jerome McGann's influential *Romantic Ideology* (1983), which decreed that "cooptation must always be a process intolerable to a critical consciousness, whose first obligation is to resist incorporation, and whose weapon is analysis."[101] A more redemptive mode of reading is needed, one that does not simply note the positive features of a text or catalog its deviancy from the historical materiality it emerged from but depends instead on a dimension of performativity. A mode of reading that relinquishes the fantasy of unclothed depths and sees in aesthetics "the tradition of reflection that turns to sense experience in order to pose the question of value."[102]

This book proceeds under the assumption that "literary thinking" has its own intrinsic value, and I agree with Kevis Goodman that "literary analysis may yield a truth not available by other means, even when this analysis means yoking together heterogeneous ideas."[103] Poets are needed because, as Charles Taylor suggests, they can "make us aware of something . . . of which there are as yet no adequate words. The poems themselves are finding the words for us."[104] They offer "raids on the inarticulate."[105] Often my argument advances in a manner suggested by Gaston Bachelard, asking "a poet to provide an image that is sufficiently new in its nuance of being to furnish a lesson in ontological amplification. Through the newness of the image and through its amplification, we shall be sure to reverberate above, or on the margin of reasonable certainties."[106] Such poetic images once found can provide points of departure around which new forms of thinking can coalesce.

Ultimately, this book advocates for a speculative formalism, by which I mean a genre of philosophic or critical speculation generated through a consideration of form.[107] A criticism that is interested in how and why the formal dimensions of Romantic literature can help us see and speculate upon the significance of underappreciated aspects of both our secular age and our potential postsecular future. It is useful to do so because, as Colin Jager and others have shown, within secularity the literary has emerged "as a privileged window—perhaps the privileged window—into the inner workings of the varieties of secularism."[108] What a speculative formalism seeks to do is look through literature's "privileged window" to see what it is that can be seen through it.

In approaching Romanticism's relationship to secular and postsecular structures of feeling, landscapes of affect, and postures of attention, I also understand myself to be operating within the domain of religion and literature.[109] My interest is in writing that performs rather than merely transmits its meaning. A scholar of religion and literature is one who is interested in investigating scriptural and nonscriptural mediations (or *poiesis*) that perpetuates the performance of (religious) meaning for a community of readers. Catherine Bell argued that if "reality is experienced as a natural weave of constraint and possibility, [and] the fabric of day-to-day dispositions and decisions [is] experienced as a field for strategic action," then religious ritual and figuration can be understood as economies of gestures that affect "a practical orientation embedded in bodies."[110] Religion is, among other things, a set of techniques to "intensify joy and confront suffering" and consists in part as "a repertoire of procedures for pushing around and evoking specific affects."[111] As Mark Taylor has suggested, religion is best understood as "an emergent, complex, adaptive network of symbols, myths, and rituals that, on the one hand, figure schemata of feeling, thinking, and acting in ways that lend life meaning and purpose and, on the other, disrupt, dislocate, and disfigure every stabilizing structure."[112] Religion enables us certain affordances because, as David Nikkel has demonstrated, "religion involves as a key dimension the extension of our biological impetus to orient ourselves to our meaning-laden environment."[113]

Nevertheless, the field of religion and literature is significant even if religion is best understood as "a network of bodily practices" because, as Donovan Schaefer has helped us begin to explicate, "texts are technologies for distributing affects, while bodies are landscapes of already existing affect."[114] Thus the field of religion and literature explores the intersection of two networks of bodily practices that can deeply affect "the way things feel, the things we want, the way our bodies are guided through thickly textured, magnetized worlds."[115] This interest in the active, performative, and participatory kinds of writing around which communities and individuals organize, regulate, and extend themselves, allows the scholar to examine how the principal ideas of a culture or a religion are expressed in the materiality of the media used to transmit these ideas. Lawrence Sullivan, a historian of religion, suggests "the capacities to conceptualize and to be reflective are deeply influenced by the particular matter given primacy by a culture."[116] The medium is, in part, the message.

The affective turn experienced of late in Romanticism has corollaries in recent approaches to secularization and in contemporary religious studies. As happened in literary studies with new historicism, Jonathan Z. Smith influentially repudiated a range of ahistorical, metaphysical systems that dominated religious studies up to the 1970s, associated with figures like William James, Rudolf Otto, and Mircea Eliade. These earlier phenomenological approaches were often concerned with "the way things feel" and "presumed that religion was an ahistorical phenomenon, a transcendent source of meaning arriving from beyond human circumstances."[117] Smith inaugurated a linguistic turn within religious studies and saw religion as being "best understood as a category manufactured within human histories through the devices of human representation and cognition" (6). His approach emphasized "an epistemic orientation that viewed religion as a way of thinking and labeling certain features of the world—and thereby as inextricable from history and power" (5). This tendency within Smith's work had the consequence of locking "religious studies into an Enlightenment prism that tends to reduce religion to a series of cognitive appraisals of the world" (10). Recently, scholars such as Schaefer have pointed toward an affective blind spot within this model, with its reliance on an assumption that religious bodies "move because a particular textual regime has directed them to do so" (13). Shaefer argues that this mesmeric aspect at the heart of the "linguistic fallacy misunderstands religion as merely a byproduct of language, and misses the economies of affect . . . that are the animal substance of religion and other forms of power." Thus affect theory is a necessary tool for mapping both religion and literature, "not just because it adds to our inventory of descriptive tools, but because affect constitutes the links between bodies and power" (9–10).

Structure

The key ways in which Romanticism can open up avenues for affect beneath and beyond the model of buffered subjectivity Taylor sees as being dominant in secularity will be elaborated upon in the book's opening section, "Approaches to the Postsecular." This section offers a preparatory "toolbox" chapter that will provide the conceptual framework for the readings of particular Romantic works in the second section, "Mediating the Postsecular," which is primarily focused on the work of Samuel Taylor Coleridge and John Keats, and in the third section, "Anthropology of the Postsecular," which highlights the work of Percy Shelley and Jane Austen. The archive I engage with consists not only of the source texts of British Romanticism but also of the history of criticism that has developed around these works. One reason the study of some of the most canonical texts of the period has been so fruitful to the development of this project is precisely because so much has been written about them. It is due to the stratified layers of interpretation that have accrued around these texts over the years that enables them to now be used as hypertexts linking and providing often surprising pathways within the history of ideas. By making poetic forms the speculative focus of my inquiries, I have found it easier to forge new connections across what may at first seem like disparate ways of thinking. By doing so I hope to point toward new possibilities for scholarship and to suggest ways in which particular poetic forms within Romanticism can function as dialectical images wherein, as Walter Benjamin memorably wrote, "What has been comes together in a flash with the now."[118]

The first chapter, "Theorizing the Postsecular," proceeds by emphasizing how techniques and technologies of mediation and embodiment are central to how words are made flesh in a postsecular age. This chapter has been structured with the knowledge that, as a whole, this book draws upon a variety of interdisciplinary subjects, and I anticipate not all readers will be equally interested in every aspect. Those readers who are less theoretically or philosophically inclined may want to skip directly to the literary focus of subsequent chapters. Other readers, however, coming from fields less invested in literary criticism may find that it is this chapter and the introduction that are the most useful. Part of my intention in writing this "toolbox" chapter is to give something back to those scholarly fields I have wandered in and borrowed from by offering a concise explication of the fruits of the speculative formalism that I have practiced while writing this book.

The chapter begins by first outlining some of the basic contours of secularity. Attention then turns toward highlighting how the two dominant branches in current discussions around affect theory—the ontological and cultural approaches—help articulate how an affectively potent poetics can, on the one hand, produce participatory experiences of breakthrough that potentially bring readers into a more intimate connection with the world around them, and on the other, can be used to line readers up with cultural structures and patterns that extend beyond the confines of their limited buffered selves and the fixations of the present moment. Focus is then placed on why Romanticism is seen by many of the most prominent media theorists as a movement of "far-reaching socio-cognitive reorganization," which was characterized by the emergence of print as a "general" medium, and which was accompanied by a series of changes that radically reoriented readers and the modern world.[119] Shifts in mediation play an important part in how Romanticism's "subtler language" is articulated because, as Friedrich Kittler puts it, "Around 1800, the book became both film and record simultaneously—not, however, as a technological reality, but only in the imaginary of readers' souls."[120] Of particular interest is how these shifts encouraged the emergence within Romanticism of a protocinematic form of poetry that develops, at least initially, due to the movement away from rhymed poetry and toward the "blanking" of verse. The next two sections of the chapter then work to recuperate for Romanticism a cinematic form of empiricism that is often implicit and sometimes explicit in Hume's work, which is much more intriguing than the camera obscura–based empiricism earlier advocated by John Locke. It is this cinematic form of empiricism that becomes the basis for understanding the conception of the mediated soul that is advocated in different ways in subsequent chapters, and particularly focused on in the chapters on Coleridge and Keats.

The chapter ends with a consideration of two philosophies of the flesh that attempt to conceptualize that part of our being that is so deeply affected by affect. Here I coordinate Merleau-Ponty's notion of flesh with the working of ontological affect and Eric Santner's scriptural or psychotheological reading of an incarnational flesh with cultural approaches to affect. Part of what I build toward with this interest in the "flesh" is a better understanding of how Romantic poetry, and literary and scriptural writing more generally, can enable and mediate how a wide variety of postures of attention can be put on.

Noel Jackson argues that by "estranging the reader's habitual and automatic associations of sensations to ideas," Romantic poetry learned to access "powerful bodily rhythms that tend to pass unnoticed," and is thus better able to "put us in touch with this level of our bodily functioning."[121] Such a *poiesis* has the ambition to act on and to alter the sensibilities of its readers through lyric experiments that begin to help "construct and make available the intellectual-emotional apparatus for accessing, and to that extent helps make available the social material of, the new."[122] Such experimentation recognizes literature as a media technology, one that functions like a set of virtual reality glasses that can make the past (or alternative points of view) virtually present. What particularly interests me is how the technics of the printed word can produce the postures of attention we associate with them and how, when, and why such postures may be productive to put on.[123]

The first two chapters of the second section, "Mediating the Postsecular," focus on Coleridge's interests in both religion and literature. "Poetic Faith," explores Coleridge's critique of bibliolatry and the articulation of his own scriptural reading practices, while "Coleridge's Parable of Modernity" uses "The Rime of the Ancient Mariner" as a lens to focus attention on Coleridge's critique of secular subjectivity and on the alternative he offers. Both chapters respond in various ways to an underling secular "investiture crisis," caused when the traditional patterns for making meaning within a community have been disrupted or rent.[124] The word investiture means both the act or ceremony of investing a person with a rank or an honor and the action of clothing or robing (i.e., putting on the thing that clothes or covers). The procedures of investiture and divestiture thus name the processes by which words are made flesh and by which they are unmade: the way symbolic identities are figured and disfigured as second nature. Problems, however, accrue when the stability of previous models of distributing and investing this charge are challenged within modernity as new forms of science, industry, mediation, and cultural practices flourish. This destabilization affects the traditional understanding and routines of those habits and practices that constituted what was perceived to be "true religion," without however eliminating the functional need for a form of life capable of adequately regulating, distributing, and investing with meaning that excess or surplus that is "immanent to and constitutive of life itself."[125]

Chapters 2 and 3 explore responses to this underlying investiture crisis within modernity through a reconsideration of how Coleridge approaches both Scripture and literature as mediums that can deeply affect and orient not only readers' postures of attention but also their ways of navigating within a wider world of concern. Chapter 2, "Poetic Faith," considers how Coleridge's reevaluations of biblical reading practices in *Aids to Reflection* and "Confessions of an Inquiring Spirit" contribute to his understanding of what it means to possess a "poetic faith." Coleridge critiques those who see the Bible as an object that functions like the "glittering eye" of the mariner—a conduit that holds us spellbound with its charged presence and captivating tale. Coleridge advocates instead for a projective method of reading that enables reciprocal exchange, one where subjective experience becomes objectively available through its correspondence with the figures of Scripture and where objective truths can become subjectively realized. For Coleridge, Scripture enables readers to reflect upon their own lives via the mediation of its figures and symbols, and through this process Scripture's dead letter is reborn through the reader's inspired attention. "True religion" is experienced as a pleasurable unity, identity, or crossing of the subjective and objective; it is through this crossing or "lining up" that the Christian reader can find sufficient evidence for belief without recourse to outside authority. The end of this chapter explores what Coleridge means by reflection and suggests that Johann Gottfried Herder's understanding of reflection (*Bessonenheit*) as the navigation of a linguistic dimension that is in pursuit of the right words, is crucial for clarifying not only what Coleridge is up to in *Aids to Reflection* but also for the model of subjectivity advocated for in "The Rime of the Ancient Mariner," as will become evident in the next chapter.

In chapter 3, "Coleridge's Parable of Modernity," my reading of the "Rime" builds upon the work of Jerome McGann and Thomas Pfau, and like Pfau, I see the poem as a response to the "shipwreck" of skeptical empiricism. However, unlike Pfau's gnostic reading of the poem, I suggest that the poem actually accepts and even celebrates the free exercise of the will as something more than sin. In order to tease out the implications of the "Rime," I turn to the related case of Daniel Schreber, a successful German jurist who suffered a breakdown after receiving the offer of becoming Senatespräsident and who eventually became the basis for Freud's classic study on paranoia. Both Schreber and the mariner experience a kind of homoludic epiphany, which manifests itself in gothic visions and paranoid delusions written out in a kind of "nerve-language." What the "Rime" provides is a virtual environment in which readers can simulate "the loss and intended recovery of the orienting a priori of the body" and learn to form judgments that are disinterested and thus devoid of "deluded enthusiasm."[126] Such exercises in reorientation are useful because they help readers step out of the regimen of habitual thinking and into a virtual "state of exception." Ultimately, readers must decide what this disruption means and it is toward this act of decision-making that the whole poem is a preparation. This chapter is also interested in how both Schreber and the mariner experience a kind of "soul-murder," in how and why the mariner recovers from this experience by blessing the sea snakes and in exploring the broader implications of the mariner's recovery of his mediated soul.

The fourth chapter, "'To See as a God Sees': Keats and Cinematic Subjectivity," continues to be interested in what it means to have a mediated soul and opens by detailing how Keats's "vale of Soul-making" functions as a model of investiture. I then investigate how an ethics and potentially a politics of wonder animates Keats's poetry by considering the ways in which his two "Hyperion" fragments correspond to the divergence between the strolling flâneur and the gawking badaud, between the blank verse of Milton and the psychedelia of Dante, and to the related break Gilles Deleuze finds in the history of cinema between the movement-image and the time-image. Put simply, the difference between these two sets of phenomena is that the former tends to move viewers along a single train of thought while the experience of the latter is much more likely to be jarring, disruptive, and open-ended. By approaching the Hyperion project in this way, this chapter explores how best to understand what it means to "see as a god sees." What ultimately becomes apparent through this approach is that the dynamism found in the movement from "Ode to Psyche" through "To Autumn" during Keats's annus mirabilis of 1819 has a great deal to do with how his *poiesis* works to first fold and then unfold his own mediated soul.

The next two chapters, explore the possibilities of a more open countermodernity, one in which, as Jager has observed, increased "sensory capacities" help move the mind from "anger and hatred and revenge" to "other occupations—love, trust, hope, and endurance."[127] In these two chapters, I remain interested in how shifts in mediation and political theology contribute to the development of this countermodernity but also focus on how tragedy and comedy, two genres rooted in misrecognition, can be useful for learning to recognize and navigate the diverse forms of connection we inhabit. I argue that these two genres give us insight into a postsecular anthropology because both help us realize what our supreme fictions are doing, while also offering practice in developing the habit or skill of soul-making.

The penultimate chapter, "'Awful Doubt': Shelley's Tragic Skepticism," starts by considering how and why Shelley produces "imageless images" designed to encourage readers to move beyond a "savage" sense of necessity and toward a "philosophic" sense.[128] The chapter explores the way in which Prometheus "clothed" Jupiter in *Prometheus Unbound* and how precisely Prometheus's suffering body, the site where the hurt of history is remembered, can be unbound. Prometheus clothes Jupiter because he is emblematic of the suffering body politic that provides the field or flesh, in the psychotheological sense of the word, through which mutability weaves its dominion of empire and superstition. Shelley recognizes that in order to fashion "the new," a poetics of divestment is needed to loosen the hold of old patterns. Prometheus needs to be unbound because in order to be free one must be released from the excitation past actions hold over our affective, conceptual, and imaginative lives. However, rather than focus on *Prometheus Unbound* itself, I use Shelley's play *The Cenci* as a lens through which to view Shelley's overall poetic and intellectual development during his own great year of 1819. The advantage of *The Cenci*, which is written in the middle of the composition of *Prometheus Unbound*, is that it provides a particularly embodied form of the kinds of "imageless images" that are so significant to Shelley's philosophical view of reform. By loosening the hold past affections have over the body, Shelley shows us how a spacing can be found for a sense of justice yet to come.

The book's final chapter, "'Open-Hearted': *Persuasion* and the Cultivation of Good Humor," offers a consideration of how good humor, a quality advocated for by Hume after his own quick recovery from the skeptical crisis experienced at the end of book 1 of his *Treatise*, is exemplified by Anne Elliot's journey in Austen's *Persuasion*. Here I connect Austen's representations of bodies in *Persuasion* to earlier notions of the humoral body, discuss how *Persuasion*'s "voyage of discovery" is more Romantic than sentimental, and clarify how and why good humor can be understood as the ideal disposition for a vehicular consciousness—one alert to its surroundings and quite capable of skillfully steering "the vital sensorium that supplies the soul's moving vehicle."[129] Ultimately, I find *Persuasion* to be a novel that integrates the various lessons and concepts found throughout the chapters of *Words Made Flesh* and can thus serve as a final guide for how best to navigate the postsecular potential of our current moment. The short coda that follows closes the book by suggesting the broader implications of this postsecular potential.

PART I

Approaches to the Postsecular

* 1 *

Theorizing the Postsecular

Although some critics consider religion, or "creed(s) outworn" more generally, to be fantasies that distort our perception of "real life" and should thus be stripped away so that the world can be seen more nakedly, these outworn creeds are better understood when one recognizes that it is only through the imagination that fragmentary sense perception is organized into a coherent gestalt in the first place. It is only through fantasy that we encounter the real. In *On the Psychotheology of Everyday Life* (2001), Eric Santner argues that fantasy is what "organizes or 'binds' the bombardment of sense perceptions into a schema, a distinctive 'torsion' or spin that colors/distorts the shape of our universe, how the world is disclosed to us."[1] Fantasy is not something that could be peeled away so that the real can be revealed beneath its distorting influence. Rather fantasy or the imagination is the medium through which the world is viewed. This is not to say that all fantasies or ideologies are healthy or desirable but only that the world must be clothed in some necessary or "supreme fiction" if it is to be apprehended coherently at all.[2] What is needed is a form of aesthetic education that can properly develop our capacity for putting on and taking off various forms of belief—those postures, orientations, affective textures, or words made flesh that help us better navigate the turbulence of being.

Within secularity, the instrumentalization of inherited images or ideas opened up a new set of questions—namely what should be done with these newfound capacities for wringing new effects from inherited forms. In *The Mystic Fable* (1982), Michel de Certeau traced how doctrine became "an *instrument* that makes possible the fabrication of social bodies, their defense and their extension." Even within the context of religious practices, "the task of *educating* and the concern with *methods* characterize the activity of the religious 'parties' and of all the new congregations."[3] It is by recognizing the instrumentality of language and ritual that the art of fabricating social bodies becomes fashionable. How this art of fabricating social bodies with meaning—or investiture—should be practiced is the subject of an aesthetic education. From the time of Friedrich Schiller to that of Matthew Arnold there was an increasing awareness of the role that culture and aesthetics play in forming citizens for the modern state.

Aesthetic education is conceived as a pedagogy based on aesthetic judgment that furnishes "an ethical training devoted to the 'educing' of the citizen from the human being."[4] It is the method in which the subject is interpellated into and invested in culture. Part of the point of an aesthetic education "is to permit the recognition of laws that are never represented, in effect, the recognition of something that acts like the law but can never take the form of a law."[5] In this way, such education aims to produce "nothing less than a body at one with the law."[6] An aesthetic education attempts to regulate the healthy functioning of a community by providing occasions for the recognition of something that transcends representation. It is in these moments of recognition that access is provided to "a sense sublime / Of something far more deeply interfused" (*WPP*, "Tintern Abbey," 96–97) that can be felt in the flesh but is nevertheless beyond reason's reach.

In order to better understand how and why the Romantic writers under consideration in this book began to tailor their own forms of aesthetic education, the focus of this chapter is on how conceptions of the secular and the postsecular are better understood when the debates and revisions of the secularization thesis are read in conjunction with both affect theory and the history and theorization of mediation. Doing so clarifies how the way in which the cultural imaginary is mediated is central to how a culture sees itself and how such mediations affect and are affected by those who inhabit it. This consideration of the role of mediation in relation to both secularization and Romanticism leads to a discussion of how Romantic poetry can be considered protocinematic and how and why this form of *poiesis* is particularly good at altering the sensoriums of its readers. The chapter's penultimate section then pushes further by advocating for a reading of Hume's cinematic empiricism as a form of subjectivity that is much more conducive to life in a postsecular age than the model of the buffered subject, which Charles Taylor describes as being dominant in *A Secular Age* (2007). The chapter concludes with a focus on two different theorizations of the flesh: the phenomenological and the psychotheological. Overall this chapter seeks to clarify the conceptual toolkit that is operative in subsequent chapters and is interested, on the one hand, in those seismic states that can break through the film of familiarity that can obscure the wonders of the world before us and, on the other, the ways in which our settled dispositions can be made to line up with assemblages and networks of regard that extend us beyond the limits of own particularity.

Secularity

Traditional readings of secularization suggest that history has been a progression from a kind of naïve ethos or groupthink experienced as natural and necessary to a modernity populated by enlightened and liberated individuals who finally abandon such outdated modes of thought and become self-determining, self-fashioning, and ultimately self-sufficient. The underlying assumption here is that the secular is the essential and intrinsically true reality that would be universally accessible if only the outworn creeds of the past could be stripped bare so as to reveal the truth these creeds merely cloaked. One problem with approaching secularization in this way is the underlying assumption that there is some conception of rational religion, justice, or human rights at the root of human experience that can be universally agreed upon. This is because, as many recent critiques have articulated, this notion of an underlying universal secularity is itself the product of the particular interests and history of a Western, largely Judeo-Christian genealogy.

I argue instead that we should approach secularity much more modestly, and one way secularization can be thought of is as the process through which we come not only to tolerate but also to appreciate other people's stories (i.e., recognize the value *for us* of *their* patterned response to the constitutive too-muchness that characterizes human existence). Minimally, to live responsibly in a postsecular age requires a tolerance of the fashions of others, but to live well may also require the cultivation of a willingness to allow ourselves to put on (and exchange with) the fashions of others, even if only for a moment. Why this should be the case is one of the questions this project addresses. Contrary to those "subtraction stories" that once dominated thinking about secularization, Charles Taylor argues that modernity cannot be explained by narratives of how humans progressively "lost, or sloughed off, or liberated themselves from certain earlier, confining horizons, or illusions, or limitations of knowledge." Instead, modernity and secularity are better understood as "the fruit of new inventions, newly constructed self-understandings and related practices, and can't be explained in terms of perennial features of human life."[7] Central to these new inventions are new forms of subjectivity and new understandings of how life is best governed.

The study of Romanticism has itself long been caught up in ideas of secularization. In *Natural Supernaturalism* (1971), M. H. Abrams presented his influential thesis that Romanticism was a progressive movement that translated and humanized earlier religious impulses and is thus a secularized revision of religious themes and images. His book's central claim was that much of what distinguishes writers we call Romantic "derives from the fact that they undertook, whatever their religious creed or lack of creed, to save traditional concepts, schemes, and values which had been based on the relation of the Creator to his creature and creation, but to reformulate them within the prevailing two-term system of subject and object, ego and non-ego, the human mind or consciousness and its transactions with nature."[8] Abrams links ideas of aesthetic education (or *Bildung*) to the search for value through a kind of prodigality and finds repeated throughout Romantic writing forms of a circular journey of losing one's way and spending one's resources that ultimately educates as to where real value lies. For Abrams, the repetition of this pattern or motif in Romantic literature is illustrative of an effort to make manifest to contemporaries a new, accessible translation of a perennial philosophy of idealism that stretches from at least as far back as Plato and Scripture, through Neoplatonism and medieval mysticism, to German Idealism, and finally to a wider modernity through the agency of Romanticism.

Within the recent study of Romanticism, however, Colin Jager has been at the forefront of those arguing that the account of secularization Abrams relies upon is open to a series of objections, the foremost of which is that "the historical change that the word 'secularization' tries to capture does not reside solely or even primarily at the level of ideas and beliefs (where Abrams places it), but incorporates habits, dispositions, and postures that are themselves carried out and performed within changing institutional contexts."[9] Although there is certainly still value in reading Abrams's book, nevertheless it is true that we are now in a better position to question his emphasis on seeing secularization as the translation of propositional content (i.e., that within Romanticism traditional concepts, schemes, and values were reformulated into the prevailing language of subject/object distinctions and nature philosophy, mediated primarily through the vocabulary and concepts of German Idealism). This understanding of secularization as a grand translation process that reformulates religious ideas into secular and philosophical language, with its underlying assumption that religious practices would decline as a result, has become increasingly untenable in recent years given the continued and widespread prevalence of religious expression in the modern world.

Following the distinction José Casanova makes in *Public Religions in the Modern World* (1994), a book that was an important catalyst of the recent efforts to reevaluate secularization, the secular, secularization, and secularity can be defined as follows: "the secular" is a central modern epistemic category, "secularization" is an analytical conceptualization of modern world-historical processes, and "secularism" is a worldview.[10] For Casanova, secularization should be seen as leading not to the disappearance of religion but rather to the narrowing of the influence of institutional religion and to the "differentiation" of society, which results in the emancipation of various forms of cultural authority from the control of institutional religion. Secularization entails a shift from a domain wherein everyone shares the same basic assumptions about the world to a more differentiated society with a variety of subjective private religions and beliefs. Such differentiation "forces a turning inward, and the exploration of one's subjectivity can be seen as necessarily linked, if perhaps only negatively, to the control exercised not just by ecclesiastical and political authorities but also by monetarization, by the new ways of measuring time, and by the ongoing rationalization of everyday life, particularly of economic activities."[11] As everyday life becomes more rational, there is both increased differentiation and also a greater readiness to escape the demands of a rationally ordered world through increased exploration of subjective experience.

In order to better understand the secular as a concept, here is a quick gathering of the language various critics have used to describe some of its key aspects. The secular "brings together certain behaviors, knowledges, and sensibilities in modern life."[12] The term refers to "rudimentary attitudes toward the human body, contributes to specific ways of training, cultivating, and structuring the senses, and grounds operative conceptions of the human."[13] Secularism is "not simply . . . the doctrinal separation of the church and the state but the re-articulation of religion in a manner that is commensurate with modern sensibilities and modes of governance."[14] In part, "*secularization* concerns what can be taken for granted when exchanging reasons in public settings." Secularization is not the relinquishment of religious belief but is instead "the fact that participants in a given discursive practice are not in a position to take for granted that their interlocutors are making the same religious assumptions they are."[15]

Jager argues that if after secularization the sacred structures that had given a subject meaning no longer apply as decisively as they once did and now new ways must be found to "remember that subject into a network of significance," then it is shifts in habits and practices rather than simply propositional content that will enable the subject to "save the system that gives him meaning."[16] If the secular is a way of "apprehending the world—imagining the future, feeling for the nation, picturing oneself as an agent, experiencing love, hatred, and desire—then it involves the act of perception itself."[17] Focus should thus be shifted from what the secular *is* to what it *does*. If the secular is a mode of apprehending the world, then how is this act of perception patterned, and does it offer the best posture of attention to adopt? Religion, atheism, and secularism more generally have less to do with "cognitively-held beliefs or non-beliefs" and more to do with "postures, arrangements, dispositions, embodied techniques, [and] disciplined actions."[18] Fortunately, as Jager argues, within certain aspects of Romanticism the impetus can be found to produce a "reordered sensorium" that educates "the body, increasing its sensory capacities so that anger and hatred and revenge will be recognized as modes that characterize bodies lacking other, better experiences" (628). What is needed within secularity are new forms of aesthetic education that can reconfigure the body and reorder the sensorium of our vehicular consciousness so that we can better direct our contemplative souls toward the good.

While most accounts of secularity fixate on what is written on the tablets of rationality and conceptual thinking, William Connolly claims more attention should be paid to those "arts of the self" that draw upon and experimentally shape the stream of "thought-imbued intensities moving below linguistic sophistication, consciousness, and reflective judgement as well as through them."[19] Learning to cultivate those arts of the self that can shape these intensities in productive ways is the key to legislating new ways of being in the world. The advantage of these "technologies of the self," as Foucault called them, is that they "permit individuals to effect by their own means or with the help of others a certain number of operations on their bodies and souls, thoughts, conduct, and the way of being, so as to transform themselves."[20] By doing so these "technologies of the self engender questions about how we might transcend the limits imposed on us by anonymous structures, networks of knowledge, and social and cultural institutions."[21]

In *Why I Am Not a Secularist* (1999), Connolly calls this visceral register "from which conscious thoughts, feelings, and discursive judgments draw part of their sustenance," the infrasensible.[22] Like Kant's notion of the transcendental or the suprasensible, the infrasensible is not visible in the world of appearances, but rather than operate in an ideal domain above, behind, or beyond the sensible, the infrasensible functions beneath and between everyday perceptions. Following Deleuze (as well as Spinoza, Nietzsche, Freud, and others), Connolly argues that thinking "operates on more than one level; it moves on the level of the virtual (which is real in its effectivity but not actual in its availability) and that of the actual (which is available to representation, but not self-sufficient)" (40). Whereas Abrams's *Natural Supernaturalism* influentially posited Romanticism as the fortunate recipient of a perennial philosophy that serves as the prototype of all worthwhile articulations of human thought and various new historicists critiqued all such transcendental moves as mystification and sought instead to save appearances through a vigilant historical materialism, Connolly's concept of the infrasensible, like Merleau-Ponty's notion of the body schema, enables us to conceive of Romanticism as a set of cultural practices that operate at least in part on a virtual field "below and within culturally organized registers of sensibility, appearance, discourse, justice, and identity" (40).

The advantage of this model is that it helps explain more precisely how and why a Romantic poetics can be designed to affect those energies that are "too multiple, finely meshed, and fast to be captured entirely in the coarse nets of explicit identity, conscious representation, and public appearance" (40). Romantic writers can become the "unacknowledged legislators of the world" by tapping into and shaping these infrasensible energies through poetry that provides "a reservoir from which *surprise* sometimes unsettles fixed explanations, new *pressures* periodically swell up to disrupt existing practices of rationality, and new *drives* to *identity* occasionally surge up to modify the register of justice and legitimacy upon which established identities are placed" (40). Romantic writing is often an attempt to experimentally access and reprogram this virtual dimension of infrasensible energy because by doing so it becomes possible to project virtual effects into the actual world of conscious thinking and judgment.

Two Branches of Affect Theory

To better understand how such unacknowledged legislation can be accomplished, it will be useful to briefly delineate how and why two different branches or approaches to affect theory have developed in recent years. As we shall see, one branch is particularly interested in exposing and accessing the infrasensible, as well as the body that is "a drag on signification," which operates beneath the field of representation, while the other branch tends to be more concerned with those enduring affective textures that help shape human identities and experiences across populations and can be passed from generation to generation.[23] Affect theory, in general, is useful for my argument, because, as Shaefer puts it in *Religious Affects* (2015), a book at the forefront of recent efforts to use affect theory to reenvision religious studies, such thinking "provides a new locus for studying the binding relationships between bodies and power."[24] In their introduction to *The Affect Theory Reader* (2010), Melissa Gregg and Gregory Seigworth claim that affect is ubiquitous and can be "found in those intensities that pass body to body (human, nonhuman, part-body, and otherwise), in those resonances that circulate about, between, and sometimes stick to bodies and worlds, and in the very passages or variations between these intensities and resonances themselves."[25] Affect is a form of modification produced by a feeling or encounter with difference—to be affected is to be "altered, changed-by the impact of an encounter, be it with another subject or an object."[26]

The two approaches to affect that have been most prevalent in recent criticism—the ontological and the cultural—can be traced back to two essays published in 1995—one by Brian Massumi ("The Autonomy of Affect") and the other by Eve Sedgwick and Adam Frank ("Shame in the Cybernetic Fold"). The ontological approaches use affect to name a general property of the structure of reality as such. In this view, "affect is non-anthropocentric even though it seems to infuse much of human life; this is because affect infuses much of everything."[27] This strain of affect theory can be traced back to Gilles Deleuze and his readings of Spinoza. Critics in this camp are often found working outside of literature departments and include figures such as William Connolly, Patricia Clough, Erin Manning, John Protevi, Steven Shaviro, and Isabelle Stengers.

An affect is not a personal feeling: "Feelings are personal and biographical, emotions are social, and affects are prepersonal." Nevertheless, without affect

"Feelings do not 'feel' because they have no intensity, and without feelings rational decision-making becomes problematic."[28] What is modified by an affect is aligned with what Spinoza called the *conatus*, which can be thought of as a form of willful excitation generated through "a process of repetition or recurrence of the self."[29] Thus affects can be considered as fluctuations of intensity in conatus or will. What Spinoza means by *affectus* is "the affections of the body by which the body's power of activity is increased or diminished, assisted or checked, together with the ideas of these affections."[30] In his philosophy, "our body is a determined set of relations of movement and rest, and our mind is the idea of our body."[31]

How the conatus or will is attuned becomes the basis for feelings of joy (*laetitia*) and sorrow (*tristitia*). Those experiences we call good increase the power of acting, and those we call bad decrease the power of acting. Joyful affects "cause a greater desire and confer on the individual strength, courage, curiosity, wonder, and the will to act and to think." Sorrowful affects, in contrast, "imply boredom, hatred, envy, anguish, and melancholy; they alienate the power of acting and check it in various ways" (39). Sorrow is the name of "the interruption of movement" that corresponds to "a low degree of ideal reality," while joy "signifies the unity between bodily activity and ideal integrity and degree of perfection" (40). Thus one way to understand what it means in the "Rime" for the wedding guest to wake up sadder and wiser in the morn is that this is an indication that listening to the mariner has altered the attunement of his affective being in more than one way—first by decreasing and then by potentially increasing his power of action.

Such ideas resonate with the forms of Romantic string theory surrounding the Aeolian harp, a resonance explored by both Coleridge and Shelley—two thinkers keenly interested in what happens when the conatus or will "like a musical instrument, is played with more or less intensity."[32] In his *A Defense of Poetry*, Shelley famously argues that "man is an instrument over which a series of external and internal impressions are driven, like the alternations of an ever-changing wind over an Æolian lyre, which move it by their motion to ever-changing melody."[33] Nevertheless, Shelley also goes on to argue in the *Defense* that we are not merely passive beings because there "is a principle within the human being, and perhaps within all sentient beings, which acts otherwise than in the lyre, and produces not melody alone, but harmony, by an internal adjustment of the sounds or motions thus excited to the impressions which excite them."[34] Shelley's thinking on the Aeolian harp may have been influenced by materialist philosophers of sensation, who formulated a view that "perhaps all sentient being(s)" were like Aeolian harps diversely framed, each "vibrating in tune with (or out of tune with) some other entity."[35] Sentience in this view is a form of attunement.

The correlation of ontological affect theory and Aeolian string theory is suggestive because it advocates an experimental poetics wherein both writer and reader approach the text via a method of gradual adjustment, because, as Charles Rzepka argued, each "cannot know exactly what array of specific settings will enable the wind passing through the strings to produce harmony (though one may have a good guess), so one must keep re-adjusting them until harmony is in fact produced." The only confirmation that the "adjustments are correct is the harmony itself, the 'deep power of joy' that suddenly leaps forth like a released magnetic or electrical charge."[36] Given all of this, however, the key question becomes how then are we to determine the best way to adjust our sets? How then can we learn to hear the "undertones" of those "Aeolian modulations" that produce "the deep music of the rolling world, / Kindling within the strings of the waved air" (S, *Prometheus Unbound*, 4.186-90)?

Suggestions for how best to answer these questions will have to wait for later chapters, but here it is worth noting some of the critiques to the ontological approach to affect. A particularly influential one has been voiced by Ruth Leys, who is concerned by its tendency to divorce "emotion from intention and meaning, making emotion and cognition separate systems."[37] She also questions the commitment to the theorization of a "half-second delay" between "the subject's affects and its cognition or appraisal of the affective situation," which is often found in both this strain of affect theory and in various forms of neuro- and cognitive science.[38] Sara Ahmed has similarly pointed out how the "analytic distinction between affect [in the singular], and emotion risks cutting emotions off from the lived experiences of being and having a body."[39]

This is one reason Ahmed has advocated for what she calls a feminist cultural studies of emotion and affect, which emerges out of the work of Sedgwick and Frank and has been subsequently advanced by figures, often working within literary studies, such as Teresa Brennan, Ann Cvetkovich, Lauren Berlant, and Kathleen Stewart. In this cultural approach, "affects surge through bodies, producing semistable structures that become the tough, raw materials" of subjectivity and cultural identity.[40] In this view, each of us emerges out of a "cradle of subjectivity" woven from an "interlacing dynamic between feelings, thoughts, words, habits, images, and sensations."[41] In contrast to the ontological branch, these thinkers are more interested in "embodied cognition" and insist on "on tracing affect as something felt, something that rises into embodied spheres of awareness."[42] As Ahmed argues, through our emotions each of us participates in an "affective economy" of circulation, with the subject as "only one nodal point in the economy."[43] From this perspective, "Consciousness itself is an emotional reaction to the intrusion of the outside," and emotions "produce the very surfaces and boundaries" that buffer self and society.[44]

Schaefer suggests that one helpful heuristic for distinguishing between the two branches is in terms of the stability of affective structures. The ontological approach tends to emphasize "the granular modulations of behavioral forms," and so affects are "the molecular forces that coalesce to form soft structures—sand castles—always subject to erosion and mutation." Here there is an emphasis on "plasticity, the fundamental reconfigurability of bodies under the influence of the overlapping systems of forces within which they are embedded." The cultural approach, in contrast, tends to emphasize "sustained attachments—the firm shapes of experience that emerge out of embodied histories." From this perspective, rather than as sand castles continuously "susceptible to radical reformation by the action of multidirectional waves washing over them," affects are better understood as "semistable, complex formations of embodied sensation that have coalesced through the advance of ancient evolutionary processes operating in deep time."[45]

Another way of framing this debate between the ontological and cultural branches of affect theory is to notice how a disagreement between Massumi and Richard Grusin about the nature of affect resonates with aspects of Keats's "Ode to a Nightingale." As Schaefer explains, in a discussion generated just after Massumi gave a lecture on "how evolution could be understood in terms of Deleuzian affect" as a sort of "improvisational flow made up of endless becomings," Grusin suggested that there were forms of continuity that weren't being taken into account in Massumi's model. Grusin offered the example of how certain songbirds "returned to his backyard year after year, often nesting in the same tree." Massumi, however, was doubtful and proposed they changed location every year or that they were different birds singing the same song. Whereas Grusin emphasized "the stable patterns embedded in the durable relationship between the animals and their material worlds, Massumi emphasized the granular modulations of behavioral forms."[46]

For Massumi, "Affect is a sort of finely granulated field of vital energy sifting through bodies" (40). In this view, it would make perfect sense to say,

> Thou wast not born for death, immortal Bird!
>   No hungry generations tread thee down;
> The voice I hear this passing night was heard
>   In ancient days by emperor and clown:
> Perhaps the self-same song that found a path
>   Through the sad heart of Ruth, when, sick for home,
>   She stood in tears amid the alien corn. ("Ode to a Nightingale," 61–67)

For Grusin, in contrast, there is a greater consideration of "sustained attachments—the firm shapes of experience that emerge out of embodied histories."[47] Similarly, it is due to this capacity for sustained attachments that when the poetic speaker of the ode hears this "self-same song" "opening on the foam / Of perilous seas, in faery lands forlorn," the very word "forlorn"—a word suggesting excessive affect—becomes "like a bell / To toll me back from thee to my sole self!" Part of what is being registered in this ode, in other words, is the interplay between the two branches of affect theory, between experiencing the particular nightingale as just another modulation in an endless flow of improvisational becomings of the "self-same song" (perhaps because all members of the same species share the same "atoms of perception" as Keats will call them in the "vale of Soul-making" letter) and the firm shape of a "sole" self emerging out of a particular embedded experience of history.

Another hint of how this disjunction may relate in surprising ways to the broader political debates out of which Romanticism emerged is indicated by trying to map these two branches of affect theory onto the debates between Thomas Paine and Mary Wollstonecraft, on the one hand, and Edmund Burke, on the other, over the meaning of the French Revolution. The way cultural theorists of affect see behavior as being "built from chunks of psychological texture" and are interested in the way these textures form "a compendium of preexisting shapes that project their own potentials and limitations into the behavioral field" sounds a lot like Burke's "wardrobe of a moral imagination."[48] And the emphasis on reconfigurability and the plasticity of subjective dispositions aligns quite well with some of the assumptions of Paine and Wollstonecraft.

I will return to the political dimension of affect in the chapters on Coleridge and Shelley because both writers, albeit in different ways, are concerned with what Henri Bergson described as the processes by which experience can be "acquired by successive generations, deposited in the social environment, and [at least potentially] given back to each of us" in one form or another through aesthetic education, or some other medium of morality and/or religion.[49] Both poets were invested in what Bergson called "myth-making," or "fiction." Such acts of literature are significant because "if its image is vivid and insistent," these fictions can "masquerade as perception and in that way prevent or modify action" (109).

Mediation

This capacity to alter perception and organize action, which can be found in both religion and literature, gives credence to Talal Asad's claim that imagined communities are "mediated through constructed images."[50] As a result, the forms of media used "are not simply the means through which individuals imagine their national community; they *mediate* that imagination, construct the sensibilities that underpin it" (5). Thus Romanticism, like the Enlightenment, may be best understood as "an event in the history of mediation."[51] Mediation is meant here in the broadest sense to include "everything that intervenes, enables, supplements, or is simply in between" (5). Emergent mediations took the form of new infrastructures constructed to enable the transmission and communication of information, whether these forms consisted of bodies physically gathered together in new patterns of assemblage (the coffeehouse, the scientific society) or through the proliferating power of the printing press and other media technologies. Through these shifts "man became a new kind of tool—a tool whose power now lay in its insistence on using its 'own' understanding to change itself" (20). Or as Marshall McLuhan succinctly stated, these new mediations, "by altering the environment, evoke in us unique ratios of sense perceptions. The extension of any one sense alters the way we think and act—the way we perceive the world. When these ratios change, men change."[52]

Raymond Williams claimed that all media "have to be seen finally as alternative modes," since they all "frame" or filter perception in their own way.[53] Media theorists such as McLuhan, Walter Ong, and Friedrich Kittler all saw in the Romantic period a crucial moment of "far-reaching socio-cognitive reorganization," which was characterized by the emergence of print as a "general" medium, and which was accompanied by a series of changes that radically reoriented readers and the modern world in general.[54] Ong, for instance, argued that "the Romantic period marked a decisive shift from the orally centred culture . . . to a dominant vernacular print culture, a shift that precipitated a realignment of Western societies towards the values of the autonomous subject, abstract thought, and the dominance of the visual and spatial sense" (344). He found this emergent media environment as abundantly noetic and capable of restructuring the way in which we think and perceive. Kittler similarly saw Romanticism as being caught up in a processes of "alphabetization," which was accompanied by a series of changes in reading practices, pedagogy, and discursive networks that reoriented readers in ways that "transformed the abstract marks of the printed page into a fluid and continuous stream of experience."[55]

Celeste Langan and Maureen McLane argued that Romanticism coincides with a moment in which "poetry no longer had to serve the needs of information storage but could rather range more freely, untethered by age-old requirements of mnemonic repetition."[56] Before this shift, "man still necessarily carried a heavy load of detail in his mind" and so "memory systems flourished until typography had its full effect—until romanticism." However, when knowledge is "fastened down in visually processed space, man acquired an intellectual security never known before."[57] Through these changes, Romantic poets were granted the resources and the impetus to "reinvent poetry as a middle," or medium, that could "mediate between orality and print."[58] This enabled not only a movement away from the stock phrases and "pre-established codes of decision" as demanded by Wordsworth and Coleridge, but through this shift it was possible to reconsider the "relationship between thought processes and formulary expressions in the broad sense of pre-existing, fixed phrase."[59] In this way, Romanticism emerged at a moment not unlike the one Eric Havelock saw as providing the preface to Plato, one that arises out of a second orality, wherein the tradition of spoken poetry and rhymed verse is challenged and where new forms of print technology begin to offer alternative ways of separating the "knower from the known" and thus enabling new mediums for soul-making.[60]

The emergence of print culture and a "print mentality" is a key element that enables the movement away from an analogue world based in mimesis (as above; so below) and toward the new noetic abundance of a digital age.[61] The being of the analogue is based on copying a "continuously variable impulse or momentum that can cross from one qualitatively different medium into another."[62] Digital media, in contrast, entails "the perpetual, that is, repeated invention of the new."[63] The digital is defined as "of, pertaining to, or using digits," and a digital medium takes "the form of digital or similar discrete elements," such as the moveable type of the printing press.[64] In his book *Bodies in Code* and elsewhere, Mark Hansen has explored in suggestive ways how digital technologies have the potential to "expand the scope of bodily (motor) activity," "broaden the domain of the prepersonal," "create a rich, anonymous 'medium' for our enactive co-belonging," and transform "the agency of collective existence."[65] One advantage of digital technologies is that they can be manipulated in ways that enable the user to "reassert some control over the production of new presencings" and thereby "help personal consciousness intervene creatively and substantively in the production of . . . lived reality itself."[66]

Kittler claims that by the turn of the nineteenth century, writing had a virtual monopoly on perception: "As long as the book was responsible for all serial data flows, words quivered with sensuality and memory. It was the passion of all reading to hallucinate meaning between lines and letters: the visible and audible world of Romantic poetics."[67] As a result of the process Kittler called alphabetization a new "print mentality" emerged, which rewrites the code for core social and individual experiences.[68] Cut "off from the old, high transcendental truths," Alan Liu argues that a new notion of literature emerged as "a self-contained 'form' whose internally programmed complexity had to be 'closely read' with technical attention." In this way, imaginative literature could be understood as functioning in the manner suggested by the Romantic fascination with the Aeolian harp, as a "special kind of algorithmic computational instrument on a par with the Babbage machines and Jacquard looms of the time ancestral to the digital computer." Although "poiesis is not the same as technology, communication, or computation," it "combines all these to imagine the identity tales . . . that mediate 'us' in relation to the others who are part of our generative kernel."[69] One response to these shifts led to a "sustained effort to reimagine poetry not as a genre—a literary kind among kinds—but as a medium." A medium is "a middle layer; a means; an intermediary; a transmitting conduit; an impeding conduit; a solution or solvent; a physico-technical apparatus; a route; a conductor; an instrument; a means of communication; a physical object for the storage of data."[70]

Significantly, around the time of Romanticism, "driven by and driving the greater availability of letterpress printing, the generalization of silent reading promoted an effective interiorization of the medium of language." Such silent reading appears to offer "immediate access to the thoughts of another" (241). In her influential essay "Understanding Media in 1805: Audiovisual Hallucination in The Lay of the Last Minstrel," Langan argues that this is one reason why Romantic poetry in particular is so apt for experimentation. By silencing "actual speech differences—class, provincial, and gendered vocal inflections—print [became] the medium of a virtual community of speakers," and this new reliance on the printed word transformed many things, including poetry.[71] Building on the work of Kittler, Ong, and McLuhan, Langan argues that within Romanticism the medium of poetry responds to these shifts by becoming itself "a kind of digital code, of stress patterns."[72] "Blank" instead of rhymed verse emerges as the dominant form of a digital poetics—one that can deeply affect a reader's "body in code."[73] What occurs as a "result of this 'blanking' of the auditory screen, . . . is startling: a greater variety of audiovisual hallucinations." When read silently "the poetic figure seems that much more a sculptural or pictorial form; and, no longer subjected to the immediate sensory input of verbal melody, the silent reader gains access to the mediated (i.e., narratively evoked) musical scene of the poem."[74] As McLuhan also recognized, "the visual dimension of romantic poetry ('like shooting scripts for some contemporary documentary film') is attributable to the effect of 'equitone' prose on poetry."[75] This is one reason why in Kittler's view "around 1800, the book became both film and record simultaneously—not, however, as a technological reality, but only in the imaginary of readers' souls."[76] In this way Romantic poetry can be seen as a protocinematic technology.[77] Various implications of this protocinematic shift will be a particular concern of chapter 4, but throughout this book I explore the variety of ways Romantic poetics enables readers to use textuality as a form of prosthesis that can instigate and potentially help navigate technologic modifications of their mediated souls or vehicular consciousnesses in ways that can alter and expand one's sense of the possible.

Poetry begins to function in a manner similar to cinema in part because, as David Trotter has argued, now "regular meter and rhyme were neither an encumbrance nor an expressive support, but precisely a frame, a 'prosthesis of observation.'"[78] Rhythm functions as "a fragment of myth or ritual which [holds] the personal and the impersonal in productive (and possibly even cathartic) tension" (252). The selective usage of the regularity of rhyme and meter acts as a kind of frame for eye and ear alike. Here "all the passion of reading consisted of hallucinating a meaning between letters and lines."[79] Such poetry possesses a capacity for glamour, in Walter Scott's sense of the word, "the magic power of imposing on the eyesight of the spectators, so that the appearance of the object shall be totally different from the reality."[80] For Giorgio Agamben, the poem becomes a kind of "organism or a temporal machine that, from the very start, strains toward its end."[81] Particularly through its development of blank verse, Romantic poetry becomes cinematographic: "a device (and the necessary apparatus) by which a series of instantaneous photographs of moving objects taken in rapid succession are projected on a screen in similarly rapid and intermittent succession so as to produce the illusion of a single moving scene."[82]

Cinema, Hansen writes, "comprises the paradigmatic 'temporal object' in relation to which consciousness is able to take a distance from itself and reflect on its own temporal flow, the inner self-affection by time that, for western philosophy from Kant onward, constitutes the very content of 'inner sense' or 'internal time consciousness.'" Within modernity, political and cultural industries attempt to coopt this inner sense by "controlling and directly capitalizing the time of consciousness itself."[83] Fortunately, despite these efforts to capture and hold our attention like the "glittering eye" of the Ancient Mariner one benefit of the way Romanticism participates in the general digitalization of information and media is that "by engaging the body's capacity to affectively sense the passing of time in the present," it begins to suggest ways to "allow consciousness to live time (at least to some extent) according to its own rhythms."[84]

Protocinematic Poetry

Sensibility and Romanticism are two forms of *poiesis* that emerged in the eighteenth century and are rooted in protocinematic technologies. The aim of this section is to make clear how the trajectory of Romanticism, and the trajectory of the arguments of this book, acknowledge, yet diverge from, James Chandler's efforts, in *An Archaeology of Sympathy*, to trace how the sentimental disposition first emerges out of a philosophic and theological conception of the sensorium or "sentimental soul," then developed through aesthetic advances in the form of the novel in the eighteenth century, which are ultimately adapted by Charles Dickens and others in the nineteenth century, into techniques that help order and organize classical narrative system of early Hollywood.[85] Significantly, Chandler specifically aligns these developments in the history of mediation with Deleuze's notion of the movement-image, which is articulated in the first of his two volumes on *Cinema*. Chandler is right to emphasize the movement-image in his analysis of this sentimental lineage because, whether what is viewed is the tender embrace of reunited lovers or the twists and turns of a car chase, within the movement-image a rational structure is wedded to a linear narrative by closed framings, reasonable progressions, and continuous juxtaposition. This has been the standard form for both novels and cinema. Through a strategy of montage that emphasizes a logical chronology of narrative cues, the movement-image trains us to see a "train of ideas succeeding one another in our minds."[86] The typical response to such works is, to use Wordsworth's words, to "oft perceive / Fair trains of imagery before me rise, / Accompanied by feelings of delight" (*WPP, The Excursion*, 2–4). Perceivers of the movement-image "are conscious of [its] train of ideas and its movements, though they are not actively creating it and are not able to suddenly add to it at will."[87] One consequence of this perennially popular form of mediation is that, as Hume puts it, "The imagination, when set into any train of thinking, is apt to continue, even when its object fails it, and like a galley put in motion by the oars, carries on its course without any new impulse" (*T*, 1.4.2.22). This is one reason the movement-image is particularly conducive to those forms of cultural productions that are most invested in capturing attention by providing vehicles for escapism and why it tends to move the buffered subjects of modernity along well-worn grooves of consumerism, capitalism, and political passivity.

This is not to say that there are not many positive attributes to the movement-image and to the literature of sensibility more generally. One popular form of sentimental poetics was the tendency toward the deployment of personifications. Although as Jennifer Keith acknowledges, for the modern reader personifications can seem like "empty capitalized nouns," to eighteenth-century readers they were "considered powerful stimulants to sensory experience."[88] In *Elements of Criticism* (1762), Lord Kames describes intense sensory responses to poetic imagery such as personification as partaking of what he calls "ideal presence": a state of intense reverie that "can make the reader forget that he or she is holding a book, and instead 'conceive every incident as passing in his presence, precisely as if he were an eyewitness.'"[89] In this way, sensibility and sentimental literature function as early forms of virtual reality.[90] When reading a poem like William Cowper's "The Castaway" (1799), we do not merely see in our mind's eye a man drowning but may feel we too are perishing "each alone: . . . beneath a rougher sea, / And whelm'd in deeper gulfs than he" (64–66). The most effective and innovated examples of the poetry of sensibility create a mood of intimacy between reader and sufferer through a poetic practice "based on an irregular and unpredictable coincidence of sound-patterns."[91] Through this combination of eye and ear "the reader participates in an unfolding sensory experience" so that he or she is touched by what is read.[92]

Chandler argues that sentimentality concerns itself with how the sentiments are made up of "distributed feeling" or "emotion that results from social circulation, passion that has been mediated by a sympathetic passage through a virtual point of view."[93] We are sentimental when we see how someone else sees the world and we sympathize with that point of view. Points of view are the "most marked index of an embedded sensorium" (xvii). They are particular partitions of the sensible. The sentimental journeys that typify most novels and films exploit the fact that "the capacity to sympathize and the capacity to experience sensation" are bound up with each other (180). What the sentimental journeys of writers like Laurence Sterne capitalized upon is that if you want to see things in a new way then you should see new things (by looking out your moving stagecoach window, by reading a novel, or through some other form of transport). Sentimental techniques play upon the fact that the more we sympathize with someone the more likely we will be able to see things from their point of view and vice versa.

In order to clarify what is meant by sensibility and sentimentality, it is helpful to recall Friedrich Schiller's influential distinction between the naïve and the sentimental: to be naïve is to simply and directly experience the world before us, but to be sentimental is to possess the capacity and tendency to reflect upon and potentially alter the cognitive and affective impulses (or sentiments) that make up and inform how our world is being viewed and experienced. A sentiment is "an internal impulse of passion, affectation, fancy or intellect, which is considered rather as the cause or occasion of forming an opinion, than as the real opinion itself."[94] It is something sensed or felt "rather than just held or thought."[95] Sensibility refers to "that peculiar structure, or habitude of mind, which disposes a man to be easily moved, and powerfully affected, by surrounding objects and passing events."[96] Sensibility is the capacity to move and be moved. It is "an expanded model of perception rooted in the lineages of causal efficacy that stand behind and, in a sense, give body to any act of sense perception."[97] For the Cambridge Platonist Henry More, "sensibility is the essential quickness, the vital sensorium that supplies the soul's moving vehicle."[98]

The discourses surrounding sensibility emerged when they did in part because of "how the eighteenth century secularized the passions into the emotions with the development of the discipline of psychology, thus making the emotions components of the individual subject."[99] This shift is registered in Hume's philosophy when he moves from using "the passions," as he did in his *A Treatise of Human Nature* (1739), to "the moral sentiments" in subsequent essays. However, as Philip Fisher argues in *The Vehement Passions* (2002), the use of the term "sentiments" did not merely "rename the set of problems posed by earlier discussions of the passions; rather, they install an entirely new geography of the self around self-love, sympathy for others, and the motives of the active will in its endeavor to continue existing."[100] The passions, as traditionally understood, are "monarchical states of being" because "impassioned states seem to drive out every other form of attention or state of being" (43). Disrupting the ordinary flow of experience, "the passions create a state of exception. In their suddenness and intensity, they map a personal world, fix and qualify our attention, and impel our actions."[101] The passions are excited by "what occurs within a world of care and concern" that corresponds closely to that which is closest to us and are often "intolerant of the state of others and even of the consequences for others of the passion felt by the self."[102] Vehement passions install an absolute priority of the self and draw "a line around a human subject, defining and intensifying personal will, personal limits," and personal attachments.[103] There is a single-mindedness to the passions, and in this way they are "humorless."[104]

Chandler finds that the sentiments, in contrast, "spread us thin," and are "the result of a projective imagination across a network or relay of regard." "Regard" here means "attention, respect, heed, care," but also "a look or a gaze, an act performed with the eyes." Such regard always already "involves a sense of how another is regarding us, what our eyes can see in the eyes of another, or more generally in the face of another."[105] Sentiments are formed "through the process of exchanging places" within the network of regard "by means of sympathetic imagination."[106] The network of regard forms a "social mind," which John Savarese defines as "a set of strategies for attributing mental states to other people, keeping track of what different social actors think or believe, and comporting one's behavior accordingly."[107] It elaborates "a system of looking at lookers looking—even, or especially, when all this looking is taking place in the virtual space of the printed page."[108] The sentimental spectator reflects on his or her impressions. To be sentimental is to cook "raw perception" with "the receptiveness of a tutored taste."[109]

Key facets of the architecture of the literature of sensibility include *point of view*, which "develops as the sensorium is increasingly understood to be punctually located in time and space"; *mobility*, which "registers the relation between motion and emotion"; and *virtuality*, which "marks the capacity of an embodied sensorium . . . to undergo circulation among a range of imagined sensory locations." Perhaps the core component, however, is *sympathy*, "which connects one sensorium with another by enabling us to face one another, adopt one another's points of view, and modify passion into sentiment by means of virtual circulation."[110] To be sentimental is to be capable of sympathy, which is "to put oneself in the case of the other" so as to "posit a kind of virtual body or virtual set of circumstances into which one projects oneself" (271–72). Sympathy is a state of fellow feeling, which Rae Greiner finds to be relying upon "a form of thinking geared toward others, including the other that is myself as others see me."[111] The discourses surrounding sensibility became a means of determining "how a body should appear and behave in public."[112] Over the course of the eighteenth century the figure of the literary spectator is increasingly identified with a capacity for sympathy, and this posture of attention is found to be especially well suited to the rhythms and meanings of capitalist modernity, since the capacity to anticipate and approximate how others will value something is a key component to the successful negotiation of the capitalist system of exchange.

Literature is one domain in which sympathy and the moral imagination can be cultivated and exercised because, as Adam Smith influentially claimed, it enables us to "transport ourselves in fancy" to the scene of a book or historical circumstance, so that we can "enter into" the emotions of its participants and "bring home to ourselves the situation" in which their feeling takes place.[113] Sympathy is "the bridge between the social and the psychological, the faculty by which inner mental states are shared among individuals."[114] In Smith's reading of sympathy, the imagination is what brings fellow feeling into being. We identify with the suffering of others by picturing them, and sympathy is produced "by changing places in fancy with the sufferer."[115] The grounds of a moral understanding may be obtained when the activity of the imagination is powerful enough to forge connections between otherwise unshared lives. Questions of who is in my network of regard or who is my neighbor are both sentimental and deeply ethical. Fortunately, "as our moral sentiments progress, we reflectively expand our sense of sympathy, increasing the degree to which we share specific feelings with an ever-wider array of our fellows."[116]

Sympathy, as Miranda Burgess has shown, enables "the subject's imaginative movement through time and space, precisely to the extent that it depends on the medium of the imagination."[117] To engage in sympathy is, in Chandler's formulation, "to put oneself in the case of the other" and thereby "posit a kind of virtual body" that can enter a "set of circumstances into which one projects oneself." To put oneself in the case of the other, or to love one's neighbor as oneself, "requires both an act of disembodiment and (at the same time) of virtual reembodiment." However, only that which can be rendered in a medium that permits virtual experience is generative of sympathy. Only "if my circumstances can be rendered as a case—and my relation to the object world given a certain 'objectivity'—can my subject position in relation to them become intelligible."[118] Smith "explicitly banishes, from the outset, the idea that we can feel what others feel in favor of the notion that we feel according to how we imagine it would be to place ourselves in their situations" (240).

A capacity for reflection and sympathy is cultivated in the daily life of commercial civil society, because such a society is one in which participants are continually called to function as a sympathetic spectator for other people. The default posture in both commerce and culture becomes that of a "perpetually mobile attentiveness."[119] However, the overall mobility of each vehicular consciousness is perceived to operate within a field of vision observable by an impartial spectator, a term used by Smith, which Chandler defines as "an internal principle of general perception that is able to counteract our egotism (as the weak spirit of benevolence cannot) because it carries the force of recognition, the sense of truly seeing ourselves, for example, in our own littleness within the world."[120] The sentimental subject is an individual whose agency is confirmed by the force of recognition of his or her own acts of judgment and who assumes all other members of his or her social set are similarly equipped. Each sympathetic spectator sees him- or herself performing "before a social world of (likewise) potentially sympathetic spectators" (172). How each member of this social set should be judged is ultimately "decided" by the impartial spectator, that imagined virtual perspective that Smith sees functioning as a kind of "looking-glass by which we can, in some measure, with the eyes of other people, scrutinize the propriety of our own conduct."[121] One consequence of a sentimental structure of society is that "the process of aesthetic judgment allows a virtual community, a purely 'subjective universality,' to displace altogether the embodied community."[122]

Unfortunately, as John Milbank points out, there are limits to Smith's sense of sympathy. One is that although "the exercise of moral sympathy is indeed morally crucial (as the Cambridge Platonists and Shaftesbury already taught in a more subtle way), it is not spontaneously right," because we can only really sympathize with those within our network of regard—within our own affective neighborhood. Furthermore, sympathy isn't "naturally given," and so we "must always judge as to what is deserving of our sympathy—and if we imagine ourselves in the position of the other," then this is possible only "insofar as we conceive our shared but various participation, along with the other, in the objective good."[123] This is why Thomas Pfau sees sympathy working best only within a set of people that construes the "objective good" in more or less the same way: "Moral sentiments, then, are not stand-alone units of subjective experience, on the contrary, they constitute prima facie acts of 'assent' or value judgments about a social situation, and as such they do not signify an inner (mental) action but a social transaction."[124] Sympathy is not foundational, necessary, or universally shared. The absorptive dangers of sentimentalism must also be taken into account: we can sympathize with the wrong people for the wrong reasons. There is also a "peculiar qualification" of passivity to this form of sympathy in that everyone feels like he or she is "always on stage, but [each] takes himself or herself to be a mere spectator" (342). Another limitation of Smith's sympathy is that it only works if I can imagine what it would be like to be in the other's case, and thus "I" remain the (colonizing) standard and I can only love my neighbor "as" myself.

One way to right these (potential) wrongs is to adopt a posture of sympathy that emerges through a detachment, or dispossession, of one's self, so that a space can be cleared for the appearance of others. What is needed are formal techniques that can help cut, edit, or splice ourselves from conventional attachments and help us attend to those impartialities that interrupt our normative forms of common sense. In contrast with Smith, for whom sympathy was always mediated through "virtual experience" and routed through cognition, for his friend Hume, sympathy was a matter of vibration, contagion, and "force" (*T*, 1.1.6:16). In Hume's view, the sympathizer could be affected by sentiments that were not their own: "As in strings equally wound up, the motion of one communicates itself to the rest; so all the affections readily pass from one person to another" (*T*, 3.3.1:7). Nevertheless, despite this capacity to partake in another's signifying stress, Hume insists we are still "free to deliberate on the degree to which we are affected, and on what we are going to do as a result."[125] Hume's model of sympathy assumes that at least potentially anyone can "enter into the same humour, and catch the sentiment, by a contagion or natural sympathy."[126] Through such sympathy, to use Anna Gibbs's evocative description, "Bodies can catch feelings as easily as catch fire: affect leaps from one body to another, evoking tenderness, inciting shame, igniting rage, exciting fear—in short, communicable affect can inflame nerves and muscles in a conflagration of every conceivable kind of passion."[127]

The magic of this "natural sympathy" is that it can "return feeling with like feeling."[128] In this way, the divergence in the models of sympathy found in Smith and Hume is analogous to the divergence between the two great classes of sympathetic magic described in James George Frazer's *The Golden Bough* (1890): one is the magic of imitation, the other that of contact. According to Sara Ahmed, in Smith's model of sympathy "you enter into another's happiness only if you agree with it" (238). This is a "conditional sympathy," which helps orient the sympathizer within a network of regard, because "to share in the happiness of others is how we come to have a direction toward something, which is already an agreement that the object is appropriate" (239). Smith, unlike Hume, assumes "sympathy takes place through mediation—regardless of proximity and physical encounter."[129] Hume's model of sympathy is more disruptive because here sympathetic feelings "are neither mimetic nor semiotic in any way nor subordinate to statements of fact. They are quantities of force."[130]

For Hume, sympathy is "'moved' through the channels of the senses, rather than those of imaginative identification."[131] He asserts that "no quality of human nature is more remarkable . . . than that propensity we have to sympathize with others, and to receive by communication their inclinations and sentiments, however different from, or even contrary to, our own" (*T*, 2.1.11.2). This produces, as Lorri Nandrea notes, "a somewhat different picture of the way feeling might be communicated by a literary text," one wherein the text itself could be understood as "a forceful stimulus that would act directly on the reader's physical sensibilities, without the intervention of identification or imaginative projections." Instead of identification the reader repeats "the sensation the passage scripts (or allow[s] the sensation to be repeated through them) rather than copying a model."¹³² Here "sensibility produces and is produced by dynamic repetition" (117). It is the repetition of the performance that initiates and ensures the transfer of meaning from text to reader. Romanticism is one name for the cultivation of those literary devices "that are oriented purely toward affective intensification, inflecting the text" (114). Such cultivation comes to fruition in the reader's response to the text, which should be understood as a set of instructions to be acted out by the participant observer. The efficaciousness of such texts depends less on "an ability to imagine the self in the place of the other—than on sensory susceptibility—a willingness to be played upon, to be altered" (115).

Significantly, in his archeology of sympathy Chandler only briefly touches upon Romantic authors such as William Blake and Jane Austen, saying he is more interested "in that line of work for which sentiment and sensibility tend to be imbricated rather than opposed."¹³³ My interest, however, is in exploring how and why Romanticism swerves from this main line that runs from the rise of the novel to the cultural industries of our own day, a lineage which has become increasingly adept at cultivating and capturing our attention. As William Blake understood, in order to see things clearly one must first cleanse the doors of perception by unmaking the sentimental "mind forg'd manacles" that bind us to unsavory networks of regard. His *Songs of Innocence and of Experience*, for example, offer one example of how art might help in this process, since they so often engage in situations where the underlying point of view is subtly ambiguous. The *Songs* often attempt to represent conflicting emotions in such a way so as to "decompose sentiment into what he called passion and sense."¹³⁴ By doing so it becomes apparent how what makes "sense" to us both in terms of how the world is viewed and how one's own mediated soul or sensorium is experienced is ultimately a matter of how the structure and syntax of a given sensibility is assembled.

Both the point and the point of view of one of Blake's *Songs* looks different depending on how its ambiguous syntax is read. Blake's aim is to "cast the syntactic joints," produced through sensibility, as "mind forg'd manacles." To avoid being enslaved by another man's system he sought to "denaturalize the level of habitual reflection and exchange that marks the sentimental."¹³⁵ Romanticism in general can be conceived as a set of inquiries and techniques for the making and unmaking of passionate sense. It swerves from sentimentality by offering an alternative understanding of sympathy, subjectivity, and neighborliness as well as a postsecular political theology and biopolitics that is anchored by something other than Smith's "impartial spectator."

Romanticism offers tools to enable individuals to mediate their own self-understanding in ways that allow for greater agency and a more robust capacity for navigating their own vehicular consciousness within modernity. As will be discussed more fully in chapters 4 and 5, one way Romanticism does so is by tapping into the rhythms, movements, and interruptions of the time-image, Deleuze's other major categorization of cinematic form. Whereas the movement-image emphasized in sensibility is based in action and the chronology of narrative cues, the time-image focuses on perception and highlights rupture, hesitation, irrational cutting, and prolonged duration. Unlike the movement-image, which is closer to the unscrolling landscape of loco-descriptive poetry, the time-image exists not as a chronology of actions but as a much more open-ended happening. Classic examples of the time-image in cinema can be found in Alain Resnais's *L'Année dernière à Marienbad* (*Last Year at Marienbad*), Stanley Kubrick's *2001*, and more recently Terrence Malick's *The Tree of Life*. Within Romantic poetry, good examples of the time-image can be found in Wordsworth's "spots of time," Samuel Taylor Coleridge's "Kubla Khan" and "The Rime of the Ancient Mariner," Charlotte Smith's "Beachy Head," Keats's "Fall of Hyperion," Percy Shelley's *Prometheus Unbound* and "The Triumph of Life," and throughout William Blake's prophetic books.

Later in the book, during the discussions of Keats and Shelley in chapters 4 and 5, I will return to this divergence and trace the implications of how Romanticism tends toward a cinema of the time-image, while sensibility, as Chandler specifically notes, like much of the popular culture that came after it, is more firmly rooted in the form of the movement-image. One way the formal logic of the time-image will come into play is in the fifth chapter's discussion of how Shelley's poetics offers "imageless images" to readers in order to lift them up out of a "savage" sense of necessity and into a "philosophic" sense. Here there is also a train of thinking, but this "train" does not imply "regulated succession or natural consequence" but is closer to Hume's version of a "train of thinking" (*T*, 1.4.2.22) and what Shelley will call "philosophic necessity"—as "the forces and intensities of assembly that assemble discontinuous impressions."[136]

For Hume, the "train of ideas" follows the "movement between discontinuous instants that, when streamed together, generates the impression of collation."[137] This movement functions much like McLuhan's description of "reading after the invention of the printing press," in which the reader is put "in the place of the movie projector thus moving the series of imprinted letters before him at the speed consistent with apprehending the motions of the author's mind."[138] The key difference in viewing or reading the time-image, however, is that there is often no obvious or necessary causality linking one moment of perception to the next. As I explore more fully in later chapters, it is often by tapping into the rhythms and movements of the time-image that Romanticism offers tools that enable individuals to mediate their own self-understanding in ways that give them greater agency as well as more robust capacity for orienting and navigating their own vehicular consciousness within modernity.

Cinematic Subjectivity

If Romantic poetry is often cinematographic and projects a series of instantaneous impressions in a rapid and intermittent succession, then how can readers contract these impressions and experience a single moving scene? The focus of this chapter's penultimate section is on how the philosophy of Hume, as well as subsequent interpretations of his philosophy, can clarify, as well as delineate, the ways in which specific patterns of habit, body schemas, or postures of attention can be broadcast in a postsecular age and how and why such perceptual suggestions are both affective and efficacious. The model of cinematic subjectivity articulated here will be developed out of Hume's version of empiricism and will have implications for all subsequent chapters but will be particularly crucial to the arguments in the chapters on Keats and Shelley. By reconsidering subjectivity in light of this model, ways can be found of moving beyond the forms of buffered subjectivity that Taylor and others see as dominant within secularity.

Empiricism is ultimately an approach to the question of how relations contract and dissolve, in what Brian O'Keeffe calls "an ongoing, restless play of both active and passive association."[139] What is perceived to be reality actually "involves our creating continuous ties to those things and relations, identities and continuities, most proximate to us."[140] Empiricism is a philosophy of the imagination, an imagination that takes the "data-stream flowing in from the senses" and gathers and contracts these perceptions together, gradually firming up what were previously discrete or atomistic "data elements into intelligible schemas."[141] Experience strings "objects" together, and as "these strings unspool into the future; imagination and habit conjure these next objects up, and in doing so, they ... anticipate what the future holds in store for experience itself" (76). Habit is fundamental to our thinking about time and our place in it. Time itself is produced through the imagination's habitual contraction of discrete impressions.[142] The present by itself is "almost too fleeting to root itself securely into time's continuum—a rippling sand dune, shifting under one's feet."[143]

In his preface to *Lyrical Ballads*, Wordsworth describes how the "habits of mind" that enable sensibility are developed and can be suggestively passed on to others through "habits of meditation" (*WPP*, 79). The poet is the one who "considers man and the objects that surround him as acting and re-acting upon each other, so as to produce an infinite complexity of pain and pleasure," and looks "upon this complex scene of ideas and sensations," and finds "every where objects that immediately excite in him sympathies" (*WPP*, 87). The model of mind that Wordsworth finds operative in the poet as it responds to this "complex scene of ideas and sensations" is as follows:

> For our continued influxes of feeling are modified and directed by our thoughts, which are indeed the representatives of all our past feelings; and as by contemplating the relation of these general representatives to each other, we discover what is really important to men, so by the repetition and continuance of this act feelings connected with important subjects will be nourished, till at length, if we be originally possessed of much organic sensibility, such habits of mind will be produced that by obeying blindly and mechanically the impulses of those habits we shall describe objects and utter sentiments of such a nature and in such connection with each other, that the understanding of the being to whom we address ourselves, if he be in a healthful state of association, must necessarily be in some degree enlightened, his taste exalted, and his affections ameliorated. (*WPP*, 79)

As Chandler notes, Wordsworth's epistemology here is drawn directly from the opening of Hume's *A Treatise of Human Nature* (1739), "with 'feelings' substituted for Hume's 'impressions' and 'thoughts' substituted for Hume's 'ideas.'"[144]

The emphasis for each is on how feelings or impressions "are modified and directed" by thoughts or ideas, ideas that are themselves "nothing other than a surviving trace or representative of a fleeting impression" (167). Initially, appearances are only "broken appearances" (*T*, 1.4.2.36): separate, discontinuous, and interrupted. For Hume, it is only when the imagination contracts or actively assembles through habit discordant impressions that constancies can be composed "from the discontinuous impressions that life affords."[145] Ideas are formed when singular and partial impressions are subsequently contracted in the imagination through forces of contiguity, resemblance, and the like. Through this processing of previous impressions, ideas and a sense of one's own subjectivity are produced. When we contemplate ideas and "the relation of these general representatives to each other," then we engage with what Hume calls "impressions of reflection" (*T*, 1.1.2).

Taken as whole this model of epistemology functions as a three-step process. First, impressions or sensation are taken in, which are then filtered through and asked to correspond with ideas that are themselves the surviving traces of previous pressings of experience. When we reflect upon how and why such ideas recur to the mind, we engage in a secondary act of contemplation through which sentiments are produced. Sentiments are "something felt—sensed, from the Latin *sentire*—rather than just held or thought."[146] They are formed during moments in which feeling and thinking are deeply connected. Once sentiments have been developed into "habits of mind" they can be sympathetically suggested, transferred or projected toward others, to those whom we address if he or she "be in a healthful state of association" (*WPP*, 79).

"Tintern Abbey" again serves as a good model of how this structure works. In the poem, Wordsworth has returned to the area of the Abbey after five long years. He sees the same place again and realizes that although it is more or less similar, he has changed a great deal. The youth who was full of aching joys and dizzying raptures has now become a soberer and more mature man. The mature Wordsworth looks back at the youthful version of himself that was full of feeling and "glad animal movements" and realizes that this earlier feelingful sense of self is now lost to him. "For nature then / . . . / To me was all in all.—I cannot paint / What then I was" (73–76). Where once a "thoughtless youth" was passionately haunted by the crashing of a waterfall's "sounding cataract" (79), there now stands a man who must content himself with the "still, sad music of humanity," the "joy / Of elevated thoughts" (93), and "a sense sublime / Of something far more deeply interfused" (96–97). Whereas the naïve youth reveled in immediacy, the sentimental poet is the one who "*reflects* on the impression the objects make upon him, and only on the basis of that reflection is emotion founded, into which he is transported and into which he transports us."[147] Thus, in Thomas Pfau's view, the poem can be understood to be trying to teach us how "to transmute the extrinsic shock of discontinuity into the pleasure of an inward 'experience' that encompasses prospects of social ascendancy, aesthetic proficiency, and spiritual transcendence."[148]

Within "Tintern Abbey," the transferential potential of such remediation is realized through the poet's turn toward his sister Dorothy.[149] When the poet suddenly addresses Dorothy two-thirds of the way through the poem, he says, it is "in thy voice I catch / The language of my former heart, and read / My former pleasures in the shooting lights / Of thy wild eyes" (117–20). Wordsworth sees in his sister's eyes an indication of the feeling that once was his, a feeling he nostalgically recalls but can no longer directly access. However, halfway through the verse paragraph addressed to Dorothy, William begins to anticipate the day when she will, like him, similarly observe from a distance the same unmediated feelings of porousness that currently flash in the "shooting lights" of her "wild eyes." In this way, William is able to displace his feelings of loss about his previous sense of a porous oneness with nature, and his fears about what happens when he will no longer be around to catch the gleams of his past (lyric) moments, by hoping that he will not be forgotten and that future generations will continually "catch" the meaning of his work. Through his poetry, Wordsworth is attempting to find a way of reanimating some part of himself in others and in this way propagating his (lyric) identity across the chasm of time and space, becoming like "a being who had passed alone / Beyond the visible barriers of the world / And traveled into things to come."[150] He does so by anticipating the day when his current sentimental disposition can be projected onto and embodied in a future version of Dorothy and by extension the reader, if she "be in a healthful state of association" (*WPP*, 79).

One becomes reflective only after experience is mediated through some screen. The mere fact that Wordsworth has come to the abbey a second time is one way his experience is mediated, and this is why David Collings finds the poem highlighting "the tension between the affective force of what preoccupies him and its literal presence."[151] The turn to Dorothy at the end of the poem becomes another form of mediation. For Marjorie Levinson, she "functions in the poem as a final surface, the condition for the poet's ongoing reflective life."¹⁵² Dorothy becomes the screen upon which William can recognize and reflect upon the dissociation within his own sensibility as well as project into perpetuity the sense of self he currently possesses. This is significant because "lacking this screen—a kind of alienated tabula rasa—the speaker knows himself only as a fixture of the landscape; unable to reflect upon it, and therefore, by his problematic, produced by it, and, as its creature, incapable of self-reflection" (46). With this mediating screen, however, the poem can itself become a form of "perceptual suggestion."¹⁵³

Thus the poem rehearses the tripartite process described above: first, impressions are taken in, then they are processed and made to correspond with previous pressings of experience, whereby a sentimental disposition or a habit of mind is contracted, which can be subsequently transferred or projected onto others. By tapping into this dynamic, poetry functions as a medium through which such sympathies can be suggestively broadcast. The willing recipient who obeys "blindly and mechanically the impulses of those habits" transmitted in this way, "must necessarily be in some degree enlightened, his taste exalted, and his affections ameliorated" (WPP, 79). Such suggestion, according to Noel Jackson, is "a central feature of the Romantic psychology of imagination, accounting not only for the capacity of the poet to receive and to represent experiences of lively sensation but to communicate (or 'suggest') sensations to others." In this way, suggestion serves "as a term for the process by which the mind receives and orders the experiences of the senses, [and] furnishes a model for the capacity of the individual mind or of the artwork to register, give form to, and modify the sensible impressions of history."¹⁵⁴

Forms of mediation that can inform or alter such habits of self can be deeply significant because, as Deleuze suggested, the self is itself a "contemplative soul" that emerges from the contraction of "punctual impressions."¹⁵⁵ We are "habits, nothing but habits—the habit of saying 'I.'"¹⁵⁶ This "I" is modeled "as a rather loose (or at least initially loose) assemblage—a self in perpetual formation and becoming, a bundle of multiplicities and little coalescings."¹⁵⁷ As Deleuze writes in *Empiricism and Subjectivity* (1953), "We start with atomic parts, but these atomic parts have transitions, passages, 'tendencies,' which circulate from one to another. These tendencies give rise to habits" (x). According to Hume, even our sense of causality itself is only a habit. The first time I see a billiard ball I have no idea what will happen when I hit it. It is only through repetition that I contract a sense of what to expect. Through repetition there is "the transition from an exteriority of atomic instants to their contraction in habit."[158] Repetition, for Hume, "changes nothing in the object repeated, but does change something in the mind which contemplates it."[159] When given the first in a series of impressions (AB, AB, AB), I learn to anticipate the second (B), when confronted with the first (A). However, by doing so I draw a difference in the mind but do not necessarily identify something that is actually in the world. In this way, the Humean self is always in a process of becoming, and "habit is accordingly key to how we might consider both fixity and fluctuation."[160]

My approach to Hume is influenced by Davide Panagia—who sees Hume as "one of the first modern cinematic thinkers to the extent that he is a thinker of moving images—of successions of interrupted perceptions, or broken appearances."[161] Hume's "philosophy is cinematic; it is a philosophy of projection."[162] The world that is viewed outside of us, including its "enduring physical objects, power, substance, aesthetic and moral values, and more are all projected." Ultimately, for Hume, "nature and custom are the master magicians whose artifices make the world reappear, full of meaning and value and equipped with physical substances having causal powers." The first trick of Hume's skeptical empiricism is to conceptualize "experience so as to make that familiar world disappear." Nevertheless, "thanks to nature and custom, the world reappears, only in a new modality, as projection" (487).

The world as a whole is "a collection of singular partialities pressing the one upon the other and that, through various intensities of association and dissociation, are brought together or wrought apart."[163] Our self-composition as well as our imagined reality is generated and rendered through the continuous creating of ties between fleeting impressions, which are drawn by compositional forces such as "causality, contiguity, habit, and resemblance" (2). The mind is made up "of nothing other than an anonymous web of memories that inspire an array of inner sensations and ethical impulses."[164] The network of regard we find ourselves participating in is not given to us already complete but is itself built up over time through the accumulation of habit.

Panagia argues that one reason Hume seems so modern is that he was an "astute new media thinker" who attended to "the new media ontologies of transcription and inscription that flourished in his day."[165] In the case of Hume's empiricism, "cinematography begins with the printing press." What the printing press afforded him was a "medium that allows for the infinite arrangement and rearrangement of typographic units so that language stops looking like a unity and begins to look and feel quite literally as a disassembled jumble of characters." The introduction of moveable type "allowed letters, characters, words, and spaces to be conceived as permanently movable and hence discontinuous with one another." The printing press offered a form of mediation that encouraged revision, because it "allowed an author the possibility of altering one's composition by rearranging loose and discontinuous characters into a compositional whole, whose standing as a whole was as provisional as the next round of revisions, or the next scrolling of the press" (49). This new media of movable typography, which emerged out of the possibilities of the printing press, shattered "the classificatory ontology of the Great Chain of Being: after its arrival, the word of God was no longer stable and unified, but was transformed into something that could be dissected, altered, and shifted—infinitely citable and individualized" (50).

This new form of mediation suggested a new understanding of subjectivity, wherein "A self begins and ends with a perception of it: it is a punctual impression, or a snapshot along the reel of a film, if you will. It has all the aspects of a character being impressed upon a sheet of paper in black ink, and, just as such an impression exists in that space and time of its being impressed, so selves appear and disappear at indeterminate, durational intervals of perception" (66). Hume insists, "There is no impression constant and invariable" (*T*, 1.4.6.2). A self is a "moving impression, but, as such, it is also fleeting and impermanent."[166] Such a self functions like "a commonwealth where individual members, or parts, reciprocally affect one another" (70). In this sense, "the person, or self, is cinematic in that she is a stochastic series of discontinuous impressions composed and articulated according to certain intensities of association and dissociation" (68). These ongoing processes of assembly and disassembly, figuring and disfiguring, and constructing and deconstructing have ontological, political, religious, and aesthetic implications.[167]

The cinematographic model is useful because it helps us see what "the practice of writing is for Hume: a technology for repetitively impressing those apparitions he calls ideas."[168] In this model, the only constant is "the interruption of the perception" (*T*, 1.3.2.2). Hume helps us see that "existence is cinematic, that one's sense of existence is rooted in movements of assemblage, recollection, projection, splicing, editing, and the like."[169] This cinematic subjectivity is "composed of an interrupted succession of parts that glide and mingle in an infinite variety of postures, as does an actor—or any object, for that matter—captured by a camera and projected on a screen" (67). The model of cinematography "affords empiricism an ontology of impressions that enables the transformation of experience into immediate, individualized, and infinitely re-arrangeable pressure points whose relationship to one another is at once provisional and not necessary precisely because they are permanently arrangeable and revisable" (54–55).

With the cinematographic model in mind, it becomes easier to see how Hume advances beyond the forms of empiricism articulated by John Locke. Hume, like Locke, views the senses as the mediation between the mind and the world. In *An Essay Concerning Human Understanding* (1690), Locke argues that originally the mind is a blank slate, or tabula rasa, "white paper, void of all characters, without any ideas," and is thus "reliant on input from the senses for all its ideas about the world."[170] Locke draws upon the model of the camera obscura and suggests that the mind is like a dark room that receives its impressions of the outside world through the aperture of the senses. As he elaborates in his *Essay*,

> external and internal sensation [or "sensation and reflection"] are the only routes I can find for knowledge to enter the understanding. These alone, as far as I can discover, are the windows through which light is let into this dark room. The understanding strikes me as being like a closet that is wholly sealed against light, with only some little openings left to let in external visible resemblances or ideas of things outside. If the pictures coming into such a dark room stayed there, and lay in order so that they could be found again when needed, it would very much resemble the understanding of a man, as far as objects of sight and the ideas of them are concerned.[171]

For Locke, attention is simply the process whereby ideas "offer themselves" and "are taken notice of, and, as it were, registered in the Memory."[172] To be attentive, as Joseph Addison puts it in the *Spectator*, is simply a matter of "opening the eye and the scene enters."[173]

Hume similarly claims that, "the mind is a kind of theatre," but he also adds that "the comparison of the theatre must not mislead us," because it is only through the contraction of "successive perceptions" that the mind is constituted (*T*, 1.4.6.4). The key difference between Locke's camera obscura model of empiricism and Hume's cinematic thinking is that "Locke imagines the collection of images in the mind as a kind of photo album, with no animation, whereas Hume sees mental images as wholly animate motion pictures." For Hume, the self "can only be a multiplicity of streaming perceptions."[174] During the first impressions of the senses we have only "the most distant notion of the place" we are in (*T*, 1.4.6.4). It is only when a succession of impressions are woven together that we can form any idea of what we are seeing.

Thinking is cinematic because it is "a thinking of part-takings, of the conjuring of aspects that come in the form of the seriality of impression called the shot."[175] The mind, or soul, is the space, stage, screen, frame, or Elemental space "that holds memories which when threaded together provide a sense of self, an identity."[176] Although "each instance of a series maintains the haecceity (the sheer that-ness) of a material object," and "each instant of a series . . . has no necessary relation to what proceeded it or to what might succeed it," nevertheless, for Hume, and for film, "our mind responds to the fact of discontinuity by generating a 'fiction of the imagination.'"[177] What ultimately "allows us to conceive of the continuity of an object is a habit of mind" (37) wherein "the thought slides along the succession with equal facility, as if it consider'd only one object; and therefore confounds the succession with the identity" (*T*, 1.4.2.34).

Hume, however, also emphasizes that since there is no necessity to the way we assemble the "fiction of the imagination" there is no reason to "repose our senses of succession, flow, complexity, mingling, gliding, and the like upon a sense of constancy, inalterability, or necessary progression."[178] Scandalously, this ambiguity in how habits, subjectivities, customs, and societies should be formed is even at the heart of Hume's picture of Being itself. Even causality, the bedrock assumption that when I hit the billiard ball it will do *x*, is only custom, because the "transition of thought from the cause to the effect proceeds not from reason. It derives its origin altogether from custom and experience."[179] This is one reason Hume's notion of sympathy as being a potentially disruptive force can help explain the efficaciousness of certain kinds of textual encounters, because if there is a form of sympathy that can help us cut, edit, or splice ourselves from our habitual modes of engagement, then a space can be cleared for new forms of assemblage and attachment to emerge.

Some, of course, were and are wary of the implications of Hume's empiricism. In his *Biographia Literaria* (1817), Coleridge offers the "simple advice" to "be not merely a man of letters" (*BL*, 1:229), because he fears what man would become if he were capable of being infinitely reset.[180] He lamented the way Hume "degraded the notion of cause and effect into a blind product of delusion and habit," and critiqued the notion "of our whole being [as] an aggregate of successive single sensations," because "Who ever felt a single sensation?"[181] Coleridge found Hume's philosophy to be "the pillar, & confessedly, the sole pillar, of modern Atheism."[182] One reason Coleridge would advocate for the Bible as an ideal guide for secular statecraft in *The Statesman's Manual* and elsewhere is because, as Jerome McGann notes, Coleridge wanted to insist that "history, whether lived or narrated, is not a sequence of atomized movements or facts but a structured phenomenon, the praxis of a living and related set of commitments."[183] Nevertheless, other aspects of Coleridge's work, such as the "Rime" through "its very unmooring from plotted coordinates," suggest the importance of Hume's model as a stimulant to his own thinking.[184] There is a recognition in Coleridge that when considered in isolation the self can be a shallow "complexus of visual images, cycles or customs of sensation."[185] As will be explored in chapters 2 and 3, this is why Coleridge will advocate that within each of us, within our "truest self, the man in the man," there is a "house gloriously furnished" with "truths and realities" that each might glimpse through the "enlightening eye" of "Reflection" (AR, 15). Reflection, as Joshua King explored in *Imagined Spiritual Communities* (2015), is the faculty of the mind that can illuminate "those 'truths and realities' abiding at a level of the self deeper than biographical identity or daily consciousness."[186]

The political implications of Hume's model of ontology and epistemology were similarly perceived by Edmund Burke, who recognized in them a threat to the foundations of monarchic sovereignty. Burke was wary of the disruption of traditional habits experienced in the wake of the French Revolution because he saw these traditional habits and practices as foundational to an ethical life and a just society. He was so insistent in his *Reflections* on the threat of the Revolution precisely because he recognized that Hume was essentially correct when he argued that it is only "the force of habit" that ends up "reconciling us to any phænomenon" (*T*, 1.3.16.9). Burke and Hume both agree that custom is "all that reconciles us to authority and leads us to expect the future to resemble the past."[187] As Hume puts it, "Time and custom give authority to all forms of government, and all successions of princes; and that power, which at first was founded only on injustice and violence, becomes in time legal and obligatory" (*T*, 3.2.11.19). Authority, in other words, is only established through some form of normalization.

Although Burke may have accepted that tradition and the force of custom are only "pleasing illusions,"[188] he also recognized that, even if it is only a fiction of the imagination, without such a binding force "the whole chain and continuity of the commonwealth would be broken. No one generation could link with the other. Men would become little better than the flies of a summer . . . and thus the commonwealth itself would, in a few generations, crumble away, be disconnected into the dust and powder of individuality, and at length dispersed to all the winds of heaven" (81–82). Burke insists we obey the authority of custom "precisely because such authority is groundless and therefore tenuous."[189] He warned that it is only through the inculcation of correct habits and practices that the legacy of our natural inheritance becomes "second nature." Second nature functions as a regime of perception, or what Jacques Rancière calls a "partition of the sensible," which Panagia describes as being the "perceptual forms of knowledge that parse what is and is not sensible, what counts as making (i.e., fabricating) sense and what is available to be sensed."[190]

It is when things become second nature that "the mild necessity of use compels / To acts of love," and it is through this mild necessity that "habit does the work / Of reason" (*WPP*, "The Old Cumberland Beggar," 91–93). In the ideal traditional community there is no need to question how the habits of our second nature have been invested upon "our naked, shivering nature," precisely because such habits seem so natural to our sense of self.[191] Members of the community do not have to think about being good because habits that have become second nature make them good. Habits and practices that have become customary are the means by which the (covenantal) values of one generation are bound together and invested in the next. Questions only arise when the processes of investiture, which pass down habits from one generation to the next, are challenged or threatened.

Burke feared the French Revolution precisely because if successful, "all the decent drapery of life is to be rudely torn off," and "all the super-added ideas, furnished from the wardrobe of a moral imagination, . . . are to be exploded as ridiculous, absurd, and antiquated fashion" (66). He was wary of the "mechanistic rationality of the self-styled advocates of enlightenment" and felt that their "apparent rationalism only stripped away human defenses against overwhelming passions."[192] Although the word "prejudice" is now typically viewed negatively, Burke's sense of prejudice was based in those prejudgments that render "a man's virtue his habit; and not a series of unconnected acts." It is through just prejudice that "duty becomes a part of his nature."[193]

For Burke, the accumulation of prejudice is advantageous because if "we are afraid to put men to live and trade each on his own private stock of reason;

because we suspect that this stock in each man is small," then it is best when individuals can "avail themselves of the general bank and capital of nations and of ages" (74).[194] Prejudice, or the accumulated prejudgments of the past, must be retained and maintained, because to strip away "the coat of prejudice, and to leave nothing but the naked reason" is foolish, since "prejudice, with its reason, has a motive to give action to that reason, and an affection which will give it permanence." Without such prejudice man is left "hesitating in the moment of decision, skeptical, puzzled, and unresolved" (74).

Thomas Paine may have been more right than he realized when he accused Burke of filling his *Reflections* with characters "like figures in a magic lantern."[195] After the French Revolution, Burke could see that the political theology of the ancien régime had been exposed as a kind of magic trick, one that made the arbitrary seem natural; nevertheless the show must go on because without it all that now seems solid would melt into air. Hume, however, felt less threatened than Burke by the ambiguity of this general situation and recognized that since customs inevitably change, allowances must be made for "continual revolutions of manners and customs."[196] This is why it is possible to consider Thomas Paine and Mary Wollstonecraft as much descendants of Hume as Burke is.[197] Some of Burke's contemporaries, including many of the poets and thinkers associated with Romanticism, similarly realized that these same principles of empiricism could be adapted to alternative ends and were willing to tailor patterns of habit that fashion a much more singular existence.

One way of defining Romanticism is as the cultural movement that emerges within modernity from an intense desire to fashion new patterns and new forms of life. Romanticism consists of a set of cultural practices that developed and transformed formal innovations developed within the literature of sensibility in the eighteenth century and operates at least in part on a virtual field of sentiments, or what Connolly calls the infrasensible, which flow beneath and between cultural formations of identity, discourse, and justice. This infrasensible dimension of intensities moving beneath our concepts functions not unlike the soundtrack in a film; it orchestrates the underlying mood, and thereby conducts and patterns the affective reception of what is being viewed.

Notably, Hume's cinematic empiricism is also quite compatible with the general situation described by recent efforts in at least one branch of speculative realism.[198] In his "Object-Oriented Defense of Poetry," Timothy Morton argues that our relations with objects are best understood in terms established by the philosopher Graham Harman, the founder of what is now called object-oriented ontology. For Harman, "objects are ontologically prior to their relations, relations that include their appearance for other objects."[199] Objects withdraw from our view, and all that we have available to us of them are at best recordings, derivations, translations and metaphors. Furthermore, "since objects are prior to any relation, and since causality (including time and space) is just a series of relations between things, causality must be ontologically 'in front' of objects." This space "in front" of objects is the domain of the aesthetic and the manner in which the texture of this "series of relations between things" is fashioned or formulated both mediates and informs the meaning of what is viewed (206). Harman argues that due to the derivative nature of appearances, relations among things are rooted in a vicarious causality, which also suggests that the way in which the world out there is viewed is revisable depending on what schema of causality or relationality is being used as a lens.

As mentioned earlier, at the end of *The Prelude,* William Wordsworth suggests that it is the vocation of the Romantic writer, as one of the "Prophets of Nature," to teach others how to take the "frame of things" upon which we dwell and produce a mind, or soul, above it "Of substance and of fabric more divine" (*P,* 13:448, 452). If above (or in front of) the frame of things we place a "fabric more divine" (woven from mental images), then this fabric is placed "in front" of objects in the manner Harman ascribes to vicarious causality. How this fabric is tailored, therefore, like how the edited form of a motion picture is cut, patterns our view of the world.

O'Keeffe suggests that the fabric that makes up the fictions of our imagination "unrolls like a carpet, or perhaps better, unfurls like the train of an elaborate gown, and that gown is made up of various patches loosely stitched together by the elastic, contractile motions of habits." The self is "a quilted self . . . one that also has gaps and holes in the weave—holes the future of the self might fill in, perhaps, or permanent gaps that will never be filled in." But O'Keeffe also asks who is capable of "embroidering patterns upon a fabric that is only ever a surface," patterns that are woven from strands of association and "held together by the pleats and stitches of relations"?[200] Must all moral fabrics be handed down, or can they be fashioned anew? And how should the fabric of everyday life be tailored if no one pattern can be agreed upon to fit us all? Romanticism is one field of inquiry that attempts to address the question of how best to fit this fabric to the frame.

Wordsworth's use of the clothing trope resonates with Edmund Burke's notions of "second nature" and the "wardrobe of a moral imagination," wherein "ideas are organic and they are transmitted along the lines of a natural inheritance." They constitute, as Chandler points out, the "legacy of a woven moral fabric in which the naked infant of the future can be adorned and clothed."[201] Traditionally, this fabric was woven within the context of a communal religious worldview, but with the advent of secular modernity the decision about how best to fashion this fabric becomes much more personal. The intense upheaval of the French Revolution was one reason people were forced to look up from the familiar patterns of habits and practices. In *Sublime Historical Experience* (2005), Frank Ankersmit describes how in the aftermath of the French Revolution people were suddenly made aware that they had always already been "living in a world of traditions without ever having been conscious of it.... The great Revolution suddenly lifted them, so to speak, out of this world of unreflected tradition and made them aware of these traditions for the first time."[202] To be "suddenly lifted" from the "world of unreflected tradition" is to suddenly awaken out of the sleep of necessity and into a dawn where each is made more capable of becoming responsible for his or her own agency.

The procedures of symbolic investiture and the demands of singularity meet in the question of how the ethical fabric of our life should be tailored. The word "ethics" stems from the Greek word *ethos*, which means nature, disposition, or habit, and thus the fabric of our ethical life is constituted by the habits and practices of everyday life. Everyone is inevitably possessed by or invested in some ideology, and all ideologies attempt to answer the question of what constitutes a good life by providing a moral fabric in which individuals can become invested in and be made capable of addressing life's challenges. Nevertheless, as Bruno Latour suggests, if we are to form an adequate response to the ecological and political challenges we currently face, then we must resist emphasizing ideology, or what he calls Sphereology, and its critique, and shift our attention away from the globe to the loops that slowly draw it.

Literature is one way of attending to how those loops are slowly drawn. Such weaving is significant because through each loop we "become *more sensitive* and *more reactive* to the fragile envelopes we inhabit."[203] Encounters with art can help cultivate a capacity for neighborliness particularly when we approach texts that activate in us "the capacity to idealize bodies which diverge as widely as possible both from ourselves and from the cultural norm."[204]

Second natures, partitions of the sensible, and fabrics more divine should be imagined not as incarnating ideality but as "garments" that can be worn "like a removable cloak" (37). When worn in this way the art of loving one's neighbors as oneself begins to make practical sense, since the capacity to put on the sensoriums of others becomes a crucial means of extending one's own sense of self. What Romanticism at its best offers is a set of techniques and experiments that explore how best to fashion the fabric of one's habits and practices.

Philosophies of the Flesh

Some of the possibilities of Romantic self-fashioning will be explored throughout the rest of this book, and subsequent chapters will focus on the work of Coleridge, Keats, Shelley, and Austen in order to examine how, when, and why their alterations of a "fabric more divine," woven from the habits and practices of everyday life, can contribute to the building of a "wardrobe of a moral imagination" for a postsecular age. However, before proceeding I want to give one final indication of what it means to say that words can be made flesh. In order to do so I return to the tension invoked earlier between the ontological and culture models of affect but now address it in a different but not unrelated vocabulary: the language of the flesh. My inspiration for doing so is a distinction made by Kevis Goodman in her introduction to Eric Santner's *The Weight of All Flesh* (2016). Here she recognizes that there are crucial differences between Santner's use of the term "flesh" and Maurice Merleau-Ponty's conception of the "flesh of the world." For Merleau-Ponty, there is an essential porousness to his idea of the flesh, which is a term he uses to indicate the intimate fusion of the human and nonhuman worlds. Flesh is the "anonymity innate to Myself," an element "midway between the spatiotemporal individual and the idea, a sort of incarnate principle that brings a style of being."[205] For Santner, on the other hand, what is meant by flesh is mediated most directly by Ernst Kantorowicz's work in *The King's Two Bodies* (1957) but more fundamentally by Saint Paul's distinction between the body (*soma*) and the flesh (*sarx*). Whereas *soma* "describes the existence of all creatures," *sarx* "denotes fallen temporal existence" and the "historical entanglement in the world and one's relationship to other fallen creatures."[206]

To help clarify these divergent definitions, I turn first to *The Visible and the Invisible* (1964), where Merleau-Ponty describes the flesh as an intimate element of crossing over the threshold of the visible so that "the seer and the visible reciprocate one another and we no longer know which sees and which is seen. It is this Visibility, this anonymity innate to Myself that we have called flesh."[207] The flesh is the "the 'field' through which one's body is 'exposed to' the world."[208] "From this primordial being to us," Merleau-Ponty postulates, "there is no derivation"; we are not reducible to it, nor is there any break, and thus we are "intimately related to it" (15). Since "my body is made of the same flesh as the world," a living bond with the world is incorporated within my body.[209]

Merleau-Ponty sees the body as an "immediately given invariant," a "primary access to the world," and the "vehicle of being in the world." For him, the "body forms an ultimate back-ground, an absolute here, in relation to which all perceptual experience must be oriented."[210] He suggests there is a "perceptual faith," which is always already there "prior to every opinion, of inhabiting the world by our body, of inhabiting the truth by our whole selves."[211] The world touches us through our senses, and it is the apprehension of this touch that is felt prior to any interpretation as to what it might mean that secures our belief that the images that are projected inside our mind have a likeness in the world viewed.

However, despite this capacity to be in intimate contact with the world through our flesh, humans have a tendency to lose touch with these grounding experiences. Our mental images can become captivating, and even though they are derivative, and thus secondary, the manipulatable fecundity of mental imagery makes it tempting to forget the initial encounter with the world outside ourselves that touches off our thinking. Images "are meant to be maps, [but] they become screens."[212] When this occurs, what is needed is a return to the "primacy of perception," which according to Merleau-Ponty, is made available by reexperiencing "the moment when things, truths, values are constituted for us." The value of such perceptions is that they brings us in touch with "a nascent logos," one that "teaches us, outside all dogmatism, the true condition of objectivity itself."[213]

Richard Kearney argues that it is this phenomenological return to the primacy of perception that enables us to realize the "eucharistic power of the sensible." In this version of Edmund Husserl's *epoché*, there is a phenomenological return all the "way down to the lowest rung of experience (in the old metaphysical ladder, the senses)," where "the most sacramental act of communion" is discovered.[214] As Merleau-Ponty puts it in the *Phenomenology of Perception* (1945),

> Just as the sacrament not only symbolizes, in sensible species, an operation of Grace, but is also the real presence of God, which it causes to occupy a fragment of space and communicates to those who eat of the consecrated bread, provided that they are inwardly prepared, in the same way the sensible has not only a motor and vital significance, but is nothing other than a certain way of being in the world suggested to us from some point in space, and seized and acted upon by our body, provided that it is capable of doing so, so that sensation is literally a form of communion.[215]

For Merleau-Ponty, there is a "sacramental value" to these moments of encountering alterity when "I am brought into relation with an external being" because "the sentient subject does not posit them as objects, but enters into a sympathetic relation with them, makes them his own and finds in them his momentary law."[216]

This is why Wordsworth's poetry, for instance, so often attempts to produce disruptive moments of breakthrough, which can deeply affect us, shaking us out of the "lethargy of custom," and attuning readers to the "wonders of the world before us" (BL, 2:7). Here, as in Merleau-Ponty's phenomenological return, we may feel in our flesh "a sense sublime / Of something far more deeply interfused" ("Tintern Abbey," 96–97). In these moments of "sacramental sensation" there is a "a reversible rapport between myself and things, wherein the sensible gives birth to itself through me."[217] What is offered in such moments is an opportunity to "see into the life of things" ("Tintern Abbey," 50). What Wordsworth's poetry and Merleau-Ponty's phenomenology both offer is an insight akin to Kearney's interpretation of "eucharistic embodiment as recovery of the divine within the flesh, a kenotic emptying out of transcendence into the heart of the world's body, becoming a God beneath us rather than a God beyond us."[218]

The value of this phenomenological return is that it can "awaken us with wonder, not to another ideal world, but to the world before us, the life-world, 'the world in which we live, yet which we are always prone to forget.'"[219] Wonder, in Catherine Malabou's formulation, is the "affect of difference, the soul's realization that the self is not alone." It is the "emotional consequence of the intrusion of alterity into the soul."[220] It is through wonder that we break through "the film of familiarity and selfish solicitude" (BL, 2:7) and return to the site and soil of the sensible and open world.[221] This emphasis on wonder is one line of connection that runs through Wordsworth's efforts to awaken readers from the "lethargy of custom," ontologically oriented forms of affect theory, and Merleau-Ponty's form of phenomenology.

Moments of wonder produce a "breach in the membrane of awareness,"[222] which is often experienced as "a returning, sometimes with the abruptness of a sudden shock, to the world to which we always, already belong."[223] Texts that can induce wonder offer versions of what J. Hillis Miller called "linguistic moments," those "moments of suspension within the texts of poems" that produce "a form of parabasis, a breaking of the illusion that language is a transparent medium of meaning."[224] Often in such moments "forms of appearance call attention, most immediately and directly, to their own appearing, to the fact of their being encountered. One is brought to a halt by the appearance, and forced to attend to it."[225] There is something sacramental about such effects because they are instances of what Patricia Cox Miller has called the "corporeal imagination," situations " 'when everyday flesh catches fire,' a moment when blood, bones, and spirit are so thoroughly fused that they convey a certain incandescent clarity."[226]

Moments such as these can be found particularly in those aspects of Romanticism that try to better the world not through the communication of content but rather "by encouraging a state of suspension that frees sensation, enabling new links between elements of the open system of the world."[227] Morton suggests that encounters with certain "synesthetic works of art" can "disrupt our sense of being centered, located in a specific place, inhabiting 'the body' from a central point."[228] Works that disarticulate our commonsense ways of seeing are valuable because by doing so they call attention to the postures of attention we normally occupy, thereby helping us accept responsibility for the fact that, as Panagia puts it, "The bendings of the frames of our bodies, the turnings of our heads, the raisings of our eyes, the pricking of our ears, and the opening of our mouths—are acts of ethical reconfiguration; they are part of the work we do on ourselves that allows us to live in, and endure, the impact of appearances."[229]

As we shall see in a variety of ways, Romanticism differs from modes of writing associated with sensibility and sentimentality because at its heart is a poetics, or *poeisis*, that "dissolves, diffuses and dissipates" forms in order to "re-create" them (*BL*, 1:202). Rather than working to bind or weave readers into a public with a shared common sense, Romantic poetics are often radically open-ended. Through such poetry we can not only obtain insight into the formal "structuring and destructuring processes at work in textual production" but also expose what Joel Faflack calls the "radically chaotic moment" that is at the fantastic heart of every cultural discourse.[230] An anarchic "potential space" can be found at the core of many Romantic texts, which can offer attentive readers opportunities to speculate upon things as they are and how they might be made different.

Such moments of disinterest, disfiguration, and dissensus are potentially political moments because they invite occasions and actions for reconfiguring our associational lives. Panagia argues that politics happens "when a relation of attachment or detachment is formed between heterological elements." However, before new "political relations may be forged," an "interruption of previous forms of relating" must occur.[231] Romanticism is one name for those processes through which the figuration, disfiguration, and reconfiguration of the sensible can occur. In such moments of openness a lightness is experienced, which momentarily lifts the burden of the mystery and offers an opportunity for absolution, alteration, and revision. Such moments can be experienced as therapeutic or even redemptive because, as Julia Kristeva wrote, "A state of flesh appears to underlie the therapeutic act, but it can become a true therapeutic act only if language is led to the reversible and chiasmic sensation that supports it."[232]

As with culturally oriented versions of affect theory in relation to ontologically oriented versions, Santner's conception of flesh shares some of the same premises of Merleau-Ponty's but also differs in significant ways. Here the emphasis is less on those seismic states that can disrupt our sense of self and awaken us to the wonders of the world and more on those processes by which we put on and take off the affective textures and sustained attachments that can be found in the "wardrobe of a moral imagination."[233]

As Goodman notes, there is a scriptural element in Santner's reading of the flesh, one in fact that is not far from Coleridge's own: "The reflection of the Logos in the true self and the possibility of becoming this self in human community exist because the Logos has taken 'flesh' to 'assume our humanity personally' in Jesus" (AR, 323). From this perspective, it is "the life, death, and resurrection of the historical Jesus" that provides "the basis and universal pattern for each person's communion with the eternal Logos."[234] A comparable logic can be found in the sermons of John Donne and within the context of the Christian tradition more generally. Here the story told is that during the Fall, man discovered himself as naked, but because death was also admitted into the world at this time he could be clothed from the flesh of animals. To conquer death, God (in the figure of Christ) clothed Himself in man's flesh and allowed His body to be sacrificed. After this Incarnation, Christ's flesh or fabric is made available and can be worn by man, thus making him acceptable in the eyes of God. This flesh is in one sense the historical form of Jesus, but more importantly it is the example of Christ as he is inscribed into Scripture.

What believers need to do is put these words on for themselves and thereby learn to "eye Christ in every step" (AR, 203).

> And from this . . . putting on Christ as a garment, we shall grow up to that perfection, as that we shall *Induere personam,* put on him, his person; That is, we shall so appeare before the Father, as that he shall take us for his owne Christ; we shall beare his name and person; and we shall every one be so accepted, as if every one of us were all Mankind; yea, as if we were he himself. He shall find in all our bodies his woundes, in all our mindes, his Agonies; in all our hearts, and actions his obedience.[235]

Through the imitation and identification with Christ's example in the Gospels, man has a pattern from which to mend his life. However, after adopting the appearance of Christ we must then "grow" inwardly so that Christ's garment will fit. "There is then a double *Induere,* a twofold clothing; we may *Induere,* 1. *Vestem,* put on a garment; 2. *Personam,* put on a person. We may put on Christ so, as we shall be *his,* and we may put him on so, as we shall be *He.*"[236] Having the outward appearance of Christ is not enough, however; outward signs must be in harmony with inner faith. The Christian must move (as much as possible) from the imitation to the reincarnation of Christ: "We may put him on so . . . we shall be *He*" (128). Through this process his Word becomes our flesh.

Clearly, what is being conceptualized in this scriptural understanding of flesh "is not the physical body, not the corporeal matter beneath our skin that we gain and shed over our life span" but rather "something in the body that is more than a body yet is not simply spirit."[237] This understanding of flesh is concerned with that domain in which issues of signification and representation are coordinated with affective pressures felt in the nerves. Santner argues that the various intensifications of the body felt in modernity "can be correlated with disorders or shifts in the resources of representation available to subjects and in the capacities of subjects to use those resources, to discharge the normative pressures they introduce into the life of subjects."[238] The signifying stress of these normative pressures on our creaturely life is inscribed on what Santner calls our "flesh," a flesh that is constituted by the fact that human subjects possess animal bodies that also "inhabit the space of reasons."[239] Through the flesh the metaphors we live by are made manifest, and it is in the flesh that the failure to find the right words is felt.

Both Freudian psychoanalysis and Foucauldian biopolitics are concerned in different ways with the uncanny dimension of a "flesh that forms at the jointure—the 'X'—of the chiasmic relays of enjoyment and entitlement."[240] Psychoanalysis and biopolitics may approach the flesh from different angles—from the perspective of the individual and the sociological—but both are concerned with how the processes of symbolic investiture and divestiture are instrumental in establishing "not simply the jointure of body and office—a new suturing, as it were, of the somatic and the normative," but also in generating at "the locus of that suture, the pressure of a surplus carnality, of an additional bit of flesh, that can be—and historically has been—elaborated and figured as a kind of second, virtually real and, indeed, glorious body."[241]

The idea that each of us possesses two bodies, one carnal and the other "glorious" and "virtually real," is rooted in medieval notions of political theology and the doctrine of the king's two bodies: the idea that the king possesses a human body while at the same time being, like Christ, the earthly incarnation of a divine presence. With respect to the king's two bodies, Slavoj Žižek argues that "what is at stake is . . . not simply the split between the empirical person of the king and his symbolic function. The point is rather that this symbolic function redoubles his very body, introducing a split between the visible, material, transient body and another, sublime body, a body made of a special, immaterial stuff."[242] Out of these theological doctrines develops a counterargument, namely the critique of traditional sovereignty mounted by Hobbes, Spinoza, Locke, and others in the seventeenth century. According to Santner, the threshold of modernity is marked by the movement away from previous forms of sovereignty, a transition figured in the famous frontispiece of Hobbes's *Leviathan* (1651), wherein the sovereign's body is literally made up from an amalgamation of the bodies of the citizenry. Within modernity the king's sublime body is divested of its power, but in such a way that the remnants of this shift—from the king to the "people" as the bearer of the principle of sovereignty—is "written in and with the flesh [of the people], that 'part' of us inflamed by the normative pressure of the bonds at issue."[243]

In the long nineteenth century a more radical stage in this secularizing process of "immanentization" occurs, because as Santner argues, here "the divine charisma that had still stuck to the sovereign becomes disseminated throughout the social space as an 'exciting' phantasmorgorical presence—as a dimension of *surplus value*—attaching to objects and bodies that thereby become the focal points of ceaseless economic cultural, and political administration."[244] The French Revolution in particular marked a period of transition from kings to "people" as the bearer of the principle of sovereignty, which mobilized "the modern reorganization of the 'physiology' of the body politic." Ultimately, within modernity a biopolitics emerges to manage this field of phantasmagoric dissemination. In this "new physics of power," the maximum intensity is felt not in the person of the king but in the bodies that make up the body politic.[245]

In the shift from political theology to biopolitics, the split that was formally personified in the king's two bodies is increasingly felt to be distributed throughout the body politic (a shift also registered in T. S. Eliot's notion of a dissociation of sensibility) in ways that are both advantageous (increased freedom of movement both literally and for the individual's vehicular consciousness) and disadvantageous (a sense that the world is too much with us). To give a clearer indication of what biopolitics might mean in practice, it is useful to consider what it is we are really arguing about as a society when we discuss torture, abortion, internment camps at the border, bathroom bills, cults of personality, and the suffering of racial, gendered, and queer bodies in general. These heated exchanges seem to be about something more than mere policy differences. As Elaine Scarry argues in *The Body in Pain* (1987), human pain and the "obscenely . . . alive tissue" (31) of the human body is too often used "as a source of verification and substantiation of the symbolic authority of institutions and the social facts they sponsor." Particularly, when "there is a crisis of belief or legitimation in a society," the human body becomes the suffering site that allows "invented ideas, beliefs, and made objects to be accepted and entered into as though they had the same ontological status as the naturally given world."[246] These and many other aspects of our political climate are not just remnants but also examples of the continued significance of political theological thinking within modernity.

The biopolitical strand of modernity's philosophic-political tradition is interested in how, in Roberto Esposito's words, "political organization depends, not on the voluntary and rational choice of individuals united in a foundational pact, but on the inextricable knot of strengths and instincts that are innervated in the individual body and even more, in the ethnically determined traits of different populations."[247] One challenge for biopolitics is that these knots are often difficult to untangle. With the rise of secularity in the West comes an accompanying "secularization of the body,"[248] which manifests itself through the rise of a "disciplinary" society in which the body is "directly involved in a political field," and in which power relations "invest it, mark it, train it, torture it, force it to carry out tasks, to perform ceremonies, to emit signs." Michel Foucault envisioned modern biopolitics as a "system of subjection" whose "micro-physics of power" is exercised on the body as a strategy to instill new "dispositions, maneuvers, tactics, techniques, [and] functionings."[249] The biopolitics of the state generally "takes over the management of embodied life: through various media, through networks of officials and spies, through medical innovations and humanitarian organizations it observes, measures, distributes, and supervises its subjects."[250]

But one question that emerges among all of these biopolitical maneuverings is who are we if so much of who we are is a put-on? If the "self" is merely some special effect produced by the machinations and systems of subjection of a social world operating outside the individual's control? Is an "affirmative biopolitics" possible, or must we simply rage against the biopolitical machine?[251] This is a key question for Romanticism, because if Romanticism is an event within the history of mediation, then it is important to remember that for the human the first medium is the body. As subsequent chapters will clarify, Romantic authors worked in a variety of ways to find forms through which an "affirmative biopolitics" might be realized.

PART II

Mediating the Postsecular

* 2 *

Poetic Faith

This chapter explores the implications of Coleridge's poetic faith. It does so in several ways: first, by examining the alteration in biblical reading practices that Coleridge articulates in *Aids to Reflection* and its companion essay "Confessions of an Inquiring Spirit." Here the interest is in how and why Coleridge rejects bibliolatry, or the approach to Scripture that assumes the Bible functions like the "glittering eye" of the Ancient Mariner—as a conduit that holds us spellbound with its charged presence and captivates us with the tale it tells. A central problem with this approach is that it turns readers into mere automatons who must necessarily follow the intentions of a "superhuman . . . Ventriloquist." Coleridge argues instead that the purpose of the Bible, and the Christian religion more generally, is to "rouse and emancipate the soul from this debasing slavery to the outward senses" (AR, 406). Such an awakening results from the active assertion of each individual's will, and by the will Coleridge means that facet of ourselves that can be used to steer our vehicular consciousness or mediated soul toward the right words. Encounters with Scripture can serve as aids to reflection, which facilitate this active orientation of the soul toward the "Truth operating as Life" (AR, 406–7) and thereby elevate inquiring spirits into an intuition of religion that is beyond the limits of reason alone.[1] The chapter's final section considers more closely what is meant by "reflection," and particular emphasis will be placed on Johannes Gottfried Herder's conception of reflection (*Besonnenheit*), which is understood as the capacity to gather one's attention in such a way so as to learn to control the flow of the imagination. Unlike those who passively follow the connections triggered in them by whatever chain of necessity they feel themselves caught up in, only those who become expert with the sail and oar of reflection can avoid shipwreck within what Herder calls the "ocean of sensation."[2]

Scriptural Alterations

In his 1611 poem "Anatomy of the World," John Donne was already acknowledging a new modernity where "all coherence" was "gone," and voyagers "in this world's sea stray . . . needed a new compass for their way" (213, 225–26). In a previous age, to ensure that a feeling of embodied certainty was secured in the desired way, believers were disciplined by the prevailing religious order and taught to exercise their "spiritual senses." There was no need to speculate as to the source of inspiration because the divine word, both written and spoken, was housed in the materiality and performance of the text, thus allowing the inspired words to be the object of reverence and enabling the bodies of those who witnessed the text to be the conduits through which inspiration was channeled. Talal Asad argues that traditionally the disciplines and spiritual exercises of religious praxis cultivated the body "to listen, to recite, to move, to be still, to be silent, engaged with the acoustics of words, with their sound, feel, and look." For the participant "practice at devotions deepened the inscription of sound, look, and feel in his sensorium. When the devotee heard God speak, there was a sensuous connection between inside and outside, a fusion between signifier and signified. The proper reading of the scriptures that enabled her to *hear* divinity speak depended on disciplining the senses (especially hearing, speech, and sight)."[3] The sense of fitness and embodied certainty that animated presecular culture can still be heard reverberating in a 1625 sermon preached by Donne:

> If he aske me an Idea of my Sermons, shall I not be able to say, It is that which the Analogy of Faith, the edification of the Congregation, the zeale of thy works, the meditations of my heart have imprinted in me? But if I come to pray or to preach without this kind of Idea, if I come to extemporall prayer, and extemporall preaching, I shall come to an extemporall faith, and extemporall religion; and then I must looke for an extemporall Heaven, a Heaven to be made for me; for to that Heaven which belongs to the Catholique Church, I shall never come, except I go by the way of the Catholique Church, by former

Idea's, former examples, former patterns, To believe according to ancient beliefes, to pray according to ancient formes, to preach according to former meditations. God does nothing, man does nothing well, without the Idea's, these retrospects, this recourse to pre-conceptions, pre-deliberations.[4]

In his sermon, Donne suggests Scripture still served as the central, authoritative text established by God (albeit mediated through the authority and liturgical practices of the church), one which provided the blueprint and pattern for all meaning. Writing, praying, and preaching can only be done properly if they follow "former Idea's, former examples, former patterns." Nothing can be done well without recourse to what is traditional, established, and ordinate.

Scripture, says Donne, cannot be reformed to fit man's needs; man must be mended to fit the pattern laid out in Scripture. Scripture functions as a kind of wardrobe in which different possibilities of proper moral attire are suggested. The preacher's role is to help fashion spiritual clothing fit to wear. This fashioning is the process of interpreting Scripture in ways that will be intelligible to the common man. "This is *Scrutari Scripturas, to search the Scriptures*, not as though thou wouldest make a *concordance*, but an *application;* as thou wouldest search a *wardrobe*, not to make an *Inventory* of it, but to finde in it something fit for thy wearing" (148). The preacher's job is not to treat Scripture as a kind of accent or *ruffle* on the dress of Christian life. The Bible is the central patterning force of creation; it is the fixed star by which the soul's sailing is navigated. Mending occurs when we "turne over all the folds, and plaits of thine owne heart, and finde there the infirmities, and waverings" of faith—so that we may better fit God's pattern (148). A successful preacher facilitates the process of mending and inspires his flock to, as Donne says at the end of one sermon, "Be a little better now, then when you came, and mend a little at every coming" (155). Experiencing the cut of God's pattern in the eloquence of the preacher's words, the congregation could be inspired to mend themselves to match this pattern, and in this way the preacher was understood to be the tailor of man's soul.

But what happens to Scripture when it is no longer mediated by the materiality of the text's liturgical performance within the space of the communal church? Within England, processes of secularization gained momentum during the reigns of Henry VIII, Edward VI, and Elizabeth I as attempts were made to spiritualize and purify the "true faith." Pilgrimages, relics, and the like were seen as superstitious and ornamental decadence, which Protestant radicals and iconoclasts sought to strip away so that a pure faith could emerge. However, as Graham Ward traces in *True Religion* (2003), the unintended consequences of these attempts resulted in a profound disruption of the liturgical understanding of the world:

> To abrogate holy days was to change the nature of time and the relationship between work, leisure and worship. To take over church lands, dissolve monasteries, call for the destruction of statues even of patronal saints, and forbid pilgrimages and processions, was to change the nature of space and the relationship [between] one's home and sacred place. The mapping of holy loci, therefore the networking of sacred power, was redrawn. To rethink the sacraments and ceremonies as symbols or "mere outward forms" (1549 Book of Common Prayer) was to transform the nature of materiality itself, rendering the natural world opaque, silent and inert.[5]

These attempts to overturn or abandon the sacramental and liturgical systems that had previously mediated experience resulted in radical transformations of space, time, and nature. Materiality was emptied of spiritual significance, and the praxis of Christian ritual became the management of mere "outward forms." The secular becomes the emptied space or immanent frame upon which a variety of outward forms could be staged. As John Milbank notes, prior to this emergence the *saeculum* was not a space but a time—"the interval between fall and *eschaton* where coercive justice, private property and impaired natural reason must make shift to cope with the unredeemed effects of sinful humanity."[6] The modern concept of the secular develops out of a shift from seeing the world as an intimate correspondence of the seen and unseen to a relational world where meaning is thought to be produced through the circulation of ideas.

In contrast to the logic of using the materiality of the preacher's language and performance to alter the congregation's behavior to fit the patterns preconceived by Scripture, Asad argues that "the mythic method used by the Higher Biblical Criticism rendered the materiality of scriptural sounds and marks into a *spiritual* poem whose effect was generated inside the subject as believer independent of the senses."[7] Once Scripture is no longer experienced solely through the mediation of ritual and communal spaces, then scriptural effects became almost mesmeric—they slip beneath the doors of perception (and are thus subliminal). After this dissociation, faith, which had been a virtue, now acquired an epistemological sense. "Faith became a way of knowing supernatural objects, parallel to the knowledge of nature (the *real* world) that reason and observation provided" (38–39).

By the 1790s, Coleridge recognized that a new basis had to be found for saving the appearances of religious experience. Accepting Gotthold Ephraim Lessing's famous claim that "contingent historical truths can never serve as proof for necessary truths of reason," Coleridge recognized that the authority of historical religions, including Christianity, could not rest upon assertions of God's miraculous interventions within the order of nature.[8] A new foundation had to be established if religion was to flourish in a secular age. What was needed was a way of reading the Bible that recognized that "if it was written by diverse men at various times, then one must find out the different ways in which they felt themselves to have been moved by the spirit."[9] For the inquiring spirit, Coleridge claims, the true meaning of the Bible could only be realized when readers investigated the "state of [their] own mind" and realized the significance of their own affective responses to "whatever finds me" in the text.[10]

While at the University of Göttingen during his sojourn in Germany in 1798–99, Coleridge heard the lectures of Johann Gottfried Eichhorn, who had already challenged the constructedness of the Old Testament in his *Einleitung in das Alte Testament* (3 vols., Leipzig, 1780–83) and was now arguing about the belatedness of the New Testament, written as it was decades after the events it describes and by authors who were not firsthand witnesses. Elaine Shaffer argues that it was from Eichhorn that Coleridge derived his revisionary understanding of the biblical canon: that "the writings to be included in the Bible were not laid down by the Holy Spirit, nor by the authority simply of the Church, but by 'tradition,' interpreted as the continuing assent of the Christian community."[11] This is a significant shift from the traditional notion that the Bible's textual authority derived from a plenary inspiration spiritually dictated by the Holy Ghost, and this shift justified the practice of treating Scripture with the same scrutiny as any secular historical text. Such scrutiny was acceptable because if plenary inspiration is not the source of Scripture's value, then it is in no way scandalous to inspect how the text is constructed.

Influenced by the new "higher criticism" that was being espoused around him, Coleridge drew from a number of sources tools that would facilitate a more literary approach to the Bible. Like Baruch Spinoza, Coleridge recognized that biblical narratives could serve "as powerful exercises of imagination" and when "sensibly used" could serve as "appropriate vehicles for the communication of shared wisdom about how best to live." Nevertheless, that these same texts could also become "vehicles of superstitions" was a cause for concern, which could happen when interpreters used "biblical stories to induce intense emotions of hope and fear" in their followers "in order to allay fear and invite hope in ways that reinforce their own power."[12] From Robert Lowth's *Lectures on the Sacred Poetry of the Hebrews* (Lat. 1753/ Eng. 1787), Coleridge could see how Scripture's "parabolic style" coupled with the "the spareness and emotional intensity" of scriptural language could use "the clarity and energy of its diction and imagery" to throw open the "secret avenues," "inmost conceptions," and "interior recesses of the soul."[13] As Johann Gottfried Herder similarly articulated in *The Spirit of Hebrew Poetry* (1782), biblical language opened to view "the childhood and youth of the human race" because its languages were "closer to the senses, more concrete, sensuous, and image-laden than modern languages." Thus readers of Scripture could "by a kind of literary magic, become Hebrews for a time, feeling the force of their language, and of the poetic spirit that animated them from within."[14] Through the process of *Einfuhlung*, or "feeling one's way in," readers could feel their way not only into history but also into a shared biblical sensibility.

In "Confessions of an Inquiring Spirit," an essay originally designed to accompany *Aids to Reflection* (1825), Coleridge asks whether the first principle of Christian faith is to "insist on the belief of the divine origin and authority of all, and every part of the Canonical Books" or if "the due appreciation of the Scriptures collectively [is] more safely relied on as the result and consequence of the belief in Christ?" (CIS, 1116). In other words, is the appreciation of Scripture the cause or the consequence of belief in Christ? For Coleridge, this is not an idle question, and by unpacking this idea a clearer sense is obtained of the implications of Coleridge's attempt in his later work to convince himself and others that the Bible is its "own sufficient evidence" (CIS, 1128).

Before explicating more precisely how Coleridge means to ground the Bible as its own "sufficient evidence," it is useful to understand what he is reacting against—bibliolatry. Bibliolatry, the excessive adherence to a literal interpretation of the Bible, is related to a distinction Coleridge makes in his earlier work between the Bible and "fetisches." In *The Statesman's Manual* (1816), for example, Coleridge contrasts the Bible with objects and actions that convey to the believer the powers of a higher authority: "amulets, bead-rolls, periapts, fetishes, and the like pedlary" (CW, 6:64–65). Mark Canuel has suggestively explored this aspect of Coleridge's thinking and describes how "the totems of religious ritual mentioned here [the fetishes and the like] function as '*specific and individual*' signs that achieve meaning only because they are charged with carrying and compelling specific beliefs; their meaning, in other words, is to be discerned in their power as discrete, autonomous objects."[15]

To treat the Bible as a charged or fetishized object, as the bibliolatrous do, is to suggest that the text is a vehicle for "carrying conviction from author to reader" through the distribution or channeling of "particular kinds of sensations and particular kinds of shock or outrage" (956). To be bibliolatrous is to justify through sensation what is presumed to be easily—even transparently—understood in Scripture. The ideal reader in this fetishistic approach to the Bible "is an idolatrous worshipper who sees language only as '*noise*,' as isolated 'empty *sounds*' that are communicative only by virtue of their momentary ability to become charged with supernatural authority which in turn commands specific kinds of beliefs from the reader."[16] Here we are not far from a rhetoric of mesmerism: the Bible, for the bibliolater, is an object that functions like the "gleaming eye" of the mariner—a conduit that holds us spellbound with its charged presence.

While Coleridge agrees that "whatever is contained in the Bible is Religion, & [was] revealed by God" (CIS, 1140), he is unwilling to reduce Scripture to a direct and transparent conduit to divine authority. The pernicious problem of accepting the Bible as being written with infallible authority is that this doctrine "petrifies at once the whole Body of Holy Writ" (CIS, 1134). Such petrification takes the "breathing Organismus" and "glorious *Panharmonicon*" of Scripture, which previously seemed to "stand on its feet as a Man" and as a vital organism and turns it "at once into a colossal Memnon's head, a hollow Passage for a Voice, a Voice that mocks the voices of many men and speaks in their names and yet is but one voice and the same!—and no man uttered it, and never in a human heart was it conceived!" (CIS, 1134). An object that seemed most human becomes "a 'Comedia Divina' of a superhuman . . . Ventriloquist." The Bible and the mortals who wrote it become simply masks or instruments worn or used by a superior presence that lies outside the text. Even David, that "Royal Harper" and writer of the Psalms, to whom Coleridge in his reading had submitted himself "as a 'many-stringed Instrument,' for [David's] fire-tipt fingers to traverse," even "this sweet Psalmist of Israel" becomes himself as "mere an instrument as his Harp, an *automaton* Poet, Mourner, & Supplicant" (CIS, 1136). The consequence of a literal view of the Bible is that the first cause or prime mover that stands outside and authorizes the text necessarily pulls the strings and all believers—readers and writers alike—become, like the mariner's ghastly crew, mere automatons and slaves to the intensions of a master who sits elsewhere.

Clearly this is a troubling view—it depicts the relationship between God and man as that of master and slave. However, there may be some insight to gain from the perspective of the bibliolatrous if we recall the critique of fetishism as it has developed along Marxian and psychoanalytic lines. If the point of Karl Marx's critique of fetishism is that "beliefs, superstitions and metaphysical mystifications . . . are embodied in the 'social relations between things,'"[17] then belief is external and it is not subjects *but the things themselves* that believe. Contrary to the common understanding of belief as something interior, it may be that belief "is radically exterior, [and] embodied in the practical, effective procedure(s)" and habits of a people. To use an example borrowed from Slavoj Žižek, speaking of Tibetan prayer wheels: "You write a prayer on a paper, put the rolled paper into a wheel, and turn it automatically, without thinking" (34). Likewise, it may be that by "following a custom, the subject believes without knowing it" (40). Habit can do the work of reason. The externality of a symbolic machine (or object) like the Bible is therefore not simply external; it is

> at the same time the place where the fate of our internal, most "sincere" and "intimate" beliefs is in advance staged and decided. When we subject ourselves to the machine of a religious ritual, we already believe without knowing it; our belief is already materialized in the external ritual; in other words, we already believe unconsciously, because it is from this external character of the symbolic machine that we can explain the status of the unconscious as radically external—that of a dead letter. Belief is an affair of obedience to the dead, uncomprehended letter. (43)

Thus somewhat provocatively we might say that what the media environment of bibliolatry produces is the unconscious as it is described by Lacan: "the automaton (i.e. the dead, senseless letter), which leads the mind unconsciously with it" (37).

Coleridge is able to move beyond the slavishness of bibliolatry in part because he recognizes a gap between the Spirit or the Word and the dead senseless letter. For him, the purpose of the Christian religion is "to rouse and emancipate the Soul from this debasing Slavery to the outward Senses, to awaken the mind to the true Criteria of Reality, viz. Permanence, Power, Will manifested in Act, and Truth operating as Life" (AR, 406–7). The Bible is conducive to this struggle for emancipation from "the dead, uncomprehended letter"[18] because through familiarity with Scripture it is possible to acquire an "early and habitual association with Acts of the Will" (AR, 292), and it is only by activating the will within us that we will be set free from the path of the bibliolatrous.

Here it is worth noting how Coleridge's critique of bibliolatry is reminiscent of his critique of those forms of associationism articulated by David Hartley that had influenced Coleridge's early thinking. Hartley was the principle philosopher of the rational Unitarian Christianity to which Coleridge converted while a student at Cambridge. The Unitarians were in the vanguard of intellectual life after the French Revolution, making advances in social reform, science, and the historical critique of religious doctrine and ritual. Nevertheless, their "vision of a material, mechanistic universe directed by divine providence to an inevitably happy ending for all . . . threatened to founder on the kind of sceptical objections raised by Hume."[19] Ultimately, the challenge for Unitarianism is that is "strips away the divine mystery of transcendence, making God purely immanent," and this makes it hard to talk about God at all (525).

The problem with both Hartley's necessitarian schemes and bibliolatry is that their models of causation leave no room for freedom, and thus due to their "impoverished model[s] of the sensorium," both systems of thinking turn people into automatons.[20] Although Coleridge had once declared himself "a compleat Necessitarian,"[21] by the time he was writing *Aids to Reflection* he found necessitarianism deeply problematic, chiefly because it assumes that "motives act on the Will, as bodies act on bodies; and that whether mind and matter are essentially the same or essentially different, they are both alike under one and the same law of compulsory Causation" (AR, 139). In fact, the example Coleridge uses in the *Biographia Literaria* to point out the absurdity of the causal logical of Hartley's associationist thought could be applied equally well to the bibliolatrous:

> According to [Hartley's] hypothesis the disquisition, to which I am at present soliciting the readers attention, may be as truly said to be written by Saint Pauls church, as by me: for it is the mere motion of my muscles and nerves; and these again are set in motion from external causes equally passive . . . in interdependent connection with every thing that exists or has existed. Thus the whole universe co-operates to produce the minutest stroke of every letter, save only that I myself, and I alone, have nothing to do with it, but merely the causeless and effectless beholding of it when it is done. Yet scarcely can it be called a beholding. . . . It is the mere quick-silver plating behind a looking-glass; and in this alone consists the poor worthless I! (*BL*, 1:118–19)

What role is there for the individual to play beyond that of the idle voyeur in a world based on either necessitarian or bibliolatrous schemes?

Coleridge is willing to assume that, "For the Animals, their Nature is their Law," but humans must have the capacity to be "moral and rational agents," and so their "Will constitutes, or ought to constitute, the Law." Moral agents have a privileged role in creation because through the exercise of their own personal will they can comprehend "the *idea*, as a Reason," and give "causative force to the Idea, as a *practical* Reason." Each of us has the opportunity to properly express our own free will when our "Spirit comprehends the Moral Idea, by virtue of its rationality, and it gives to the Idea causative Power, as a Will: In every sense therefore, it *constitutes* the Law, supplying both the Elements of which it consists—viz. the Idea, and the realizing Power" (*AR*, 300). The individual is not a mere voyeur made of "quick-silver plating" (*BL*, 1:119) but instead has a significant role to play in creation. As Gerard Manley Hopkins would later suggest in "As Kingfishers Catch Fire," "*myself* it speaks and spells, / Crying *What I dó is me: for that I came.*" The "just man justices," and "Acts in God's eye what in God's eye he is—/ Chríst—for Christ plays in ten thousand places, / Lovely in limbs, and lovely in eyes not his / To the Father through the features of men's faces" (7–14).

In contrast to the necessitarian perspective of both Unitarianism and bibliolatry, Coleridge argues that the key to agency is the Will, which is activated at the level of reason and reflection and thus escapes the limits of our understanding, for "the Judgments of the Understanding are binding only in relation to the objects of our Senses, which we *reflect* under the forms of the Understanding" (*AR*, 218). Objects of nature conform to the categories of our understanding because they are "representable in the forms of Time and Space, and subjected to the Relations of Cause and Effect," but "whatever originates its own acts, or in any sense contains in itself the cause of its own state, must be *spiritual,* and consequently *supernatural*" (AR, 251). The Will is supernatural in this sense because the Will must be self-originating and not necessitated by any outside cause if it is to be free. The Bible, therefore, stimulates both our understanding and our reason in that it occupies space and takes time to read and understand, while also recording and representing Acts of Will that strain understanding and force us to reflect upon what may lie beyond understanding's limits and the sensuous logic of time and space and cause and effect.

It is this twofold nature that accounts for the Bible's potential significance as an object that can function as an aid to reflection and as a tool for soul-craft: it is "spiritual and yet at the same time outward and common to all" (CIS, 1154). For Coleridge, this commonality is demonstrated by the fact that "men of all ranks, conditions, and states of mind have found in this Volume a correspondent for every movement toward *the Better* felt in their own hearts" (CIS, 1154). For a believer, under certain conditions, such a feeling of correspondence can produce a "state of enduring bliss" (AR, 170), wherein an epiphanic feeling is accompanied by a sense of being addressed by the text and elevated to a life of grace. Such charged moments seem to justify the believer's efforts and ensure that he or she is on "the right road" (AR, 170). Nevertheless, in Coleridge's view to remain here is to be stuck with tautology and bibliolatry. Disagreeing with those Christians "whose Christianity, as matter of belief, is wholly external, and, like the Objects of Sense, common to all alike," Coleridge claims that Christianity cannot be "wholly *objective,* to the exclusion of all its correspondent *subjective.*" To read the "dead letter" only "by its own outward glories without the light of the Spirit in the mind of the Believer" is to be left with just the husk of religion (CIS, 1167). Christianity can only be a living faith if the "correspondent subjective" is maintained by not only bearing witness to "whatever finds me" (CIS, 1123) in the text, but also by addressing the text myself. By doing so the reader has the potential of recognizing that "the value of the Biblical text is that it does not conform to the prejudices" applied to it.[22]

When reading thoughtfully and actively rather than as a passive recipient ready to receive Scripture's stamp, the reader will find that the Bible does not conform to expectations—and this failure to conform is a serious obstacle or blockage that inhibits understanding. Scripture often defies the projections of significance placed upon it and thus opens a gap between objects and things or between objects and the "correspondent subjective" human gaze that makes it into a thing. The encounter with this gap or tension becomes a potential opportunity for recognizing and perhaps re-cognizing the gaze with which we look at the world. In these moments we catch a glimpse of ourselves looking—and "crossed by gleam / Of our [own] image" (*P*, 4:258–59), this can make all the difference.

This gap or tension between the textual object and the "correspondent subjective" is present because the Bible's meaning exceeds its enunciation: it possesses a surplus value that "cannot be the object of . . . direct and immediate Consciousness; but must be *inferred*" (*AR*, 79). The Act (or Acts) of Will that set in motion the symbolic machinery of the Bible, like the Act of Will that originates the world, cannot be understood because in each case "the Operative Cause is *transcendent*" and because it lies "beyond the information contained in the enunciation of the Fact, it can be characterized only by the *Consequences*" (*AR*, 319). The problem with bibliolatry is that it "mistakes the causes, the conditions, and the occasions of our becoming *conscious* of certain truths and realities for the truths and realities themselves" (*AR*, 15). In other words, it mistakes a transcendent cause that is "beyond our Comprehension and not within the sphere of sensible experience" and perceives it as an efficient cause—one understandable under the sensible logic of cause and effect (*AR*, 321).[23] What must be recognized in Coleridge's view is that the causes and occasions of our "becoming conscious" (*AR*, 15) of certain truths are not those truths themselves—the thing in itself continually eludes our understanding. This is to say that for Coleridge the Bible is not an object that we should fetishize but is instead a sublime object that requires us to reflect beyond the sensible limits of our understanding.

Scripture can serve as an "aid to reflection" because it can elevate inquiring spirits into an intuition of a religion beyond the limits of reason alone. As Shaffer has argued, here Coleridge builds upon Kant's "rejection of all the usual forms of the religious supernatural," but acceptance of certain aids to grace as long as our embrace of them is "reflective" and not "dogmatic."[24] The aids Kant accepted were prayer, churchgoing, baptism, and communion. He does so because "Prayer renders us willing to be well-pleasing to God; churchgoing is an aid to the appearance of a universal ethical commonwealth; baptism aims at initiating the development of a citizen in a divine state; and communion expands the mind towards the idea of a 'cosmopolitan moral community'" (211). Coleridge wants to expand the realm of acceptable aids and carefully explores the results of using them in the experimental manner already justified by Kant. Scripture could also serve as an aid because it functions as a sublime object, which is, to use the language of Kant, "an object (of nature) the representation [*Vorstellung*] of which determines the mind to regard the elevation of nature beyond our reach as equivalent to a presentation [*Darstellung*] of ideas."[25] The sublime, therefore, is "the paradox of an object which, in the very field of representation, provides a view, in a negative way, of the dimension of what is unrepresentable."[26]

We need a *via negativa* because, just as we cannot look upon the sun directly—for to do so results in blindness—we can only gain insight into the sublimity of a transcendent cause by reflecting backward from the effects.[27] We turn toward the sun or transcendent cause only by turning away from the effects. Such a turning occurs through a conversion, which, as Coleridge informs us, is "an act of the WILL *to turn towards* the true pole, *at the same time* (for this is the force of the preposition *con*) that the understanding is convinced and made aware of its existence and direction" (AR, 35). We do not turn to the true pole because we understand—the turning and the understanding coincide. What Coleridge is suggesting is necessary in the life of a Christian is akin to a Copernican Revolution in subjectivity—we must turn away from envisioning our creaturely selves as the center of all things and instead, like Dante's pilgrim at the end of the *Divine Comedy*, to be willing to revolve around the one true pole and roll "onward, like a wheel / In even motion, by the Love impell'd, / That moves the sun in Heaven and all the stars."[28] Coleridge assumes that all readers can find a "Moral Law within . . . the proof of which no man can *give* to another, yet every man may *find* for himself" (AR, 136). For him the ethical springs from the aligning of the will with the indwelling *logos*. Coleridge assumes we can know the good, which says something of the nature of God, and the goal of life should be to align ourselves with this goodness.

The difficulty lies in the fact that what Coleridge is asking us to enter into relation with has in some sense not yet taken place. If the origin and true meaning of the Bible transcends our understanding and is beyond the categories of time and space and cause and effect—then where or when is it—how do we find it? For Coleridge, the meaning of the Bible is always in excess of its enunciation, and to be proper Christians we must enter into relationship with this excess. But we can only approach such transcendence by examining and reflecting upon how the signs of this excess are woven into the twists and turns of the normative space of Scripture. In other words, like a black hole, a transcendent cause can only be detected by the way it bends what is perceivable—in the case of a black hole light is bent; in the case of an original text language is bent or troped. The transcendent excess or surplus value of such a text cannot be capitalized upon (or mastered) by unmasking the secret behind the form but can only be recognized when we enter into an exchange (or negotiation) with the secret of the form itself. In order to profit from the reading of Scripture, we must address the text that addresses us and put on its meaning. This is a reversal of the view found in bibliolatry—the implications of which implied that the human agents who wrote the Bible were simply masks worn by a superhuman ventriloquist. For Coleridge, it is instead we who wear the mask, and through our reading and reflection upon the text it is we who put on and perform Scripture's meaning—a meaning that only becomes sensible and thus understandable when we reflect upon how the text tropes us and affects our lives. What the text ultimately means is something we must labor to produce.

The question is how to read this surplus—the signifying stress of an "elsewhere" or beyond that paradoxically is so central to our sense of self. "To be *ours*," Coleridge writes, such an excess "must be referred to the mind either as motive, or consequence, or symptom" (AR, 13). Lacan suggested that Marx, in his analysis of capital, was the inventor of the symptom, meaning a condition where there is an original referent that is absent, and whose absence is made known through a crisis as to what this original referent might be. For psychoanalysis, the absent original referent "is a normal subject constitution, which is interrupted by the symptom and its cause and through which normalcy is [produced in analysis through negotiation], as its retroactively presupposed original referent."[29] Coleridge deduces a comparable logic when he suggests that in our exchange with Scripture our inability to match spirit and letter is symptomatic of the absent original referent that eludes and transcends our understanding. For Coleridge, this absent original can only be presupposed retroactively as a consequence of our reflections upon and negotiations with Scripture—and only as a product of our putting on the passionate crisis of the original referent in our own lives. This is how we move beyond the fixed attentiveness of bibliolatry and begin a life of Thought. "We may learn arithmetic, or the elements of geometry, by continued attention alone; but *self-knowledge*, or an insight into the laws and constitutions of the human mind, and the *grounds* of religion and true morality, in addition to the effort of attention requires the energy of THOUGHT" (AR, 14–15). For Coleridge, with attention alone we simply "submit to an impression [and] we keep the mind steady in order to *receive* the stamp." With thought, we seek instead "to imitate the artist" (AR, 14) and attempt to "eye Christ in every step" (AR, 203) of our life. Looking to him as the "pattern both in doing and in suffering, and drawing power from him for going through both: being *without him* able for nothing" (AR, 302).

Reflection

In order to see more clearly how the reader of Scripture can learn to "eye Christ in every step" (AR, 203) the remainder of this chapter will work to unpack what is meant by reflection, the means by which the will finds the right words to name or be brought back in relation with the "absent cause" whose meanings stimulate yet exceed Scripture's capacity to signify.[30] The importance of a habit of reflection was already apparent in Coleridge's 1795 lectures where he describes the ideal figure of Religion as being one who "displayed deep Reflection animated by ardent Feelings."[31] Coleridge develops his interest in reflection in part to overcome the theological difficulties that emerged in the wake of John Locke's empirical philosophy, which from Coleridge's perspective problematically proclaimed that "the universality of the law of cause and effect contravened the freedom of the will, and this in turn meant that moral responsibility was impossible."[32] Locke had his own conception of reflection, and begins book 2 of his *An Essay Concerning Human Understanding* (1690) by stating that "all ideas come from either sensation or reflection."[33] Ideas of sensation are closely coordinated to the sensations themselves, but ideas of reflection are those "the mind gets by reflecting on its own operations within itself."[34] It is this capacity to reflect upon its own operation that, for Locke, allows philosophy to take place at all.

Locke's model of subjective experience functions much like a camera obscura. It presupposes a passivity to the human mind and assumes that perception takes place "in a kind of cavern, with the mind only able to see what came to it through the 'inlets' of the senses."[35] Through these inlets reality is experienced in an atomized way as a series of particulate bits or "impressions." Empiricist skepticism emphasizes how "this level of information could be isolated from a later stage in which these bits were connected together, for example in beliefs about cause-effect relations."³⁶ As with the phenomenologist's *epoché*, or bracketing of all previous presuppositions, in empirical skepticism there is a desire to return to a natural attitude toward experience. To think clearly and distinctly it is necessary to separate out the basic level of sense impressions from the too-hasty conclusions about them that we too often leap to. What ultimately binds these bits together is the imagination as well as the habits and customs that emerge and cohere over time from these initial acts of imagination. Nevertheless, as Hume in particular emphasizes, there is no absolute certainty that guarantees these imaginative productions. Although the principles of association may seem to us to be "the cement of the universe," there is no necessity to these principles—even in our notions of causality.³⁷ Coleridge recoils from such thinking and responds to such skeptical disbelief by asking, "How can we make bricks without straw? Or build without cement?" (*BL*, 1:142).

A response to the disbelief of the empiricists offered itself to Coleridge as a result of his trip to Gottingen in 1798–99, where among those he meets "all are Kantians" (*CL*, 1:444). By 1801, Kant "took possession of [him] as with a giant's hand" (*BL*, 1:153), and through the study of Kant's work he is also able to overthrow "the doctrine of association, as taught by Hartley, and with it all the irreligious metaphysics of modern infidels, especially the doctrine of necessity" (*CL*, 2:706). By doing so Coleridge begins to be able to articulate a space for free will between the Scylla and Charybdis of necessity and empirical disbelief. Kant helps him respond to the skepticism of the empiricists by arguing that there is a "background understanding which underpins all our perceptual discriminations." As Charles Taylor puts in *The Language Animal* (2016), to really be sensed, a sensation must already have an "aboutness" and "intentionality" to it. For example, "The buzzing in my head is discriminated from the noise I hear from the neighboring woods, in that the first is a component in how I feel, and the second seems to tell me something about what's happening out there (my neighbor is using his chain saw again)."³⁸

In the Kantian model, "knowledge results from the synthesis of the universal forms of intuition and categories of understanding and the particular data of sense experience."³⁹ The imagination (*die Einbildungskraft*) is the faculty through which this synthesis occurs. Apprehension is the active aspect of the imagination that is "immediately directed to perceptions," and, according to Mark Taylor, since the "imagination has to bring the manifold of intuition into the form of an image, it must previously have taken the impressions up into its activity, that is, have apprehended them" (106). Apprehension is the act of capturing or gathering up sense experience into an image. The imagination operates "at the edge or on the border between understanding and sensation," and since according to Kant the imagination can cross or bridge this gap, it thereby responds to the threat of Humean skepticism by being guided by the regulative ideas of God, self, and world, and by a "transcendental schema" (106–7). According to Kant, this schema maps the manifold of the sensible in a manner that is universally intelligible and thus accessible to all subjects.

There are, of course, potential critiques to Kant's approach. One obvious question is what happens in a secular age when a universally acceptable transcendental schema no longer seems available and the regulative ideas that traditionally patterned social order become far less compelling? But a more basic critique of Kant's notion of an a priori schema that all sensations must map onto can be made with reference to child psychology, since it does not seem to be the case that at first the infant is even able to discern where it begins and the mother ends. It is only after the first months of development that there is a shift from what child psychologist Allison Gopnik calls an unfiltered "lantern consciousness" to a more focus "spotlight consciousness,"[40] and it is only in this latter more developed mindset that the baby would be able to discern "aboutness" and "intentionality." This suggests that most if not all of what Kant assumes to be a priori may actually be learned behavior that has developed through custom and habit much as Hume suggested. Even those facets that are "hardwired" may simply be another form of habit, which has developed gradually and intergenerationally through evolution.

Despite these potential concerns, part of Kant's appeal for Coleridge was that he reversed "the empiricist assumption that the human mind must conform to external objects" and argued instead that "objects of the senses must conform to our mental faculties."[41] In contrast to the blank-slate logic of the camera obscura model of the mind, Kant argued that what is inside and outside the mind fundamentally correlate, and with this "background understanding of aboutness" in place, he "sweeps away the empiricist atomism of experience."[42] By doing so he gained access to a form of reason that was beyond the understanding of the empiricists—beyond an understanding that could merely draw empirical conclusions through the processing of sense perceptions. For Kant, in contrast, reason was capable of making "universal and necessary, a priori judgements (such as the propositions of geometry)" and thus could send the reasoner "beyond the limits of experience, seeking the unconditioned." [43] However, in seeking the absolute, despite the fact that reason inevitably posits certain transcendental ideas such as "God" and "free will," Kant does not think reason can directly establish their truth. We can only have an "intuition" of the moral law, an intuition that is expressed whenever we say, "I ought." Nevertheless, even given these limitations "we must behave as if God and freedom were established" (527). Part of what gives reason the room to maneuver in this way is the imagination, which "creates, as it were, another nature out of the material that actual nature gives it" and through this process "we feel our freedom from the law of association." [44] Despite this feeling, however, as Shaffer acknowledges, Kant's view of freedom is still quite limited because for him "freedom implies adherence to the moral law of reason." Within phenomenal experience itself, "there can be no freedom; all we can hope for is to be self-determined." Self-determination appears as freedom only from a "timeless noumenal standpoint" and a man's character would only appear to be "a unity determined by him if it were viewed not as we must view it in nature as a succession of determinations each necessitated by the last, but through an intellectual intuition, as one timeless moment." [45]

Coleridge incorporates aspects of the Kantian model into his own, but he also seeks to move beyond it in a variety of ways. In 1819, he declares that his own philosophy is "built on the distinction between the Reason and the Understanding" (CL, 4:1049–50). Coleridge's concept of "Understanding" is akin to what Locke called reason: "the Faculty by which we reflect and generalize" from "impression[s] on the Sense" (AR, 224–25). What Coleridge calls reason is a higher capability that is able to detect the presence of the divine "logos" in all things. He maintains that "reason is the irradiative power of the understanding, and the representative of the infinite." [46] Here Coleridge is subtly revising Kant's fundamental distinction between Understanding (*Verstand*) and Reason (*Vernunft*), or between a "lower" reason (*Verstand*) and a more complete imaginative knowledge (*Vernunft*, i.e., "secondary imagination," "vision"). Understanding (*Verstand*) refers to those inductive and deductive operations that relate "the outer world to the subject, but not the subject to the outer world" because this form of knowledge "excludes the feelings and emotions of the subject and is therefore mechanical." [47] Reason (*Vernunft*) includes subjective experience and can thus gain access to what lies beyond the limits of reason alone. Coleridge swerves from Kant by aligning the Christian faith with *Vernunft*, boldly insisting that the "CHRISTIAN FAITH IS THE PERFECTION OF HUMAN REASON."[48]

The distinction between reason and understanding becomes a focal point of Coleridge's thought. One aim of *Aids to Reflection* is to "substantiate and set forth at large the momentous distinction between REASON and UNDERSTANDING," in order to "exhibit a full and consistent scheme of the Christian Dispensation."[49] When looked at only though the sensible eyes of understanding, "All experiencing, feeling, and intuiting is in and of itself mute and requires a mediating organ to gain expression."[50] This "mediating organ is Reason (*Vernunft*), which sees what is immediately experienced mediately, as if in a mirror!"[51] For Coleridge it is this higher, mediated form of reason that can "be safely defined as the organ of the Super-sensuous; even as the Understanding wherever it does not possess or use the Reason, as another and inward eye, may be defined the conception of the Sensuous, or the faculty by which we generalize and arrange the phænomena of perception." It is through Reason as an "organ of inward sense" that the human mind, or soul, has "the power of acquainting itself with invisible realities or spiritual objects" (*CW*, 6:156).

By suggesting that the human mind has access to the noumenal realm, Coleridge "calculatedly opens the floodgates to the kind of enthusiastic discourse that Kant had tried to banish by showing clearly the limits of our knowledge."[52] For Kant, ideas of God or the "Moral Law" were only regulative and could only be used as regulations or guides to our practical conduct. Coleridge, on the other hand, wants to consider how such ideas could be experienced as constitutive, that is as "objects of possible experience" (527). For Coleridge, "Whether Ideas are regulative only, according to Aristotle and Kant; or likewise CONSTITUTIVE, and one with the power and Life of Nature, according to Plato, and Plotinus . . . is the highest problem of Philosophy'" (*CW*, 6:113–14).

The capacity that helps us see the supersensuous in the mediating mirror of reason is called reflection. Although a dominant meaning of reflection in the eighteenth century merely equates it with serious thought, Coleridge used the term in a much more robust way. It is the faculty in which knowledge is reflected upon and envisioned. Through reflection the mind's eye functions as a mirror or screen in which one can glimpse the underlying pattern experienced only serially in sense perception. Each momentary flash of insight recorded by the mediums of memory, technology, and art make it possible to see a patterned whole out of the passing multitude of momentary insights. Reflection can offer a view of eternity, because through intuitive vision what would otherwise pass by our understanding in too quick a succession or would normally be unavailable for comprehension can be suddenly seen in a concentrated immediacy. As Coleridge writes in an 1806 letter, "For Reflexion seems the first approach to, & shadow of, the divine Permanency; the first effort of divine working in us to bind the Past and Future with the Present, and thereby to let in upon us some faint glimmering of that State in which Past, Present, and Future are co-adunated in the adorable I AM" (*CL*, 2:1197). Reflection is the "key to an understanding of the significance of the Word or Logos, forming part of a conception which links central elements in outwardly perceived nature to the nature of Being, and so to the Absolute Being who is God."[53] Reflection is the "masterlight of all our seeing."[54] For Coleridge, this light "is the eye of [the] soul" (*AR*, 15).[55]

In "The Concept of Criticism in German Romanticism," Walter Benjamin highlights one way to understand the significance of reflection within the period. He writes, "Reflection expands without limit or check, and the thinking given form in reflection turns into formless thinking which directs itself upon the absolute."[56] In this view, "Art, bestowing shape from the impulse of striving spirituality, binds the latter in ever new forms with the occurrence of the entire life of the present and the past. Art fastens not on particular self—perfecting mankind, it draws the complex of events together, rendering them unified and manifest."[57] In this way, for Benjamin as for Coleridge, "reality does not form an aggregate of monads locked up in themselves and unable to enter into any real relations with one another"; on the contrary, "they are so far from being shut up in themselves and free of relations that through the intensification of their reflection . . . they can incorporate other beings, other centers of reflection, more and more into their own self-knowledge" (146).

Another key model of reflection from the period that should also be kept in mind when contemplating the concept is Johann Gottfried Herder's description of "reflection," or "*Besonnenheit*." In *The Language Animal*, Taylor has a useful discussion of Herder's approach, which emerges out of a distinction Taylor makes between two types of language theory: designative and constitutive. And here we should recall that whether ideas are regulative or constitutive is, for Coleridge, "the highest problem of Philosophy" (*CW*, 6:114). In the designative or "enframing" approach to language, which Taylor associates with the work of Hobbes, Locke, and Condillac, language is viewed as an instrument or "set of connections which we can use to construct or control things."[58] In this view it is the invention of language that gives humans "control over the whole process of association" for the first time. Thus what language ultimately affords us is "dominion over our imagination" (5). This capacity for dominion is developed through the acquisition of knowledge—a knowledge that consists in having the representations in our head match or correlate with the material reality outside of it. Language is what allows our ideas to be in touch with reality, and the better our picture of the world is, the more control we will be able to exercise over it. Knowledge "consists in having the representation actually square with the reality" (4).

Herder's work belongs to the other side of the debate, which offers a constitutive theory of language. This view sees language as a means of lifting "the mind from 'blank' perception to an awareness of the mind's own constitutive role."[59] From this perspective, language is not simply a tool for producing adequate representations of the world "out there," because the association "between sign and some mental content is already there with the animal [or infant] cry (what Condillac calls the 'natural sign')."[60] Herder argues that since even "prelinguistic beings can react to the things which surround them," language must be more than merely a representation, association, or correlation made between some mental context "in here" with the world "out there" (6). For Herder, what the linguistic or "instituted sign" enables is for the sign user to "focus on and manipulate the associated idea, and hence direct the whole play of their imagination" (5). What the constitutive theory argues is that what language makes possible is not merely representation, or access to regulative ideas, but an entirely different kind of consciousness, which Herder calls "reflective" (*besonnen*).

It is this capacity for reflection that gives users access to a "linguistic dimension" in which sensitivities to issues of rightness come into play. A parrot may be able to mimic a language user, but because the bird has no capacity for reflection, we do not think it has access to the linguistic dimension "no matter how unerringly it squawked out the 'right word'" (7). A human speaker, however, does have access to this dimension. A creature is "operating in the linguistic dimension when it can use and respond to signs in terms of their truth, or descriptive rightness, or power to evoke some mood, or recreate a scene, or express some emotion, or carry some nuance of feeling, or in some such way to be *le mot juste*."[61] Reflection is the "gathering of attention" that helps us find the right word.[62] We may not always be consciously focusing on the issue of rightness, but its significance comes to the fore "when we get uncertain and are plumbing unexplored depths of vocabulary" (7). It is when we are uncertain, confused, or otherwise left speechless that we become most concerned with finding the right words. We might even call this the poetic impulse.

Reflection (*Besonnenheit*) can thus be understood as another way of describing the Aeolian string theory of Romantic poetics discussed in chapter 1, wherein both writer and reader approach the text via a method of gradual adjustment, because each "cannot know exactly what array of specific settings will enable the wind passing through the strings to produce harmony (though one may have a good guess), so one must keep re-adjusting them until harmony is in fact produced." The only confirmation that the "adjustments are correct is the harmony itself, the 'deep power of joy' that suddenly leaps forth like a released magnetic or electrical charge."[63] Similarly, within reflection it is a sensitivity to rightness, to finding *le mot juste,* that functions as the rudder we use to steer our vehicular consciousness through the linguistic dimension and toward the right words. As Herder memorably puts it,

> The human being demonstrates reflection when the force of his soul operates so freely that in the whole ocean of sensations which floods the soul through all the senses it can, so to speak, separate off, stop, and pay attention to a single wave, and be conscious of its own attentiveness. The human being demonstrates reflection when, out of the whole hovering dream of images which proceed before his senses, he can collect himself into a moment of alertness, freely dwell on a single image, pay it clear, more leisurely heed, and separate off characteristic marks for the fact that this is that object and no other.[64]

Entering this linguistic dimension and "being able to focus on objects by recognizing them, creates, as it were, a new space around us." Rather than "being overcome by the ocean of sensations as they rush by us, we are able to distinguish one wave, and hold it in clear, calm attention." It is this "new space of attention, of distance from the immediate instinctual significance of things, of focused awareness," that Herder calls reflection (87).

By developing a capacity for acts of reflection, one can learn to control "the flow of their own imagination, [unlike those who] passively follow the connections which are triggered off in them by the chain of events" (as is the case for the mariner's ghastly crew in the "Rime").[65] Reflection is what allows our souls to not become shipwrecked in the "ocean of sensations." Furthermore, our reflective "stances are literally bodily attitudes or actions on or toward objects." When language is used in this way, it is an "'expressive' action, one that both actualizes this stance of reflection and also presents it to others in public space" (30). Reflection in this sense is the key to understanding the true significance of the world before us, because it contributes to a conception that "links central elements in outwardly perceived nature to the nature of Being, and so [at least for Coleridge] to the Absolute Being who is God." [66]

* 3 *

Coleridge's Parable of Modernity

In his 1936 essay "The Storyteller," Walter Benjamin argues that the art of storytelling is coming to an end "because the epic side of truth, wisdom, is dying out."[1] Wisdom is "counsel woven into the fabric of real life," and a storyteller could tease wisdom out of this fabric because he was of the same locality as the listener and thus the fabric of their daily habits and practices were held in common (86–87). When the fabric of life is no longer shared, however, and is instead differentiated into a variety of lifestyles, cultural perspectives, and imagined communities, then it becomes increasingly difficult for the storyteller to disseminate wisdom. Benjamin, however, did not lament the decline of storytelling, saying that "nothing would be more fatuous than to want to see in it merely a 'symptom of decay,' let alone a 'modern' symptom"; rather, he suggests we see the decline of storytelling as a "concomitant symptom of the secular productive forces of history, a concomitant that has quite gradually removed narrative from the realm of living speech and at the same time is making it possible to see a new beauty in what is vanishing" (87). The secular productive forces of history unlock new narrative formations and an altered sense of temporality. Just as narrative shifts from the storyteller's reliance on shared experience and an epic investment in past tradition to new forms of narrative whose cultural value is produced through the circulation of its performance of novel speculations, so too does historical consciousness awaken from the communal repetition of the liturgical year. In each case it is a turn toward the future that makes possible the vision of a new beauty being born in what is vanishing.

Nevertheless, as Eric Santner argues, if our capacity for pleasure is "linked to a sense of fit with the world," then it is this "sense of jointure or fitness" that is "under assault in modernity."[2] Modernity brings about a dissociation in sensibility, which is often experienced as the loss "of feeling libidinally implicated in the world" (122). The posts and beams of this modernity include the "ideals of reciprocity and universality," the requirement to act "from an integration of one's inclinations" and not "from any one strongly felt momentary passion," to have interests rather than passions, to assume "that all units of future time have equal value,"[3] and to accept "the attenuation of modes of ritual time, ancestral time, and higher time and their displacement by a monochronic idea of secular time."[4] These shifts have obvious benefits in terms of social progress and individual liberties, but there are costs. As Wordsworth suggests, we have given our hearts away—and this may indeed be a sordid boon. Two consequences of living in a dispassionate world are tendencies toward disenchantment and disengagement.

A society's stability is dependent upon the healthy functioning of these processes of investiture, which serve as the *"performative magic*—whereby individuals 'become who they are.'" For Santner, the threshold of modernity is felt to be crossed, and an investiture crisis is experienced, when the attenuation of traditional "social bonds becomes chronic, when they are no longer capable of seizing the subject in his or her self-understanding." The disruption of the normative functioning of the social order and "generalized attenuation of symbolic power and authority can be experienced as the collapse of social space and the rites of institution into the most intimate core of one's being."[5] The threatening affect generated by such a crisis is not an anxiety of absence and loss but of overproximity. The world, in other words, is felt in the flesh of each individual to be too much with us. At the root of the trauma of an investiture crisis is the subject's inability to satisfyingly express, in Joel Faflack's words, "an unmasterable exteriority encrypted within themselves."[6] This "unmasterable exteriority" consists of those ideological discourses and normative pressures that get under our skin, and thus affect our flesh, through the processes of investiture, and thereby subliminally establish the matrices through which we perceive the world.[7]

Trauma can be suffered when the subject's orientation in the world becomes violently divorced from any cultural, linguistic, and social context that could meaningfully ground experience within a wider matrix of significance. In order to alleviate the trauma of a world that was in some way too much with them, Romantic writers often sought new ways of grounding, rebinding, or rereading the too-muchness of their subjectivity. As we shall see, one of the crucial questions Romanticism engaged in is how best to mind the fold or "'gap' between our biological being and 'the historical forms of life' in which human communities unfold."[8]

"The Rime of the Ancient Mariner" functions as a poetic response to the underlying investiture crisis of modernity and could be said to be staging, or scripturalizing, the seismic psychic disturbance that accompanies the shift from a porous to a buffered consciousness that Charles Taylor describes as transpiring over the last five centuries. It is a parable of a traumatic entrance into modernity and the way this trauma can be felt in that element of flesh that registers, in Santner's formulation, "the virtual yet unnervingly visceral substance of the fantasies that both constrain and amplify the lives of modern subjects."[9] Fortunately, the poem also attempts to offer a way of intervening into this space of unnerving agitation by modeling a form of exodus and by showing how literature can help cultivate the forms of sympathy and reflection that are needed to uncouple us from patterns of behavior that are no longer desirable and rebind us to forms of human purposiveness informed by new models of moral and political trajectory.

My reading of the poem acknowledges Thomas Pfau's interpretation of it as a parable that confronts the "shipwreck" of skeptical empiricism within modernity, one that functions as a gnostic indictment of free will. However, I ultimately swerve from this reading and argue that the "Rime," rather than gesturing backward toward some presecular world of Christian harmony, instead points forward toward a potentially much more optimistic reading of what religion can mean for a postsecular age—one that accepts and even celebrates the free exercise of the will as something more than sin. Drawing upon the related case of Daniel Schreber, the German jurist who has a nervous breakdown at the end of the nineteenth century and served as the basis for Freud's classic case study of paranoia, I demonstrate how both Schreber and the mariner suffer from a kind of soul murder, which is experienced when there is no space left in which a reflective vehicular consciousness can maneuver. It is due to this attenuation of spacing within the self that "vitality comes to be registered as an invasive excitation of nerves."[10] Fortunately, the "Rime" does not simply diagnosis a crisis but also suggests a cure, and I focus on how and why the blessing of the sea snakes episode at the heart of the poem serves as the moment in which the mariner and ultimately the reader can confront a form of neighborliness that moves beyond seeing the other as nothing more than a material support for the tormenting monologue of our own subjective projections. In this way, the foci of chapters 2 and 3 work together to consider the significance of the ways in which encounters with neighbors, Scripture, and literature, all have the capacity to force us out of ourselves and into a wider world of concern by their very resistance to the projections we place upon them.

Alone on a Wide Wide Sea

The overall pattern of the "Rime" is that of a movement that begins by singling out an individual and ends in an invocation of a broader community. The poem opens with the mariner picking the wedding guest out from a group and holding him captive with his "glittering eye" (3). Once the wedding guest's attention is caught, the mariner leads him on an imaginative journey that begins by describing how the mariner's "soul hath been / Alone on a wide wide sea / So lonely 'twas, that God himself / Scarce seemed there to be" (597–600) and ends with the mariner suggesting something far "sweeter than the Marriage-feast" (601), which is

> To walk together to the kirk
> With a goodly company!—.
> To walk together to the kirk
> And all together pray,
> While each to his great Father bends,
> Old men, and babes, and loving friends,
> And youths, and maidens gay! (603–9)

But if the poem ultimately culminates with a "goodly company" bending toward the "great Father" (607), then how does the poem encourage this radical reorientation? Is this reorientation still desirable to us today? And given the fact that the mariner himself seems cursed to be never fully at home in this "goodly company" (604) is such a reorientation even possible?

The central plot of the "Rime" probably originated with Wordsworth, who claims to have suggested that Coleridge represent the mariner "as having killed one of these birds on entering the South Sea, and that the tutelary Spirits of these regions take upon them to avenge the crime."[11] And the basic narrative of the plot is familiar: the mariner must periodically, "at an uncertain hour" (582), go and use his "strange power of speech" (587) to tell his tale to one who appears in need of its telling. The story told is that of a mariner who after killing an albatross enters a nightmarish landscape of spectre-bark, undead shipmates and polar spirits.

By giving us this poem the poet makes us ask: What do you want from me? If the "Rime," like his conversation poems, "reveal[s] Coleridge's increasing concern with the function of the will to lift the mind from 'blank' perception to an awareness of the mind's own constitutive role," then what act of interpretation will enable readers to lift their wills up out of the "blank perception" readers typically feel in their initial response to the poem?[12] Clearly, in the "Rime" the shooting of the albatross is foundational, and every interpretation of the overall discourse must ultimately attend to the question of why the mariner shot the albatross. But what this might mean is difficult to discern in part because, as Pfau explains, "the narrative is but an accretion of isolated episodes strung up like so many beads with the help of the ever-same conjunctive phrases: 'And now there came both mist and snow, / And it grew wondrous cold: / And ice, mast-high,'" etc.[13] Marvelous things are related but the psychological connection of the events is not forced upon nor even clearly suggested to the reader. What binds the narrative together is not a sense of necessity but only the "sheer charisma or 'feel' of an experience that continues to dominate the Mariner's (and his listener's) consciousness with traumatic force."[14]

Like the mariner's crewmates, who, as Coleridge's gloss tells us, "make themselves accomplices in the crime" by attempting to justify the albatross's death, readers of the "Rime" become invested in the poem's spectral discourse to the extent that they feel compelled to justify the poem's originating act.[15] The problem with overly contextual readings of the "Rime" is that they often seek to map out and in some way rationalize and thus stabilize the poem's spectral imagery. The "Rime" is better understood as an experiment in language that offers readers an imaginative itinerary within which to exercise their will so they can decide for themselves the meaning of these "reliques of sensation" (*BL*, 1:113) the poem forces them to feel. Those unable to make this decisive interpretative leap may share in the fate of the mariner's traveling companions. Unlike the mariner, who is somehow singled out and alone survives the ordeal, the rest of the "ghastly crew" (*CPP*, "Rime," 340) raise "their limbs like lifeless tools" (339), becoming the automatons of a controlling yet lifeless agency. These "dead men" (334) are without wills of their own but are instead compelled by outside forces to act as they do. As a result, by the end of the third section of the "Rime" their "souls did from their bodies fly" (220).

This difference between the mariner and the "ghastly crew" suggests that at least in some respects the poem is a critique of certain forms of mediation.[16] Robert Mitchell has highlighted how Coleridge was "suspicious of any form of suspension that affected the will, and he vilified 'modern' mass-media institutions that he felt encouraged trances."[17] He saw such undesirable reading practices as likely leading to "a sort of beggarly Day-dreaming, in which . . . the mind furnishes for itself only laziness and a little mawkish sensibility, while the whole Stuff and Furniture of the Doze is supplied ab extra by a sort of spiritual Camera Obscura, which (*pro tempore*) fixes, reflects, & transmits the moving phantasms of one man's Delirium so as to people the barrenness of a hundred other trains [of associations] . . . under the same morbid Trance, or 'suspended Animation,' of Common Sense, and all definite Purpose."[18] Although the "Rime" is clearly a form of mediation that at one level works by fixing and transmitting "moving phantasms," it also tries to teach its readers how to lift their wills up out of the temptation to linger in the suspended animation of blank perception.

The poem is keenly interested in the mesmeric quality of the reading experience. As Miranda Burgess has argued, reading often invokes a form of transport that encourages "a kind of automatism in which books make their readers move precisely to the extent that they make their readers feel."[19] Through this "strange power of speech" the subject's mind becomes "the projector of a hallucinatory cinema."[20] Just like the "glittering eye" of the mariner that captivates the wedding guest, the sublime style of the poet can be used to create images of sense that take control over a responding subject by inducing a particular reading experience.

Although within the poem there is a clear need for the piercing of illusions—a separating of "the certain from the uncertain, day from night" (*CPP*, 59)—the decision about what the poem ultimately means can only be made by one who has already suspended disbelief. Readers must be willing to become lost in the sea of the poem's spectral signifiers if they are going to find their own meaningful way out. The reader finds these right words by first feeling disoriented along with the mariner but then learning to secure meaning through a recovery from this disorientation. The reader, in other words, must learn how to become reflective in relation to the poem in the sense ascribed to Herder in the previous chapter, by willingly entering into its ocean of sensations and learning to successfully navigate its linguistic dimension. Although the mariner himself is doomed to the repetition compulsion of having to tell his own tale in fits and starts, for readers it is possible to transcend at least momentarily the paranoiac immersion in "blank" perception because we can learn to exercise our will and form (aesthetic) judgments about the mariner's delusions and the overall significance of the poem.

This training in meaning making can come in the form of a poetics that offers what Wolfgang Iser described as "a state of unending oscillation by means of which closed positions are opened up again and apparent finalities are outstripped."[21] The challenge of interpreting the "Rime" is that any hypothesis one might have for what the "Polar Spirit" might signify will inevitably complicate one's reading of the albatross and vice versa. The interpretive situation here resembles "That dolphin-torn, that gong-tormented sea," invoked by W. B. Yeats in the last line of "Byzantium." Every attempt to interpret the rippling implications of any one of the "Rime's" dolphin-torn images interferes with the interpretations of others, as well as the "gong-tormented" desire to apprehend the concentric orderliness of the poem's complete pattern. The way out of this interpretative confusion can only occur if we can find the right words to break "the deadlock, the vicious cycle, of empty and confused ruminations."[22]

There is of course a long history of attempting to explicate the *Rime*'s meaning, but the poem's parabolic style has frustrated attempts at achieving interpretative closure. One reason for the persistent focus on this poem stems from its centrality for understanding not only Samuel Taylor Coleridge's poetic and intellectual development but also the enduring significance of Romanticism itself. In this analysis, I discuss two particularly strong readings of the poem by Jerome McGann and Thomas Pfau and use their work to highlight how a postsecular reading of the poem diverges from theirs. Like Pfau, I see the "Rime" as a parable of modernity, but whereas he reads the poem as a gnostic warning about the sinfulness of free will and seems to want to return to a presecular Christian sensibility, I argue that the poem points forward (perhaps further than Coleridge himself intended) and suggests the role religion can still play in a postsecular age. The poem is not simply an allegory concerning a skeptical crisis brought on by empiricist thinking but also offers a positive response to the sometimes traumatic conditions of modern secularity.

First, however, I want to use aspects of McGann's influential reading of the Rime as a way of orienting my approach to the poem. He sees the structure of the "Rime" as forming a stratified text buffered by a series of textual emendations to an original experience and argues that in the "The Rime of the Ancient Mariner," particularly in its 1817 revision, there are "four clear layers of development" that can be distinguished:

(a) an original mariner's tale;
(b) the ballad narrative of that story;
(c) the editorial gloss added when the ballad was, we are to suppose, first printed;
(d) Coleridge's own point of view on his invented materials.[23]

In these stratified layers can be found attempts to both contain and clarify an originary experience that was *too much* for words to bear. Given this structure, McGann sees the "Rime" functioning in a manner similar to the method for reading the Bible advocated by the higher criticism, which worked to reveal the various "layers" of the work. The poem serves as a kind of "English national Scripture" in the way it "imitates a redacted literary text which comprises various material extending from early pre-Christian periods through a succession of later epochs of Christian culture, and the ultimate locus of these transmissions is England" (160).

The "Rime" functions as a response to an investiture crisis and could be said to be staging, or scripturalizing, the seismic psychic rupture that inaugurates the shift from a porous to a buffered consciousness that Charles Taylor describes as transpiring over the last five centuries. Taylor's general time frame for this shift resonates with the dating McGann and other critics have given to the various layers of the "Rime." Using internal textual evidence these critics date the original mariner's tale as describing an event that must have occurred after Columbus but before Magellan (ca. 1492–1517) and take the ballad narrative as well as the subsequent glosses as additions that accrued to the original tale over the subsequent centuries. Given this similarity in time frames, it seems justifiable to at least consider that the entire stratified frame of the "Rime" acts as a kind of commentary on the overall shift from the porous consciousness Taylor describes as being dominant in 1500 to the forms of buffered consciousness endemic to the nineteenth century.

McGann assumes that Coleridge "takes it for granted that an 'Enlightened' mind of his or a later period will not believe that the spectre-bark ever had a concrete and objective existence or that the creatures called Death and Life-in-Death ever did what the poem reports or ever existed in the ordinary sense." Readers should instead "recognize such phenomena to be mental projections of the mariner's delirium." All of the "fabulous events" of the poem are best understood as "phenomena mediated either by the mariner, or by the balladeer(s), or by some still later editor or scribe, like the writer of the gloss" (163). However, the poem does not then become a mere fabric of errors because when intuited as a whole, these stratified layers of mediated misrecognitions reveal, at least according to Coleridge, "that the entire system (or history) of the mediations is organized a priori and that the history of the mediations is an evolving process whereby the original (God-instituted and redemptive) system is raised up into human consciousness by the processive acts of human consciousness itself" (164).

This logic of stratified progression (or dialectical materialism) is not unlike the dominant strategy of Friedrich Schelling's *Die Weltalter* (*Ages of the World*), or for that matter the approach a critic might take when contemplating the implications of a canonical work of art. In either case, one attempts to produce a new reading of the world or a work by first tracing the fault line that runs through successive layers of interpretation and then by intuitively and reflectively glimpsing the figure (or situated void) of that fault line, which then serves to ground a new strata of interpretation about what it all means. Of course each new production in some way extends the fault line further, so "at an uncertain hour" ("Rime," 582) when "Hieronymo's mad againe" the whole process will need to be repeated.[24] This is why, according to McGann, "given a coherent cultural tradition, the text which exhibits marks of its historical passage (in the form of later interpolations, glosses, and other textual additions and 'impurities') retains its ideological coherence despite the process of apparent fragmentation."[25]

McGann argues that the poem "dramatizes a salvation story, but it is not the old story of our salvation in Christ; rather, it is the new story of our salvation of Christ" (156). Part of what the "Rime" helps us see is how Christian ideas could "find a new birth of freedom, not in the fact of Christ's resurrection, which is the traditional Pauline view, but in the symbol of the resurrection, in its meaning" (164). What Christ comes to represent is not necessarily a historical actuality but rather a way of reading in which the dead letter of tradition is redeemed and illuminated by the way its words are made flesh.[26] To put this into the language of mediation the question becomes: "Is the Christ-medium still the bearer of a transcendent message or has he, so to speak, completely absorbed the message into his very mediality? And if so, can this mediality then be uncoupled from his 'person,' be dispersed into other media, systems, and objects?"[27] These are questions that get at the heart of what it means to study both religion and literature.

Despite such provocations, however, what seems to be missing in McGann's approach is precisely an understanding of what Coleridge calls the "correspondent subjective" (CIS, 1123)—that part of me that responds to whatever finds me in a text. Although in practice McGann is clearly a subtle and sensitive reader, his more doctrinaire statements about criticism tend to assume "the phantasm of the reader-interpreter as sovereign"—and that the job of the critic is to be the one who knows and who can pierce the veil of all illusions.[28] This is evident, for instance, when he says, "We willingly suspend our disbelief only when disbelief, or critical distance, is the ground of our response" and that "Criticism must penetrate those illusions" that have been built up around the "Rime."[29] To me this doesn't seem very neighborly, and although such a hermeneutics of suspicion has its place, it shouldn't necessarily be the only or even the dominant mode of literary criticism.

In contrast to McGann's suggestion that "cooptation must always be a process intolerable to a critical consciousness, whose first obligation is to resist incorporation, and whose weapon is analysis,"[30] I argue that a better way to approach the "Rime" is in the context of what Michel de Certeau calls "mystic fables." In *The Mystic Fable* (1995), Certeau argues that with the advent of modernity and the loss of the cosmological tradition a new way of proceeding became necessary—a new *mystics*. And whereas physics refers to the methods and discourses that name and categorize physical reality, the modern discipline of mystics "assembles and orders its practices in the name of something that it cannot make into an object (unless it be a mystical one)."[31] According to Certeau, one way this new formality expressed itself was in what he calls mystic fables—and within this term he groups a variety of spiritual and mystical texts that began to be written in the sixteenth and seventeenth centuries (Meister Eckhart is a notable precursor, but Certeau is most focused on the period from Teresa of Ávila to Angelus Silesius).[32] The new way of proceeding that these authors were engaged in deployed "a language of the body," which worked to create through a "corporeal vocabulary the initial markers indicating the place in which these authors found themselves and the illumination they received."[33] Mystic fables are works that "aim at the *exercise* of language—a 'performance' and therefore, . . . the 'conversion of language into discourse.'"[34] Such texts utilize the materiality of language in an effort to invest readers into a larger discourse about meaning. And just as the itinerary of a pilgrimage is an exercise that converts instructions for bodily movement into an embodied experience, so too is a mystic text an exercise in language that attempts to pattern an imaginative experience. The reader, therefore, must recognize reading as a discipline and be willing to be coopted by the words that are read. The words must be made flesh if they are to be made meaningful. If the "Rime" functions as mystic fable, then like a pair of virtual reality glasses, the only way to really know what it is about is to put it on for ourselves. What the encounter with the poem provides is the "set and setting" of a certain kind of heightened aesthetic experience.[35]

Having established some of the basic conditions for reading the poem, I now want to consider what it means to call it a parable of modernity. Here I follow Pfau, who finds the poem to be "a parable about the philosophical predicament of modernity" and sees the killing of the albatross as the central event of the poem, one that registers the problematic implications of free will when it is coupled with skeptical empiricism.[36] However, although Pfau's overall argument that the poem can and is perhaps best read as a parable of modernity is convincing, it is also telling that in his long and otherwise careful reading of the poem he only makes passing reference to the mariner's blessing of the sea snakes in part IV, which is the second major event around which the mariner's tale pivots.[37] By taking into account the importance of this blessing a different understanding of modernity becomes available, one that acknowledges but also goes beyond a mere critique of empirical skepticism and that draws more fully upon interconnections between Coleridge's thoughts about philosophy, theology, and mediation.

Nevertheless, there is much that is compelling in Pfau's approach, and he rightly observes that the mariner "becomes the archetypal figure for a modern, deracinated, and aimless existentialist vision, the nightmare of Charles Taylor's 'buffered self' that ever since has been the stuff of dystopic (proto-) modernist narrative from Coleridge through Kafka" (498). Pfau reads the killing of the albatross as a "synecdoche for the scientific and commercial exploits that modernity so often captures in the master-trope of seafaring and shipwreck." He finds the killing of the albatross deeply troubling because it is a purely volitional act "whereby the solitary individual shatters the cosmos by turning it into an inventory of disaggregated objects to be subjected to (inherently skeptical) analysis and experimentation" (455). In other words, for the mariner the net result of shooting the albatross is becoming lost in a sea of signification. For Pfau, an over-reliance on empirical thinking is problematic because it perpetuates a form of curiosity that "harbors no expectation of 'wonder,' such as would imply some impending, all-consuming revelation" (423). It is a form of thinking that has lost touch of any unifying logos that binds the world together into a meaningful whole. As in the case of Victor Frankenstein, the exercise of mere curiosity produces monstrosities because it "destroys the ancient notion of community as a normative (non-negotiable and non-contingent) framework."[38] In this way, the "Mariner's defining act of skepticism and its consequent inauguration of modernity as epoch" (984) proves to be "nothing less than sin."[39]

The idea that free will is sinful is a major emphasis within Pfau's analysis. But why should this be the case? In *Aids to Reflection*, Coleridge writes that "a Sin is an Evil which has its ground or origin in the Agent, and not in the compulsion of Circumstances. Circumstances are compulsory from the absence of a power to resist or control them" (AR, 266–67). Thus sin can only occur through an act of will, because if one is compelled by circumstances to do something, then it cannot be a sin. The will is "a primal and ineffable force that creates a new reality rather than reacting to the one given"; it is "the power of originating a state."[40] The will is "ultimately self-determined, or it is no longer a *Will* under the law of perfect Freedom, but a *Nature* under the mechanism of Cause and Effect" (AR, 285). However, when an individual will "deviates from the Absolute Will, it negates itself." The individual "participates in the noumenal reality only when he is one with it."[41] Therefore, to exercise free will is sinful because it deviates from and thus falls out of a harmonious participation with the absolute will. This is why, for Pfau, the "Rime" is a parable of the loss of the spiritual integrity of the premodern Christian world, and "whatever spirituality the modern individual may be able to achieve, it will be a creed categorically different than the one that had prevailed prior to modernity's sinful inauguration of the free will."[42]

Pfau recognizes that to claim that "there is free will in any sense is to deny necessity and claim that men can break out of the chain of cause and effect."[43]

However, he reads such attempts not as moments of liberation but as repetitions of the "metaphysical dilemma first broached by Gnosticism" with its "demiurgic conception of the will." From this perspective to exercise free will is to participate in "the sudden deterioration of a putatively benevolent deity into a menacing and demonic force."[44] To exercise free will is to participate in the workings of a false god. It is a sinful mistake that can be made only because of "the constant possibility of human beings to disavow the Logos in an act of free, sinful choice" (442).

Although there are certainly moments in Coleridge's wide corpus that seem to resonate with such thinking, the problem with reading the "Rime" through the lens of Gnosticism is that it returns Coleridge to the situation that he was critiquing in Hartley's necessitarianism and in bibliolatry. Is it really the case that the only role for the human to play that is not sinful is as the passive "quick-silver plating behind a looking-glass" (*BL*, 1:119)?

For a clearer sense of what is at stake in this debate, I want to briefly reflect upon the central moment of "Frost at Midnight," when the poet turns to his infant son and says,

> But *thou*, my babe! Shalt wander, like a breeze,
> By lakes and sandy shores, beneath the crags
> Of ancient mountain, and beneath the clouds,
> Which image in their bulk both lakes and shores
> And mountain crags: so shalt thou see and hear
> The lovely shapes and sounds intelligible
> Of that eternal language, which thy God
> Utters, who from eternity doth teach
> Himself in all, and all things in himself.
> Great universal Teacher! he shall mould
> Thy spirit, and by giving make it ask. (59–69)

The poet had already lamented how his own urban upbringing had buffered his subjectivity reared as he was "In the great city, pent 'mid cloisters dim" (57), but he now describes how he wants his own "babe" to "wander, like the breeze, / By lakes and sandy shores, beneath the crags, / Of ancient mountain, and beneath the clouds, / Which image in their bulk both lakes and shores / And mountain crags" (59–63). The chiasmatic imagery here is significant and suggests a subtle model of the role of reflectivity in subjectivity.

"To wander like the breeze" is to possess a self that is quite different from the billiard-ball-like solidity suggested by Taylor's notion of the buffered self. The fact that in this poem the self depicted moves by lakes "which image in their bulk both lakes and shores / And mountain crags" suggests that such a self is something akin to a subtle disturbance or interference pattern that moves between a perceptual imaging apparatus and that which is imaged. To wander like a breeze is in some sense to be a disruptive force—to disturb the waters of creation—because the breeze's measured motion would interfere with any mimetic identity with "The Infinite I Am." Why such errancy might be a desirable human attribute and not simply a sin can be clarified by reconsidering what it is meant by reflection. It is not the mere passive mirroring of what is but is instead the active search for finding the right word. If, as described in the last chapter, reflection is to enter the "linguistic dimension" and if the will can function as the rudder that pilots our vehicular consciousness, then it is an activity that is likely to make waves. God, by giving us the eternal language of nature, and the poet, by giving us the elusive language of the poem, makes us ask—What is it for? To find the right words to respond to this demand, the reader must become "expert with sail and oar" over their own vehicular consciousness.[45]

One way of distinguishing my reading of the "Rime" from Pfau's is to return again to the closing line of W. B. Yeats's "Byzantium" that describes "That dolphin-torn, that gong-tormented sea." Although the first impulse of nature—perhaps made by God brooding over the waters of creation—may have produced patterns akin to those Dantean fields of concentric circles drawn when a stone is dropped into water, nature's overall image is not static or orderly—it is dolphin-torn. For Pfau, with his understandable desire for the harmony that was once promised by a presecular Christian worldview, there seems to be a "gong-tormented" longing for nature and man to conform to the ordinate design that emanated from the first impulse as it brooded over the waters of creation, and a strong sense of disapproval for how subsequent human impulses and desires torment this rage for order by continually tearing and disrupting the smooth surface of nature's turbulent sea like leaping dolphins. From this perspective, it makes sense to consider free will sinful. For an individual psyche or soul these distortions will only cease when all rival objects of desire are banished or emptied of their attractiveness, and when this occurs, man will naturally choose and desire God. This choice will become necessary despite man's freedom, because the field of competing attachments will have been narrowed to one, and God will be left as the only object that attracts the will.

This reading of the situation certainly resonates with aspects of Coleridge's thinking, and he will argue in his later work that complex bodies are actually cooperating assemblages of simple bodies, and power increases as more parts are assembled into greater and greater congregations. Thus the more bodies any one body can associate with the better, and this is one reason that Coleridge becomes increasingly interested in ecclesiastic and political bodies in his latter work on church and state. If in Coleridge's view, the great end of nature is to congregate all things into "the ultimate production of the highest and most comprehensive individuality,"[46] and if this cosmic composite could in fact be constructed, then there would indeed be "One life" concentrically ringing out from a unified will that freely participates in the continual reiteration of the primal ex-citation of "I am that I am."

Nevertheless, when Coleridge is telling his infant son to "wander like the breeze" is he telling him to sin? Clearly the syntax of the eternal language Coleridge wants his son to see and hear consists largely of "parallelism, chiasmus and repetition."[47] But if this is the case, then what can a person be except a sinful disturbance in the divine resonance of creation? It seems that Pfau's account privileges Coleridge's definition of the primary imagination—"a repetition in the finite mind of the eternal act of creation in the infinite I am"—but discounts the role of the secondary imagination: 'an echo of the former, co-existing with the conscious will, yet still as identical with former in the kind of its agency, and different only in degree, and in the mode of its operation' (BL, 1:304). The primary imagination is "a receptive phase of perception," which is followed by a secondary "expressive phase of recreation."[48] In Pfau's account, the active role of the secondary imagination appears to be equated with the Gnostic demiurgic conception of the will. But if free will is sinful and if all we are when we exercise it is a disruption, then wouldn't it be better if we were nothing more than "quick-silver plating behind a looking-glass" (BL, 1:119) or perhaps nothing at all? This may be my own sinful nature talking, but that doesn't seem right.

Although I start with some of the same premises as Pfau, I argue for a different reading of the "Rime" and a different reading of what religion can mean for a postsecular age—one that accepts and even celebrates the free exercise of the will as something more than sin. A succinct way to understand how my reading of the "Rime" diverges from Pfau's is to consider the last line from

Gerard Manley's Hopkins's "Pied Beauty": "He fathers-forth whose beauty is past change: Praise Him." Pfau's traditional and primarily Catholic worldview aligns in a perfectly sensible way with a reading of this line that emphasizes the permanence and universality of a God the father, who transcends or is "past change." While I can certainly appreciate the harmonious beauty suggested by such a reading, I experience myself living in a world that is much more dolphin-torn and suggest that if we are still able to think of God at all, then it is likely that we do so as the accumulation of "past change." This is not a god who stands aloof in her transcendence but rather a god of immanence whose beauty is made up of, and is perhaps nothing more than, past change. Or, if we do not want to go quite that far, it is at least a god whose beauty lies in the poetic ambiguity inscribed in the last line of Hopkins's "Pied Beauty."

Admittedly, in highlighting this ambiguity I may be straying from Coleridge's more settled views on such matters as well as Pfau's and anticipating instead Percy Shelley's articulation of God as the form of "the collective energy of the moral and material world" that may only be glimpsed through Aeolian modulations of the "chords" of human perception and imagination.[49] Nevertheless, to linger in this anticipation of Shelley for one moment more, here it may be worth considering that if there is something to Demogorgon's claim in *Prometheus Unbound* that "the deep truth is imageless" (II, iv, 116), then whether the kind of God figured in this "deep truth" can be related to the view of God Jacques Derrida describes in *The Animal That Therefore I Am* (2008). A God "who doesn't know what he wants with respect to the animal, that is to say, with respect to the life of the living as such, a God who sees something coming without seeing it coming, a God who will say 'I am that I am' without knowing what he is going to see when a poet enters the scene to give his name to living things."[50]

Orienting Oneself in Thinking

To read the "Rime" readers must suspend disbelief so that they are affected by the poem's experimental nature and enter into its "ocean of sensations." To experience the poem effectively and affectively one must be willing to become lost in its sea of signifiers. Rather than resisting incorporation a better approach is to recognize why Allen Grossman argues that "the principle motive of strong poems of the post-Enlightenment modernity" is typically the "narration of the loss and intended recovery of the orienting a priori of the body (assurance of mind-body connection, imagination—*Einbildung*—that Kant in some measure built)."[51] What a poem like the "Rime" attempts to do (or "Frost at Midnight," "Mont Blanc," *The Waste Land,* H. D.'s *Trilogy,* and many, many other poems), is overwhelm our typical postures of attention so that we lose "recourse to the networks, practices, and relays of attachment that sustain representation" and suddenly revisit the moment prior to the decision about what things mean.[52] By disrupting the networks that normally capture and coordinate conviction, such poetry helps us see that the way we frame things matters.

While making his own case about the value of poetry, Grossman recalls Kant's 1786 essay "What Does It Mean to Orient Oneself in Thinking?" which explores how such orientation might be possible without "the deluded enthusiasm of *Schwärmerei.*"[53] *Schwärmerei,* or enthusiasm bordering on self-deception, literally means "going off in swarms" and is an obvious threat to any form of enlightened rationality. Kant wants to secure a mode of orienting oneself that does not succumb to delusion, and he argues:

> In the proper meaning of the word, to orient oneself means to use a given direction (when we divide the horizon into four of them) in order to find the others—literally, to find the sunrise. Now if I see the sun in the sky and know it is now midday, then I know how to find south, west, north, and east. For this, however, I also need the feeling of a difference in my own subject, namely, the difference between my right and left hands. I call this a feeling because these two sides outwardly display no designatable difference in intuition.[54]

For Kant, orientation is ultimately based on the "feeling of a difference in my own subject."[55] Grossman argues that, as a consequence, "truth in Kant's world (the ground of critique, sociability, and all possible knowledge of the highest human good, the moral *summum bonum* and explicitly God) is built (a ground without metaphysical requirement) upon the perishing basis of our common life—our corporeal singularity, our physical subject nature, our body as it is the bearer of recognition and intelligibility" (8). Grossman goes on to suggest that this kind of knowledge is of the same order as "poetic knowledge," and that through such a process of orientation the "body secures the *sensus communis* and makes it possible for us to find the way—*die Richtung*—of which the only authority is the sunrise" (8).

What the "strong poems of the post-Enlightenment modernity" provide are textual environments in which it is easy to become lost. Readers must practice at reading these poems in order to successfully orient themselves among their difficult terrain. Such poems provide a virtual experience in which readers can simulate "the loss and intended recovery of the orienting a priori of the body" and learn to form judgments that are disinterested and thus devoid of the "deluded enthusiasm of Schwärmerei" (8). In both the "Rime" and "Frost at Midnight," for instance, as Noel Jackson argues, what needs to be disrupted is "the very medium of self-consciousness (its 'film,' in Coleridge's idiom), as a constitutive outside that structures perception imperceptibly from within."[56] What needs to be disrupted is the film, flesh, or fabric of habits and practices woven by common sense that both enables and constrains how we see the world. The ultimate revelation of a more ideal "sensus communis (an aesthetic or social community) in these poems thus depends crucially on the seeming violation of a common sense (a normative structure of perception) that erroneously trusts to the integrity and self-sufficiency of one's perceptions in the first place" (122). Ultimately, what poetic "originality" means is the "intention to interrupt the continuity of cultural understandings."[57] Such exercises in reorientation are useful because they help readers step out of the regimen of habitual thinking and into a virtual "state of exception," a moment when "the power of real life breaks through the crust of a mechanism that has become torpid by repetition."[58] Ultimately, the reader must decide what this disruption means, and it is toward this ritual of decision-making that the whole poem is a preparation.

Avoiding the Shipwreck of Skepticism

Nevertheless, as Pfau recognizes, to become a proper reader of the "Rime" does require avoiding the shipwreck of skepticism. Pfau rightly invokes the skeptical crisis brought on by the development of empiricist philosophy as one of Coleridge's principle concerns in the poem. In the well-known conclusion to book 1 of *A Treatise of Human Nature*, Hume is brought "almost to despair" by the skepticism his philosophy brought him to and momentarily resolves "to perish on the barren rock, on which [he is] at present, rather than venture [himself] upon that boundless ocean, which runs out into immensity" (*T*, 1.4.7.1). Such skepticism developed in response to the realization that there was no way to know anything with certainty—even the basic structures of cause and effect. A parallel crisis can be found in the philosophy of Spinoza, and Coleridge will similarly find in the "Wreck" of Spinoza's philosophy "a warning for us if only we are at once wise and charitable enough to use it aright, and to exclaim as we pass sail by—See! By the a merciful Providence the Wreck has become a Sea-mark for us and for all future Mariners."[59]

Clearly, the "Rime" is written at least in part as a response to these earlier examples. One potential way to navigate past this skeptical crisis is suggested by Kant in his *Prolegomena*, which also invokes Hume's doubts: "Yet even [Hume] did not suspect such a formal science but ran his ship ashore, for safety's sake, landing on skepticism, there to let it lie and rot; whereas my object is rather to give it a pilot, who, by means of safe astronomical principles drawn from a knowledge of the globe, and provided with a complete chart and compass, may steer the ship safely, whither he listeth."[60] Kant's solution to the crisis of skepticism is to offer his own schema of reason, intuition, and a priori knowledge as the map that can help us steer all of our ships of self to safety.[61] However, Coleridge's way of moving beyond the skeptical crisis is not as easy as simply following Kant's map. Ultimately, what the "Rime" offers is not a map but an itinerary—a suggestion of a way of moving through the world that can produce meaning.[62] According to Certeau, the perspective of the map is that of a universal and simultaneous gaze upon the "formal ensemble of abstract places," a perspective that leaves little room for the representation of subjective experiences and feelings.[63] An itinerary is a "spatial story" used to mark out a route, often for a pilgrimage. Rather than survey the terrain upon which he is to travel as a whole, "the pilgrim moves through particular spaces, tracing a narrative through space and time by his or her movements and practices."[64]

To have a clearer sense of how and why Coleridge's poetic itinerary is patterned as it is it is useful to step back for a moment and reconsider what is at stake in the "Rime." Pfau convincingly asserts that it makes sense to read the poem as invoking a skeptical crisis and as charting the transition from a porous to a more buffered form of subjectivity. However, in order to better contemplate the postsecular implications of the "Rime," I suggest that a better way of reading the poem as a parable of modernity is to also recognize a fundamental kinship between the mariner and the case of Daniel Schreber—the German jurist who had a nervous breakdown at the end of the nineteenth century and served as the basis for Freud's case study of paranoia. Schreber had a severe nervous breakdown six months after being appointed as *Senatspräsident* of the Supreme Court of Saxony. His elevation to this high office brought on an investiture crisis that produced profound levels of paranoia, which was accompanied by auditory and visual hallucinations along with a "belief that he was becoming a woman, that he was in direct contact with God, that the divinity wished to copulate with him once his 'unmanning' was complete, and that it was up to him to save humanity and restore the proper Order of the World (*Weltordnung*)."[65]

The applicability of the Schreber case to Coleridge's poetic practice has been previously noted by Celeste Langan, who explored how the "nerve-language" displayed in Schreber's memoirs resonates with the "sounds and visions of dubious origin, spiritual possession, a family curse, and, of course, a scene of transgender or homosexual seduction" found in "Christabel."[66] Schreber's case is similarly applicable to the "Rime" for a number of reasons. First, and most obviously, because Coleridge's depiction of the mariner's spectral state of consciousness so closely resonates with the psychoanalytic conception of paranoia. Freud writes that "people become paranoiac over things [*Dinge*] that they cannot put up with" and instead project onto the external world, as the mariner does in Coleridge's poem.[67] Furthermore, as Kenneth Reinhard notes, by failing to judge the thing "that they cannot put up with," paranoiacs also refuse "to articulate the space of symbolic difference" and thus become "lost in the specter of realized signifiers, the materiality and grammatical patterns of language deprived of signification."[68] The mariner, I argue, is similarly lost in the "specter of realized signifiers" after his murder of the albatross. What is blocked from symbolic expression returns in the Real.

In an early letter to Wilhelm Fleiss describing paranoia, Freud says paranoiacs "love their *delusions as they love themselves*. That is the secret."[69] Paranoiacs, in other words, instead of learning to love their neighbors as they love themselves confuse the distinction between inside and outside, and their projected delusions are thought to be objectively true. Paranoia is the failure to recognize or articulate a space or gap between subjectivity and objectivity, precepts and affects, or the "two natures—/ The one that feels, the other that observes" (*Prelude*, 1805, XIII, 326–31). What the paranoiac lacks is the "'spacing' that has no interiority but marks the irretrievable distance between being and the subject."[70] In such a situation, the world is often felt to be too much with us. Additionally, it is worth noting, Hannah Arendt's work suggests that totalitarianism is one potential political outcome of the paranoiac's failure to recognize the proper spacing between self and other.

From Eric Santner's perspective, what Schreber's case discloses is that "an inability to inhabit and to feel libidinally implicated in the space of representations had the effect of transforming his entire being into a bundle of excitable flesh."[71] I argue that the mariner is similarly afflicted or, more precisely, that what the "Rime" explores is the feeling of such affliction and the way to work through its implications. What Schreber experiences is a kind of "soul murder," which resulted from "the collapse of the symbolic dimension of even so-called performative speech acts into some form of actual manipulation or influence, some form of direct psychophysical inscription."[72] The mariner suffers from a similar collapse and is left "Alone, alone, all, all alone, / Alone on a wide wide sea! / And never a saint took pity on / My soul in agony" (232–35). Both Schreber and the mariner experience a kind of "literalization of the concept of the *performative* as understood by speech-act theory," where "all speech came to be experienced as the performing of an action and, indeed, as the performing of an ultimately mechanical and nonsensical action *directly on [their] nerves.*"[73]

In a moment I will clarify further what "soul" might mean in this context, but first I want to recall two other invocations of the Schreber case that have bearing on the "Rime"—one from the history of mediation and the other from political theology.

The relationship to mediation becomes clearer when we recall how Schreber's systematic account within his memoir of the "inscription system" (*Aufschreibesystem*) that affected him in such terrifying and disturbing ways during his illness was taken up by Friedrich Kittler in his history of mediation and placed at the heart of his "understanding of the drastic shift from one system of inscription to another that took place following the development . . . of apparatuses that allowed the storage and manipulation, not just of words, but of sound and of moving image."[74] According to Kittler, in 1800 "voice is still conceived as Aristotle conceived it in his *De Anima*, the sound of that which has soul in it," and all writing is still held "to conduce or aspire to the condition of voice." By the end of the nineteenth century, however, "the seamless continuity of mind, hand and word . . . is broken apart," as the typewriter and cinematographic technologies, break "language down into separate units." Whereas "the curves of the pen caress the page, monitored attentively by the eye of the writer; the keys of the typewriter blindly impact and incise it" (119). Thus within these shifts in mediation there is already a kind of soul murder occurring.

Kittler sees Schreber's delusional inscription system as a symptomatic awareness of new and more insistent recording and broadcasting technologies, which bombard the modern sensibility and drown out the soulfulness of an earlier epoch of mediation. That Kittler is on to something with this argument is evident by the way each new advance in mediation (newspaper, radio, television, cable television, internet, social networking) is accompanied by the often legitimate concerns about how these new developments are affecting our social, political, and personal lives in ways that are not always beneficial. However, it is also worth noting that there are already forms of paranoid schizophrenic writing, in and around 1800, that are remarkably similar to Schreber's. One early example of what Victor Tausk has called the "influencing machine"—"the systematic fantasy of a mechanism that systematically controls the sufferer's own thoughts and powers of imagination"— emerged in the case of "James Tilly Matthews, who is writing, and having his words transcribed by his doctor, James Haslam, in the very heart of Kittler's 1800 dispensation."[75] Thus the disturbing effects of these shifts in mediation are already being felt within the time of Romanticism.

There is also a political theological dimension to these developments in mediation because, as Kittler observed, through these shifts writing and other media practices become more capable of producing mesmeric effects and increasingly serve as a means for "transmitting thoughts from one individual to another."[76] Mesmerism itself is of course named after the work of Franz Anton Mesmer (1734–1815), who posited a "universally distributed and continuous fluid . . . of an incomparably rarefied nature."[77] This fluid connects all things together in a manner similar to the "'mutual influence' between magnets," and it was because of this that the work Mesmer did was also called "animal magnetism."[78] The intense preoccupation with mesmerism in the decades leading up to the French Revolution is one reason why Robert Darnton calls mesmerism a "camouflaged political theory."[79] Santner similarly argues that mesmerism is part of the afterlife of political theology and suggests that mesmerism "represents not so much a pseudoscientific condensation of the multiple invisible forces of nature; it functions rather as one of the names of the flesh at the point at which the matter and charisma of the King's sublime body . . . becomes dispersed into the new locus of sovereignty, the people." [80] The mesmerist becomes a stand-in for the one who can affect the "sacred" materiality that once belonged to the king's "sublime physiology" but which now perturbs the space of immanence (99). It is the "flashing eyes" and "floating hair" of the mesmerist that now marks him as the one in possession of "the supernatural aura which surrounded those crowned heads"—the one who possesses a "royal touch" that can so profoundly affect our flesh.[81]

It is within the crosscurrents of these broader shifts in secularity, mediation, and political theology that both Schreber and the mariner experience a kind of soul murder. But what does "soul" mean in this context? As discussed earlier, the soul can be considered a form of mediated consciousness that is sufficiently detached from immediate experience that it can make connections backward and forward in time and is thus able to "retrace the long path of developments from the present back into the deepest night of the past."[82] The soul can do so because, as Deleuze puts it, "The soul is what has folds and is full of folds."[83] The soul is folded in the sense that is formed when a single surface is folded into two layers: nature and second nature.

If we think of soul in terms of mediation, then there is a real question whether there is a soul if we adopt Locke's camera obscura model of subjectivity. There the self is essentially a naïve collection of impressions that have been received from the outside. This same problematic is also true of mesmerism. In either case, there isn't much room for a contemplative soul because the self functions much like the "quick-silver plating behind a looking-glass" (BL, 1:119) Coleridge invokes in his critiques of necessitarian and unitarian thinking. A notion of the soul is, however, much more compatible with the form of cinematic empiricism explored in chapter 1, particularly if what a soul is is that aspect of our self that holds time enveloped within it.[84] A contemplative soul is formed by the way our imagination contracts the series of punctual impressions that our experience of the world exposes us to and strings these impressions together into a meaningful montage or moving picture.[85] The way one's sensibility is ultimately projected provides the "essential quickness, the vital sensorium that supplies the soul's moving vehicle."[86]

Thinking of the soul as a vehicular consciousness resonates with one way Plotinus explains the relationship between body and soul:

> It is . . . said that the soul is in the body as the steersman is in the ship; this is a good comparison as far as the soul's ability to be separate from the body goes, but would not supply very satisfactorily the manner of its presence, which is what we ourselves are investigating. For the

steersman as a voyager would be present incidentally in the ship, but how would he be present as a steersman? Nor is he in the whole of the ship, as the soul is in the body. Are we then to say that it is present as the skill is in the tools, in the rudder for instance?[87]

My response to this last question is yes. Although for Plotinus the soul/ship analogy ultimately fails to provide an adequate metaphor for the relationship between body and soul, he does suggest that "whenever and wherever it chooses to operate, [the soul] does in much that way move the body."[88] We develop our soul to the extent we become "expert with sail and oar."[89] It is our skill and use of the rudder of our will than enhances our capacity for what was described in the last chapter as reflection (*Besonnenheit*), which allows us to go off in search of the right word within the whole "ocean of sensations" we are exposed to. From Dante's "little bark" to Rimbaud's "drunken boat," from Coleridge's Ancient Mariner to becoming "expert with sail and oar" in *The Waste Land,* what poetry is often offering is an environment in which to explore how best to develop, and exercise, the will in ways that enable us to become more capable captains over our own vehicular consciousnesses.

Nevertheless, there is always the danger of shipwreck. A capacity for reflection is not guaranteed, and this is why Karl Jaspers argued, "Man cannot sink back into an unreflective immediacy without losing himself."[90] What soul murder is is the loss of that spacing within ourselves that allows us to detach from the stream of immediate sense experience and that grants us the con-sciousness [*Mitt-Wissenschaft*] to sail off into a wider world of concern. It is this capacity for reflective transport that is threatened when the world is too much with us. The "Rime" is a parable of modernity precisely because it is concerned with crises that stem from this sort of catastrophe—from what Santner describes as "the collapse of the symbolic dimension of even so-called performative speech acts into some form of actual manipulation or influence, some form of direct psychophysical inscription."[91] At the heart of the "Rime" is a mesmeric crisis, wherein messages are inscribed directly upon the "psychophysical" flesh or infrasensible substratum of the psyche. This results in a kind of soul murder, which is experienced when there is no space left in which a reflective vehicular consciousness can maneuver.

Blessing the Sea Snakes

Fortunately, the "Rime" is also a parable about how to respond to such crises. Although his crewmates succumb to the same disturbances the mariner is exposed to and become soulless automatons, the mariner is able to find a way to return home. He is able to do so because he blesses the sea snakes. But why should this blessing be so efficacious? The central problem in all of the various crises the mariner is facing is one of spacing—they all produce a world that is in some way too much with him. The skeptical crisis of empiricism suggests that any way of making sense of sense perceptions is always something of a put-on, and so there is no way to be assured that our response to the bombardment of atomized sense impressions is actually reasonable. The mesmeric crisis associated with shifts in both mediation and political theology is similarly experienced as the collapse of a symbolic dimension, which results in a nightmarish experience of intensities that are felt directly on the nerves. Through the various attenuations of this spacing vitality comes to be registered as pure nervous excitation.

Evidence that Coleridge is thinking about the "Rime" precisely along these lines can be found in the excerpt from Thomas Burnet's *Archaeologiae Philosophicae* (1692) used as an epigram in the 1817 edition of the "The Rime of the Ancient Mariner." The epigraph uses Burnet's Latin original, which functions as a kind of thesis for the poem, and its translation is as follows: "I do not deny that it is helpful sometimes to contemplate in the mind, as on a tablet, the image of a greater and better world, lest the intellect, habituated to the petty things of daily life, narrow itself and sink wholly into trivial thoughts. But at the same time we must be watchful for the truth and keep a sense of proportion, so that we may distinguish the certain from the uncertain, day from night" (*CPP*, 59). For Coleridge, it is in the mind, and within the imagination, that "the image of a greater and better world" can be glimpsed, and only a mind that is attentive and "habituated *to the Vast*"[92] can counteract the deadening influence "of the petty things of everyday life," which cause the intellect to "narrow itself and sink wholly into trivial thoughts." However, a trivial and automated life is only one danger faced in the "Rime," another is paranoia—the failure to "keep a sense of proportion, so that we may distinguish the certain from the uncertain, day from night" (*CPP*, 59). The poem, in other words, attempts to expose its readers to the Vast while at the same time leading them through the space between automation and paranoia, between the failure to think for oneself and the failure to think of anything else.

Jacques Lacan claims that the paranoiac fails to judge, and thus recognize and accept responsibility for, the spacing between self and other, because "the paranoiac *fails to believe*, not in one reality or another, but in the transcendental element (the Name of the Father) that should demarcate the difference between *das Ding* and the world of representation and hold the space between them open."[93] If this demarcation is successfully made and the subject is willing to recognize a perspective outside the closed circuit of specular reflection, then the travails of paranoia can be traversed. In fact, Lacan suggests that the secular "structure of the human world" is predicated on just this transcendence of "paranoiac knowledge."[94] What the "Rime" offers is the articulation of one way the travails of paranoiac knowledge can be traversed and a transcendent element recognized. This is not to say that Coleridge's response to these issues is the only or even the best response, but it is a response worth considering. What is needed is to find some way to acquire or regain a sense of proportion so "that we may distinguish the certain from the uncertain, day from night" (*CPP*, 59).

Where this response is most fully articulated is in the blessing of the sea snakes scene, an episode that is easy to describe but difficult to discern. After killing the albatross, the mariner finds himself adrift on a (skeptical) sea, and when he "looked to heaven, and tried to pray; / But or ever a prayer had gusht, / A wicked whisper came, and made / [His] heart as dry as dust" (244–47). Fortunately, he then sees some sea snakes swimming "beyond the shadow of the ship" (272). These may be the same creatures described earlier in the poem as those "slimy things [that] did crawl with legs / Upon the slimy sea," as "The water, like a witch's oils, / Burnt green, and blue and white" (125–30). Now, however, when looked at beyond the shadow of the ship, "They moved in tracks of shining white, / And when they reared, the elfish light / Fell off in hoary flakes" (274–76). As the snakes writhe beyond the shadow of the ship their spectral bodies are irradiant, but when their bodies rear up, an "elfish light" falls off in hoary flakes. The creatures are revealed to be contributing to a luminescent light show "often observed near ships at sea, in the night."[95] As the mariner's attention shifts to the area "within the shadow of the ship," and he continues to watch the swimming snakes, the colors shift again: "Blue, glossy green, and velvet black, / They coiled and swam; and every track / Was a flash of golden fire" (279–81). What was initially repulsive "is eventually shown to have been the result of the Mariner's flawed perception, not their intrinsic nature."[96] The same thing looks different depending on when and how it is looked at.

As the mariner continues watching the vibrant display of "their rich attire" (278) he finally exclaims,

> O happy living things! no tongue
> Their beauty might declare:
> A spring of love gushed from my heart,
> And I blessed them unaware:
> Sure my kind saint took pity on me,
> And I blessed them unaware.
>
> The selfsame moment I could pray;
> And from my neck so free
> The Albatross fell off, and sank
> Like lead into the sea. (282–91)

By blessing the sea snakes "unaware," the mariner is in the same moment free to pray and is released from his bondage to the albatross. The sight of the sea snakes unlocks his ability to pray. It does so for at least two reasons. First, because in them the mariner recognizes a space between their bare thingness and the vibrant light that seems to adorn their bodies, and thus the sea snakes offer the mariner an opportunity to recognize a space between their naked materiality and the "rich attire" that the mariner's perspective projects upon them. What is revealed is the space, gap, or vacancy between their thingness and the glorious lights that seem to emanate off their bodies.

By blessing the sea snakes unaware, the mariner spontaneously assents to the realization that there is more happening in the world than he can put into words himself. By confronting the radical inadequacy of his ideas to phenomena, the mariner is forced to acknowledge there is something beyond himself that demands recognition while at the same time evading conceptualization. The mariner's recognition of the gap between the sea snakes' serpentine *das Ding* and the situationally experienced phenomenon of the "elfish light" (275) produces a kind of breakthrough, which releases a gushing "spring of love" (284) from the mariner's heart.

A second contributing factor to this affective release is the "beauty" no tongue might declare. The wondrous recognition of the natural beauty before him helps "interrupt the continuity of cultural understandings" and encourages the mariner to step out of a regimen of habitual thinking and into a virtual "state of exception."[97] This is because, as Santner argues at the end of *On the Psychotheology of Everyday Life* (2001), beautiful objects "are disarming not in the sense of releasing us, once and for all, from the 'too much' of excitation that is, at some level, constitutive of human life, but rather in the sense of loosening our defenses, opening beyond our stuckness in an especially rigid and defensive organization of this pressure." Such beauty should not be viewed as being based on a "harmonization of parts within an ordered whole," but is instead the singular representation of "a self-interrupting whole—one animated, as it were, by a 'too much' of pressure from within its midst."[98] Beauty revitalizes because "the combination of quickening and release occasioned by a beautiful object," its shock and awe, loosens those defensive postures within us that have damned up vitality (137).

By blessing the sea snakes the mariner experiences a moment when the "separation of the knower from the known" is realized.[99] Such a moment is wonderful because this experience of beauty coupled with a recognition of a vacancy or gap between how things look and how things are produces what Catherine Malabou calls a "pure openness to the extraordinary," where extraordinary refers to "alterity as such, everything that is not the soul and interrupts its self-identity."[100] The affective release felt in such moments of wonder or joy is "a gift that comes from the absolute outside of being." This outside or exteriority of being is "characterized again as a 'space' or a 'spacing' that has no interiority but marks the irretrievable distance between being and the subject" (25). Such an affection "is not a feeling, but rather is the opening of a space in Being, of a map, a surface of inscription" (42). The blessing of the sea snakes is a wondrous moment that "marks the opening of the self to experience" (32). However, such an affective opening "cannot be my decision but [is] an ontological movement, impersonal and anonymous." What is experienced is a form of grace wherein it is "existence itself that gives me the feeling of existence, not 'me'" (25). In this moment a generosity is experienced that "allows one to configure, and think together, the gift (or rather the offering), decision, spacing, and freedom" (24). It is by opening onto the space of being in this way that our soul is given room to breathe.

This wondrous moment is what opens the mariner "to energies beyond its habituated limits" and is an example of why "Sympathy" is "an Action" (*CN*, I 1705), and the fact that "Love itself" involves "an inward FIAT of the

Will" (AR, 63). The mariner blesses the sea snakes unaware because it is done in a spirit of generosity—it is a "gift gratuitously given."[101] Such generosity is grounded in the Cartesian recognition "that nothing really belongs to us other than the free disposition of our volitions," as well as a "firm and constant resolution to use them well.'"[102] The mariner's experience of this "spring of love," which is "a species of wonder combined with love," deeply affects him and allows him to recognize alterity through the difference he sees in the sea snakes as they swim in and out of the shadow of the ship.[103] In such affective experiences something touches me so that "I don't know what 'me' means," when there is an "interruption between me and myself," which appears to be a spacing, a spacing "which is the genuine spatiality of the breached affected subject" (24).

Loving the Neighbor

Another way to clarify what happens during this moment of generosity that gives the mariner back his soul is to recognize it as an experience of neighborliness. The sea snakes function as a figure of what Freud called the neighbor, or *Nebenmensch*—the fellow or adjacent being that "falls apart into two components, of which one makes an impression by its constant structure and stays together as a thing [*als Ding*], while the other can be understood by the activity of memory—that is, it can be traced back to information from [the subject's] own body."[104] The figure of the *Nebenmensch*, or neighbor, joins together the objectivity of a thing with the subjectivity of memory and perspective and is thus a peculiar configuration of inside and outside. One reason the encounter with the neighbor is important is that it can force us to look beyond the narrowness of our own perspective. The danger of a narrow perspective is particularly acute in cases of paranoia, since paranoiacs confuse the distinction between inside and outside and assume their projected delusions are objectively true. This is why in the letter to Fliess describing paranoia, Freud says paranoiacs "love their *delusions as they love themselves.*"[105] What the logic of loving the neighbor, or the blessing of the sea snakes, provides is a means of working through such paranoid fantasies by recognizing the gap between self and other. Reinhard has argued that "when the proximity of the neighbor collapses, paranoid delusions and hallucinations emerge, often precisely in the place and the guise of the (missing) neighbor."[106] The paranoiac loves his delusions as he loves himself because he fails to properly recognize the *Nebenmensch* and is thus lost in the enthusiasms of undifferentiated signification. This is also the lesson of the "Rime."

The neighbor has had a long history in political-theological thought, stemming in large part from the commandment in Leviticus 19:18 to "love your neighbor as you love yourself." This history developed out of the scriptural traditions and has been revitalized in modernity by a variety of thinkers including Kant, Hegel, Nietzsche, Kierkegaard, Freud, Weber, Durkheim, Rosenzweig, Levinas, and Lacan. More recently, reevaluations of the concept by Santner, Kenneth Reinhard and Slavoj Žižek in *The Neighbor: Three Inquiries in Political Theology* (2005), have sought to extend our understanding of the neighbor by exploring how it has become a privileged locus for the reinvention of both the ethical and the political in late modernity.

The dual process of judgment and memory that is taken up in the encounter with the neighbor reinscribes the double gesture of the commandment to love thy neighbor as thyself. But the question remains, when I love my neighbor as myself, how is the perplexing relationship between subjectivity and objectivity untangled? In other words, how do I relate to the other in a manner that is not delusional? What is needed is a way of recognizing a transcendent element (the gaze of the third, Lacan's "the name of the Father") that demarcates the difference between the objective thing and the subjective memories and representations projected upon it. One realization that results from this recognition is that what I call my "self" is aporetic, asymmetrical, and nonidentical with itself—I am split between subjectivity and objectivity just like my neighbor. Literature is one place we can learn to mind this gap, and thus literature can potentially provide a form of aesthetic education wherein we learn to become responsible for our own projections.

Rather than approach the "Rime" as a gnostic warning against the sinfulness of free will and of modernity in general, I read the poem much more optimistically and as pointing forward rather than backward. Admittedly, I find myself concerned by the suggestion in the poem that we all must ultimately "walk together to the kirk, / And all together pray, / While each to his great Father bends" (605–7), and I question why the mariner even after he has blessed the sea snakes may be headed home but never seems to gain full control over his own vehicular consciousness. These concerns are likely an indication that my personal sympathies are ultimately more in line with the second generation of Romantics than the first. Nevertheless, Coleridge offers great insight into how to consider both religion and literature in a postsecular age: why it is crucial for our own salvation to remember that "He prayeth best, who loveth best / All things both great and small" (614-15) and how it is that by becoming a better neighbor that one learns to acquire and develop his or her soul.

What is lost when one cannot pray is the possibility of addressing that pure will that continues to address us but to which we may no longer have the right words to respond. The inability to pray is another version of an investiture crisis. The paradox of such a crisis is that one is in the midst of a loss one cannot really name, "for when you lose a concept you also lose the capacity to name what has been lost."[107] This is problematic because, as the mariner experiences, what is lost in the symbolic returns in the Real. What is enacted in the "Rime" is the crisis of representation experienced when no mediating mode of discourse can be found to replace what was lost. Too often we are locked in the stimulations of the present moment and, like the mariner's crew, feel like automatons whose movements are being orchestrated by forces outside our control. Too often the encounter with the other is merely an encounter with oneself, because we fail to look beyond seeing the other as anything but a material support for the "tormenting monologue" of our own subjective projections.[108]

Fortunately, both our encounters with neighbors and our encounters with literature have the capacity to force us out of ourselves by their very resistance to the projections we place upon them. What is returned to us in such a moment is the reserve we maintained in keeping up appearances—when this reserve is suddenly relaxed, we feel at least momentarily redeemed. Both the neighbor and literature can function as screens or masks whose very solidity can block out that world that too often is too much with us, thus offering, like a gift, that space—that elsewhere—through which and in which we can recognize the way we look at things. Such experiences expand the degrees of freedom in one's own existence, and "frees us from the movement of the flow of things, that is to say, from the rhythm of necessity."[109] Through this release the space of inscription, or soul, within us is opened up to the extent that we are attentive not only "to the flow of external sensations and events" but also "to the way in which memories coincide with or diverge from 'present' perception(s)."[110]

The "Rime" functions as a parable of modernity that suggests how literature, like Scripture, has the potential to provide instances "of repose from our tormenting monologue, and an experience in which we are given more chances, compared to reality, to encounter really another gaze."[111] Literature possesses such potential because it is here readers experience pleasure in encountering neighbors who routinely defy the projections of significance placed upon them and thus open gaps between what the fictional figure is for himself or herself and the correspondent subjective memories and impressions the reader projects upon the figure. Literature can interrupt my sameness because, as Georges Poulet argued, "Whenever I read, I mentally pronounce an I, and yet the I which I pronounce is not myself."[112]

Like Freud's *Nebenmensch,* literature like the "Rime" joins together the objectivity of the textual artifact with the subjectivity of the reader's own memories in such a way that readers can encounter the gap or tension between subjectivity and objectivity, between I and thou, and this encounter becomes an opportunity for recognizing, and perhaps re-cognizing, the particular perspective from which the reader looks at the world. These moments of recognition are potentially pleasurable because a feeling of epiphanic excess or surplus can be experienced—one that recognizes an excess of signification within the world that is manifestly before us.

* 4 *

"To See as a God Sees"

Keats and Cinematic Subjectivity

In the "vale of Soul-making" letter written to his brother George and his wife in April of 1819, John Keats recognizes as "misguided and superstitious" the notion that the world is "'a vale of tears' from which we are to be redeemed by a certain arbitrary interposition of God and taken to Heaven" (*LJK*, 2:101–2). Nevertheless, although Keats did not believe that redemption was achievable through the arbitrary power of a sovereign deity, nor was he attracted to Christian theology and practice in the way Coleridge was, he still wanted to comprehend the processes by which a concept of the soul could be saved within modernity. How and why Keats thought that a soul develops when an individual's "atoms of perception" are altered by affect will be the first focus of this chapter. After establishing how best to conceive Keats's version of a contemplative, or mediated, soul, I then clarify how his view coordinates with cinematic empiricism, as well as two contrasting forms of protocinematic versions of Romantic poetry, which, on the one hand, I associate with the walking *flâneur*, Milton, and the movement-image, and, on the other, with the gawking *badaud*, Dante, and the time-image. A central concern of this chapter is how Keats, by constructing an experience of seeing as "a God sees" (*F*, 1:304), brings us to the limits of wonder and negative capability. Such experiences may not be able to change the world, and we may have to wait for the next chapter on Shelley for a poetics more capable of instigating real reform, but nevertheless, there is still great value in the forms of mediation Keats presents. Through his protocinematic poetry, readers can project in the "cathedral cavern" (*H*, 1:86) of their own imagination images of their own "glorious" bodies or souls.¹ In doing so, readers are encouraged to learn how to loosen or absolve themselves from the confines of their own isolated, buffered, and suffering bodies and learn to navigate within a much wider world of concern.

Vale of Soul-Making

In his "vale of Soul-making" letter, Keats identified the "three materials" necessary for "forming the Soul or Intelligence destined to possess the sense of Identity," as "the Intelligence, the human heart (as distinguished from intelligence or Mind) and the World or Elemental space suited for the proper action of Mind and Heart on each other" (*LJK*, 2:102). Intelligences "are atoms of perception—they know and they see and they are pure, in short they are God." Pure perception, in other words, is one version of what it means to see as a God sees. A soul only develops when an individual's atoms of perception are altered by affect, but prior to such alteration the individual lacks identity. The "world or Elemental space" is what provides the medium in which the Mind and Heart can interact with each other. If a child dies before developing a soul, then his "Spark or intelligence returns to God without any identity—it having had no time to learn of and be altered by the heart." Keats suggests that the heart "is the Minds Bible, it is the Minds experience, it is the teat from which the Mind or intelligence sucks its identity," and the world is "a School instituted for the purpose of teaching little children to read." The implication of Keats's argument is that by writing in the "horn book" of the heart, it becomes possible to cultivate the landscape of one's affect and thereby produce a soul.²

The soul is the particular fold or cut of an individual's ethical character; it is the part of the self that has become second nature. "As various as the Lives of Men are, so various become their souls, and thus does God make individual beings, Souls, [from] the sparks of his own essence." Although Keats recognizes that "man was formed by circumstances," he doesn't think that bearing witness to these circumstances is enough to know a man's soul. Circumstances are insufficient, Keats argues, because the real significance lies in how the individual faces those "proovings of his heart" that serve as "touchstones" and are "fortifiers or alterers of his nature." Identities are made "through the medium of the Heart," and the soul is the "altered nature" that is produced through these "proovings." Before being invested with a soul, one is merely "an intelligence-without Identity." An identity can only be made

"Through the medium of the Heart. And how is the heart to become this Medium but in a world of Circumstances?" A vale of soul making is needed because it is only through some process of investiture that we become who we are. As Keats writes in his letter to his brother, "Do you not see how necessary a World of Pains and troubles is to school an Intelligence and make it a soul?" (*LJK*, 2:101–3).

In James Engell's view, "The discovery of the soul, of the inner life or psyche, proved to be a major turning point in the brief career of Keats."[3] This is why the "Ode to Psyche," which is the first of the great odes, and often considered a versification of the "vale of Soul-making" letter, inaugurates "the extraordinary productivity of Keats's final five months of writing."[4] As James Chandler has carefully traced, Psyche's promotion to divine status in the mythology of late antiquity coincides with a historical moment that is "marked by a skepticism that we may hold responsible for the faintness of the older Olympian gods and the fading of their hierarchy." Psyche can be seen as "the apotheosis not of fideism but of skepticism, or at least of an empiricism that insists on the proof of the senses." A sense of the continued connection between Psyche and empiricism within the eighteenth century is evident from Voltaire's *Philosophical Dictionary*, which "informs its readers that 'the Greeks had invented the faculty Psyche for the sensations.'"[5] Chandler also notes that the rise of Psyche in the mythological writing of Apuleius in the mid-second century AD was roughly contemporaneous with the Christianization of Rome, at which time Christianity began to take "over the doctrine of the immortality of the soul" while at the same time removing it "from the history in which, from Plato himself to the writer Keats refers to as 'Apuleius the Platonist,' it was developing" (414). However, "Ode to Psyche" cannot simply pick up where the pagan Apuleius left off, "since the skepticism implicitly celebrated in his account led first, as it were, to the blind faith of Christianity and then to the sensational skepticism of an Enlightenment that, in certain moments, lost sight of the soul altogether" (415).

Although I will not attempt to do justice here to the subtleties of Chandler's argument in *England in 1819* (1998), I do want to highlight one of his conclusions, namely that "The 'neglect' of Psyche that Keats playfully describes himself as too 'orthodox' a heathen to countenance is thus a double neglect: the neglect of the pagan-Platonic 'Psyche' in favor of the Christian soul and the neglect of the Psyche/soul in any form by the mechanist strain in Enlightenment moral philosophy" (415–16). How should we understand

Psyche—or the mediated soul—in a way that is not necessarily Christian or strictly mechanistic? What does it mean for Keats to "mount resistance at once to enlightenment and to Christianity?" (418). Why is it that Keats, like Wordsworth, turns to mythology when trying to cope with a world that is too much with us?

The argument of this chapter is that part of the answer to these questions has to do with mediation in general and with a cinematic form of subjectivity in particular, one that is already being modeled in "Ode to Psyche." This modeling of a cinematic subjectivity occurs within the ode in at least two ways. First in the shift that occurs in the second and third stanzas, where there is a movement from a listing of Psyche's lacks to the speaker's dedication of himself as the Goddess's instrument.

> Nor virgin-choir to make delicious moan
> Upon the midnight hours;
> No voice, no lute, no pipe, no incense sweet
> From chain-swung censer teeming;
> No shrine, no grove, no oracle, no heat
> Of pale-mouth'd prophet dreaming.
>
> . . . .
>
> I see, and sing, by my own eyes inspired.
> So let me be thy choir, and make a moan
> Upon the midnight hours;
> Thy voice, thy lute, thy pipe, thy incense sweet
> From swinged censer teeming;
> Thy shrine, thy grove, thy oracle, thy heat
> Of pale-mouth'd prophet dreaming. (30–35, 43–49)

In this moment of reflective doubling (or folding), the poet vows to project internally what Psyche lacks externally, and be "by my own eyes inspired." The poet elects to be "thy priest, and build a fane / In some untrodden region of my mind, / Where branched thoughts, new grown with pleasant pain, / Instead of pines shall murmur in the wind" (50–53). Within the midst of his own "wide quietness / A rosy sanctuary will [he] dress / With the wreath'd trellis of a working brain, / With buds, and bells, and stars without a name" (58–61). Through this process "the 'mind' of the speaker becomes an internalized landscape, a projected domain in which 'shadowy thought' and the 'working brain' can recreate an alternative world."⁶ It is a world where a better future can be projected.

The logic of inner sensuousness operative in the Ode is akin to one of Wordsworth's characteristic structural devices for his own lyrics: "'thoughtless' vision, followed by meditation, followed by a revisiting of the scene of the first stanza 'in thought.'" Even the "I wander'd in a forest thoughtlessly," contained in the ode's first stanza echoes the famous opening to Wordsworth's "daffodil" poem: "I wandered lonely as a cloud." Functioning in this way, Keats's "Psyche," like Wordsworth's poetics more generally, "projects a home for spirit not in nature but in the inner life evident in our creative responses to nature."⁷

In a suggestive reading of "I Wandered Lonely as a Cloud," Charles Altieri explores how the poem transmits and mediates a form of "inner sensuousness." Wordsworth's poem opens with the lyric "I" first floating "high o'er Vales and Hills," as it "wandered lonely as a cloud," when "all at once" it sees "a crowd, / A host of dancing Daffodils; / Along the Lake, beneath the trees, / Ten thousand dancing in the breeze" (1–6). The speaker sees "Ten thousand" at a glance, as "the waves beside them danced," but the daffodils "outdid the sparkling waves in glee" and "a Poet could not but be gay / In such a laughing company." The poet "gaz'd—and gaz'd—but little thought / What wealth the shew to [him] had brought" (6–12). Significantly, during this moment of first impressions the poet "cannot be one with the daffodils at all, since he cannot be conscious of being not conscious."⁸ The logic here is not unlike Lacan's version of the cogito: "I am not wherever I am the plaything of my thought. I think of what I am where I do not think to think."⁹ It is only when this spontaneous overflow of powerful emotions is recollected in tranquility, when the poet is in "vacant or in pensive mood," that "they flash upon that inward eye / Which is the bliss of solitude, / And then [his] heart with pleasure fills, / And dances with the Daffodils" (14–18). Paradoxically, the "union with nature comes only afterwards and in a lonely room."¹⁰

Altieri claims Wordsworth is offering readers practice in putting on an alternative posture of attention. He focuses on the doubling of "I gazed—and gazed" within the poem and the way it rhymes with "waves." Through this "turn by the mind on its own state," a reflexive doubleness emerges, and a fold is made in the poetic speaker's mediated soul. The Romantic spectator becomes a participant observer within his or her own lucid experience of a virtual event. Such "gazing positions the mind while retaining its freedom and mobility," becoming "in human space what dancing is in the world of nature."[11] Although in "I Wandered Lonely as a Cloud" the speaker "gazed and gazed" during his first exposure to the scene, he only really dances with the daffodils after the initial event is reexperienced in the theater of the mind's eye. Only alone in a darkened room does "the mind's 'Dancing' retain the sense of physical action projected in the mass of flowers and in the waves" (291). What Wordsworth's and Keats's poems ultimately demonstrate is that "some forms of attention to the world cannot be attributed to simple perception but reveal elaborate work done by self-consciousness eager to share what it has recognized" (294). These forms of inner sensuousness can then be shared through a poetics that projects moving images, which can then cinematically affect readers.

It is also worth noting how "Ode to Psyche" and "I Wandered Lonely as a Cloud" both diverge in significant ways from a Lockean model of subjectivity, where attention was rendered as being relatively passive. To put it in the terms of the "vale of Soul-making" letter, Locke's camera obscura model of empiricism could articulate how intelligences are atoms of perception, but would have a much more difficult time conceiving what it means to school an intelligence and make it a soul. Fortunately, the models of cinematic subjectivity advocated in Romanticism can move beyond this limitation in early empiricist technology.

One reason for the Romantic divergence from the camera obscura version of subjectivity is that this model of vision became far less compelling after the emergence of physiological optics and as it became clear that "perception was not a matter of a relatively passive *reception* of an image of an exterior world, but that the makeup and capacities of an observer contributed to the *making* of perception."[12] As Jonathan Crary details in *Techniques of the Observer* (1990), the profound impact of a wide variety of protocinematic and optical devices (from the magic lantern and phantasmagoria to the panorama and kaleidoscope), which emerged in the late eighteenth and early nineteenth century, was to reposition the observer "outside of the fixed relations of interior/exterior presupposed by the camera obscura and into an undemarcated terrain on which the distinction between internal sensation and external signs is irrevocably blurred."[13] This repositioning of the observer undermined the epistemologies of the Enlightenment and is perhaps best exemplified by Goethe's experimental closing of the aperture through which light entered the camera obscura, done so that attention could be focused on the sensations of color that are thereby experienced. As research begins emphasizing such "afterimages," models of vision begin to focus on physiological rather than mental actions. The persistence of vision phenomenon, which offers an illusion of continuous motion, becomes the basis for an assortment of optional amusements, such as the anorthoscope, the phenakistoscope, and the zoetrope, all of which were invented in the late 1820s and early 1830s.

Crary's emphasis is on how the proliferation of optical devices collapsed the distinction between interiority and exteriority and increased the reach of what Michael Foucault calls subjection—the process by which subjects incorporate those ideological codes that structure a rationalized and disciplined society. Nevertheless, as Simon During argues in *Modern Enchantments* (2002), this rendition of the relationship between visuality and modernity is only one side of the coin. During finds this emphasis on biopolitical incorporation and discipline significant but an incomplete accounting of what these new forms of mediation made possible, and he supplements Crary's account by acknowledging the enduring importance of a wide variety of cultural practices through which subjective interiority was itself projected and externalized. He suggests we should take seriously those visual technologies and special effects that have been "designed to realize fictions of the real."[14] Examples of such technologies can be found in theatrical stage craft, stage magic, sleight-of-hand tricks, peep shows, seances, and the phantasmagoria. In effect, what all of these "magic assemblages" have in common is that they offer at least momentary access to a "veiled, supernatural order separated from everyday life by a barrier which is also a threshold" (37). Unlike Crary's emphasis on subjection and incorporation, here the focus is on projection, and to enter the world of secular magic "is to access a domain which, unlike science's nature, is regulated in terms of human desires and meanings" (37).

As Friedrich Kittler observed, these technologies of magic assemblage played a significant role in the culture of the Counter-Reformation. The Jesuits, for instance, deployed the magic lantern and the phantasmagoria in a search "for a new medium to work against Luther's bible," and by doing so "brought back the old religious images in a redressed or stronger form, no longer as icons or painted panels [*Tafelbilder*] on church walls, no longer as pious miniatures of saintly legends, but as psychedelic visions which the soldiers of Christ (as the Jesuits called themselves) could evoke more effectively (which means more unconsciously) than the old-fashioned drawings in this war of beliefs."[15] Kittler also recognized how certain kinds of "physical poetry (*physikalische Gedichte*)" had strong connections to these early optical technologies and that they were capable of "producing an author's perspective [in a way] that enables its audience to view objects without seeing them."[16]

Wordsworth and Keats both produce this sort of "physical poetry," poetry that is capable of producing psychedelic effects, and each of these poets try to save their own souls as well as those of their readers "against the backdrop of enlightenment attempts to dissolve the soul into the mechanics of the body."[17] Just as Keats is trying to build a fane for Psyche "in some untrodden region of [his] mind," Wordsworth declares "the Mind of Man, / My haunt and the main region of my song" (*WPP, The Excursion*, preface, 40–41). What the soul means here can be coordinated quite closely with how the soul was discussed in previous chapters. The soul is what "has folds and is full of folds."[18] The soul is folded in the sense that is formed when a single surface is folded into two layers.[19] It is the "affective fabric" that, like cinema, is woven through the processes of mental picturing. The soul is that aspect of our self that holds time enveloped within it, and it is the faculty that enables the human mind to become mobile and achieve vehicular consciousness. The question for both Wordsworth and Keats is that if above (or in front of) the frame of things we place a "fabric more divine" (woven from mental images), then how should this fabric be tailored (*P*, 13:452)? If the poet is the one capable of "embroidering patterns upon a fabric that is only ever a surface," patterns that are woven from strands of association and "held together by the pleats and stitches of relations," then what is the best pattern or posture of attention to put on?[20]

The fold of the soul is figured through that process of doubling that occurs between stanzas two and three of "Ode to Psyche." When the poet builds a fane in some untrodden region of his mind, initially, this process might seem to parallel that of the camera obscura, but because Fancy "breeding flowers, will never breed the same" (62), such repetition is always with a difference. Mental picturing finds its own form as the external world is "folded" into mental space. The intelligences or "atoms of perception" are altered as they are mediated by the human heart in the "World or Elemental space" in which Mind and Heart meet. This internal landscape is, ultimately, a work of both the heart and head—the part "that feels, the other that observes" (*P*, 13:326–31).

Giuliana Bruno has suggestively described how this "interior landscape moves, creases, and folds in tangible ways. It is, in many ways, designed—woven as if it were handmade. Frames of mind can be said to be fabricated, tailored to a specific subject and suited to a particular intersubjectivity. Mental images are fashioned as cloth is—haptically, out of the texture of our world: they are pictured with the material, stretchy, malleable, creative quality of its fabric."[21] These mental images are woven into canvases of unfolding images, and these moving images are "thus not only a language of mental motion, but also a language for emotion—a moody, atmospheric way to fashion affects in transmittable fabrics" (227). These fabrications become "our second skin, our sensory cloth. They house the motion of emotion. They make mood, [which] unfolds as an ever changing space. It is driven by the tissuelike rhythm of unreeling as state of mind" (216). What unfolds here is the actual movement of the affective fabric—"Draped around and unreeling . . . one discovers that the design of the fold fashions inner life. It is, ultimately, the very architecture of the soul" (221).

If deprived of sensibility's capacity to use the affective alteration of perception to fashion the inner folds of our interior lives, then the poet would not be able to dedicate the fane of his mind as a shrine to Psyche, and instead the poet would simply be an automaton or a fanatic. The question of whether what Keats is up to in the "Ode to Psyche" and elsewhere is the work of a poet or a fanatic is highlighted at the beginning of "The Fall of Hyperion." For

> Fanatics have their dreams, wherewith they weave
> A paradise for a sect; the savage too
> From forth the loftiest fashion of his sleep
> Guesses at Heaven; pity these have not
> Trac'd upon vellum or wild Indian leaf
> The shadows of melodious utterance.
> But bare of laurel they live, dream, and die;
> For Poesy alone can tell her dreams,
> With the fine spell of words alone can save
> Imagination from the sable charm
> And dumb enchantment. (F, 1:1–12)

What then is the difference between the poet and the fanatic? If the fanatic weaves dreams for the "paradise of a sect," then why is this act of fabrication found wanting? Perhaps because a fanatic is one who cannot separate "the certain from the uncertain, day from night."[22] The advantage of poetry seems to be that although it may cast a "fine spell of words," it can still save the imagination from "sable charm / And dumb enchantment."

There is something about literature that enchants but does not mesmerize, something that is able to maintain the proper spacing between what is and what seems to be. As discussed in the preceding chapter, literature, like Freud's *Nebenmensch*, joins together the objectivity of the textual artifact with the subjectivity of the reader's own memories in such a way that readers can encounter the gap or tension between objectivity and subjectivity—"Do I wake or sleep?" Such encounters become opportunities for recognizing, and perhaps reassembling, the particular perspective from which the reader looks at the world. Nevertheless, as the next lines indicate,

> Who alive can say,
> "Thou art no Poet; may'st not tell thy dreams?"
> Since every man whose soul is not a clod
> Hath visions, and would speak, if he had lov'd
> And been well nurtured in his mother tongue.
> Whether the dream now purposed to rehearse
> Be Poet's or Fanatic's will be known
> When this warm scribe, my hand, is in the grave. (F, 1:2–18)

If every soul has visions, and perhaps what it means to have a soul is to possess this capacity for vision, then who can say that only poets should tell their dreams? Who is to say that "The Fall of Hyperion," the poem in which these lines appear, is the work of a poet and not a fanatic?

The focus of the rest of this chapter is on exploring the implications of these questions, first by suggesting at least one of the ways the poetics of Wordsworth and Keats tend to diverge from each other and situating this divergence within the visual milieu of their day and then by focusing on how Keats's Hyperion fragments in particular can teach us to reevaluate what it means to have a soul in a postsecular age. The final section of the chapter considers how the two Hyperion fragments coordinate with the distinction Gilles Deleuze makes in his two volumes of *Cinema* between the movement-image and the time-image. By doing so, a bridge will be built to the discussion in the next chapter of Percy Shelley's efforts to release readers from a sense of "savage" necessity through the intercession of "imageless images."

Walking and Gawking

In his 1823 essay "On Londoners and Country People," William Hazlitt resists "Mr. Blackwood's" definition of "Cockney" as "a person who has happened at any time to live in London, and who is not a Tory."[23] Instead, Hazlitt pictures the Cockney as "a person who has never lived out of London, and who has got all his ideas from it" (1:155). The Cockney is portrayed as being "confined to one spot, and to the present moment" (1:155). For him, everything is near and seen in "hasty succession" so that "the world turns round, and his head with it, like a roundabout at a fair, till he becomes stunned and giddy with the motion. Figures glide by, as in a camera obscura. There is a glare, a perpetual hubbub, a noise, a crowd about him; he sees and hears a vast number of things, and knows nothing. He is pert, raw, ignorant, conceited, ridiculous, shallow, contemptible. His senses keep him alive; and he knows, inquires, and cares for nothing farther" (1:155–56).[24] The Cockney feasts upon the ocular delights offered up by the "perpetual hubbub" of a vital cosmopolitan city. Even a shopman may be "nailed all day behind the counter: but he sees hundreds and thousands of gay, well-dressed people pass—an endless phantasmagoria—and enjoys their liberty and gaudy fluttering pride." Another may be a mere "footman—but he rides behind beauty, through a crowd of carriages, and visits a thousand shops" (1:160).

For Hazlitt, these vivid glimpses of the always turning social world are valuable because they facilitate man's recognition of himself as a "public creature." This is important because, in addition to defining "Cockney," another aspect of Hazlitt's effort in "On Londoners and Country People" is to rebut Wordsworth's portrait in the preface to *The Excursion* of "men in cities as so many wild beasts or evil spirits, shut up in cells of ignorance, without natural affections, and barricaded down in sensuality and selfishness."[25] Hazlitt argues that this would be true if city dwellers were really disconnected from one another, but this is not actually the case. The Londoner may know fewer details about other people's private lives, but in London "he has better opportunities of observing its larger masses and varied movements," because the city's streets are a "stream of human life," and "the public amusements and places of resort are a centre and support for social feeling." For the Londoner, "a playhouse alone is a school of humanity, where all eyes are fixed on the same gay or solemn scene, where smiles or tears are spread from face to face, and where a thousand hearts beat in unison!" In London "there is a public; and each man is part of it" (1:178).

Wordsworth's contrasting response to "the mighty city" (7:697) is captured in the "Bartholomew Fair" section of book 7 of *The Prelude*. Here the poet encounters a "blank confusion" (7:696) while experiencing what it would be like to be one of those

> ... thousands upon thousands of her sons,
> Living amid the same perpetual whirl
> Of trivial objects, melted and reduced
> To one identity, by differences
> That have no law, no meaning, and no end (7:701-5)

For Wordsworth, to live amid the "second-sight procession" of the city's "perpetual whirl" is to risk becoming submerged in an enthusiastic but ultimately lawless collective identity. It is important to note how threatening Wordsworth finds these "fears of amalgamation."[26] To return to an undifferentiated world is to lose one's very sense of self and is thus a form of death—"a hell / For eyes and ears" (7:659-60). Fortunately, Wordsworth is able to avoid this fate due to a chance encounter with a blind beggar "who, with upright face, / Stood propped against a wall, upon his chest / Wearing a written paper, to explain / The story of the man, and who he was" (7:612-15). The poet's mind turns round at the sight of this surprising spectacle, and as he gazes upon the beggar's "fixèd face and sightless eyes" he feels "as if admonished from another world" (7:622-23). Wordsworth feels admonished in part because he sees in the beggar's "fixèd face and sightless eyes" a reflection of his own gawking at London's perpetual whirl. Catching himself in the act of looking in this way makes him ashamed of what he sees, while also enabling him to speculate upon how some unknown other could at any time be looking at him in precisely the same way he now looks at the beggar.

The encounter with the blind beggar is significant because, as Neil Hertz memorably argued, it is this exposure to the potential of a gaze more encompassing than his own that keeps the poet "from tumbling into his text."[27] The blind beggar functions as an emblem of blockage within the sublime scenario, because he is "propped against a wall" between seeing and knowing—between the sensuous eyes of the body and those more worthy eyes capable of reading the story the beggar wears on his chest. The beggar is an emblem of the minimal difference between gawking and seeing with discernment, and it is precisely this difference that troubles Wordsworth about his own response to the city's second-sight procession. By recognizing the beggar as his double or neighbor, the poet is able to triangulate the possibility of a panoramic perspective that he may lack himself but from which London's perpetual whirl would seem sensible. Within the environs of Bartholomew Fair, Wordsworth may lack the means to obtain this perspective for himself, but he can nevertheless subjugate himself to the power he intuits in such a gaze.

Alberto Gabriele has made the visual stakes of book 7 even more explicit by coordinating Wordsworth's poetic practice with Dzinga Vertov's 1929 movie *Man with the Movie Camera*. The protocinematic quality of Wordsworth's lines lies in the way they function as "the photographic recording of a specific point of view, the individualized point of view of random glances captured in the city by a moving observer."[28] Gabriele ultimately associates this individualized point of view with the figure of the flâneur, that dweller within the Romantic metropolis "who gazes on shop windows that rouse his appetites and walks streets that 'conduct [him] into a vanished time.'"[29] What the eye of the flâneur registers is the rhythm of the sensational shocks "imparted by the fleeting glimpses at humanity in constant movement, by the passing look at signs, advertisements, and street scenes that rapidly parade in front of the stroller or the coach rider."[30] However, since these visual shocks lack any organizing narrative or schema, there is a radical leveling out of any hierarchy of perception, and Gabriele argues that in an environment where every view is substitutable with every other, "the contemplative mode of vision of Wordsworth's poetry implodes" (7).

Nevertheless, Gabriele understands the two modes of seeing Wordsworth displays in his encounter with the blind beggar—bare perception and the intuition of a panoramic perspective that can gaze upon a scene and perceive the totality of the situation despite the apparent fragmentation of its details—as a precursor to the cinematographic techniques and technologies developed later in the century. Both models of mediation are rooted in the form of psychological perception involved in the montage effect—the ability "to create cogent narratives and recurrent binding symbols out of the scattered stimuli" that bombard viewers in everyday life (xviii). Montage, according to the famed Russian director Sergei Eisenstein, is "a theory of the interval," and the "juxtaposition of two shots by splicing them together resembles not so much the simple sum of one shot plus another—as it does a creation."[31] The way montage generates new elements out of the collision of other elements opens a space where perception "can be fitted together in an infinite number of ways . . . because they are not oriented in relation to each other."[32] While montage techniques are often used in a manner that isn't jarring, providing instead a narrative flow that is completely sensible to the spectator, the collision of two contrary images in montage can also be used to create an explosion famously described by Walter Benjamin as "the dynamite of the tenth of a second."[33]

Gabriele argues that montage effects could not only be found in a wide variety of nineteenth-century visual entertainments but are also expressed in aspects of print culture ranging from the popularity of serialized sensational fiction to the modes of spectatorship encouraged by the regular reading of periodicals. One reason for this pervasiveness of these effects within contemporary media is that they were coincident with and illustrative of how the increasingly urbanized sensorium of the nineteenth century was reforming the perceptions of its inhabitants in new and shocking ways.

Although I agree with Gabriele's overall analysis, this chapter explores an alternative mode of looking that was also available during the nineteenth century—the badaud. The badaud is "the curious observer, the rubberneck, the gawker" and is thus closer in character to Hazlitt's Cockney than Wordsworth's stroller of the streets.[34] Ultimately, I align the figure of the badaud with the peculiar form of gawking that goes on at the end of John Keats's "The Fall of Hyperion" and suggest that Keats's Cockney efforts in the Hyperion project are directed toward finding an alternative means of negotiating the kind of speculative crisis that animates book 7 of *The Prelude*.

While there are certainly aspects of Keats's poetry that fit the profile of the flâneur, I want to focus attention on the ethical and political potential that the wondrous gaze of the indolently gawking badaud may play within the context of the Hyperion project. The badaud differs from the flâneur, for whom a suprasensible totality may be intuited through the aesthetic mediation of a series of discrete encounters, because the badaud willingly lingers in the sensuous pleasures of pure perception. Although at first glance this willingness to linger would seem to be the opposite of political action, I argue that this may in fact not be the case. Here I am in agreement with Noel Jackson's efforts to link Keats's poetics of pure presence to Paul Fry's concept of ostension.[35] Ostension defines an experience that stretches duration and disrupts the rule of consciousness, thus opening "our awareness to something that may be more primary or even essentially other to it."[36] This feeling of openness is "characterized by an unwillingness to project final meanings or to produce a sense of completion" (21).

Hazlitt defines the Cockney as one who "sees and hears a vast number of things, and knows nothing.... His senses keep him alive; and he knows, inquires, and cares for nothing farther,"[37] a definition that calls to mind Keats's own delineation of negative capability, which "is when man is capable of being in uncertainties, Mysteries, doubts, without any irritable reaching after fact and reason."[38] In *Looking Away* (2009), Rei Terada provides a helpful model of negative capability, one rooted in how the aesthetic instance of the chameleon poet "takes place before any determinate judgement can fix the experience with reference to either ethics or epistemology" and as such, "it occurs as a moment of freedom before the imposition of an ethical or epistemological code and allows the space for a different form of vision to emerge."[39] According to Terada, the negative capability of this enabling space is generated when the gap between object perception and fact perception is kept open. Drawing this distinction from analytic philosophy, she explains that "perceiving an object (it passes across my field of vision) isn't the same as perceiving the fact of the object (I recognize that it's there, what it is); and it is perceiving the fact of the object that's generally taken to produce, seamlessly, knowledge of and belief in the existence of the object" (15). Since only fact perception induces belief, Terada is interested in exploring what happens when one suspends belief and lingers in object perception. Thus we can say that unlike Coleridge, whom Keats criticizes for "being incapable of remaining content with half knowledge," the chameleon poet, like a gawking badaud, lingers luxuriantly in appearances, savoring the moment prior to the imposition of having to declare the meaning of what he sees. This lingering in object perception is pleasurable because it is a form of absolution—it is the enjoyment of phenomena that have yet to be tied down to facts.

There is a lightness felt in withholding judgment as to the meaning of an appearance, because such refraining also suspends the subtly persistent pressure to assent to the world as it is. In the loosening of feeling that accompanies this sense of absolution, one learns to bask in pure perception—and see as a god sees, as Hyperion does at the end of "The Fall." There is an underlying politics in such lingering because in these moments of openness a renewed vitality is experienced, momentarily relaxing of the burden of the mystery and thus quieting the chains of associations that normally inhibit one's freedom to imagine alternative modes of being. The value of art that is as negatively capable as Keats's is that it can tease us out of thought and offer an opportunity to see the world with opened eyes.

In the following three sections, I first explore the applicability of coordinating the two fragments of Keats's Hyperion project—"Hyperion" and "The Fall of Hyperion"—with the figures of the flâneur and the badaud and discuss the relationship between protocinematic technologies and poetic practice more generally. I then consider how the two fragments draw upon either Milton or Dante for their respective stylistic inspirations and why doing so helps "The Fall" in particular to facilitate a feeling of wonder. The final section focuses on how Gilles Deleuze's discussions of the difference between the movement-image and the time-image can help further highlight how "Hyperion" and "The Fall" diverge.

Protocinema

There is at least a family resemblance between Hazlitt's Cockney and the pose of the strolling flâneur, influentially defined by Charles Baudelaire as one who "enters the crowds as though it were an immense reservoir of electrical energy, or we might liken him to a mirror as vast as the crowd itself; or to a kaleidoscope gifted with consciousness, responding to each one of its movements and producing the multiplicity of life and the flickering grace of all the elements of life."[40] Nevertheless, there is a subtle but significant difference between the Cockney and the flâneur, since the flâneur is in the crowd but not of the crowd. The flâneur observes the city with intelligence and distinction, turning "his overdeveloped sensibilities to dwell on mysteries and telling details."[41] For the flâneur, the "joy of watching is triumphant" and this is why Walter Benjamin compares him to an amateur detective.[42] However, although most critics have followed Benjamin's example and lavished attention on the flâneur as a means of understanding the rise of mass culture, Gregory Shaya argues that the role of the badaud—"the curious observer, the rubberneck, the gawker"—is of even greater importance to this development. For "if the flâneur was the model for the Baudelairean poet," then "the badaud offers a model for the crowd he passed through" (49).[43]

In his own discussion of the flâneur and the badaud, Benjamin delineates the difference between the two types by citing Victor Fournel, who argued that "the simple flâneur is always in possession of his individuality, whereas the individuality of the badaud disappears. It is absorbed by the outside world ... which intoxicates him to the point where he forgets himself. Under the influence of the spectacle which presents itself to him, the badaud becomes an impersonal creature; he is no longer a human being, he is part of the public, part of the crowd." [44] It is the gawking badaud that is of closest kin to the Cockney. The badaud is one "given to idle observation of everything, with wonder or astonishment." [45] The badaud, like Hazlitt's Cockney, "sees and hears a vast number of things, and knows nothing." [46] The "impersonal" badaud lacks detachment, and it is the ethical and political potential of this absorptive anonymity that I wish to explore.[47]

All of this is important for understanding the Hyperion project because the difference between "Hyperion" and "The Fall of Hyperion" coordinates with the difference between the flâneur and the badaud. Whereas "Hyperion" is an attempt to narrate an epic based on the projection of a psychologized theogony, "The Fall" stages a single episode of a ritualized metamorphosis designed to induce a visionary experience of enhanced awareness and wonder through the striking representation of a Hyperion ablaze with abundant power. In this way, "The Fall" functions in the manner of protocinematic technologies like the magic lantern, which advances beyond the camera obscura by introducing a technology for projecting or broadcasting images.

As Vincent Newey observes, there is an underlying discipline that "pervades The Fall and invests the religious aura of its rites of initiation, which take place in an 'old sanctuary' before an 'altar' spread with 'lofty sacrificial fire.'" [48] The poet-initiate is challenged to ascend Moneta's altar step, a "hard task" that requires "prodigious" toil, which when accomplished admits him into a new order of perception (F 1:120–21). By going through this ordeal, the initiate temporarily absolves himself of the burden of the mystery and in this moment of openness and loosening affect a lightness is experienced, which releases cognitive tension and revitalizes imaginative vision. Rather than displaying the calm detachment of the flâneur, in "The Fall," the initiate does not so much see Hyperion as stare into the kaleidoscopic potential of his "hard gem-like flame." [49] To peer through Hyperion's image is to feel empowered, and it is this ability to influence affect that makes "The Fall" a means of intimating "the right mood or landscape of affect," which must be in place if a particular set of moral principles is to actually be lived out.[50]

Nevertheless, the eye-opening effects presented in Keats's poetry were just one of many competing avenues to delight available within the giddy London of Hazlitt's Cockney: a place of light, color, and possibility. A new cosmopolitan environment was being created in which consumption was king and visual stimulus was being harnessed "to convert passersby into gawkers, and gawkers into purchasers," and in this way "the link between visual pleasure and a commodity culture was forged."[51] Modern urban spectatorship was fostered by a burgeoning entertainment industry that offered ample opportunity for viewers to feast on the visual delights of technologically achieved "special effects." It is due to the enormous popularity of devices such as the kaleidoscope, the panorama, and the phantasmagoria that Tom Gunning, a scholar of the emergence of cinema, argues that "decades before the cinema, urban experience and an emerging commodity culture had already carved out a visual receptivity into which the film experience crept like a hermit crab" (32).

Gunning emphasizes the importance of the badaud for understanding this visual receptivity into which cinema crept, and he finds in the kaleidoscope, the "philosophical toy" David Brewster invented in 1815, a model for the badaud's "purely visual delight in a constantly changing spectacle irrelevant to the knowing gaze of the classical flâneur" (32). The kaleidoscope's purely visual spectacle employed "the visual materials of desire—color, glass and light" to create striking effects, which "combined order and transformation by creating an aleatory and unpredictable movement within a highly structured visual composition and consistent frame" (32). The attraction of such experiences is attested by the popularity of Brewster's invention, which spread quickly across early nineteenth-century Europe creating a frenzy that Percy Bysshe Shelley dubbed "Kalleidoscopism."[52]

Later in the century, when early filmmakers made their initial forays into cinema, perhaps surprisingly, it was often city street scenes that most interested audiences. As Gunning puts it, "nearly all early film shows presented a mise en abyme of audiences filling vaudeville theaters from busy city streets in order to see projected on the screen—busy city streets."[53] Although one may suppose that the first audiences would have simply watched anything available, Gunning argues that "the street scenes embody another way of seeing the phenomenon of motion pictures." (35) This alternative approach is connected to the gazes of both the badaud and the Cockney, as well as to the phenomenology of the kaleidoscope, in that these films similarly "combined order and transformation by creating an aleatory and unpredictable movement within a highly structured visual composition and consistent frame" (32).

Unlike the narrative-driven cinema we are now familiar with, the city scenes exhibited by Lumière Cinematographe and its imitators in Paris, London, and New York seesawed "between the delight in kaleidoscopic movement of the gawker and at least some vestige of the flâneur's attempt to master the visual array through technologically aided observation" (35). The street scenes "gloried in the reproduction of a various and recognizable surge of life" (35). Lacking dramatic hierarchy, these early films call for a different sort of gaze than is required to follow the chronology of narrative because, as Gunning argues, here "one must scan the surface of the image for various centers of interest using what Noël Burch has called a topographical reading. Once focused, however, the pleasure one finds in a face, a gesture, an odd mode of transport, a bit of architecture, gives no guarantee of being sustained. Further, these points of pleasure are simultaneous with other possible points of interest; one is peripherally aware of all one is missing. New centers of interest bob into the frame unexpectedly, while others depart beyond reclamation" (36). In this way the early cinema was closer to the badaud's disappearance into the image then the flâneur's theatric detachment.

Contemporary audiences, however, are often bored by these early films. The modern spectator has been trained to follow the patterns of prediction and anticipation that drive narratives, but these early street scenes frustrate any attempt to impose narrative order. The cinema we have become accustomed to has followed the route of the flâneur, and the classically conceived spectator of cinema functions like a detective "attentively observing the unfolding images for narrative enigmas, testing them with anticipatory schemata, predicting narrative outcomes and processing the image for its relevant narrative information and cues" (36). Unlike the gawker, the cinematic detective "is involved in reading and interpreting all he observes," blessed with the certainty that it is possible to make sense of what is seen. The cinema of the badaud, in contrast, is akin to the kaleidoscope, in that the frame of the camera's eye does not impose an order upon what is visible but instead captures it "in a form which allows endless repetition, opening the way for a studied apperception" (35).

Ultimately, as Orrin Wang recognized in his trailblazing article on Keats and cinematic sensation, the question is whether by inhabiting this "moment of inter-medial discontinuity" one experiences "a moment of freedom or quotidian repetition."[54] A great many gawking gazes would of course fall under the category of quotidian repetition, and it is not difficult to see how a good deal of capitalist modernity is predicated upon stupefaction and mass spectacle. Nevertheless, by taking seriously the possibility that under certain circumstances a freedom can be experienced in such moments of immediacy, it is worth considering how this possibility affects our understanding of Keats's Hyperion project.

The protocinematic elements of the Hyperion project can also be situated within the longer history of loco-descriptive poetry, a trajectory that stretches back to at least John Denham's 1642 poem "Cooper Hill" and extends through works such as Alexander Pope's "Windsor Forest" before being transformed in James Thomson's *The Seasons* in ways that prepare for later Romantic revisions by Charlotte Smith, Wordsworth, and others. The guided visualization of a traditional loco-descriptive poem is designed to map onto the literary spectator's gaze, which surveys the virtual landscape of a specific locale like Windsor Forest as if it were painted on an unspooling canvas, but in such a way that there is a subtly insistent transferential coordination between the poetic speaker's ideological description of what is seen and the "landscape" of each reader's affect. What typically happens in a loco-descriptive poem is a kind of investiture crisis—a moment when the status of one's own identity is called into question. According to Tim Fulford, these texts tend to be linked by the sense that "the writer's authority as an observer of nature is in some respects threatened."[55] Although loco-descriptive poetry provides the representation of a commanding view, this view serves as both a test and a spur to the exercise of authority. On the whole, however, loco-descriptive poetry tends toward conservatism, and the lyric speaker generally finds himself returning to the place he started "but with an altered mood and deepened understanding."[56] The reader too is expected to share in this transformation to some degree.

A similar dynamic can be found within the structure and style of what M. H. Abrams called "the greater Romantic lyric," by which he meant those lyrics in which there is a transferential coordination between speaker and landscape so that a "change of aspect in the landscape evokes a varied but integral process of memory, thought, anticipation, and feeling" in the speaker (201). The Hyperion fragments share some characteristics with both loco-descriptive poetry and the greater Romantic lyric, particularly in the way the two fragments similarly structure transferential scenes in which pathos is projected onto an external canvas so that it can be perceived and interpreted. One key difference, however, between these forms of projection is that in both loco-descriptive poetry and the greater Romantic lyric the speaker's achievement of insight is typically mediated by a more or less "natural" landscape, whereas in "Hyperion" insight must be drawn from a mythopoetic theogony staged within the "cathedral cavern" of the imagination itself (H, 1:86).[57]

In other words, the landscape painted as if on an unspooling canvas is now being entirely projected inside the "cathedral cavern" of the mind.[58] Such internalization is advantageous, because it offers greater control over how one's landscape of affect is mediated and mapped. By presenting an internalized landscape of mythological dream vision these poems offer, in the forms of Apollo and Hyperion, phantasmagoric models by which to alter mood and deepen understanding. Once the poet has internalized the means of imaginative production and no longer has to coordinate their gaze to an already given landscape, then he or she is free to project new models of empowerment. What to do with this power is another question.

The Hyperion Project

Between the fall of 1818 and the end of September 1819, Keats made two attempts to write a mythopoetic epic, one designed to depict an intergenerational struggle between those Titans who once ruled creation and their Olympian successors. According to his friend Richard Woodhouse, the focus was to be on "the dethronement of Hyperion, the former God of the Sun, by Apollo,—and incidentally of those of Oceanus by Neptune, of Saturn by Jupiter, etc."[59] Keats ultimately produced only fragments of what he originally envisioned. Undoubtedly, the reasons Keats abandoned this project are overdetermined. The slow but final demise of his brother Tom in December 1818, coupled with Keats's own deteriorating health, surely had a role to play, as did the much more pleasant distractions of a brightening romance with Fanny Brawne. But perhaps the roots of the epic's incompleteness can be traced back to Keats's earliest conceptions of his epic.

In a letter to his friend Benjamin Robert Haydon in January of 1818, Keats suggests that the great contrast between *Endymion* and his new epic is that in *Endymion* the "mortal is led on, like Buonaparte, by circumstance whereas the Apollo in Hyperion being a fore-seeing God will shape his actions like one" (*LJK*, 1:207). Ultimately, however, representing Apollo's "fore-seeing" nature proved too challenging, and "Hyperion" ends in mid-sentence precisely at the moment Apollo is to adopt the mantle of an Olympian. Keats was unable to realize the image of this Olympian ideal, and "Hyperion" ends abruptly with Apollo shrieking and his celestial limbs writhing:

> His very hair, his golden tresses famed
> Kept undulation round his eager neck.
> During the pain Mnemosyne upheld
> Her arms as one who prophesied.—At length
> Apollo shriek'd;—and lo! from all his limbs
> Celestial. (H, 3:131–36)

The Miltonic style Keats deploys in "Hyperion" is best suited for the representation of action. Its limitations become evident when the poet tries to depict something that cannot be represented by actions and agents.

For a better sense of the strengths and limitations of this Miltonic style for a protocinematic form of poetry it is useful to recall how Eisenstein, the great early twentieth-century Russian film director, delved deep into the archeology of film in an effort to recover "the montage culture that so many have lost."[60] Montage is the art of juxtaposing elements within and between shots in such a way that the spectator must labor to assemble disjointed fragments into a whole. Suggestively, Eisenstein cites both Keats's *Endymion* and Shelley's "Julian and Maddalo" to make some of his points but finds in *Paradise Lost* a whole school of montage.[61] He is particularly interested in Milton's use of enjambment, which Milton defined as "the sense variously drawn out from one verse into another."[62] In these line endings, Eisenstein finds "a contrapuntal design of non-coincidences" between the limits of rhythm and representation and suggests that it is through enjambment that poetry mobilizes techniques of montage.[63]

In *The Film Sense* (1943), Eisenstein produced a cinematic reading of *Paradise Lost* in which he resegments the poetic text into a shooting script, with an identical number of lines and shots. Eisenstein turns Milton's words into pictures, which compresses action into a set of "privileged instants or pregnant moments."[64] The presence of enjambment produces juxtaposition, and "as it suspends, extends, and exceeds those instants or pregnant moments, the enjambment provides the link between different frames, dynamizing them into movement" (3). When confronted with montages of dynamically linked movements, the reader/viewer produces chains of associations, which transform a multitude of still images into one moving whole.

Eisenstein's exercise demonstrates how *Paradise Lost* was cinematic avant la lettre and had always in some way been a set of instructions for visualization. The Hyperion fragments are similarly cinematic, and approaching the poems as protocinematic media helps clarify why "The Fall of Hyperion" is such a departure from "Hyperion" in terms of its technique of visualization. "Hyperion" itself is a montage of tableaux, wherein emblematic scenes of arrested action are linked together to produce a continuous narrative, like individual stills joined together in a film reel. The poem becomes "an interval of arrested reactions—soliloquy (Saturn), anxiety (Hyperion), and oration (Oceanus, Enceladus)."[65]

The figures arranged within these tableaux often approximate statuary, as in the scene where Saturn and Thea are introduced:

> these two were postured motionless,
> Like natural sculpture in cathedral cavern;
> The frozen God still couchant on the earth,
> And the sad Goddess weeping at his feet. (H, 1:85–88)

Nevertheless, it would not be difficult to rework these lines into a shooting script like the one Eisenstein made for *Paradise Lost*, because although the overall stillness of these two figures suggest painting or statuary, Keats's attention to the precise description of action contributes to an overall sense of movement or duration. In this way, when

> old Saturn lifted up
> His faded eyes, and saw his kingdom gone,
> And all the gloom and sorrow of the place,
> And that fair kneeling Goddess. (H, 1:89–92)

Each element is individually framed (Saturn lifting, faded eyes, lost kingdom, gloom and sorrow, kneeling Goddess) but linked together by juxtaposition and enjambment into a feeling of movement—in a manner not unlike how a film reel generates a "motion picture" out of a series of still images. "Hyperion," however, abruptly ends at the moment when Apollo is "trembling with light," and "made flush" by "wild commotions." The young Apollo has the "fierce convulse" of one about to "die into life" (H, 3:120–30), but Keats cannot seem to represent what this new life might look like. Limited by his use of a poetics of Miltonic blank verse, the poem's final "Celestial" moment is left in a state of suspension, and the poet is unable to picture what comes next. Keats ultimately abandons this version of the project.

"The Fall," in contrast, differs in that it depicts a scene of initiation, which purposefully suspends narrative flow, halts the habituated performance of normative identity, and exposes the poet-initiate to the wonder of pure perception. As many critics have argued, there is compelling evidence that Dante's encounter with Beatrice in *Purgatorio* serves as a template for the initiate's meeting with Moneta, and reading Dante likely assisted Keats in his general swerve away from the attraction that Milton held over "Hyperion."[66] Much like Keats's "hieroglyphic visioning," the *"visibile parlare"* of Dante's dazzling contrapassos and spiritual psychedelia points toward a poetics that can represent psychic states in a manner that enables some sense of the underlying mood or tendency of the state to be transferred to the reader despite the fact that what is being depicted is at the threshold of intelligibility.[67] It does so by "peering beyond word and symbol and concept altogether into the unsayable, unrepresentable, and unthinkable realm of the apophatic."[68] Although the structural devices that Keats may have learned from his study of Dante, in both the English translation by Henry Francis Cary and ultimately in the Italian original, cannot be tied down to a single derivative passage, perhaps the key difference between Milton and Dante is the divergent ways they struggle with the tension between "description and representation . . . observation and participation."[69] In other words, perhaps the crucial thing Keats learns from Dante is quite similar to what Percy Shelley expresses in his own Dantean poem "The Triumph of Life," namely, that readers must "from spectator turn / Actor or victim in this wretchedness" (303–4). What Keats learned from Dante may be akin to what William Franke recognizes as Dante's key insight, namely that the best way to express a "mystical vision and passion for what transcends the world," is paradoxically by turning "toward the world" so that "the body and specifically the flesh become the crucial site of revelation."[70] It is not enough to merely be a spectator or to witness the spectacle of a god's becoming; one must become a participant in this transformation, by putting on the ritual or itinerary of this metamorphosis for oneself. Only when words are made flesh in this way can such ritualistic alterations actually affect our lives.

Within "The Fall" it is the golden figure of Hyperion himself that offers a glimpse of what it is like "to see as a god sees" (F, 1:304). This vision is obtained after the initiate awakens from his "cloudy swoon" (F, 1:55) and finds himself in an enormous space. But first he sees far off "an image, huge of feature as a cloud" (F, 1:87). This is the goddess Moneta, who appears as a kind of phantasmagoria, with her image projected "huge of feature" upon a cloud of mist. Before her stands an altar, and from behind "white fragrant curtains" a voice is heard that commands the initiate to ascend the altar's stairs. Climbing the altar steps, however, proves challenging, and the initiate feels the "tyranny" of the hard task proposed. He feverishly strives "to escape / The numbness" that he feels, and only gains the lowest step when he is "One minute before death." Nevertheless, when his "iced foot" does touch the lowest stair, "life seem'd / To pour in at the toes," and he mounts up, "As once fair angels on a ladder flew," crying "Holy Power" (F, 1:119–36). After passing Moneta's test, the poet-seer is offered an opportunity to look upon "the scenes / Still swooning vivid" within her "globed brain," and it is by looking into Moneta in this way that the poet-seer obtains visions of both Saturn and Hyperion (F, 1:244–45).

The vision the initiate obtains of Saturn's melancholic figure is of a "frozen God still bending to the earth" while the "sad Goddess" Thea is "weeping at his feet" (F, 1:386–87). For a long time the dreaming poet stares as the "two were postured motionless, / Like sculpture builded up upon the grave / Of their own power," but eventually Saturn speaks and like "some old man of the earth / Bewailing earthly loss" moans against the circumstances that "Have chang'd a God into a shaking palsy" (F, 1:382–84; 440–41; 426). The initiate continues to scrutinize Saturn as he sat fixed "beneath the sable trees, / Whose arms spread straggling in wild serpent forms" (F, 1:446), but eventually the two titans "melted from [his] sight into the wood" (F, 1:459). The first canto ends with the initiate pausing at the "open doors" of this "antechamber" of his dream, questioning whether he dare go further. The second canto opens with Moneta explaining how she has had to "humanize" her sayings by "making comparisons of earthly things" so that she could be understood (F, 2:2–3). The initiate's attention is then turned from Saturn's "melancholy realms" to "Blazing Hyperion on his orbed fire," the last of the "whole eagle-brood" who "still keeps / His sov'reignty, and rule, and majesty" (F, 2:7–15).

By the end of "The Fall," the initiate is in a state of wonder and in the poem's last thirteen lines time itself unspools as the initiate peers through the figure of Hyperion and into the depths of time itself:

> Mnemosyne
> Was sitting on a square edg'd polish'd stone,
> That in its lucid depth reflected pure
> Her priestess-garments. My quick eyes ran on

> From stately nave to nave, from vault to vault,
> Through bowers of fragrant and enwreathed light,
> And diamond paved lustrous long arcades.
> Anon rush'd by the bright Hyperion;
> His flaming robes stream'd out beyond his heels,
> And gave a roar, as if of earthly fire,
> That scar'd away the meek ethereal hours
> And made their dove-wings tremble: on he flared. (F, 2:50–61)

Although only a few of these lines are new and the rest are recycled and repurposed from "Hyperion," the overall effect accomplishes what Keats couldn't in "Hyperion": the depiction of godlike vision. A "lucid depth" is generated from the doubled image of Mnemosyne, the goddess of memory, whose "priestess-garments" flash across the reflective surface of the "square edg'd polish'd stone." The movement of the speaker's "quick eyes" reinforces this sense of depth as his gaze runs from "nave to nave" and "vault to vault" and through "bowers of fragrant and enwreathed light, / And diamond paved lustrous long arcades." The repetitive play of light, reflection, and distances in these lines creates a spectacle of flashing jewellike beauty, and this spectacle is intensified and animated by the use of the verbs "rush'd," "stream'd," "scar'd," "flared," and the adjectives "lustrous," "bright," and "flaming." In the first fragment, Hyperion is an actor—he moves, tastes, and laments his circumstances. In "The Fall," however, Hyperion is not depicted so much as his effect is announced. Hyperion's kaleidoscopic brightness is so potent that even the "dove-wings" of "the meek ethereal hours" tremble.

As an avatar of a vibrant vitality and as an image that is nevertheless iconoclastic, Hyperion is the virtual embodiment of a state of being that "Hyperion" merely narrates. "The Fall," rather than presenting a discursive account of creation, instead offers a visual representation of continual emergence— "on he flared"—and it is the wondrous nature of this vision that has the potential to purge the "mind's film" off the initiate at Moneta's altar (F, 1:146). One reason the initiate has been chosen is because he differs from all those who "seek no wonder but the human face" (F, 1:163). For such men the world is a haven and so the feeling of release Moneta offers holds little attraction. Unlike the calm wonder of the human face, the wonder of seeing those "scenes / Still swooning vivid through [Moneta's] globed brain" (F, 1:244–45) produces nausea if approached too closely. Yet like the "immense reservoir of electrical energy"[71] that Baudelaire's flâneur encounters when he enters a crowd, it is through this unsettling exposure to an "electral changing misery" (F, 1:246) that wonder does its work.

The political efficacy of wonder has been explored by Jane Bennett, a theorist who has compellingly advocated for the ethical relevance of affect. In *The Enchantment of Modern Life* (2001) and *Vibrant Matter* (2010), she examines the "mood of enchantment or that strange combination of delight and disturbance" that accompanies certain moments of sensuous intensity. The value of such moments is that one may find in them "the motivational energy needed to move . . . from the endorsement of ethical principles to the actual practice of ethical behaviors."[72] For Bennett, "enchantment entails a state of wonder, and one of the distinctions of this state is the temporary suspension of chronological time and bodily movement."[73] To feel enchanted is to be caught up in a state of wonder or what Phillip Fisher has described as a "moment of pure presence."[74] Thought itself is arrested in wonder because the mind is unable to "move on by association to something else" (131).[75] However, although thoughts and limbs may be brought to rest, the senses themselves continue to operate in high gear. In this way, wonder holds us spellbound while at the same time transporting our senses to new heights of delight. The overall effect of such wondrous enchantment "is a mood of fullness, plenitude, or liveliness, a sense of having had one's nerves or circulation or concentration powers tuned up or recharged, a shot in the arm, a fleeting return to childlike excitement about life" (5). The political value of such moods of fullness and enchantment is that they invigorate and can generate the sense that anything is possible.

As Mary-Jane Rubenstein has traced, Plato and Aristotle both argued that philosophy begins in wonder. In the Platonic dialogues for instance, Socratic wonder (*thaumazein*) "arises when the understanding cannot master that which lies closest—when surrounded by utterly ordinary concepts and things, the philosopher suddenly finds himself surrounded on all sides by aporia."[76] Wonder is what strikes Theaetetus in the Platonic dialogue that bears his name, when "he loses his grasp on notions that had seemed utterly self-evident, sending him reeling, his head spinning."[77] Wonder "is a dizzying, vertiginous, and destabilizing experience" that threatens to upend all preconceptions. In *Theaetetus*, Socrates claims that it is in this experience of wonder that "philosophy begins and nowhere else."[78] Such wonder is a crucial aspect of how "The Fall" represents an advance over "Hyperion's" loco-descriptive depiction of an epic theogony, and how it offers at least momentary access to gaze at a "veiled, supernatural order separated from everyday life by a barrier which is also a threshold."[79]

The Socratic concept of *thaumazein* is reworked by Martin Heidegger into a "shock" and "awe" theory of wonder. Heidegger hypothesizes that there is a mood (*Befindlichkeit*) of holding-backness (*Verhaltenheit*, which is often translated as "reserve" or "restraint"). According to Heidegger, the mood of *Verhaltenheit* is constituted by two key movements: *Erschrecken*, a kind of shock, or even terror; and *Scheu*, or awe.[80] In *Verhaltenheit*, as in negative capability, one is exposed "to the sudden uncanniness of everything it thought it knew: ideas, objects, and the thinking self itself" (15). This uncanniness induces a nauseating vertigo that "then gives way to a kind of awe that anything can be at all." Wonder oscillates between a shock that "recoils at the abandonment of being" and an awe overwhelmed by the fact that despite this withdrawal things nevertheless are (15).

The shocking nature of this mood of *Verhaltenheit* helps clarify why Keats, in the October 1818 letter to Richard Woodhouse that defines the "egotistical sublime," writes that "What shocks the virtuous philosopher, delights the camelion Poet."[81] The camelion poet is the one who has recovered from the recoil of being's abandonment and is willing to communicate his awe of what remains. The nature of the camelion is to be "a very little time annihilated" by "the identity of every one in the room," and yet it is this propensity for being shocked out of an everyday understanding of things that enables the poet to be "continually in for—and filling some other Body" (*LJK*, 1:386). Ultimately, it is the negative capability that is to be found on the other side of the wonder of the "The Fall" that enables Keats's soul to absolve itself of all attachments and in turn to become in "To Autumn" one with the "twitter in the skies."

What "The Fall" depicts is the investiture crisis of a poet-initiate, who by proving himself upon Moneta's altar, becomes invested in an altered nature. Admittedly, the vision of Hyperion does not arrive at some profound discursive truth; instead, it hovers phantasmagorically at the edge of ineffability. Nevertheless, despite its clearly constructed and mediated nature the poem's conclusion is still a potential source of wonder due to the way it stages the seer's experience in encountering what Deleuze describes as a nonlocalizable pure optical and sound situation.[82] What the seer hopes to encounter is "the perpetual foundation of time, nonchronological time, Cronus and not Chronos."[83] Cronus, of course, is the Greek name for Saturn.

In a world skeptical of any claims of total understanding, the question becomes whether, when one lacks the luxury of moral certitude, an ethically meaning life can be founded upon wonder alone? Although in the end "The Fall" has no final solution to this question, and this may be one reason why it is a work of poetry rather than fanaticism, it can provide those willing to gaze into its gemlike flame a glimpse into how differently things could look. Beholding "The Fall's" kaleidoscopic climax can revitalize the gawking initiate, because "the combination of quickening and release occasioned by a beautiful object," its shock and awe, loosens those defensive postures within us that have damned up vitality.[84] In this moment of openness a sense of absolution is experienced, which momentarily lifts the burden of the mystery and offers an opportunity for alteration and revision. Like William Blake's "Moment in each Day that Satan cannot find," for the "Industrious," such moments when found can renovate "every Moment of the Day if rightly placed." [85] To witness "Cronos and not Chronos" is to be exposed to the wondrous emergence of a vitality that is both outside of chronology and at its heart.

Time-Image and Movement-Image

In this last section, I want to recognize how the divergence between "Hyperion" and "The Fall of Hyperion" is not only analogous to the difference between the flâneur and the badaud, and between Milton and Dante but also coordinates with a related break Gilles Deleuze finds in the history of cinema between the movement-image and the time-image. It is useful to explore this additional correlation, because thinking of Keats's poetry in relation to the time-image helps clarify how his project relates to the other "strong poems of the post-Enlightenment modernity" that Allen Grossman understands as being motivated by the "narration of the loss and intended recovery of the orienting a priori of the body." [86] A poetics of the time-image is already at work in Dante and is also present in various ways throughout Romanticism, with Wordsworth's "spots of time" and Charlotte Smith's "Beachy Head" being two obvious examples, before becoming increasingly ubiquitous in modernist and postmodernist works. Another reason to explore the connection to the time-image here is because it will provide a bridge to the next chapter on Shelley, who will also tap into the power of the time-image in his efforts to deploy "imageless images" capable of encouraging readers to abandon their attachment to what he calls a "savage" sense of necessity.

Like many thinkers before and since, Deleuze found film to be an exemplary means for understanding the intricacies of modernity. Walter Benjamin, for instance, similarly found in cinema a concise model of how technology can organize the shocking principles of modernity into a formal principle, whose "rhythm of reception" matches that of "the rhythm of production on a conveyor belt."[87] Likewise, Max Horkheimer and Theodor Adorno saw movies as places where intellect, sensory perception, and bodily affect were coordinated and orchestrated so as to offer up feelings of excitement and vitality to those willing to submit to its perceptual regime and narrative flow. Deleuze calls this regimen "the sensory-motor schema," and in his two influential volumes on cinema he explores how the sensory-motor schema of classic cinema guides perceptions and shapes actions.

Deleuze becomes interested in cinema, in part, so that he can explore the implicit philosophy and politics embedded in movement, and his two volumes of *Cinema* map out a disjunction he finds in the history of filmmaking between the movement-image and the time-image. According to Deleuze, in films made prior to World War II the dominant mode of filmmaking was based on the movement-image, which can be equally found in a lover waving goodbye or in the twists and turns of a chase scene. Here, characters respond to their environment via movements, explainable through linear or efficient causality. As in loco-descriptive poetry, the temporality of the movement-image is based in action (the action of narrative, causality, and rationality) and is governed by the sensory-motor schema.

The time-image, however, which becomes increasingly prevalent after World War II, breaks from this sensory-motor regime, and with this break emphasis shifts from a chronology of progressive movement to an experience of the image in itself.[88] Although Deleuze is reluctant to cite a specific film as an exemplary model, good examples of the time-image, as already mentioned in the first chapter, can be found in Resnais's *L'Année dernière à Marienbad* (*Last Year at Marienbad*), Kubrick's *2001*, and Malick's *The Tree of Life*. According to Deleuze, the advantage of the time-image is that it "gives us access to that Proustian dimension where people and things occupy a place in time which is incommensurable with the one they have in space."[89] In this Proustian dimension time is "mounting its magic lantern on bodies and making the shots coexist in depth. It is this build-up, this emancipation of time, which ensures the rule of impossible continuity and aberrant movement" (39). In the time-image "the sensory-motor schema is no longer in operation" because it has been "shattered from the inside" (40).

As linear causality breaks down "perceptions and actions ceased to be linked together, and spaces are now neither co-ordinated nor filled" (40). To cite Allen Ginsberg's "Howl," the ideal audience for such art are those

> who dreamt and made incarnate gaps in Time & Space through
> images juxtaposed, and trapped the archangel of the soul
> between 2 visual images and joined the elemental verbs and
> set the noun and dash of consciousness together jumping
> with sensation of Pater Omnipotens Aeterna Deus (70–74)

This capacity to be able to trap the "archangel of the soul / between 2 visual images" is a good description of the posture of attention readers need to put on in order to make sense of a poetics made up of "images juxtaposed" rather than ones literally and logically spread out in a more traditional narrative form.[90] The compensation for reading such difficult work is that when the "elemental verbs" are joined and the force of meaning is suddenly felt, then both the "noun" and the "dash" of consciousness jump together with sensation, and one becomes increasingly cognizant of an emphatic relationship to a whole. The experience of such moments of intense recognition can often take the form of an epiphany—the sudden showing forth of the spiritual in the actual.

Characters who are caught in the time-image's "pure optical and sound situations" are considered by Deleuze to be the "pure seers, who no longer exist except in the interval of movement, and do not even have the consolation of the sublime, which would connect them to matter or would gain control of the spirit for them."[91] The sensory-motor schema holds out the promise of a sublime consolation or climax in exchange for submitting to its regimen of spectacle. The seer, however, does not participate in this schema and thus turns away from the movement-image's linear causality to peer instead in wonder at the "non-localizable" pure optical and sound situation of the direct time-image. In the time-image the actions of characters no longer flow easily across the gaps between framed moments. Instead, the characters themselves become swallowed up in the space between frames.[92]

The aptness of applying Deleuze's work on cinema to Keats's poetry has already been suggested by Rei Terada as part of her own interrogation of the roles visuality and politics play in the Hyperion project. In her essay "Looking at the Stars Forever," she begins by highlighting a peculiar scene in "Hyperion," where "Hyperion arose, and on the stars / Lifted his curved lids, and kept them wide / Until it ceas'd; and still he kept them wide: / And still they were the same bright, patient stars" (H, 1:350–53). Terada wants to explore what this "looking does, and, if it adds nothing, why Keats describes it."[93] Such looking is found to be significant because, unlike the dominant view of Romantic visuality, which "invokes the aesthetic in order to imagine something better than what can be realized," Keats's mode of looking "seems openly absorptive, yet withholds realization" (278).

"The Fall" is viewed by Terada as a poem in which, "on the level of the plot, nothing is seen, only dreamed" (296). It is a fantasy of the kind of looking Keats would like to be capable of: "the kind of looking an eye would do if no one were operating it (the fantasy of neorealist cinema)" (296). The value of a blank gaze lies in how its view is unprejudiced and unmarred by the matrixes of ideological thinking. It is this look that Moneta asks for when she says to the poet-initiate,

> "My power, which to me is still a curse,
> Shall be to thee a wonder; for the scenes
> Still swooning vivid through my globed brain
> With an electral changing misery
> Thou shalt with those dull mortal eyes behold,
> Free from all pain, if wonder pain thee not." (F, 1:243–48)

Terada argues that by looking into Moneta's globed brain the viewer is "exposed to what things look like without our looking at them, without value."[94] To approach the scenes stored within Moneta's globed brain in this way is useful because one would then be able to observe freely and without prejudice.

Terada acknowledges that this form of beholding is akin to an experience of wonder. However, drawing upon Hegel's definition of wonder as a primitive form of perceptual tension created by a lack of determination, she argues that "if looking is scanning and contemplating, and seeing is grasping for potential use, beholding is not even yet to look." Thus, "in cognitive terms a program to produce wonder would actually be going in reverse" (298). Terada ultimately finds limitations to Keats's approach and critiques the efficacy of "The Fall's" wonder working by coordinating it with failings she perceives in Deleuze's notion of the time-image. In Terada's reading, the time-image is useful because it exposes viewers to the skeptical realization that the habits and practices through which their experience of the world is normally mediated are not in and of themselves reality. The time-image in this sense functions as a kind of inoculation against fanaticism. The downside of the time-image is that although it offers a glimpse of the "wholeness of the false," it fails to offer any way out of the underlying predicament; it can only make the momentary exposure to a vicarious loss of determination appealing. For these reasons, time-images can be seen as "reactions to sensory-motor enervation that seem more like defenses than alternatives" (285). For Terada, the time-image is ultimately of limited political value because it is essentially a defensive attempt "to restore the 'panoramic vision' of those who feel mortally threatened or lost."[95]

Eric Santner also finds value as well as limitations to the time-image, and he argues that part of what Deleuze does is help us see how a cinematic virtuality might reconnect us to the real and give us reasons to believe in the world again.[96] By short-circuiting typical habits of attention such art touches upon a domain of "flesh and nerve" that may be able to "directly relay the rhythmic mobility of an 'almost unlivable Power.'"[97] Nevertheless, for Santner, although time-images may be able to express "time as the absolute by activating an infinite relay between the virtual and the actual," because they reject "the dimension of representation that Lacan calls the logic of the signifier," they cannot ultimately affect what Santner calls the flesh and are left to "construe the field of operation of the logic of sensation as the virtual, and pantheistic, animality of meat" (135). In short, for Santner the limitation of the time-image is that it goes after the wrong kind of flesh—the phenomenological body rather than that form of Scripture in which issues of signification and representation are coordinated with affective pressures felt in the nerves.

The problem Santner sees in Deleuze's approach to the time-image, and to art more generally, is that Deleuze strives toward a liberated but "purely virtual reality, one that concerns not the lives of living creatures but rather the vitality of the process of creation itself" (135). What interests Deleuze is "the perception of creative time . . . purged of any actual creature."[98] Thus, "the time-image is . . . precisely not an image in the usual (or actual) sense of the term. It is not a relation between perceiver and perceived, so much as 'a perception as it was before men (or after).'" The time-image enables the perception of a time and space "released from their human coordinates.' . . . Crystalline perception proceeds, in other words, at the scale of cosmic creation itself" (116). By being released from human coordinates in this way the seer can apprehend alternative ways of viewing the world. These new intuitions can also restore "faith in the world" precisely by tapping into the intensity that creates it. But for Santner, the limitation of Deleuzean aesthetics is that it is directed toward "a utopian vision beyond any reference to the political theological tradition, a vision seemingly grounded in something like a perpetual state of emergence." Santner argues that by focusing on this state "of pure natality, . . . this work can never give rise to a renewed and reconfigured engagement with the forms and locations of normative pressure that define the symbolic order of modern societies."[99] Time-images are valuable because they can be engines of wonder, and like Wordsworth's poetry can help break through the "film of familiarity" and the "lethargy of custom," but they are ultimately limited if they cannot alter or affect the normative pressures that inform our gaze in some positive way (BL, 2:7).

There is much to agree with in both Terada's and Santner's critiques of the time-image, and I recognize that Keats can ultimately take us only so far and that we will have to turn to Shelley's poetics for a utopian vision that does include reference to the political theological tradition and thus may be better able to affect what Santner sees as the "right kind" of flesh. Nevertheless, I still want to propose a more positive reading of time-images and the potential of moments of wonder. Here, I am closer to William Connolly's argument in *A World of Becoming* (2010), a book about the interrelations between temporality, affect, and politics, wherein he considers how it is better to understand Deleuze's discussions of the time-image not as failing to provide a way out, but as offering an opportunity to release the affective burden of resentment and thereby restoring belief in the world. In Connolly's reading, there is a therapeutic dimension to the forms of experience that the time-image taps into, which can help assuage those resentments that are too readily "insinuated into the pores of experience."[100] Resentment is a rigidity of both body and mind, which poisons and paralyzes the public sphere. The time-image can be a remedy to resentment because the exposure to the wholeness of the false can itself act "as a shock, spurring thought on." This shock to the system jolts viewers off "the grooves of regularity," thereby exposing the artificiality of everyday habits and practices while also suddenly freeing up affective energy that can be reinvested into generating and motivating new forms of action (65). In this more optimistic reading, by lifting the mantle of melancholy and shining light on saturnine dispositions, the time-image can not only potentially relieve resentment and restore belief in the world but motivate a desire to change it as well.

Although by itself it may ultimately be a necessary but insufficient step, nevertheless, the kind of wonderous vision produced through the mediating technology of "The Fall of Hyperion" is an advanced form of the dynamics coordinated in previous chapters with Wordsworth's efforts to break through the "film of familiarity" and awaken readers to the "wonders of the world," with the ontological branch of affect theory, with Merleau-Ponty's version of flesh, and with the kind of self-interrupting beauty associated with the blessing of the sea snakes in the "Rime." Admittedly, with Keats we approach the limit of what these sorts of postures of attention can accomplish, or perhaps more precisely, what "The Fall" projects for us is what this limit looks like.

Nevertheless, at the end of "The Fall," what the iconoclastic image of Hyperion depicts is not the meaty flesh of our phenomenological body but rather a glimpse at our soul—that "second, virtually real and, indeed, glorious body" that once served as the better half of the king's two bodies.[101] Keats's Hyperion project was always an effort "To see as a god sees, and take the depth / Of things as nimbly as the outward eye" (F, 1:304–5). His mistake in "Hyperion" and in the flailing figure of Apollo was to try to picture God as a body image that could be looked at directly. In "The Fall," however, he tries a different tactic; rather than offering readers an image to look at he gives them a body schema or posture of attention to put on.[102] After all, what is it we are looking at when we "see" the imageless image of Hyperion as he "gave a roar, as if of earthly fire, / That scar'd away the meek ethereal hours / And made their dove-wings tremble: on he flared" (F, 2:59–61)?

What "The Fall" ultimately offers both the poet and the reader is a ritual of absolution. Absolution is a form of detachment, which makes sense due to the very etymology of the word: *ab* (off) + *solver* (to loosen). The absolute is that "which is loosened off and on the loose."[103] Within a religious context this logic of loosening can be seen in the sacrament of absolution performed by a Catholic priest, which is intended to loosen sin from the soul. By going through this process one becomes better prepared to see the absolute. Although notions of the absolute are often tied up with conceptions of an omnipotent and radically other God, Hent de Vries has offered a definition that is more open-ended and thus perhaps far more Keatsian: the absolute is "that which tends to loosen its ties to existing contexts" (3). The Hyperion project, I argue, is crucial to a process of absolution or letting go and thus serves as a key component to the poetry of Keats's annus mirabilis, which begins with the folding of the soul in "Ode to Psyche" and ends with the unfolding of the soul in "To Autumn."

By the time of "To Autumn," Keats had found a way to make great art that is kenotic. Such art, according to Kaja Silverman, "succeeds in soliciting" from the spectator "the love he or she normally preserves for the ideal-ego, but no longer reflects back to him or her an image which can be assimilated to the self."[104] Through this iconoclastic withholding, the meaning of the world viewed is left open-ended, and my view of the world is altered and enlarged as I assemble more and more different perspectives into my network of regard.

In "To Autumn," when Keats writes of those "barred clouds" that "bloom" in the "soft-dying day," which "touch the stubble-plains with rosy hue," there is a clear sense of a loosening off of the self (25–26). By the time we reach the ode's last three lines, the poet's soul seems to have completely unfolded and dissolved into the twittering sounds of the "Hedge-crickets," the "red-breast(s)," and the "gathering swallows" (31–33). Although to live we couldn't remain in such a state forever, nevertheless, Keats leaves us with a model of the contemplative soul that has become a "world spectator," one that can say, along with the painter Paul Cézanne: "The landscape thinks itself in me, and I am its consciousness."[105] Granted, given our own responsibilities, and a sense of life expectancy that hopefully is more prolonged than the one Keats was facing, we may not be quite ready to fully unfold our own souls quite yet; nevertheless, there is still great wisdom to be gleaned from the trajectory of his poetics in 1819.

PART III

Anthropology of the Postsecular

* 5 *

"Awful Doubt"

Shelley's Tragic Skepticism

In "The Fall of Hyperion" and "To Autumn," John Keats pushes lyric subjectivity to its limits, offering readers a model for how to lay down the gaze of their own language of desire and allow their own souls to unfold and no longer be limited by any particular identity. As rituals of absolution, this aspect of Keats's poetry has much to offer the individual reader, functioning as a kind of master class on what to do after one has graduated from schooling an intelligence and making it a soul within "a World of Pains and troubles" (*LJK*, 2:103). Percy Shelley's poetry on the other hand, although it shares many of Keats's starting premises, presses on in a much more overtly political direction. Whereas in Keats's "Ode to Psyche" the poet promises to dedicate himself to his goddess by building "a fane / In some untrodden region of my mind," in Shelley's poetry there is often a communal impulse, "and our work shall be called the Promethean" when "From the temples high / Of Man's ear and eye, / Roofed over Sculpture and Poesy," "our singing shall build / In the void's loose field / A world for the Spirit of Wisdom to wield."[1] Shelley's poetry and prose are more invested than Keats's in considering how new cultural and political assemblages are produced when resonant bodies join together to fashion new knits of identity.

In this chapter, I begin by considering why Shelley thought mental revolution could only be depicted through the mediation of outward scenes and how the "filmy" allegories of his poetry were intended to prepare for those revolutions.[2] A key concern is understanding how the poet can produce "imageless images" that may help some readers move from a "savage" sense of necessity to a philosophic one.[3] In this way, Shelley can be seen as the great proponent within Romanticism of the awful doubt of an enabling skepticism that knows that it lives a consciousness produced by its ongoing life activity—it just doesn't know precisely why it is putting on this production (i.e., the cause is absent). Shelley's poetry and prose thus present the fullest articulation within Romanticism of the personal and political implications of a cinematic empiricism. Throughout this chapter particular focus is placed on how and why Prometheus, or perhaps more precisely the "passion of revenge" that locks us into a "savage" time consciousness, must be unbound.[4] In order to better understand this process of affective unbinding, *The Cenci* will be read as a play that offers a particularly embodied form of one of Shelley's imageless images, one that can clarify how aesthetic form can help reform the suffering body politic that provides the field, or flesh, through which mutability weaves its dominion of empire and superstition.

One goal of this chapter and the next is to explore how we can begin to conceive an anthropology of the postsecular through a consideration of the continued significance of the genres of tragedy and comedy within modernity. Doing so will suggest potential paths of divergence from Charles Taylor's elevation of buffered subjectivity as the central model of human experience within a secular age. For Taylor, it was in Descartes that a profound shift in the experience and structure of consciousness within early modernity first became evident, "whereby goods previously located 'outside' in a Platonic order of things, or partially constructed through a neo-Stoic Natural Law, are fully internalized, dissected, and reconstructed from the bottom up by the power of autonomous reason."[5] After Descartes, in Taylor's reading, reason becomes the privileged faculty, one that not only establishes the contours of the buffered subject but also became the basis for both a public sphere and a notion of secularity itself as being fundamentally congruent to the structure of a pure, autonomous, and disengaged reason. From this perspective, "the properly trained, neo-Stoic subject stands 'above' the body and orchestrates the passions accordingly, guiding body and soul to the correct, rationally derived telos." Although in this model the passions and body aren't simply sacrificed on the altar of reason, they are nevertheless desirable largely to the extent that "they can further the soul's aims: e.g. by coercing the body into desiring virtue" (58). Thus the passions were to be brought under the instrumental control of reason, and the body became a sort of stepping stone upon which the soul stood, but only in an effort to ultimately climb free.

Marek Sullivan, however, suggests that there is another understanding of Descartes that needs to come into view, one that takes into account his last major work, *Les Passions de l'Âme* (*Passions of the Soul*, 1649), and which effectively challenges Taylor's understanding of both subjectivity and secularity. Here Descartes "testifies to an acute awareness of the limits of internal, autonomous reason, emphasizing the entanglement of reason in the workings of the body; the importance of external, environmental factors for the shaping of human experience and response; and the centrality of 'habit' or 'habits' to the cultivation of virtue."[6] By emphasizing this aspect of Descartes's thought a much more postrationalist, and thus postsecular, understanding of the body comes into view. Clearly, this interest in the late Cartesian emphasis on the role of habit in the cultivation of virtue and the shaping of human experience resonates with my own consideration of the possibilities inherent within a cinematic empiricism. In both models, there is an attempt to recover latent possibilities within the tradition in order to move beyond some of the normative understandings of modernity that now seem limiting. What needs to be taken into account in either case is the crucial role that habit, affect, mediation, and embodiment play in the anthropology of the postsecular and why it is that if "the passions can extend or even alter the soul's disposition, it is not because they further the soul's power directly by acting as a causal link between the soul and the body, but because they precondition the soul to interact in certain ways with the body, by inscribing memories at a deep level" (54).

Victoria Kahn has similarly noted the significance of Descartes's late work, in which an "old-fashioned aristocratic ideal of self-mastery" is replaced with "the modern individual, whose body has become a foreign territory, one that requires new indirect techniques of government." This shift is deeply significant because it inaugurates "a new regime of politics, one inscribed in the body itself."[7] One implication of this new form of politics is that what is important is "less a matter of competing reasons than the affective structure in and through which such reasons were presented."[8] The form a particular politics will take is most often determined by whoever controls the mediating forces that shape the sensoriums of the people. Consent can be manufactured "by controlling people's experiential environment, or, as it came to be expressed in the eighteenth century, 'what passed before people's eyes'" (66). Affecting the forms of mediation in this way is so effective because agency is itself rooted in "a process of behavioural self-conditioning through the manipulation of habits, themselves shaped and modified by external conditioning factors" (50). Through exposure and reiteration one can alter the deep structure of another's soul. If as Descartes argued in *Passions of the Soul*, "what we commonly call 'virtues' are habits in the soul which dispose it to have certain thoughts," then there is great power in controlling or disrupting those means of production by which habits are formed.[9]

In this final section of the book, I am interested in articulating a postsecular anthropology in order to better understand what it means to be a creature "whose welfare is, in a special and intimate way, bound up with the operations of the body, and with the feelings, sensations, and passions that arise from our embodied state."[10] If human agency is not "a simple assertion of the individual will but a *thinking-through* of the diverse sorts of connection that we inhabit," then tragedy and comedy are significant to this conversation because they are both genres of misrecognition.[11] As Rowan Williams has compellingly argued in *The Tragic Imagination* (2016), "tragedy is not about 'fate,' about external forces acting on a helpless human subject, but about a moment of the self's *misrecognition* of itself as already unified" (57). By learning to recognize this tendency toward misrecognition, we are made more open to true thinking.

Now it may be, as we will see in the next chapter, that "comic characters learn how to manage their frailty better" than tragic ones (153). Nevertheless, the key to both genres is an "awareness of how deep-rooted the fictions of the self are in the human constitution," and how incongruity is an essential aspect of human subjectivity (75). The genres of tragedy and comedy give us insight into what I am calling a postsecular anthropology because they both help us *think* through what our supreme fictions are doing, while also offering practice in developing that "habit or skill of self-recognition which has to be integrated into mature interdependence, the recognition of self in the other towards which all human action and thought moves" (74). In short, this section of the book explores what it means to be a subject in a world in which we must continue to live in community, despite the fact that we may never arrive at or agree upon a final point of view on how best to respond to those crises, catastrophes, and contingencies that both haunt and justify our existence.

Mediation Unbound

Before considering Shelley's relationship to the tragic imagination, I want to return to and build upon Kahn's claim that what is needed in modernity is a "new regime of politics, one inscribed in the body itself."[12] Shelley was well aware that by affecting what passed before people's eyes one could alter the sensoriums of the citizenry and thereby manufacture consent. As Celeste Langan and Maureen McLane asserted, for Shelley, an "imagined revolution—the overriding thematic of his poetry—was incessantly audiovisualized, its movements virtually kinesthetic, propelling spirits and readers ever onward in a shared dream."[13] Like Keats, Shelley produced a poetry that is intensely cinematographic, picturing "revolution as a stunning sound-and-light show" (257). He was a poet who looked at the world and "drew / New figures on its false and fragile glass / 'As the old faded'" (S, "Triumph of Life," 246–48). Both poets were intensely interested in how "to communicate ideas, to make them sensible, to impress them on our sensorium, via poetry."[14] As contemporaries like William Hazlitt recognized, Shelley painted "pictures on gauze ... and proceeds to prove their truth by describing them in detail as matters of fact."[15] Nevertheless, as Hazlitt also realized, the style of Shelley's "rhapsodies or allegories" are often difficult to discern, marked as they are with "the disjointedness of the materials, the incongruous metaphors and violent transitions," and the obscurity of "the drift or the moral." Looking at the end of "The Triumph of Life" Hazlitt concludes: "Any thing more filmy, enigmatical, discontinuous, unsubstantial than this, we have not seen; nor yet more full of morbid genius and vivifying soul."[16]

Part of the challenge of Shelley's "filmy" allegories is that he is trying to depict the inner workings of the human mind. As he says in the preface to *Prometheus Unbound*, "The imagery which I have employed will be found, in many instances, to have been drawn from the operations of the human mind, or from those external actions by which they are expressed" (S, 207). Such depictions were desirable despite the challenge they posed for readers, because Shelley agreed that for change to occur there had to be mental revolution. However, in contrast to William Godwin, Colin Jager argues, Shelley came to realize that "Godwin was wrong to think that the contents of one mind could be simply transferred to another." The only way to "grasp mental revolution is through the mediation of the outward scene."[17] Shelley's "rhapsodies or allegories" thus serve as forms of mediation that can facilitate mental revolution not through some form of beneficent mesmerism, but through an indirect and externalized form of coding and decoding, which encourages the "separation of the knower from the known"[18] and requires the active participation of the reader to decipher.

In his essay "On Christianity," Shelley claims that for better or worse, "All reformers have been compelled to practice this misrepresentation of their own true feelings and opinions" because "the practice of utter sincerity towards other men would avail to no good end, if they were incapable of practicing it towards their own minds." Some level of "dissimulation, or simulation, or hypocrisy, or exaggeration, or anything but the precise and rigid image which is present to the mind," is needed, because "truth cannot be communicated until it is perceived." In order for an audience to be able to adequately contemplate and examine the truth that is to be transmitted by a poet, their "state of mind" must be prepared.[19] To make Shelley's poetry meaningful, readers must "from spectator turn / Actor or victim in this wretchedness" ("Triumph of Life," 305–6). To the extent that "the mind acquires an active power, the empire" of selfishness and injustice becomes limited.[20]

The kind of poetry Shelley advocates is thus quite different from the model of poetic eloquence articulated by Wordsworth, where the poet is the one who " 'lets himself slip' into delusion, to the point that the distinction between self and other is 'confounded.' "[21] This model of eloquence was based on a capacity for identification, and so, in Robert Mitchell's formulation, "the poet's job was to enable sympathy by allowing his listeners to take pleasure in images without having to labor."[22] By doing so the poet could highlight a proper model of response to the pains and pleasures of the world. The design of the eloquent poem was to function "as the intruding sky does—that is, first to show us our lacks, then to suggest another way to dispose our psychic energies."[23] The audience can then sympathize with and ultimately emulate the eloquent model offered by the poet, and thereby establish "a form of relationality that binds the subject to an object or an imaginary," which in turn enables "ways of inhabiting the world, bodily and ethically."[24] Notably there is an implicit hierarchy to this mode of eloquent address because while sympathy can be felt by anyone, the act of poetic "identification was a skill, or gift, that only a few could master. As a result, everyone could be auditors, but only a few the authors, of poetry."[25] As Wordsworth puts it at the end of *The Prelude*, the poet is the one who is a "Prophet of Nature," and who "to them will speak a lasting inspiration" so that "what we have loved / Others will love, and we may teach them how" (P, 13:442–45). All the audience has to do is follow this advice and become the poet's "second self" when he is gone.

Shelley's poetry has a different agenda. According to Mitchell, Shelley's poems "challenged readers' powers of representation in order to expand the consciousness of time, thereby soliciting the powers of futurity."[26] Whereas Wordsworth provides the coordinates of a specific natural object, like "The Thorn" or the sheepfold in "Michael," and teaches readers to see it as a "compressed narrative" upon which to reflect upon a more encompassing situation, Shelley's "unsculptured" images give "the reader little to 'see' or think" about, and suggest a "relationship to temporality" that is quite different from that of the Wordsworthian image.[27] Shelley, like Keats, taps into the power of the time-image and does so to play with "the connection between time consciousness and perceptions of causal necessity" (194). Part of his goal is to "liberate readers from the savage understanding of Necessity" (195).

In *Sympathy and the State in the Romantic Era* (2007), Mitchell helps us see how Shelley, in a variety of prose texts such as "An Essay on the Punishment of Death," *A Philosophical View of Reform*, and *A Defence of Poetry*, and in his later verse like "The Mask of Anarchy" and the poems of the *Prometheus Unbound* volume, makes a crucial distinction between "a 'savage' mode of impoverished time consciousness that tended to confirm the causal power of the past," and a "philosophic" sense of necessity that "located the origin of the future in the present, rather than the past, and sought to enable potentials, rather than plotting probabilities."[28] Shelly makes the distinction between savage and philosophic necessity in a note to "An Essay on the Punishment of Death":

> The savage and the illiterate are but faintly aware of the distinction between the future and the past; they make actions belonging to periods so distinct, the subjects of similar feelings; they live only in the present, or in the past, as it is present. It is in this that the philosopher excels one of the many; it is this which distinguishes the doctrine of philosophic necessity from fatalism; and that determination of will, by which it is the active source of future events, from that liberty or indifference, to which the abstract liability of irremediable actions is attached, according to the notions of the vulgar.[29]

The "savage" is trapped in a temporal consciousness that is akin to the forms of necessity that Coleridge critiqued in the bibliolatrous. It is only by lifting one's will up out of the fatalism of necessitarian thinking that one can have the agency, capacity for reflection, and determination to make the future one's own.

Mitchell argues that in order to encourage readers to develop their own "capacity for a much more expansive and speculative mode of time consciousness, Shelley developed a series of 'imageless images' designed to counter the belief that individuals were indebted to the past."[30] Readers could become prepared for these "keen, awakening tones" by a poetry that affects us like the "vital alchemy" of Iris, that shape all light encountered by Rousseau in "The Triumph of Life," who when he "Touched with faint lips the cup she raised, / ... suddenly [his] brain became as sand" (404–5). Encounters with "imageless images" are scattered throughout Shelley's canon with another obvious one occurring in "The Masque of Anarchy" when Hope lays herself "down in the street, / Right before the horses' feet" and "between her and her foes / A mist, a light, an image rose, / Small at first, and weak, and frail / Like the vapour of a vale" (98–99, 102–5).

Hume was clearly a key influence on Shelley's efforts to distinguish between a savage necessity wherein "time appeared homogenous" and the past was assumed to be the origin of both the present and the future, and a philosophic necessity wherein the "*present* appeared as the origin of the future (that is, the present is 'the active source of future events')."[31] Hume similarly recognized that "consciousness of the present must be grounded in retention and protention," and that "these three aspects of time consciousness can be linked by two different modes of 'necessity.'"[32] Savage or causal necessity assumed that one thing necessarily followed another. So when the billiard ball is hit, it causes X, which causes Y, etc. Philosophic necessity recognizes that perceptions of causality are merely modes of time consciousness and that there is no actual necessity to any particular imaginative contraction of impressions. The power the savage assumes to be operative out there, in other words, is not actually in the world but in our minds. These assembled "relations are not qualities inherent in objects" and are instead "nothing but an internal impression of the mind" (*T*, 1.3.14.20). What the philosophic mind realizes is that "Our capacity to conjoin impressions ('releasing a rock' + 'rock falling') by means of the idea of causality ('releasing a rock causes it to fall') depended upon the plasticity of the imagination: that is, its ability to contract into an impression two phenomena (releasing; falling), and to ground these in an internal feeling of expectation (when I drop the rock, I expect it will fall)."[33]

Despite all expectations, one day when we release a rock it may fall upward, for whatever reason. What seems to a savage time consciousness to be inevitable is not necessarily so. The contraction occurs only in the mind that contemplates, and things as we imagine them might actually be otherwise.

Although Hume himself thought "we could not help but act as though causality were a real force in both the physical and moral worlds," Shelley is more interested "in probing the conditions of possibility for such perceptions of causality." If the default assumptions of savage necessity tend "to perpetuate existing institutions," then how could a poetics lift its reader up into the realization that things as they are could be otherwise (171)? How could a poet teach us to reread (*re-legere*) the present as the origin of the future rather than as the continuation of the past?

This is where the time-image comes in. Deleuze argued that what one sees when one peers into the time-image is "the gushing of time as dividing in two, as splitting."[34] This splitting is continuous and there is a constant exchange between "the actual image of the present which passes and the virtual image of the past which is preserved" (81). There is an "unequal exchange," or "point of indiscernability" in the time-image because "the dividing in two, the differentiation of the two images, actual and virtual, does not go to the limit, because the resulting circuit repeatedly takes us back from one kind to the other. There is only a vertigo, an oscillation" (84). What is seen in the time-image is the moment in which the relationships between perception and recollection or retention are as of yet undifferentiated—the wonder of the moment prior to the decision about what something means.

To put this in practical terms it is helpful to think of watching a film like Terrence Malick's *The Tree of Life* (2011). In this film the spectator is confronted with a montage of moments, images, and insights that kaleidoscopically shift from scattered moments across the lives of two generations of a West Texas family to depictions of the beginning of time, the creation of the earth, and the evolution of life on it. In any given moment of viewing the film it is quite easy to see what is happening—there is Brad Pitt playing a father who is somewhat estranged from his sons, here are some lingering shots of tree branches, there is a long sequence tracing the evolution of the earth, here is a scene in a church invoking the story of Job, there is a moment when the mother seems to be floating in midair, here is a scene where one dinosaur seems to spare a smaller dinosaur's life. In a normal film running on the principles of the movement-image there wouldn't be any real question as to how these pieces fit together. There may be mystery and suspense involved, but ultimately a savage necessity would smooth out the relations of the film's parts. The time-image works differently, because although it makes the actual image of the present readily available, how the virtual image of that present should be preserved in our time consciousness is left open-ended. This is one reason a film like *The Tree of Life* can be stimulating for discussion, because different viewers will likely hold divergent understandings of what they saw. The fragmented and allusive form of such an experience "isolates textual elements from one another so that each can comment on the others, rather than seeming to be part of an ostensibly harmonious whole."[35] By working in this way, time-images encourage us to make unexpected connections, between, for instance, how a seeming act of mercy among dinosaurs relates to the Oedipal drama of a family in 1950s West Texas.

The time-image loosens the links between retention, perception, and protention, and so when watching Malick's film it doesn't matter when the interactions between the dinosaurs occurred in narrative or evolutionary time: this interaction can still have something to say about the meaning of a family drama that occurs millennia later and vice versa. This is a radically different sense of how events are related, and it is this philosophic form of time consciousness that opens up the possibilities of new forms of political engagement. It is this aspect of the time-image, which Keats was also exploring in 1819, that enabled Shelley to look for a "redemptive mode of sympathy" that was dependent "upon the capacity to read the present as the origin of the future."[36]

Already in "Queen Mab," Shelley is interested in breaking "The icy chains of custom" (1:127), and freeing the heart from "withering custom's cold control" (9:201). Shelley recognized that often the best "the reformer in political and ethical questions" can hope for is to leave "a vacancy," which "reduces the mind to that freedom in which it would have acted, but for the misuse of words and signs, the instruments of its own creation." Such forms of intervention are valuable not because they offer a "new truth," but because they destroy "error, and the roots of error" (S, 507). This is why Shelley's poetry so often taps into forms of passive resistance, enjambment, reticence, and unplugging in order to deconstruct the hold the force Godwin called "institution" has over us, and thereby offering opportunities to move closer to the realization of political justice. Godwin argued that the force of an institution is found not only in its positive presence but also in its capacity to insinuate itself into the habits and practices of everyday life and thereby compel obedience. Political justice will only become realizable if this subtle but insistent binding force can be countered, dissolved, or reformed. However, if this "obscene libidinal foundation" that is the "phantasmic support" of institutional injustice can indeed be unbound, then a "glorious Phantom may / Burst, to illumine our tempestuous day."[37]

Of course a great deal hinges on our reading of the enjambment of this final couplet in Shelley's sonnet "England in 1819." Giorgio Agamben has described enjambment as the *versa* or turning point that gives poetry its versatility; it is an "ambiguous gesture that turns in two opposed directions at once: backwards (*versus*), and forwards (*pro versa*)."[38] There is a queer temporality to the poetics and politics of enjambment and to philosophic necessity more generally, because the meaning of the first word is held in suspension until the arrival of the second. The meaning of both the present and the future may not be determined by the past, but the meaning of the present is still a help in suspension and will look different depending on what the future looks like when it finally does arrive. Thus there is no guarantee or necessity that in any given situation the realization of political justice will actually occur. The "glorious Phantom" *may* burst, but then again it may not. When the events of the past are recalled and folded into present understandings, the soul or spirit of the age that then lay dormant may, or may not, now "illumine our tempestuous day." Just as to think in terms of a savage necessity is a form of false consciousness, so too must the reformer realize that a great deal hinges on how things ultimately turn out. The arc of the moral universe may be long, but it may not necessarily bend toward justice.

Awful Doubt

Shelley is the great proponent within Romanticism of the awful doubt of an enabling skepticism that knows that it exists as a consciousness produced by its ongoing life activity. Such a consciousness knows that what it is doing is a production—that it is artificial, a put-on—it just doesn't know precisely why it is putting on this production (i.e., the cause is absent). The phrase "awful doubt" comes from "Mont Blanc":

> The wilderness has a mysterious tongue
> Which teaches awful doubt, or faith so mild,

> So solemn, so serene, that man may be
> But for such faith with nature reconciled. (76–79)

Although there is a long history of questioning what is meant by these lines, perhaps the best way to understand this "awful doubt" is as the mild faith of philosophic necessity. If all humans could understand was savage necessity, then we would be caught in a world of cause and effect and would thus be "with nature reconciled." As with Coleridge's critique of necessitarianism and bibliolatry, without some way of exercising our will through reflection, philosophic necessity, or some other method of separating the "knower from the known,"[39] and thereby developing the capacity to decide for ourselves what something means, then we would at best be merely passive spectators to existence—mere "quick-silver plating behind a looking-glass" (*BL*, 1:119). Fortunately, due to our capacity for awful doubt we are free to make adjustments to how we view and navigate within the world we find ourselves in.

In Shelley's poetry and prose we see the fullest articulation within Romanticism of the personal and political implications of sympathy and a cinematic empiricism. In his "Speculations on Morals," Shelley remarks on the significance of sympathy to civilization: "An infant, a savage, and a solitary beast, is selfish, because its mind is incapable of receiving an accurate intimation of the nature of pain as existing in beings resembling itself," but "The inhabitant of a highly civilized community will more acutely sympathize with the sufferings and enjoyments of others."[40] The difference between "the selfish man and the virtuous man is, that the imagination of the former is confined within a narrow limit, whilst that of the latter embraces a comprehensive circumference" (189). So much depends on how wide our circle of sympathy extends, and thus there is great importance in facilitating the processes by which the mind "acquires, by exercise, a habit, as it were, of perceiving and abhorring evil, however remote from the immediate sphere of sensations with which that individual mind is conversant" (189). Of course, one of the challenges of developing sympathy is that "to sympathize with the sufferings of another, is to enjoy a transitory oblivion of [one's] own" (188). Sympathetic moments of transitory oblivion can feel threatening particularly if one's own sense of self has become something of an addiction.

Fortunately, Shelley suggests poetry has the capacity to enlarge "the circumference of the imagination" and strengthen "that faculty which is the organ of the moral nature of man, in the same manner as exercise strengthens a limb" (S, 517). Poets are among those who have the capacity to represent and communicate this "unusually intense and vivid apprehension of life," and when these startling apprehensions of life are received by those with ears to hear and eyes to see, then "the painted curtain" of savage necessity can be stripped away from the "scene of things," and a view of life can be retrieved that previously the "habitual sense of its repeated combinations [had] extinguished in us."[41]

Shelley's world, like Hume's, is a world of assemblage, which Davide Panagia describes as a "collection of singular partialities pressing the one upon the other and that, through various intensities of association and dissociation, are brought together or wrought apart."[42] The key to living in such a world, according to Jane Bennet, is realizing how ethical responsibility resides in how we respond to the assemblages in which "we find ourselves participating." The question becomes "[How] do I attempt to extricate myself from assemblages whose trajectory is likely to do harm? How do I enter into the proximity of assemblages [that tend toward] nobler ends?"[43] It is only by addressing these promethean questions that we may find ourselves "Possessing and possessed by all that is / Within that calm circumference of bliss, / And by each other, till to love and live / Be one" (S, "Epipsychidion," 49–52).

The assemblages we find ourselves a part of are made up and dissolved by the harmonies and dissonances produced through the internal adjustments we make to our capacity for sympathy. The power of the imagination lies in its ability to either "do away with resonance or concentrate it," altering in one way or another judgment's "pitch of perfection."[44] It is this capacity for the imaginative formation of assemblies through repetition, resonance, or the contraction of habits, that "constitutes the very essence of power or connexion" (T, 1.3.14.16). One implication of such thinking is that in order to overthrow a pernicious power that is already in effect, it is not enough to simply overthrow the tyrannical figure that embodies that power; one must also work to interrupt and rebind (*re-ligare*) the imaginative formations of assembly that constitute the very essence of that power.[45]

If there is to be the possibility of an affirmative biopolitics, then it is not enough to simply revolt against the tyrant Jupiter. What needs to be unbound is Prometheus himself, or perhaps more precisely the passion for revenge that locks us into a savage time consciousness. An affirmative biopolitics requires not just an overthrow of a particular tyrant but a recalibration of how "the law" is felt in the flesh of the body politic. As many critics have noticed, it is peculiar that within *Prometheus Unbound,* Prometheus, who appears to be the martyr, has a hand in creating Jupiter, the tyrant that tortures him. Prometheus has power over Jupiter because he "Gave wisdom, which is strength, to Jupiter, / And with this law alone, 'Let man be free,' / Clothed him with the dominion of wide Heaven" (II, iv, 44–46). It is only in Prometheus's flesh that Jupiter's authority can be made manifest. If there is to be any hope of a different, and more just, political order, then Prometheus needs to be unbound, because in order to be free one must be released from the ex-citation past actions hold over our affective, conceptual, and imaginative lives.

As Mercury tells Prometheus in act I, "there is a secret known / To thee and to none else of living things, / Which may transfer the sceptre of wide Heaven, / The fear of which perplexes the Supreme." To protect against this fear the "Supreme" Jupiter demands that Prometheus keep his will and soul bent toward the tyrant's throne: "Clothe it in words, and bid it clasp his throne / In intercession; bend thy soul in prayer, / And like a suppliant in some gorgeous fane, / Let the will kneel within thy haughty heart" (I, 371–78). Jupiter demands Prometheus bend his knee and align his will to Jupiter's own.[46] The tyrant makes this demand because he knows "the secret," namely that Prometheus "Clothed him with the dominion of wide Heaven" (II, iv, 46) and that Prometheus like "Thought / Alone, and its quick elements, Will, Passion, / Reason, Imagination, cannot die; / They are . . . / The stuff whence mutability can weave / All that it hath dominion o'er, worlds, worms, / Empires, and superstitions" (S, "Hellas," 795–801). Prometheus "clothed" Jupiter because he is emblematic of the suffering body politic that provides the field or flesh, in Santner's sense of the word, through which mutability weaves its dominion of empire and superstition.

If Prometheus can be unbound, and the ex-citations of past actions can be absolved, then that which now clothes the dominion of wide heaven can be reformed and tailored anew. In such a world, rather than being gong-tormented by past patterns, life's contingencies can be woven together into meaningful and potentially ever-more fashionable assemblages, so that "like lutes / Touched by the skill of the enamoured wind," we can "Weave harmonies divine, yet ever new" (III, iii, 36–38). However, in order to weave anew these strange combinations and harmonies divine, one must first be able to unplug from those assemblages that are overly nostalgic for the return of some previous idea of order. Within the mythopoetics of *Prometheus Unbound* this act of unplugging is figured in the form of the "mystic shell" (III, iii, 70), and when "Thou breathe into the many-folded shell, / Loosening its mighty music;—it shall be / As thunder mingled with clear echoes" (III, iii, 80–82). The effect of this mighty music is to absolve or loosen resentment—a rigidity of both body and mind that can poison the public sphere—so that "Even to the adamantine central gloom / Along [Earth's] marble nerves—'tis life, 'tis joy" (III, iii, 86–87).

The rest of this chapter will consider how the flesh of Prometheus can be unbound from the "passion of revenge," so that the "glorious Phantom" of his soul can be released. However, since within the mythopoetics of *Prometheus Unbound* how this is actually done is quite difficult to discern, in order to clarify how such an act of unbinding might be possible I turn to the tragic case of *The Cenci*, the play that Shelley writes in the middle of his composition of *Prometheus Unbound*. *The Cenci* is a work at the heart of Shelley's thinking in 1819, and as a play intended for theatrical production offers a particularly embodied model of how *poiesis* can work to facilitate the shift from a savage to a more philosophic form of time consciousness—a shift that may be a necessary step in moving beyond the remnants of those more unsavory aspects of political theology that still haunt our age.

The Cenci

In traditional Greek tragedy, the climax of the play occurs in a scene of heroic, and often horrific, self-recognition and enlightenment. Aristotle referred to this moment as the anagnorisis, and in *Suspiria de Profundis* (1845), Thomas De Quincey provides an apt definition of Oedipus's anagnorisis: it is "the recognition of his true identity, which in one moment, and by a horrid flash of revelation, connects him with acts incestuous, murderous, parricidal, in the past, and with a mysterious fatality of woe lurking in the future."[47] In this climactic moment, the tragic hero achieves a transcendent and totalizing vision of the causal web of events he has been caught up in, which finally allows him to recognize his own essential character. In this traditional model, the hero of a tragedy must fall so that the idea or realization implicit within the tragedy can find a space upon the stage to represent itself, thus offering the audience an opportunity to become persuaded as to the fitness of this representation. In other words, the man or woman who masks the idea must be sacrificed so that the idea itself can be recognized. By watching and vicariously experiencing this realization, audience members achieve a catharsis wherein their own anxieties are mimetically scapegoated and sacrificed in the tragic hero's downfall. The audience leaves the theater with renewed resolve to be fit members of society.

Perhaps what is most interesting about *The Cenci* is that in this tragedy the totalizing moment of anagnorisis never occurs.[48] The story of the Cenci family history handed down to Shelley is one where the father, "an old man having spent his life in debauchery and wickedness, conceived at length an implacable hatred towards his children; which showed itself towards one daughter under the form of an incestuous passion, aggravated by every circumstance of cruelty and violence" (S, 141). This daughter, Beatrice, who must endure his implacable hatred, vainly "attempts to escape from what she considered a perpetual contamination both of body and mind," and at length "plotted with her mother-in-law and brother to murder their common tyrant" (S, 141). In the end, her role in the parricide is discovered, and the play ends with preparations for her own execution. Beatrice is not the tragic hero of the play in the traditional sense: she never achieves the anagnorisis, and at the end of the play she instead continues in the delusional belief in her own innocence. Rather than her tragic fall revealing the truth about the way things are and persuading us in a moment of cathartic solidarity that this same truth applies to us, Beatrice's downfall represents something profoundly different. Martyred at the crossroads between the unspeakability of incest and parricide, Beatrice's inability to traverse this ordeal of the undecidable in a satisfactory manner is why her story is tragic, but it is also why her case is so fruitful for analysis.

In his preface to the play, Shelley claimed that "the highest moral purpose aimed at in the highest species of the drama, is the teaching the human heart, through its sympathies and antipathies, the knowledge of itself" (S, 142). For the audience of *The Cenci*, this pedagogic mission is accomplished through "the restless and anatomizing casuistry with which men seek the justification of Beatrice, yet feel that she has done what needs justification" (S, 142). The hope is that through casuistry—or the technique of resolving moral problems through the application of theoretical principles to particular circumstances—the audience will be able to cut the Gordian knot that the case of Beatrice, who endured incestuous rape but initiated parricide, represents to morality.[49] However, this proves to be a difficult if not impossible task, and it is the very presence of this impossible ordeal that makes *The Cenci* such a fascinating play.

Candy Schille argues that there are two central issues that have engrossed readers of *The Cenci*: "the play's contested status as a tragedy" and this question of how to respond to Beatrice's troubling insistence that she is innocent despite the evidence against her.[50] Focusing on the role of Orsino, the conniving priest who attempts to ensnare Beatrice through his various acts of deception, Schille concludes that to read the play as a tragedy is to "preclude any coherence." This incoherence is due to "the absence of true anagnorisis in the case of Beatrice, the ambivalence about its efficacy in the case of Orsino, and the resistance to it in the case of Shelley himself."[51] This lack of anagnorisis within Beatrice has also been recognized by Roger Blood, who argued that an anagnorisis is precisely what is not represented in *The Cenci*, and Michael Kohler, who argues that the anagnorisis is displaced onto Marzio, one of the assassins who carries out Beatrice's plan, who "takes on the guilt of the hero in a self-recognition and self-judgment that calls attention to its uncanny and self-consciously figurative form."[52] I agree that in order to fully understand *The Cenci* we must take into account Beatrice's lack of anagnorisis as well as the peculiar roles Orsino and Marzio play in the drama. Nevertheless, in contrast to Schille's conclusion I argue that by taking these elements into account we can in fact come to an understanding of how Shelley provides a new coherence for tragedy within modernity by encouraging its audience to prepare themselves for a new vision of the future by lifting themselves out of a savage time consciousness and by overcoming the insistent desire for revenge.

Traditional tragedy has often been understood as "a tense balance between free will and fate, the destruction of the supremely human and the revelation of a divine order."[53] In classical tragedy this balance is dramatized through the actions of a tragic hero who "most often dies in coming face to face with the powers that limit man, but out of the destructive confrontation between man's assertion of his own order and the reimposition of an extra-human and perhaps inhuman order arises an expanded sense of both man's power and of the forces that exceed it."[54] However, Jeffery Cox finds the depiction of this balance becomes problematic within modernity as the hierarchies "that defined the hero as sitting atop society were challenged, and in a time of a deep questioning of providential models."[55] It became much more difficult to assume the reality of those heroic or supernatural orders that previous forms of tragedy had been staged to reveal. Thus the problem Shelley confronted was the question of how to reimagine the form and vision of tragedy within a burgeoning democratic world that questions both social hierarchy and the necessity of divine providence.

In the following, I claim *The Cenci*'s exploration of the generic form of tragedy is not only suggestive from a literary standpoint but also has implications for our understanding of broader historical shifts in the logic of sovereignty—from political theology to biopolitics—that resulted in the formation of the modern secular state. I suggest that Beatrice's delusional refusal to take responsibility for her actions and her stubborn unwillingness to break from a social framework that had proven false is presented as a challenge to the audience's own refusal to wake up from the subliminal impulse that keeps them enslaved to the matrix of a discredited social framework. I argue that Shelley presents the case of *The Cenci* so that evidence of his countrymen's own blockages toward progressive change can be submitted into the court of public opinion. In making this argument I first build upon Walter Benjamin's analysis of the representation of sovereignty in Baroque drama and explore how it relates to *The Cenci* and then suggest how Marzio, a relatively minor character in the play, potentially opens up a logical space beyond the conceptual deadlock of Baroque sovereignty.[56] Ultimately, I suggest *The Cenci* not only dramatizes the philosophical view of reform that characterizes so much of Shelley's creative output following the Peterloo Massacre but can also help us more clearly speculate upon the role the tragic imagination has to play within modernity.

Tyrant/Martyr/Plotter

The story of Beatrice and her family, in both the historical situation of 1599 and in Shelley's theatrical representation in 1819, are representative of an experience that is outside of given norms and that traces a rupture where an older normative scheme is called into question and new forms of political, social, and religious responsibility attempt to emerge. However, it is important to note that what makes Beatrice's story so captivating is her failure to rise above her impulsive necessity for revenge and emerge as a responsible subject. This failure is due to what Shelley calls a "pernicious mistake" (S, 142), and it is because of Beatrice's steadfast desire for revenge that she remains a tragic rather than an enlightened figure.

To understand what Beatrice's "pernicious mistake" was, it is important to recognize how the play's religious, political, and aesthetic tensions were played out against the background of an increasingly secularized worldview affected by the Enlightenment, which, as Carl Schmitt argued, had experienced a shift in the basis of sovereignty and political theology from one founded upon a notion of transcendence to one of governance through immanence. According to Schmitt, the philosophy of state in the seventeenth and the eighteenth centuries subscribed to the notion of the transcendence of the sovereign vis-à-vis the state in analogy to the transcendence of God over nature. The nineteenth century, however, was increasingly governed by representations of immanence. This new world wherein immanence was privileged over transcendence had profound implications for religion, politics, and aesthetic representation; namely, how then do we understand the exceptional—that which is outside (and seemingly transcendent to) everyday life? Famously, Schmitt attempts to answer this question in *Political Theology* with the following dictum: "Sovereign is he who decides on the exception (*Ausnahmezustand*)."[57] He also links the radical nature of the sovereign's decision, executed during a state of exception, to the theological concepts of miracle and creation ex nihilo. In his view, the state of exception that constitutes the object and product of the sovereign decision is paradoxically one that threatens or calls into question the existence of the state while at the same time providing that state with its (renewed) basis for survival.

In his *The Origin of German Tragic Drama* (1928), Walter Benjamin cites Schmitt's theory of the exception and applies it to his own explication of the origins of German tragic drama or mourning plays (*Trauerspiel*) in the Baroque period. However, within this application Benjamin subtly redefines the relationship between sovereignty and the state of exception in ways that have significant implications for our understanding of *The Cenci*.[58] Benjamin disagrees with Schmitt's analogy that the sovereign transcends the state just as God transcends creation and wants to replace this analogy of being (*analogia entis*) with a more sophisticated notion of secularization. For Benjamin, the Baroque sovereign is defined by his difference from God, just as the new worldview of immanence is distinct from the medieval worldview of theological transcendence. The paradox for Benjamin is that at the very moment the political sovereign begins to successfully free himself from the grip of the church, the difference between worldly and divine power becomes apparent.

In a Baroque world that refuses any limitation of immanence, the task of the sovereign is not to decide the exception but to exclude it—perhaps by placing it beyond the realm of questioning or by concealing it altogether. The sovereign seeks the transcendence of transcendence by making it immanent, but this is an impossible task. Ultimately, the sovereign can neither decide nor exclude the exception, and it is in this failure that Benjamin locates the origin of the *Trauerspiel*. The sovereign reacts to the tragedy of his impotence by either attempting to gather all the power and thus becoming a tyrant or by going in the opposite direction and becoming a martyr crucified upon the radical disjunction of being both a sovereign and a creature at the same time. The figures of the tyrant and the martyr on the Baroque stage are "the Janus-heads of the crowned . . . the necessarily extreme forms of the princely character." [59] However, Benjamin also delineates a third stock character of the *Trauerspiel*, the plotter (*der Intrigant*), and it is he who actually holds the keys to sovereignty. The plotter knows that there is no totality within which the world is enclosed and no eschaton from which the plot can be seen as complete. In a world of immanence, there is no transcendent position from which an Aristotelian unity of action can finally justify the sovereign decision. Rather, the world is a stage upon which the "sheer arbitrariness of a constantly shifting emotional storm" blows about the figures on the stage "like torn and flapping banners." [60] The plot has been replaced by plotting, and the plotter confronts a world in which the exception has become the rule. All that can be done is to orchestrate the action on the stage in hopes of producing the best outcome.

Benjamin's political anthropology of the Baroque stage has clear resonances with *The Cenci*, and his three primary types—tyrant, martyr, and plotter—are figured in Shelley's play by Count Cenci, Beatrice, and Orsino. Explicating how these characters overlap with Benjamin's types helps clarify what is at stake in the play. In addition, I argue that Shelley introduces a fourth type in his own political anthropology, which is embodied in the figure of Marzio, and it is through Marzio that Shelley presents us with a potential opening beyond the deadlock of Baroque sovereignty, an opening that can orient us toward a potential postsecular future, but more on that in a moment.

In Benjamin's analysis, the sovereign's dilemma is that "however highly he is enthroned over subject and state, his status is confined to the world of creation; he is the lord of creatures, but he remains a creature." [61] The logical conundrum is that the sovereign is both outside of and transcendent to the world of creation while at the same time remaining embodied within this world as a creature. In other words, in the Baroque the king's two bodies, as defined by the political theology of the Middle Ages, were no longer coincident with each other, and the sovereign's ideal and creaturely bodies threatened to split apart violently. The sovereign often reacts by attempting to gather all power by eliminating all opposition and thereby becoming a tyrant. Nevertheless, as we find depicted both in the tragedies Benjamin analyzed and in *The Cenci*, the frequent result of such tyranny is that this "summit of creation, erupting into madness like a volcano and destroying himself and his entire court," finally "falls victim to the disproportion between the unlimited hierarchical dignity with which he is divinely invested and the humble estate of his humanity" (70). Count Cenci is a clear example of such a tyrant, and his compulsive need for closure and self-certainty manifests itself as a willingness to eliminate (or build a wall around) anything that threatens his sense of wholeness. He murders, desires the death of his sons, and rapes his daughter—that "particle" of his "divided being" (4.1.135)—all so he can be certain of who he is and be secure in his position as master of all.

The count's tyranny has some clear resonances with Sigmund Freud's myth of the primal horde, as well as with Carl Schmitt's theories of sovereignty and the state of exception. These resonances become evident through a comparison of Count Cenci to Kenneth Reinhard's formulation, in *The Neighbor: Three Inquiries in Political Theology* (2005), of the overlap between the analyses of Freud and Schmitt. "The sovereign is like the primal father in being stationed at the margins of the state he regulates: it is only insofar as there can be a radical exception to the law that the law can exist and be effective. The primal father and the sovereign occupy the position of extreme dictators whose word both violates the rule of the total state and promises it totality, closure, drawing a line between the inside and the outside, the native and the stranger."[62] Cenci is "like the primal father" stationed at the margins of the state he regulates. In fact, during the feast he throws to celebrate the death of his sons, he calls himself an "Anchorite," "one who has secluded himself from the world, usually for religious reasons" (S, 151). Each time Cenci secludes himself from the world, due to his various transgressive crimes, he returns by bargaining for a dispensation from the church. This is one way in which Cenci is the anchor for his community—he flagrantly transgresses the law, then pays to be forgiven for this transgression, and through this return the church becomes wealthier, and the mutually beneficial system of rationalized religion and nation-state is supported. Thus, Cenci is like the primal father who "both violates the rule of the total state and promises it totality."[63]

Throughout the play there is a confusion between Cenci, the figure of the "father" in general, and that "great father of all" (1.3.26)—God. Beatrice, for instance, after her offstage rape asks, "Thou, great God, / Whose image upon earth a father is, / Dost thou indeed abandon me?" (2.1.20–22). This suggests a confusion in Beatrice between Cenci and God, because she presumes that a father, and specifically her father, is God's earthly representative. This *analogia entis* is doubly pertinent because Cenci is also in a sovereign position politically. As we shall see, part of the reason Beatrice commits her "pernicious mistake" of revenge is due to the fact that she is unable to separate her perception of the creaturely man that her father is from the idealized sovereign position that he occupies. A similar instance of fatherly misrecognition occurs in the scene in Cenci's bedchamber when Marzio and Olimpio are about to murder the count. First, Olimpio is unable to go through with the crime because his will is quelled by the look of "an old and sleeping man; / His thin gray hair, his stern and reverent brow, / His veined hands crossed on his heaving breast, / And the calm innocent sleep in which he lay" (4.3.22–25). With this image of paternal peace before him, Olimpio is unable to carry out the murderous plot. Then Marzio, who "was bolder," brought his knife to Cenci's "loose wrinkled throat," but he too is foiled because at that moment the old man stirred in his sleep; he said "God! hear, O, hear, / A father's curse! What, art though not our father?" and then laughed. Despite having witnessed this strangely blasphemous scene, Marzio nevertheless "knew it was the ghost / Of my dead father speaking through his lips, / And could not kill him" (4.3.30–35). Both Olimpio and Marzio are stifled in their actions by their transfer of affect from a familial relationship with their own fathers to this man who occupies the structural position of "father" within the system of sovereignty.

As a tyrant, Cenci differs from other men because he is without "remorse" and has "little fear," and for this reason he does not have "the checks" that other men do on their behavior (1.1.88–89). This lack of any check is what makes Cenci so dangerous. During the feast Cenci throws to celebrate the death of his sons, a guest rises in disgust and asks, "Will none among this noble company / Check the abandoned villain?" (1.3.100–101). However, no one will—all are too fearful and too cowed by Cenci to do anything. As Lucretia later says to her stepdaughter Beatrice, "And every one looked in his neighbor's face / To see if others were as white as he?" (2.1.44–45). Even religion is no check to Cenci, in part because the pope feels that if he were deprived of Cenci's devious ways he would also be deprived "of a certain and copious source of revenue" (S, 141). Religion fails to curb Cenci because, as Shelley says in the preface, "Religion pervades intensely the whole frame of society, and is according to the temper of the mind which it inhabits, a passion, a persuasion, an excuse, a refuge"; thus, it is "never a check" (S, 143).

The only real obstacle to Cenci's will is Beatrice, who, during the feast, "alone stood up, and with strong words / Checked his unnatural pride" (2.1.49–50). She tries to entreat the men to turn against her father's tyranny and torture, but to no avail. Unfortunately, this attempted betrayal further aggravates Cenci and leads to the incestuous crime. As Cardinal Camillo points out, previously the father had already been afraid "to read upon" his children's looks "the shame and misery" he had written there (1.1.44–45). Now that Beatrice has stood up to him, however briefly, Cenci's fear borders on paranoia. He is suspicious and almost delusional, fearing "the all-beholding sun" and the "garish, broad, and peering day," which is "Loud, light, suspicious, full of eyes and ears" (2.1.186–90). In order to ease his own suffering and to avoid the gaze of judgment, the father plans "a deed which shall confound both night and day" (2.1.195). This act of incest would "soon extinguish all" and allow him to "walk secure and unbeheld towards" his purpose (2.1.200–205). Incest would allow him to "extinguish all" because the crime would erase the final prohibition that is excluded from his totalizing ambition. If incest is a crime that transcends all limits of moral purview, then by committing this crime, Cenci, from his own deranged point of view, would be able to transcend transcendence and achieve a totalizing mastery over all. Of course things do not work out the way Cenci plans, and he ends up the victim of parricide.

According to Shelley's preface, Beatrice, "the young maiden, who was urged to this tremendous deed by an impulse which overpowered its horror, was evidently a most gentle and amiable being, a creature formed to adorn and be admired, and thus violently thwarted from her nature by the necessity of circumstance and opinion" (S, 141). It is significant that Beatrice is called a "creature" in this description. The word "creature" is derived from "the future-active participle of the Latin verb *creare* ('to create'); creature indicates a made or fashioned thing but with the sense of continued or potential process, action, or emergence built into the future thrust of its active verbal form." The creature is a thing always in the process of creation, always open to change and "subject to transformation at the behest of the arbitrary commands of an Other."[64] However, as the preface informs us, it is exactly Beatrice's "gentle and amiable" creaturely openness that is "violently thwarted" by "the necessity of circumstance and opinion" (S, 141). This openness is thwarted because Beatrice is fixated on, and even mesmerized by, the impulse to kill her father in revenge.

As mentioned earlier, the concept of creature is also important for Benjamin in his definition of the sovereign's dilemma: "He is the lord of creatures, but he remains a creature."[65] Benjamin sees the creature as being internally divided into two overlapping forms of too-muchness, in a manner similar to the dilemma of the king's two bodies. As Lupton puts it, "From one point of view the Creature is too much body, collecting in its leaden limbs the earthenness and passionate intensity of mere life uninspired by form. From another the Creature suffers from too much soul, taking flight as 'speculation,' as reason soaring beyond its own self-regulating parameters toward a second-order materiality of signifiers unfixed to signifieds."[66] The creature is divided because it is burdened with the uninspired and unredeemed materiality of the body, while at the same time desiring to move beyond the body and into a world of ideal speculation. In a sense this is the flip side of the sovereign dilemma, and one reason why Beatrice as martyr is the "Janus-head" of her father's tyranny. The tyrant is willing to give up the ideal so he can become all body, while the martyr will give up the body in order to become all ideal.

Beatrice is led toward the path of martyrdom because of Cenci's incestuous crime against her body, and she begins to develop a creaturely double consciousness because "her spirit apprehends the sense of pain, / But not its cause" (3.1.38–39). After her father's crime, Beatrice asks herself, "What thing am I?" She "can feign no image" in her mind "of that which has transformed" her, and she feels alone in her "formless horror" because "if another ever knew aught like to it," then that other died like Beatrice will die, leaving the thing "without a name" (3.1.121–30). We are told that before her father raped her, he said "one little word" (2.1.69). However, the audience never learns what this word was, nor can Beatrice speak it. If she could name the crime, and "find a word that might make known / The crime of my destroyer; and that done, / My tongue should like a knife tear out the secret / Which cankers my heart's core" (3.1.172–75). Beatrice is even willing to mutilate herself to achieve the anagnorisis that will grant her self-knowledge, but she cannot find the word that will give her (cathartic) release. Frustrated from achieving release through self-knowledge, she chooses a more perilous path and plots the parricide of her father, the bodily cause of her mental distortion. In this pursuit, she is "urged to this tremendous deed by an impulse which overpowered its horror" (S, 141). Following this impulse is a "pernicious mistake," because doing so binds Beatrice to a set of relations whose consequences are beyond her control.

As discussed earlier, Beatrice had a tendency to confuse her earthly father and sovereign lord with God himself. As she said after her rape, "Thou, great God, / Whose image upon earth a father is, / Dost thou indeed abandon me?" (2.1.20–22). This confusion of signs between father, sovereign, and God keeps Beatrice committed to an idealized system of relations despite her own father's betrayal of that system. When her earthly father behaves in a manner reprehensible to his position as God's sovereign representative, she feels compelled to set in motion her father's death; however, her continued fixation on the position of sovereignty itself makes her unable to either take responsibility for her actions or to have enough guile to avoid getting caught. This is evident in her final exchange with Legate Savella: "Guilty! Who dares talk of guilt? My Lord, / I am more innocent of parricide / Than is a child born fatherless" (4.4.136–38). She claims innocence because surely her father's actions prove he is not her father, for her true father could do no such thing. And even after Marzio has confessed the crime and implicated Beatrice in it, she nevertheless claims:

> That poor wretch
> Who stands so pale, and trembling, and amazed,
> If it be true he murdered Cenci, was
> A sword in the right hand of justest God.
> Wherefore should I have wielded it? Unless
> The crimes which mortal tongue dare never name
> God therefore scruples to avenge. (4.4.148–54)

In other words, she and Marzio were simply instruments implementing God's will and thus bear no responsibility for the crime. She will only admit to having "desired his death" but lays no claim to the outcome:

> 'Tis true I did believe, and hope, and pray,
> Ay, I even knew ... for God is wise and just,
> That some strange sudden death hung over him.
> 'Tis true that this did happen, and most true
> There was no other rest for me on earth,
> No other hope in Heaven ... now what of this? (4.4.160–65)

In essence, what Beatrice is willing to admit is the inverse of Cenci's prayer for his sons' deaths. Cenci, the tyrant, justifies his totalizing power by God's fulfillment of his prayers, while Beatrice, the martyr, legitimates her innocence and purity by God's fulfillment of her desire. Of course, both father and daughter are delusional. The count is not all powerful, nor is Beatrice all pure.

Beatrice's inability to break the spell of her subliminal "impulse" toward parricide or take responsibility for her actions leads to her downfall. As Shelley writes in the preface, "Undoubtedly, no person can be truly dishonoured by the act of another; and the fit return to make to the most enormous injuries is kindness and forbearance, and a resolution to convert the injurer from his dark passions by peace and love. Revenge, retaliation, atonement, are pernicious mistakes" (S, 142). What Shelley is describing here is the radical logic of the law of reflection—to turn the other cheek. This logic suggests that if we are injured, then we must decathect from the drive toward revenge and strive to make ourselves the example or occasion that figures or reflects through a form of passive resistance the dark passions of the injurer so that the other can see things as they really are and thus act upon and improve this reality. And "if Beatrice had thought in this manner she would have been wiser and better; but she would never have been a tragic character" (S, 142). Beatrice is a tragic character because she, like most of us given the same situation, could not live up to this neighborly ideal.

However, Beatrice is a tragic figure in an untraditional way. Rather than her tragic fall revealing the truth about the way things are and persuading us in a moment of cathartic solidarity that this same truth applies to us, Beatrice's downfall represents something profoundly different. Her delusional refusal to take responsibility for her actions and her stubborn unwillingness to break from a social framework that has proven itself false is presented as a challenge to the audience's own refusal to wake up from the subliminal "impulse" that keeps them enslaved to the matrix of a discredited social framework. Shelley presents the case of *The Cenci* so that evidence of his countrymen's own blockages toward progressive change can be submitted for analysis in the court of public opinion.

The implications of Beatrice's "pernicious mistake" become clearer when compared to remarks Shelley makes about the French Revolution in "A Philosophical View of Reform." Here Shelley argues,

> The oppressed, having been rendered brutal, ignorant, servile and bloody by slavery, having had the intellectual thirst, excited in them by the progress of civilization, satiated from fountains of literature poisoned by the spirit and the form of monarchy, arose to take a dreadful

revenge on their oppressors. Their desire to wreak revenge, to this extent, in itself a mistake, a crime, a calamity, arose from the same source as their other miseries and errors, and affords an additional proof of the necessity of that long-delayed change which it accompanied and disgraced.[67]

Shelley critiques the desire to wreak revenge displayed in the aftermath of the French Revolution and traces the source of this desire to a tendency to bind their "passions as well as judgements" to the external form of things, a tendency instilled in them by cultural institutions and a national literature that Shelley calls "weak, superficial, vain, [and] with little imagination." Shelley argues that their "institutions made them what they are" and incapacitated them "from arriving at the exercise of the highest powers to be attained by man." The French Revolution was ultimately unsuccessful because although it "overthrew the hierarchy, the aristocracy and the monarchy, and the whole of that peculiarly insolent and oppressive system on which they were based," it nevertheless "only partially extinguished those passions which are the spirit of these forms," which resulted in a reaction that "restored in a certain limited degree the old system."[68] In other words, the French Revolution failed because it did not fully reform the passions that affected the flesh of the body politic, and the people were thus unable to arrive at the soulful exercise of "the highest powers to be attained by man." One can only arrive at this pinnacle through a skeptical divestment from passionate attachment.

A philosophical view of reform requires the reformation of the passions because affective attachment is the missing link that drives the symbolic machinery of the law. Our passionate attachments are how words are made flesh; they embody the processes "by which a made world of culture acquires the characteristics of 'reality.'"[69] As Eric Santer argues with respect to Benjamin's essay "*Zur Kritik der Gewalt*" ("Critique of Violence"), the "rule of law is, in the final analysis, without ultimate justification or legitimation, . . . the very space of juridical reason within which the rule of law obtains is established and sustained by a dimension of force and violence that, as it were, holds the place of those missing foundations."[70] Not unlike Shelley's Anarchy, who says "I AM GOD, AND KING, AND LAW" (S, 317), Benjamin understands the rule of law to be supported by a tautological enunciation: "The law is the law."[71] Such tautological assumptions can only be supported by a passionate attachment to the truth of this proposition, an attachment inculcated in subjects through the threat of violence as well as through more subtle forms of institutional persuasion. The challenge political reform faces is that such passionate attachments are essentially subliminal or infrasensible and endure even after the particular arrangements of a given institutional order are overthrown.[72]

What is necessary for a more lasting transformation of the social order is what Santner has called "unplugging," which is theorized "as an interruption not so much of the law's rules and regulations but of the meaningless force it exerts upon us."[73] It is only through an interruption of our passionate attachments that we can respond more appropriately to those states of exception, which serve as the violent, unlawful foundation of the law itself. However, such unplugging does not expose the real nature of things. Instead, it only enables us to drop the "allusion to some external point of reference which eludes the Symbolic."[74] Nevertheless, by dropping this allusion we can turn away from the tautology assumed in a form of sovereignty that decides its own exception and towards more neighborly forms of responsibility, ones that encourage us to unplug from the hypnotic hold our passionate attachments often have over us. However, despite the optimism of this effort the tragedy of secular responsibility is that a full and honest appreciation of our passionate attachments is at the very least difficult and such analysis may in fact be interminable, thus potentially postponing indefinitely the exercise of free decision.

Nevertheless, I argue that Shelley intends *The Cenci* to be a dramatization of the need for precisely this kind of unplugging or divestment from the forms of passionate attachment that underlie belief. Although Beatrice through her "pernicious mistake" eluded the experience of an enlightened emergence of responsibility, her extreme case still helps articulate how in a similar circumstance one might be able to break the hypnotic hold of both tradition and the desire for revenge, experiencing instead a progressive form of anagnorisis. If this is done, then it becomes possible to tap into the enabling skepticism of an "awful doubt."

Our understanding of the implications of Beatrice's downfall can be advanced by recognizing how the use of religious belief as a form of justification is challenged in Shelley's drama by the playwright's implicit recognition of a disconnect between what characters say they believe and how they act. This question of imposture is evident in *The Cenci* in the behavior of both the count, who despite his belief is not really in the same position as God, and Beatrice, who despite her protestations to the contrary is not entirely innocent either. The disconnect exhibited in the impostures of both father and daughter is illustrative of the profound tensions in both their creaturely lives, lives that are being split apart into the too-muchness of an unredeemed body and the too-muchness of a wildly speculative mind. The tyrant attempts to resolve this crisis by embracing materiality and ignoring the intellect, while the martyr renounces the body in a flight toward the speculative.

Within Benjamin's political anthropology of the *Trauerspiel* the plotter (*der Intrigant*) is the third that emerges from the cleaving of sovereignty into tyrant and martyr. The plotter is so important for this form of the tragic because with the dissolution of a unified concept of sovereignty comes the dissolution of the unity of action and character that was the basis of the Aristotelian theory of tragedy. The tragic plot is no longer a movement from ignorance to acceptance of a divine providence or of fate, which in a moment of anagnorisis is seen to be the true organizing force of our lives. Rather, the plot is now a rhythm of arbitrary events that blow about the figures on the (world's) stage "like torn and flapping banners."[75] Only the plotter takes advantage of these events, because he is the only one who recognizes that they are not based on rules or on any necessity—they are all arbitrary exceptions to what we naïvely assume to be the fixed rules of reality. This arbitrariness is evident throughout *The Cenci*: the count escapes death at the chasm by passing the appointed spot an hour too soon; the two murderers initially stumble in their crime when Cenci begins talking in his sleep; the pine tree catches the body of Cenci before it hits the ground, thus preserving the evidence that his death was not by suicide; the two murderers are caught because the light reflecting off Marzio's golden coat gives away their position; Beatrice and her family are implicated in the crime because the murderers kept Orsinio's letter on them; and if Savilla had arrived an hour earlier with his execution orders for Cenci, then there wouldn't have been a crime at all. If any of these things had happened differently, there would not have been a tragedy. However, there is no indication in the play that any of these events were fated to happen; they were all arbitrary or contingent events. Had Beatrice not been so desperately fixated on revenge and shown at least a little cunning, she could probably have carried out her plot without detection by constructing a plan that built into it at least some calculation of the potential risks. She fails to do so because by being a slave to her desire she is unable to act rationally or be open to contingency.

Within the logic of *The Cenci*, Orsino is the character whose role is closest to the ideal of the plotter. Of all the characters, only Orsino, by accepting that he lives in a world where the exception has become the rule, seems free to calculate and orchestrate the action on the stage in the hope of producing the best outcome. Admittedly, he is not the noblest of creatures and his motivations are base, but he is able to see through the imposture of his social system. He has no confusions about sovereigns being gods or about all fathers being good. His motto is take what you can when you can, but get away when you must, and thus he is self-conscious in his scheming. He is the one who continually—and consciously—sets actions in motion through his plotting. He is the one who first desires to bed Beatrice, and it is through him that the plot to kill Cenci advances. He attempts to acquire what he wants by indirectly using others as his agents:

> When dread events are near, stir up men's minds
> To black suggestions; and he prospers best,
> Not who becomes the instrument of ill,
> But who can flatter the dark spirit, that makes
> Its empire and its prey of other hearts
> Till it become his slave . . . as I will do. (2.2.166–71)

Orsino does not attempt to enslave others to his will as a tyrant does, nor does he allow himself to become an instrument of ideology the way a martyr might. Rather, he manipulates events so that others become enslaved by the greed or naïveté of their own "dark spirit[s]." In essence, Orsino is in different ways the prototype of both the modern capitalist entrepreneur and the modern political spin doctor. He has the ability to advance an enterprise by his calculation of risk, and he is adept at manufacturing consent through subtle acts of influence, framing, and statesmanship. Of course, in this particular case things did not go as planned, and while Orsino was hoping for a "solemn comedy," he received instead "a net of ruin" due to the interference of "a Power / Which graspt and snapped the threads of [his] device" (5.1.85–90). However, this power is neither that of divinity nor fate but is rather an invocation of the sheer arbitrariness of events themselves. Nevertheless, in the end he is free to slip away in his own act of imposture "wrapt in a vile disguise; / Rags on my back, and a false innocence / Upon my face, thro' the misdeeming crowd / Which judges by what seems" (5.1.93–96). Orsino is able to escape because he recognizes the space between what is and "what seems," and it is through this crack that he slips away and exits the play a free man.

Marzio's Minor Gesture

But if Orsino ultimately fails us, where then should we turn for a way out of the Janus-faced deadlock of the tyrant/martyr dynamic we find in *The Cenci*? I argue that Marzio is the key, particularly in those scenes toward the end where he is tortured. In the play, torture functions as a kind of substitute for the anagnorisis, where in a terrifying manner the tortured are forced to accept the fitness that what the system they are fated to live under says is true, is true. Those undergoing torture are compelled to proclaim the truth of what the state says about them, and, as Santner has argued, the "torture victim's abject body is the 'privileged' site of politicotheological epiphany," an epiphany that keeps the secret that the state is really based on a tautology: "the law is the law."[76] The law is the law because in moments of divine violence it can compel us that this is so. Beatrice protests against this very aspect of the "wicked farce" of torture when her family is threatened with forced confessions via torture after her father's death (5.2.38). The problem with torture as a means of learning the truth is that when "some obscure and trembling slave is dragged / From sufferings which might shake the sternest heart / And bade to answer, not as he believes, / But as those may suspect or do desire," then the torturer's questions "suggest their own reply" (5.2.50–55). As long as the rack is the medium of communication, the tortured will say whatever the torturer tells him to say. Using torture in this way is pointless, because the questioner may not learn anything more than what he is already suggesting is the truth, but effective, because the tortured will confess to anything the torturer wants, whether it is true or not.

Torture ultimately "bottoms out, touches on a dimension of vicious circularity that cannot be avowed if these social facts are to continue to enjoy credibility, if the social field structured by them is to remain consistent for the subject."[77] In this way, torture is similar to mesmerism because torture confuses the two poles of torturer and the tortured, and as a result the tortured merely passively (but painfully) ventriloquizes the answers to the torturer's demands. However, as the case of Marzio demonstrates, there are exceptions to this rule. What is particularly interesting is that in effect Marzio is trapped between two diametrically opposed forms of compulsion. At first Marzio confesses everything upon the rack, but a change occurs when he is brought before Beatrice to directly present evidence against her. When confronted with Beatrice's "solemn tones," Marzio "shrinks from her / regard like autumn's leaf / From the keen breath of the serenest north" and trembles on "the giddy verge / Of life and death" (5.2.130–39). Beatrice then presents a speech that makes him change his tune by using "a keener pain" to wring a "higher truth" from his "last breath" (5.2.190–91). In this speech, she reflects upon how her father had "stabbed with one blow" her "everlasting soul" and how, after this act of soul murder, her hate "became the only worship [she] could lift to our great father" (5.2.150–51). She then demands that Marzio not use his words to kill "her and all her kin" because although "her wrongs could not be told, not thought," nevertheless, "she endured what never any / Guilty or innocent endured before" (5.2.162–66). In other words, she is an exception that cannot be found guilty because the crime committed against her was so heinous that it is beyond not only the rule of law but also that of language and thought as well.

Beatrice suggests that the "little word" that would name what she endured transcends the system of signifiers and cannot be brought into the totality of what can be spoken or thought (2.1.69). However, although this "little word" is exceptional in every way, to exclude it would be to exclude that "which is the life of life" (4.4.170). To conclude her argument, Beatrice says to Marzio:

> *Think*, I adjure you, what it is to slay
> The reverence living in the minds of men
> Towards our ancient house, and stainless fame!
> *Think* what it is to strangle infant pity,
> Cradled in the belief of guileless looks,
> Till it become a crime to suffer. *Think*
> What 'tis to blot with infamy and blood
> All that which shows like innocence, and is,
> Hear me, great God! I swear, most innocent,
> So that the world lose all discrimination
> Between the sly, fierce, wild regard of guilt,
> And that which now compels thee to reply
> To what I ask: Am I, or am I not
> A parricide? (5.2.167–80; emphasis added)

In effect, Beatrice is asking Marzio to "think," and argues that if he uses his words to accuse her, then he is closing the totality of law, life, language, and thought to the possibility of this "little word"—to this exception to the rule. If Marzio speaks what he is compelled to speak by his torturers, then the world will "lose all discrimination," and there will be no space for individual agency within the savage necessity of the modern state, even if this agency is only that of a "sly, fierce," and guilty conscience. This argument proves to be at least momentarily convincing because following it Marzio proclaims Beatrice's innocence, although whether Marzio changes his mind freely or because of Beatrice's use of a "keener pain" is an open question. Nevertheless, this second shift leaves Marzio placed precariously between the demands of two mutually exclusive claims, and so when he is once again taken to be tortured into reaffirming the truth of his former position, he utilizes the one option left open to him: he smiles "as one who baffles a deep adversary; / And holding his breath, died" (5.2.212–14).

Marzio was trapped between two forms of tautology—between the state's secret that "the law is the law" and Beatrice's suggestion that she did not commit a parricide because her father's actions prove he is not her father. Faced with deciding between two competing tautologies, Marzio does a perplexing thing: he withholds his breath and smiles. By withholding his breath in this way, he refuses to realign his flesh with the state's violent persuasiveness and thus breaks the hypnotic hold that the state's threat of violence has over his passionate attachments. Furthermore, Marzio withholds not only his spirit or will but also his smile or pleasure, and this withholding has the potential of making us conscious of that blind spot that institutes a coherent field of ideological vision. For in a sense, ideology is taking pleasure in a particular tautology. Marzio accomplishes this affective anagnorisis by placing his tortured body at the greatest possible distance from the demands that he is called upon by the state to embody. This can be considered an instance of affective anagnorisis, because rather than imbibing a revelatory rush of positive knowledge, all Marzio's actions assume is that in a world that can never be seen from a totalizing perspective the ultimate justification of one's own passionate attachments becomes a matter of critical concern.

In *The Tragic Imagination* (2016), Rowan Williams suggests that what tragedy at its best offers is not a finished narrative but only "the continuing exposure of ourselves to ever-new perspectives on the danger concealed in where and who we think we are." Nevertheless, this simple act of "liturgical showing-forth" can enable us to witness disaster in ways that can change "the world we inhabit" (27). What tragedy ultimately reveals is a form of "thinking that arises from the 'passion' involved in digging down to the level of affect where our habitual forms of self-relatedness are buried" (54). One way tragedy does so is by staging the downfall of figures like Beatrice and the count, or in a not unrelated way, Antigone and Creon. These characters fall because they are too "invested in their convictions in a way that denies or subverts the possibility of truthful thinking." The problem with these passionate convictions is that they became so central to their sense of self that these characters can only see themselves as "aesthetic objects, as sharing the static givenness of the images of the divine which they look to" (58). What these figures fail to recognize is that self-identity is always something of a put-on.

In the end, the tyrant and the martyr both fail because each feels equally justified: "Each will maintain an unflinching commitment to what they believe is right because it is felt as a commitment to their own identity or integrity" (59). By making themselves fixed objects of contemplation they can only maintain their own integrity through a "terminal rivalry with the claims of other selves," which dooms them to destruction (66). What these figures fail to realize, but what Marzio's minor gesture at the end of the play may suggest, is the significance of a postsecular neighborliness within modernity, one that finds "meaning and integrity in the shared enterprise of thinking, the unfolding of 'spirit' in mutual recognition and misrecognition" (63). Thus I ultimately read *The Cenci* as a tragedy rather than a *Trauerspiel*, because like all good tragedy it helps us identify "the universal and unavoidable moments in the evolution of the conscious self when we create selves" (69).

For Benjamin, the *Trauerspiel* was a mourning play because it lamented the loss of a coherent universe and contemplated "the unyielding hostility of the cosmos to human subjectivity" (146). This form of the tragic narrates suffering and offers spectators an opportunity "to reflect on subjectivity and its trials, the modern subject adrift from shared meaning, let alone cosmic meaning." In Benjamin's reading, these dramas sketched the deep chasm between the meaningful subject and the meaningless world, a gulf that could only be crossed "by 'divine violence,' by the apocalyptic arrival of a justice or order so radically transcendent that it cannot be spoken of in advance—revolutionary terror or messianic reconciliation" (145).

In *The Origin of German Tragic Drama*, Benjamin writes that "the only word which can breathe is unknown [*Aber eines ungekannte allein*]. Heroic defiance contains this unknown word, locked within itself."[78] Benjamin saw this kind of tragic silence as an instance of hubris, defined as "the hero's refusal to justify himself in the face of the gods," a refusal which marks the site of that decisive confrontation [*Auseinandersetzung*] said to structure the space of tragedy. However, in his view this silence is not the result of a failure of language; rather, such silence can be considered "language in its most originary and proper sense."[79]

If we only had the story of Beatrice and her father, then *The Cenci* would fit more fully in the *Trauerspiel* tradition, since, as Jeffrey Cox noted, the play "offers the period's most complex dramatization of the romantic protagonist's turn to the interior in the wake of the collapse of social and cosmic order."[80] The play's final focus on Marzio, however, suggests a different way of understanding the tragic imagination. In this view, the world that is "properly and adequately 'thought' is a world in which the subject recognizes itself in the other and is not competing with the other to define shared meanings."[81]

If for Benjamin the plotter is the figure on the Baroque stage who functions in the space between tyrant and martyr, then for Shelley Marzio embodies the space between the passionate but naïve belief of the vengeful Beatrice and the calculating but potentially terrifying governmentality of secular authority. To be made conscious of this narrow space—the only space left for Marzio's soul to occupy—forces the audience to make a decision: where should he or we align our pleasure? With the state? With Beatrice? How can we decide what this play means? Marzio's act, of withholding his own breath while also offering a smile, redistributes responsibility for the decision. The answer is not given to us. Instead, to make sense of the play and Marzio's place in it, each reader must redeem its meaning for themselves.

In his preface to *The Cenci*, Shelley highlights the importance of redemption to his play when he cryptically writes that the "imagination is as the immortal God which should assume flesh for the redemption of mortal passion" (S, 143–44). In other words, the imagination must find a way to embody or make manifest that unspeakable "little word" whose presence, when recognized, will break the hypnotic hold the pernicious powers of the world have over our passionate attachments and thus redeem our creaturely natures. But how can this be done? A clue is provided by Marzio's response to finding himself in the untenable situation of being compelled by two opposing forces—one that acts upon his body and the other his mind. With no way out of this ordeal of the undecidable, Marzio smiles "as one who baffles a deep adversary; / And holding his breath, died" (5.2.182–83). This smile is both a "minor gesture" and an extreme act of passive resistance, one that provides insight into the potential for a new form of politics.[82]

Through his death, Marzio instantiates an extreme case of self-redemption—one that radically revises the sovereign logic of the king's two bodies. At the moment of his death, he recognizes that there is still a space to exercise his free will within the gap between his own "two bodies." The insight he embodies in this moment is also articulated in a poem by Emily Dickinson that begins

> No Rack can torture me—
> My Soul—at Liberty
> Behind this mortal Bone
> There knits a bolder One—
>
> You cannot prick with Saw—
> Nor pierce with Cimitar—
> Two bodies—therefore be—
> Bind one—
> The Other fly.[83]

A further explication for the implications of Marzio's affective anagnorisis can be found in Shelley's essay "On Life": "What follows from the admission? It establishes no new truth, it gives us no additional insight into our hidden nature, neither its action nor itself. . . . It leaves, what it is too often the duty of the reformer in political and ethical questions to leave, a vacancy. It reduces the mind to that freedom in which it would have acted, but for the misuse of words and signs, the instruments of its own creation" (S, 507). It is this insistent articulation of an awful doubt that at least potentially forces Shelley's audience into a position where they must take responsibility for the play's performance and labor to produce a political answer to the problem it exposes. Through Marzio's example, Shelley forces his audience to seek, within the space of their own souls, the anagnorisis the play refuses to supply. By doing so, Shelley articulates one model of a postsecular politics and the quest for justice—one where we must acknowledge our responsibility for the ideologies we take pleasure in. One where each must decide which words are the words we will ultimately choose to make flesh.

∗ 6 ∗

"Open-Hearted"

Persuasion *and the Cultivation of Good Humor*

The essence of both the tragic and the comic lies in the self's fundamental misrecognition of itself. In each there is the exhibition of moments when self and truth fall apart. However, in comedy characters generally learn to manage this frailty more successfully. If tragedy is the wound that exposes the soul at the heart of human experience, then comedy "imagines a restored body where the wounds are not ignored or belittled or explained away, healed rather than cured."[1] In this last chapter, I explore the form the comic takes in Jane Austen's *Persuasion,* so that we can better envision a world where wonder is still possible despite, or perhaps because of, our "awful doubt." If we can recognize in good humor the fact that our concepts do not fit the objects we attach them to as securely as we might think, then there will still be opportunities to experience a sense of immanent transcendence whenever the expectations of a limiting point of view are popped and the world before us is seen anew.

Austen, like Shakespeare, taps into the "biological-mythical roots of comedy,"[2] a genre that in both writers' hands always ends in marriage. However, marriage is never only a matter of individual preference nor a simple submitting to the way things are; rather, marriage marks a moment when the form one will take within a given social set is decided—a moment where two bodies become one flesh. Marriage lends itself to comedy so easily because both are built through "interruptions and breaks, a continuity that constructs with discontinuity."[3] Comedy, like marriage, is concerned with how things are joined together, and it is in *Persuasion* that we find the most mature version of Austen's comic vision.

One reason to explore the significance of the comic for a postsecular age is because good humor is a key aspect of Hume's own response to the affective "shipwreck" experienced within modernity in the wake of skeptical empiricism, which is described at the end of book 1 of his *Treatise,* and which "The Rime of the Ancient Mariner" may also be allegorizing. Although the reception history of Hume has often emphasized melancholic catastrophe and the tragic impasse of skeptical doubt, we should remember that within the account recorded in his *Treatise* Hume liberates himself from such sorrowful dispositions simply by altering his mood. After doing so, he then says to any would-be followers of his philosophy, "If the reader finds himself in the same easy disposition, let him follow me in my future speculations. If not, let him follow his inclination, and wait the returns of application and good humour" (*T*, 1.4.7.14). The "hopeful and carefree frame of mind" experienced by those in good humor is a vital prerequisite for navigating life's turbulence.[4]

One of the pleasures of reading Jane Austen's *Persuasion* is the way it draws readers "into the world of [Anne Elliot's] thinking, feeling, and willing, [and] invites us to participate in a learning of romance that is colored by the passions without being blinded by them, that is both intellectually and emotionally true, and that is increasingly independent of surrounding circumstance." In this way, Austen's writing offers "a mature romance which derives its spiritual splendor from selfless intentionality, *and* the ordering power of a directed will."[5] Although *Persuasion* as a whole may represent for the reader a "reality thickened with retrospection,"[6] it is particularly in the second half of the novel during moments of "high-wrought nervous tension" that readers are exposed to an intimate view of Anne Elliot's external "reality." Marilyn Butler argued that in these moments of intensity the felt presence of Anne's sensorium is suggested by the author's textual "distortion of the two 'normal' outward dimensions: time is recklessly speeded up, space grotesquely contracted."[7] What interests me most about *Persuasion* is the way these intense moments of dislocation can enable readers to witness and vicariously participate in both Anne and Captain Wentworth's gradual realization of an "openhearted" good humor (*PS*, 175). Such humor can be understood in at least three ways: as the cultivated ability to appreciate what is funny or comical, as recalling older understandings of the bodily humors, or as referencing a temporary state of mind or feeling (a posture of attention). Humor takes its place with wit and irony as one of the key components of comedy and the comic, and this chapter explores the way that it can be variously understood through attention to Austen's *Persuasion* and why it is that a posture of good humor may be so well suited to navigating a postsecular age.

Persuasion

Part of what makes *Persuasion*'s lead romantic characters' gradual realization of good humor possible is that each key moment of Anne and Captain Wentworth's renewed courtship takes place through intense moments of dislocation or wonder. These exceptional instances of close contact are often "accompanied by overwhelming moments of access to the outside world."[8] A key example of such a moment can be found in the party scene when Captain Wentworth and Anne have a conversation that reveals to Anne both Wentworth's lack of attachment to Louisa Musgrove and the depth of his continued feelings for her. Upon hearing his speech and realizing the potential implications for her own situation, "Anne, who, in spite of the agitated voice in which the latter part had been uttered, and in spite of all the various noises of the room, the almost ceaseless slam of the door, and ceaseless buzz of persons walking through, had distinguished every word, was struck, gratified, confused, and beginning to breathe very quick, and feel a hundred things in a moment" (*PS*, 199). Afterward, in response to this "interesting, almost too interesting conversation," Anne finds herself filled with "exquisite, though agitated sensations" but is nevertheless "in good humour with all," having "received ideas which disposed her to be courteous and kind to all, and to pity every one, as being less happy than herself" (*PS*, 200–201).

Although Anne is admirably rational in many respects, as Alan Richardson notes she is also "highly susceptible to influxes of feeling from sources not always consciously present to Anne herself, registered instead in the body, in ways that at times become so pressing as to overwhelm the conscious subject."[9] When overwhelmed in this way the illusory unity of a buffered subjectivity is punctured or made permeable by the actions of an embodied mind. Richardson argues that "Austen's famously innovative style for conveying the heroine's impressions in *Persuasion* speaks as much to a new psychological appreciation of unconscious mental life and embodied cognition as to a new esthetic mode for representing the flux of conscious experience." In his reading, these moments of dislocation that are so vividly rendered throughout *Persuasion* are meant to "mark the collision of conscious awareness with unconscious thoughts and feelings and the intense physiological sensations that accompany them" (102). These "invasions of feelings,"[10] as John Wiltshire calls them, are felt in Anne's flesh and are registered in the novel's "rapid and nervous syntax designed to imitate the bombardment of impressions upon the mind."[11] This is why *Persuasion* "is as notable for its hidden throbs as for its external embodiment of desire."[12]

How then are we to understand Anne's good humor in this and similar scenes? Jill Heydt-Stevenson argues that Austen's comic irreverence and bawdy humor "announces her 'knowingness,' since laughter, like sexuality, is associated with agency."[13] Invoking such memorable moments as the innuendo implied in *Pride and Prejudice* when Darcy responds to Caroline Bingley's suggestion that he allow her to mend his pen for him since she "mend[s] pens remarkably well" by saying "Thank you—but I always mend my own"[14] or the suggestiveness of Mary Crawford's joking reference in *Mansfield Park* to naval "Rears, and Vices," Heydt-Stevenson offers an intriguing model of the role the comic plays within Austen's work, which is exemplified by Fanny Price's use of the phrase "slipping into the ha-ha" within *Mansfield Park*.[15] Although "imperceptible from a distance, the ha-ha was a 'sunk fence' that prevented livestock from crossing from the park into the garden, while also allowing the viewer to maintain the fiction that the grounds were seamlessly connected." The ha-ha receives its name for the sudden surprise and laughter that might erupt when one recognizes they have been duped by a trompe l'oeil. Heydt-Stevenson convincingly argues that Austen's own bawdy "slip" into the ha-ha "extends and expands the space normally allowed to a woman during this period," but implicit in her model is the perhaps even more provocative suggestion that in the comic there is a crisis of coherency wherein the "necessary" connection between elements is suddenly called into question and where the slipping away of the fiction that things are seamlessly connected is suddenly felt.[16]

Heydt-Stevenson's approach helps us see how Austen's comedy "opens up interstices that prevailing assumptions about women ... have sutured"[17] and how Austen announces her "knowingness" through double entendres or "unbecoming conjunctions" that are scattered throughout her novels. These conjunctions can be useful because they are "elastic" structures that can "allow for the simultaneous apprehension of paradoxical responses." However, although this emphasis on unbecoming conjunctions is helpful, it also comes with certain limitations. An "unbecoming conjunction" is "what happens when two ideas or images or people, set side by side, reveal unforeseen similarities,"[18] and these suddenly seen similarities can surprise, shake up conventions, and even provide an "outlet" for pent up "hostility toward ideologies that dominate women" (206). Nevertheless, I argue that the heights of "good humour" that Anne achieves at several key moments in *Persuasion* can take us a step further still.

There is, I argue, a therapeutic dimension to the forms of experience that the second courtship, and the novel as a whole, taps into, which helps assuage those resentments that are too readily "insinuated into the pores of experience" and threaten to calcify both body and mind. After the failure of the initial courtship Wentworth was "on his side, totally unconvinced and unbending" and, "feeling himself ill-used by so forced a relinquishment," leaves the country in consequence. In Anne's case, "her attachment and regrets had, for a long time, clouded every enjoyment of youth; and an early loss of bloom and spirits had been their lasting effect" (*PS*, 19–20). For both, some degree of rigidity or melancholia descends. What is needed is some shock that can jolt one off their "grooves of regularity" and thereby expose the artificiality of typical postures of attention, while also suddenly freeing up affective energy, which can then be reinvested into generating and motivating new forms of action.[19]

The Comic

A helpful introduction to the mode of comedy I have in mind comes from Henri Bergson, for whom laughter occurs when we see how "some rigidity" or another has been "applied to the mobility of life," but we are ourselves capable of moving beyond this stasis.[20] Often the pleasure produced in a comedic situation erupts when "we have a clear apprehension of this putting the one on the other" but are able to produce a pleasurable friction from "the rubbing together of two alternative perspectives."[21] In *The Odd One In* (2008), Alenka Zupančič argues that the immediacy comedy produces is not the necessity of a smooth, imperceptible passing of one thing into another but that of a pleasurable realization of a material cut between them. From this perspective, wit is one of the basic building blocks of the comic because it is the pleasurable yoking of two disparate images, and comedy, more generally, helps us see and find pleasure in "the cut" between two or more objects or frames of reference. When the comic is effective, there is "a moment of disorientation, a momentary suspension in which the subject vacillates between

[her] being and [her] meaning" so that "it is no longer clear on which side [she is] standing."²² Although this rhythmic oscillation between being and meaning undermines understanding, it can nevertheless be therapeutic because such moments can overwhelm typical postures of attention so that we lose "recourse to the networks, practices, and relays of attachment that sustain representation," suddenly revisiting the moment prior to the decision about what things mean.²³

Immanuel Kant argued that what is most significant about a comic response is this sudden shifting of "the mind now to one standpoint and now to the other" that the subject must undergo in order to "contemplate its object."²⁴ Kant further claims that this moment of disorientation may ultimately correspond to the movement of the body through a "reciprocal straining and slackening of the elastic parts of our viscera, which communicates itself to the diaphragm (and resembles that felt by ticklish people), in the course of which the lungs expel the air with rapidly succeeding interruptions." Through this experience of a feeling of the "loss and intended recovery of the orienting a priori of the body" there is a ticklish exercise in elasticity that is "beneficial to health," and like the Burkean sublime, albeit for different reasons, can help clear out blockages that inhibit us from becoming our best selves (162).²⁵ For Kant, "laughter is an affect arising from a strained expectation being suddenly reduced to nothing."²⁶

In *The World as Will and Representation* (1819), Arnold Schopenhauer similarly argues for incongruity as the basis of the comic, suggesting that "laughter results from nothing but the suddenly perceived incongruity between a concept and the real objects that had been thought through it in some relation. . . . All laughter therefore is occasioned by a paradoxical, and hence unexpected, subsumption."²⁷ The implication of this incongruity theory is that at the heart of the comic is the recognition of an astonishing misfit between concept and object. This amusing misalignment often takes the form of wit ("when we consciously apply a concept to an object which does not measure up to it") or folly ("when an agent does something that fails to satisfy his concept of what he is about," like Don Quixote tilting at windmills).²⁸ However, I suggest that in Austen's comic vision, as in Kant's, the comic is not only a cognitive but also a physiological experience—one that is felt in one's flesh.

Kant agrees with earlier thinkers like Frances Hutcheson that humor derives from an intellectual recognition of incongruity, but he also adds a physiological theory to explain why we have a pleasant reaction to that intellectual recognition. According to Kant, we laugh at absurdities not because the intellect itself finds pleasure in that which frustrates it but because the intellect's attempt to reconcile an absurd conjunction of ideas causes a physical response that is found to be pleasant. A jest "must have something in it capable of momentarily deceiving us," but "when the semblance vanishes into nothing, the mind looks back in order to try it over again, and thus by a rapidly succeeding tension and relaxation it is thrown to and fro and put in oscillation."[29] Good humor often enables a moment of wonder, which "is a dizzying, vertiginous, and destabilizing experience" that threatens to upend all prejudices and preconceptions.[30] When the comic approaches wonder in this way, it becomes a potentially potent phenomenon that can help cut, edit, or splice one from conventional attachments and help one attend to those impartialities that interrupt normative forms of common sense through a pleasurable oscillation of losing and finding oneself.

The comic can sometimes stage a disorienting moment of seeing nothing, because "comedy is the moment in which substance, necessity, and essence all lose their immediate—and thus abstract—self-identity or coincidence with themselves."[31] Comedy can help us see that A does not equal A and that our concepts do not fit the objects we attach them to as securely as we might think. Comedy puts into practice one crucial point: "We really encounter nonsense only when and where a sense surprises us."[32] Seen in this light the comic can be compared to what Jacques Rancière has called dissensus, or as Davide Panagia has formulated it, "an aesthetico-political moment that results in the reconfiguration of the regimes of perception that seize our attention, so that we can no longer assume the legislative authority (or logical priority) of any one form of perception." A comic moment of dissensus can momentarily disrupt "the mechanisms that enable the fluidity of the operation" of those regimes of perception that typically mediate the meaning of experience.[33] Doing so may introduce something exceptional into the common world of perceiving and thereby confound habitual postures of attention. This sudden experience of a state of exception can be significant because before a new partition of the sensible can be fashioned or adopted, an interruption of previous forms of relating must occur.

Knowing Our Own Nothingness

But what then are we to make of Anne Elliot's good humor if not a wise passiveness? How does *Persuasion* offer something beyond the apophatic experiences of wonder detailed in the previous novels—from Catherine Moreland's "motionless wonder"[34] produced when she, to invoke Byron's critique of Keats,[35] absent-mindedly *frigs* her own imagination through habitual misrecognition, to Elizabeth Bennett's wretched perplexity after receiving Darcy's letter, to Emma's "amusement" while gazing outside the door of Ford's while shopping with Harriet, with "a mind lively and at ease, [that] can do with seeing nothing, and can see nothing that does not answer"?[36] Like Emma, Anne is capable of possessing a "mind of winter" so that being nothing herself she "beholds / Nothing that is not there and the nothing that is."[37]

This posture of attention of a "mind lively and at ease" that "can do with seeing nothing" and sees "nothing that does not answer" is worthwhile, in part because it can generate new intuitions and restore faith in the world precisely by tapping into the intensity that creates it. To be caught up in wonder is to experience a "moment of pure presence" where thought itself is arrested because the mind is unable to "move on by association to something else."[38] Nevertheless, the wonder felt in these moments of seeing nothing is insufficient in itself. Even though wonder can often consist of a pleasurable loss of perspective, one must nevertheless work to avoid the temptation "to indulge in indecision and indeterminacy, and to retreat into a self-reflexivity that marvels at our capacity to defer judgment endlessly, as though that were itself our end."[39] Although the potentially infinite possibility of revising reflective judgment can become an excuse to continually delay its exercise, one must recognize that to indulge in a process of infinite deliberation and reflection, as Fanny Price realizes in *Mansfield Park,* is also a refusal to act.

Even at the beginning of the novel, Anne, who at twenty-seven is already far more mature than any of the other Austen heroines, has already learned the lessons the other heroines receive during the course of their own stories. This is made clear early on when Anne is among the Musgroves at Uppercross and she reflects on how the "removal from one set of people to another, though at a distance of only three miles, will often include a total change of conversation, opinion, and idea" (PS, 45). She wishes her foolish father and older sister could recognize how "unconsidered" their preoccupations at Kellynch Hall were at Uppercross. For herself, she is surprised that when she came "with a heart full of the subject which had been completely occupying both houses in Kellynch for many weeks," there were only passing remarks on these issues. She is reminded that "she must now submit to feel that another lesson, in the art of knowing our own nothingness beyond our own circle, was become necessary for her" (PS, 45).

Clearly, some of the autumnal tone of *Persuasion* can be traced back to this need to learn how to know one's own nothingness, but there is also a fanciful facet to this art of knowing as well, because Anne also acknowledges "it to be very fitting, that every little social commonwealth should dictate its own matters of discourse." Furthermore, if she did not want to be an "unworthy member" of the community she has been transplanted into, then "it was highly incumbent on her to clothe her imagination, her memory, and all her ideas in as much of Uppercross as possible" (PS, 46). With this recognition of a chameleonlike need to clothe the imagination in a manner fitting the context of present circumstances, one feels justified in speaking of a Romantic Austen, perhaps one who, like Anne Elliot, "had been forced into prudence in her youth, [but] learned romance as she grew older" (PS, 32).

The art of knowing one's own nothingness is needed because, as Hume suggests, all appearances are "broken appearances": discontinuous, separate, and interrupted. One's sense of existence is "rooted in movements of assemblage, recollection, projection, splicing, editing, and the like." Images do not "bind" themselves, and so the faculty of the imagination is needed to draw upon causality, contiguity, habit, and resemblance in order to "artifice strategies of composition in the face of ontological discontinuity."[40] In this way, all politics flows from the power and possibilities of assembly, and this is how and why "every little social commonwealth" can stitch together the discourse that will clothe its own imagination. One's sense of self "comes into existence only as the result of a laborious stitching together of disparate parts," and such acts of religion (*re-ligare*, binding again) affect and are affected by how we see ourselves oriented in the world.[41]

By the end of the novel, Anne will ultimately recognize the need for a philosophic sense of necessity when trying to impartially judge the actions taken in response to any given event. Reflecting upon the advice of Lady Russell for Anne to not marry Wentworth during the initial courtship, and the fact that this advice was heeded, Anne explains to Wentworth that, "I was perfectly right in being guided by the friend whom you will love better than you do now. To me, she was in the place of a parent. Do not mistake me, however. I am not saying that she did not err in her advice. It was, perhaps, one of those cases in which advice is good or bad only as the event decides" (PS, 267–68).

Humoring the Body

Critics interested in how Austen represents the processes by which sense and sensibility are stitched together and invested with meaning have often been influenced by Michael Foucault. In "The Tittle-Tattle of Highbury" for instance, Casey Finch and Peter Bowen consider how free indirect discourse is itself the language of self-surveillance, in part because it exposes how the language of the private self must be expressed in terms of an always already public language."[42] Similarly, Mark Canuel has suggested that the household of a place like Mansfield Park enables "a technique of social organization that lends persons and their actions a privileged form of legibility."[43] Other critics have explored the ways in which Austen represents the breakdown of these "technologies of classification" and other processes of investiture. David Southward, for example, has investigated those "little zigzags of embarrassment"[44] that are experienced when one is felt to be "doing wrong and being looked at."[45] These moments of embarrassment are memorable because they incorporate the sensation of "the confused halting of the social machinery, an awkward lack of direction in speech and behavior, the contagious darting from person to person; in short, the 'little zigzags' of a mind looking inward in its sudden self-consciousness and outward as it scurries to rectify the situation."[46]

In order to both offer a somewhat different approach and to further explicate what all of this has to do with humor, I turn to Jonathan H. Grossman's inquiry into how Austen participates in what Norbert Elias called the "civilizing process." Elias defines "the civilizing process" as the set of practices that result in the pacification of behavior and the control of one's emotions.[47] Part of the labor of the leisured is to give body to social values through the establishment of polite culture. The uncanny socializing force of politeness is due to the fact that, as Pierre Bourdieu puts it, "nothing seems more ineffable ... than the values given body, made body by the transubstantiation achieved by the hidden persuasion of an implicit pedagogy, capable of instilling a whole cosmology."[48] In other words, as in the example of Wordsworth's "The Old Cumberland Beggar," when values such as charity become second nature "habit does the work / Of reason" (91–93). Principles "embodied in this way are placed beyond the grasp of consciousness" because the "body has beliefs" that are "submerged below the level of consciousness—embedded, for example, in the habits of muscle memory or speech patterns, or in manners."[49] In this way, such principles become words made flesh.

Although Grossman is primarily interested in how good manners subtly make even a weak patriarch like *Emma*'s Mr. Woodhouse compelling, I want to connect the flesh of this body that has beliefs to earlier notions of the humoral body because doing so helps clarify the implications of Austen's comic vision. Learning the "arts of the self" that can shape these submerged intensities in productive ways is the key to legislating new ways of being in the world. Part of the pleasure and power of Austen's writing, and perhaps also of Romanticism more generally, is not only the way it offers frequent albeit fleeting glances at these sensations beneath syntax but also in how it offers occasions for reforming them as well.

In *Humoring the Body: Emotions and the Shakespearean Stage* (2004), Gail Kern Paster delineates a model of an early modern understanding of the humoral body, or the body with beliefs that the civilizing process is thought to affect. In a cosmos permeated by passions, or those "forces that are at once extremely powerful and actually or potentially beyond our control," the humoral body was "characterized not only by its physical openness but also by its emotional instability and volatility, by an internal microclimate knowable, like climates in the outer world, more for changeability than for stasis."[50] To be in good humor required behaving in such a way so as to satisfyingly balance the four qualities of cold, hot, wet, and dry within one's own personal microclimate. These forces "constituted the material basis of any living creature's characteristic appraisals of and responses to its immediate environment; they altered the character of a body's substances and, by doing so, organized its ability to act or even to think."[51] This is an ecological view of subjectivity, rooted in the "dynamic reciprocities between self and environment imagined by the psychophysiology of bodily fluids." There is a porousness felt between circumstance and character because "circumstance engenders humors in the body and humors in the body help to determine circumstance by predisposing the individual subject to a characteristic kind of evaluation and response."[52] In this understanding of the humoral body, "the passions are the winds and waves of the body, producing internal changes that the subject suffers as if they came from the outside," and it is due to these passionate persuasions that the humoral body is "characterized by corporeal fluidity, openness, and porous boundaries."[53]

Like the humoral body, the sense of self that triumphs in *Persuasion* is fluid and dynamic. Throughout the novel Anne is frequently crowded in on and even overcome by her environment. Upon her first reintroduction to Wentworth, for instance, "a thousand feelings" rush in on Anne, and her normal rhythms of perception are so affected that "the room seemed full—full of persons and voices" (*PS*, 64). The feelings of porousness Anne frequently experiences in Wentworth's presence are not unlike those Sigmund Freud discusses at the beginning of *Civilization and Its Discontents* (1930), wherein there is a "sensation of 'eternity,' a feeling as of something limitless, unbounded—as it were, 'oceanic.'"[54] The crucial question remaining at the end of *Persuasion* is, given this sense of self, how then should each of us steer "the vital sensorium that supplies the soul's moving vehicle."[55]

This is the crux of the conversation Anne has with Captain Harville near the end of the novel concerning whether men or women are more prone to being inconstant in their feelings. Harville puts forward his belief "in a true analogy between our bodily frames and our mental; and that as our bodies are the strongest, so are our feelings; capable of bearing most rough usage, and riding out the heaviest weather." Anne responds by arguing that men's "feelings may be the strongest," but women's are the most tender in part because man may be "more robust than woman, but he is not longer-lived" (*PS*, 253). She continues by suggesting that it would be too hard on men if it were otherwise, because "You are always labouring and toiling, exposed to every risk and hardship. Your home, country, friends, all quitted. Neither time, nor health, nor life, to be called your own. It would be too hard indeed" (with a faltering voice) "if woman's feelings were to be added to all this" (*PS*, 254). It is at this moment of faltering that a "slight noise" calls their attention to Wentworth's side of the room. He had been writing a letter but dropped his pen. When the sentiments and tones of Anne's faltering voice reached him, he had under an "irresistible governance . . . seized a sheet of paper, and poured out his feelings" (*PS*, 262). He could now finally fully abandon the "madness of resentment, which had kept him from trying to regain her" (*PS*, 263).

This spontaneous overflow of powerful emotion doesn't fit with the model of subjectivity first advocated by Wentworth early in the novel when he compares Louisa's "character of decision and firmness" to a "beautiful glossy nut," which, "blessed with original strength, has outlived all the storms of autumn." At this point Wentworth's ideal subjectivity is that of a buffered self with "not a puncture, not a weak spot any where" (*PS*, 94). He learns of the limitations of this model at the moment of Louisa's accident. The words Louisa utters just before her fall could serve as the motto for her variation on the Cartesian cogito: "I am determined I will" (*PS*, 118). It is also significant that it is Louisa who is ultimately transformed through her surprising courtship with Captain Benwick "into a person of literary taste, and sentimental reflection" (*PS*, 182).

Anne is different because she is not as "determined" as Louisa, and Anne is able to move beyond the merely sentimental in part because she is perpetually in the process of losing and suddenly finding herself again. The locution Austen frequently deploys when "Anne is addressed by the outside world is 'Anne found herself': in the carriage on the way home from Lyme, Anne 'found herself' being addressed by Wentworth. At Uppercross she 'found herself' having the child removed from her back."[56] The kind of cogito that Anne exemplifies is far closer to the Lacanian model than what is typically understood as the Cartesian: "I am not wherever I am the plaything of my thought; I think of what I am where I do not think to think."[57] It is precisely this capacity for oscillating between seeing and knowing and between being and thinking that is the mark of good humor.[58]

One of Anne's moments of wondrous dislocation in *Persuasion* helps further demonstrate the advantages she holds over Austen's other heroines. While talking with Wentworth, Anne discovers "that he had a heart returning to her at least; that anger, resentment, avoidance, were no more," and that "he must really love her." When she subsequently walks into a room with her sister Elizabeth both are "very, very happy," but we are told that "it would be an insult to the nature of Anne's felicity, to draw any comparison between it and her sister's; the origin of one all selfish vanity, of the other all generous attachment." Whereas her sister, like her father, is almost cartoonishly trapped in the aesthetic, so that nothing either wishes for seems to them to be out of reach, Anne felt the value of her own openhearted disposition. "Anne saw nothing, thought nothing of the brilliancy of the room. Her happiness was from within" (*PS*, 201). For her, happiness is not the clutching after satisfaction of this or that desire but a deep openness to the possibility that something good can happen. Such happiness, Joel Faflak argues, "elicits an 'ambient attention' to one's surroundings, something at once deeply felt, interpersonal, and anonymous."[59] In another moment of romantic happiness, Anne is found "sporting" with her own delightful musings "from Camden-place to Westgate-buildings," and these musings are "almost enough to spread purification and perfume all the way" (*PS*, 208).

In the fullness of such moments, Anne is acutely attentive to her ambient environment.

Key facets of good humor are exemplified by two of the secondary characters met in *Persuasion*. The first is Mrs. Smith, a childhood friend Anne reconnects with only after a series of misfortunes had befallen her. Despite the fact that Anne "could scarcely imagine a more cheerless situation in itself than Mrs. Smith's," for she has lost her affluence, her husband, and her health, "Anne had reason to believe that she had moments only of languor and depression, to hours of occupation and enjoyment. How could it be?" Anne watches, observes, and reflects "and finally determined that this was not a case of fortitude or of resignation only," but that Mrs. Smith possessed "the choicest gift of Heaven"—an "elasticity of mind, that disposition to be comforted, that power of turning readily from evil to good, and of finding employment which carried her out of herself, which was from Nature alone" (*PS*, 167). The person possessing it "takes and resigns what they give with equal cheer, and makes her- or himself malleable to their impressions."[60] Such (neuro-)elasticity and affective plasticity can be related to notions of disinterest, as long as disinterest is understood not as viewing from an impartial Archimedean perspective, but rather as at least momentarily adopting an apophatic posture of attention—one that recognizes that there can be "no a priori criteria of interest or structures of part-taking that govern why or how one object, organ of perception, or structure of feeling might command our attentions."[61]

However, in addition to elasticity another element needs to be incorporated in order to make sense of the model of good humor offered in *Persuasion*. This additional ingredient is perhaps most succinctly exemplified in the scene where Anne and the Crofts are traveling by coach and Mrs. Croft seems to praise the Musgrove girls as "Very good humoured, unaffected girls, indeed," but does so in such "a tone of calmer praise, such as made Anne suspect that her keener powers might not consider either of them as quite worthy of her brother." Just then Mrs. Croft is alerted to an approaching danger, saying to her husband, "My dear admiral, that post!—we shall certainly take that post." However, "by coolly giving the reins a better direction herself, they happily passed the danger." Anne finds "some amusement at their style of driving, which she imagined no bad representation of the general guidance of their affairs," and in this she is likely correct (*PS*, 62). This scene is notable because it illustrates an almost ideal vehicular consciousness—one alert and attentive to its surroundings and quite capable of skillfully steering "the vital sensorium that supplies the soul's moving vehicle."[62]

Although a good-humored posture of attention may involve "a self-emptying or kenosis," it is not adopted out of a "mindless desire" for novelty but rather as "an achievement, a habit of focused seeing and participating in what gives itself to us."[63] It is by being able to "subdue [our] minds to [our] fortunes" in this way that Austen's readers may also "learn to brook being happier than [we] deserve" (PS, 269). Good humor is good because it cultivates a sensibility in which each can become "expert with sail and oar" over their own particular vehicular consciousness.[64] Thomas Pfau suggests that to attend in this way is to glimpse a realm full of a "yet unconsummated form of the good" but a good "that will be realized only if we unconditionally and habitually bestow our attention on what presents itself to us, and that will be lost if we don't."[65] By encouraging a childlike (or absolving) forgetfulness of the ties between particular events, good humor fosters a capacity to look at any given situation with a renovated eye. Such apophatic postures of attention offer occasions to overcome the fallacy of misplaced concreteness by attending anew to that "crux of embodiment: the turning point where bodies may be said to emerge into our fields of perception, meaning, language—into a world."[66]

Good humor, in this way, can offer us a different understanding of what an experience of porousness might mean in a postsecular age. Many of Anne Elliot's experiences in *Persuasion* resonate with what Catherine Keller has termed "aporetic probity," wherein "passages blocked in the moment of doubt, of defense, clear and open like pores." In this model the self is still buffered, folded, or distinct but the folds that make it up "are pores, passages in and out of becoming creatures that have no substantial boundaries. Yet in their singular freedoms they expose endless layers of porous surface, faces of the deep." This new porousness "is an embodying perspective that can give valence to life and meaning, a vertical dimension in which ordinariness incandesces, flaming and flowering."[67] To be a humorist, as both Anne and Wentworth are at the end of *Persuasion*, means becoming openhearted by cultivating a capacity for losing the plot and finding it again subtly or surprisingly altered.

The Politics of Good Humor

By the end of *Persuasion*, and perhaps at the end of this book as well, not only a new sense of self, but a new kind of politics seems to be animating the main characters—a politics of good humor. Ultimately, I argue, there is something Machiavellian about such politics. Blakey Vermule is right in suggesting that "in modern literature especially, Machiavellian reasoning reflects the sense that we are at once captive to the swirl of the social and psychologically detached from it."[68] However, Vermule emphasizes Machiavellian narratives that "tend to feature a person who sees or thinks he sees farther than anybody else—let us call this person the mastermind. The mastermind, as denizen of comedy or tragedy, stands as the powerful fantasy of someone able to master others through analytical reflection" (222). This is the Machiavelli of *The Prince*. Within the Austen canon it is Emma Woodhouse who most clearly attempts to be the mastermind of her particular social set. Yet what she must learn is that it is precisely this fantasy of mastery that must be sacrificed if one is to live ethically.

The Machiavelli that may be most applicable to a postsecular age is the one found in his later work, *The Discourses*, wherein he argues that composite bodies, by which he means "states and religious institutions," but which can also signify human bodies, "are better constituted and have a longer life whose institutions make frequent renovations possible. . . . For it is clearer than daylight that, without renovation, these bodies do not last."[69] Such renovations "reduce them to their starting-points," which is beneficial because "a man who is accustomed to act in one particular way, never changes. . . . Hence, when times change and no longer suit his ways, he is inevitably ruined" (431). To be Machiavellian in this sense is to recognize "that political effectiveness requires choosing the right action and the right style of action at the right time, and to do this one must be alert to the role of impersonal (*fortuna*) as well as personal (human intentional) forces at work in 'real time.'"[70] Given the uncertainty of what to do next in such a world, perhaps the best thing to do is cultivate good humor.

A good-humored disposition helps us see that our concepts do not fit the objects we attach them to as securely as we might think. However, this tendency toward misfits is not felt to be tragic, because although the comic may operate within a horizon of immanence that has abandoned reference to anything beyond itself, it nevertheless includes the wondrous possibility of an immanent transcendence that is experienced whenever the expectations of a limiting point of view are burst and the world before us is seen anew. The logic here recalls William Blake's notion that "reason is the bound or outward circumference of energy." Reason's limit provides us with something to collect in, to gather our strength, a form in which to bind, and from which to reflect upon our imaginative energies. But in certain moments our rigid defenses against the too-muchness that forms our turbulent core are suddenly relaxed and an energetic excess unfolds and extends past the boundaries of our current sense of rationality. Within these spontaneous overflows of powerful emotion, a new horizon for the world is intuited, a new world that waits to be recollected and bound by the rationality of a new limit. And at least potentially this process can be repeated indefinitely.

CODA

Postsecular Romanticism

In an 1818 letter to John Hamilton Reynolds, Keats provides a "simile of human life" by offering the model of what he calls the "Mansion of Many Apartments." In this large mansion he can describe only two rooms, "the doors of the rest being as yet shut upon me." The first he calls "the infant or thoughtless Chamber, in which we remain as long as we do not think." We remain in this room until we are at length "imperceptibly impelled by the awakening of the thinking principle," at which time we enter "the Chamber of Maiden-Thought." Here we "become intoxicated with the light and the atmosphere" and see "nothing but pleasant wonders, and think of delaying there for ever in delight." However, in time there is a tremendous sharpening of "one's vision into the heart and nature of Man—of convincing one's nerves that the World is full of Misery and Heartbreak, Pain, Sickness and oppression." Through this process, the Chamber of Maiden-Thought becomes "gradually darken'd and at the same time on all sides of it many doors are set open—but all dark—all leading to dark passages—We see not the balance of good and evil. We are in a Mist—We are now in that state—We feel the 'burden of the Mystery.'" Keats claims that it is to this point that Wordsworth has come, and it seems to him that Wordsworth's "Genius is explorative of those dark Passages." Keats also claims that "if we live, and go on thinking," we shall also explore these passages (*LJK*, 2:280–81).

However, Keats may be too humble when he says that Wordsworth "is a Genius and superior [to] us, in so far as he can, more than we, make discoveries, and shed a light in them." Indeed, the suggestion of this book has been that Keats, along with Coleridge, Shelley, and Austen have all contributed to the "grand advance of intellect" in their own right, advancing, in their own often more negatively capable and iconoclastic ways, beyond the model of eloquence Wordsworth provided (*LJK*, 2:281). By doing so they realized their own ways to peer through the dark but open doors leading from the Chamber of Maiden-Thought and by doing so helped expand the wardrobe available to our moral imaginations by fashioning new ways to make words flesh.

One of the blind spots of secularism is its failure to thematize those "affects and dispositions operating below the threshold of consciousness."[1] A postsecular approach should recognize how not only religious cultures but aesthetic and political cultures function through processes of investiture that attempt to draw "the formal or representative disposition in every individual out of each person's concrete particularity."[2] To approach religion or literature in this way is to see them as forms of what Hume understood as a "promise," which perhaps surprisingly he specifically compares to "transubstantiation, or holy orders, where a certain form of words, along with a certain intention, changes entirely the nature of an external object, and even of a human creature" (*T*, 3.2.5.14). By promising, the promiser is fundamentally altered by the form the promise takes.

Instead of seeing religion as a set of potentially fictious propositions or beliefs to which the individual gives assent, a postsecular approach suggests that religion is not simply a different way of thinking but is also an alternative manner of being—a promise of a different way of life. Religion is largely formulated by and articulated in those relationships that bind or rebind (*religare*) the practitioner into a *schesis* or set of habits. Schesis is "the manner in which a thing is related to something else," which Aristotle conceptualized as capturing a sense of "the embodied habitation and intimate proximity that imbues such a relation."[3] The Latin word *habitus*, similarly suggests "a bodily condition or temperament that undergirds a particular modality of relation" (847). Pierre Bourdieu saw habitus as the determining power in the social field, which consists of those "durable, transposable dispositions" that make up socialized subjectivity.[4] Habitus is what Thomas Aquinas called those "deep-structural" patterns of action, which are understood to be "indispensable for an education into the virtues."[5] What the forms or mediums of religion and literature can potentially provide are ways through which the devote user can forge, access, or speculate upon a habitus and thereby plug into a "pious sensorium, that is, the embodied aptitudes and affects necessary for the achievement of a virtuous life."[6] The transmission of what Wordsworth called "habits of meditation" through the media of both religion and literature is possible because, as Henri Bergson suggested, "the structure of the mind remains the same" and so "experience acquired by successive generations, deposited in the social environment" is given back to successive readers each time a withered leaf is quickened to a new birth.[7]

Throughout this book I have been invested in advocating for a view of literature that sees it as an essential component to ethical practice. As Colin Jager has noted, the study of literature "makes possible a reflective activity that offers practice at negotiating among differing conceptions of the good."[8] Part of the potential of the literary classroom experience specifically, and the study of literature more generally, is that it offers opportunities to stage ourselves as different identities, thereby enabling a communal space to emerge within which joyful encounters can occur. In the classroom, texts should serve not simply as objects for us to read, study, and critique but also as events that can make something happen. Such a pedagogy cannot merely be about critical thinking skills but should also offer opportunities for encountering alterity and for developing a capacity for both wonder and reflection. More work is needed in demonstrating how even engaging in rational discourse, as Bruno Latour has suggested, "is not to treat everything in the same dispassionate tone, but to learn how to detect the different tones adjusted to the different situations so as to be able to sing all of them in the right tune."[9]

One challenge for pedagogy, like that of the clerisy more generally, is discovering ways to draw readers into a communal participation in this happening—this event that is the making and unmaking of passionate sense. It may be that a more ideal or postsecular form of neighborliness will only emerge as a result of a pedagogic practice that can properly instruct, exercise, and evaluate how we put on our postures of attention. Such dispositions are words made flesh, which are at least as much made as given. To be members of a just society it is essential that more of us become more fully aware of how and why it is that by uttering certain words and adopting certain bodily dispositions we can attune ourselves to different arrangements of the good life.

ACKNOWLEDGMENTS

The word horde out of which this book emerged was gathered after much travelling in the realms of gold. I owe a great deal to many people who have helped me think in new and different ways. I was fortunate to spend my graduate years as part of the Henry R. Luce Program in Scripture and Literary Arts at Boston University. Here I enjoyed the wonderful and nurturing interdisciplinary environment fostered by the director of the program Peter Hawkins. I was also blessed with the time and space afforded by being the research assistant to Ray Hart, who provided me with an ideal model of the scholar and who was gracious enough to serve as my dissertation director. Although there are many friends, classmates, and colleagues that I remember fondly from those years, I am particularly grateful for the many fruitful conversations I had with Garth Green. While at Boston University I also fell under the spell of Romanticism and benefited enormously from the wisdom and insight of David Wagenknecht—a brilliant thinker and conversationalist. Thanks as well goes to Charles Rzepka who provided an exemplary model of scholarly engagement and who organized the long-running Romantic Symposia. It was in those conversations that I was first able to orient myself as a potential Romanticist. Appreciation is also due to John Paul Riquelme, who codirected my master's thesis on W. B. Yeats and helped me realize what it meant to write in an academic way.

My ability to engage in the wide-ranging project this book has become stems not only from my interdisciplinary training but also from the variety of scholarly communities I have had the good fortune to participate in. The foundations of this book were hammered out during my time as a junior visiting fellow at the *Institut für die Wissenschaften vom Menschen* in Vienna. The posts and pillars of this project were established in a variety of scholarly communities that I subsequently had the good fortune to participate in. A very productive summer was spent at Cornell University as a member of the School for Criticism and Theory, where I enrolled in Victoria Kahn's seminar "Early Modern / Post Modern: Political Theology, Secularism, Literature." Two additional summers were spent, first at the National Humanities Center and then in Berlin, where I was a member of a seminar moderated by Thomas Pfau and David Womersley on "Scenes from the History of the Image: Reading Two Millennia of Conflict." Another important stepping stone was my participation in a National Endowment for the Humanities summer seminar led by Lori Branch and Mark Knight titled "Postsecular Studies and the Rise of the English Novel." Further aspects of my interests were explored during a summer program titled "Religion, Culture, and Society" at the *University Centre Saint-Igantius Antwerp* in Belgium and during a seminar led by Michael Taussig titled "Thought-Images, Body, and Mimesis in Walter Benjamin" at the Institute for Critical Social Inquiry. These experiences were invaluable and deepened my understanding of how the overall argument of my project addresses and contributes to a wider scholarly conversation. Together, these fellowships offered ideal opportunities to work through the key conceptual engines of my book project while in daily conversation with an international community of diverse scholars.

Since graduate school I have been very fortunate to have found a position at the University of Arkansas, situated within the thriving and picturesque environs of Fayetteville. While here I have benefited enormously from my participation in a welcoming and caring department. I am also particularly grateful to all of the students who have participated in my courses, which have so often served as the workshop, the laboratory, and the testing ground for so many of the ideas found in this book.

My appreciation is also directed to all of the editors, anonymous readers, and staff at the University of Virginia Press who have helped turn my musings into a book. Although many facets of this book have their origin as conference papers or as material written for or in response to various summer seminars, a few aspects were previously published in an earlier form. Parts of the argument in chapter 4 are reworked from material that first appeared in a 2012 Studies in Romanticism essay entitled "'Blank Splendour': Keats, Romantic Visuality, and Wonder." Sections of chapter 5 are drawn from "*The Cenci: Tragedy in a Secular Age*," which appeared in the journal *ELH* (2012). Chapter 6 incorporates the argument from "'Open-Hearted': *Persuasion* and the Cultivation of Good Humor," which appeared in *Jane Austen and Comedy* (Bucknell University Press, 2019). My thanks go out to the original editors and anonymous readers of those essays.

Finally, and most importantly, I am thankful for my wife Lisa, who has been such a steady presence throughout this whole process. Her example, support, and patience have enabled me to finally cross the great water. My heart goes out as well to my two daughters, Iris and Ada. Together they have provided the joyful familial axis around which my world turns.

* NOTES *

INTRODUCTION

1. Jager, *Unquiet Things*, 33.
2. Influential readings of this genealogy can be found in the work of various seminal thinkers of secularization (particularly Karl Löwith, Hans Blumenberg, Michel Foucault, and Jürgen Habermas), as well as in the advances and critiques posed more recently by a diverse group of scholars (including Charles Taylor, Vincent Pecora, Thomas Pfau, José Casanova, Talal Asad, Saba Mahmood, and the "radical orthodox" thinkers Graham Ward and John Milbank).
3. Fisher, *The Vehement Passions*, 40.
4. Santner, *The Royal Remains*, 115.
5. Feelings of dissociation become acute in modernity because, as T. S. Eliot recognized, something "happened to the mind of England between the time of Donne or Lord Herbert of Cherbury and the time of Tennyson and Browning" (*Selected Essays*, 287).
6. Bernstein, *Against Voluptuous Bodies*, 7.
7. Santner, *The Royal Remains*, 117.
8. Mahmood, "Religious Reason and Secular Affect," 861. For useful overviews of the relationship between secular and postsecular studies and literary studies see Branch, "Postsecular Studies"; Conway and Harol, "Toward a Postsecular Eighteenth Century"; and Jager, *Unquiet Things*, 19–23. For an overview of the relationship between Romanticism and religion see Mason, "Romanticism and Religion." Admittedly, I am not entirely comfortable with the term "postsecular," but I use it here because for the moment at least it has scholarly currency. As with postmodern, the post- in postsecular seems too reliant on a temporal distinction. I would be more inclined to adopt a term like "transsecular," which could be used

in a manner similar to transgender, which is in some ways a more apt description of what is actually at stake with this concept. However, here too the fit is not quite right, since the secular/religious binary is part of what we are trying to think beyond, and so having "secular" be part of the conceptual term is also problematic. Since by postsecular I do not necessarily mean something post- nor secular, the need for a better term is clear, even if finding one is not the purpose of this particular argument.

9. Habermas, "What Is Meant by a 'Post-Secular Society,'" 63.
10. My use of "naïve" and "sentimental" is drawn from Friedrich Schiller's essay "On Naïve and Sentimental Poetry," which will be discussed more fully later in this introduction.
11. Taylor, *A Secular Age*, 2–3.
12. As J. Hillis Miller similarly argues while considering the work of T. S. Eliot, "Romanticism in poetry and idealism in philosophy" seems to result in a situation wherein "each man seems destined to remain enclosed in his separate sphere, unable to break out to external things, to other people, to an objective time and space, or to God. All these exist, but as qualifications of the inner world which is peculiar and private to the self." *Poets of Reality*, 143.
13. Taylor, A Secular Age, 15.
14. Hansen, *Bodies in Code*, 38.
15. Connolly, "Refashioning the Secular," 167.
16. Simpson, *Merleau-Ponty and Theology*, 38.
17. Merleau-Ponty, *Phenomenology of Perception*, 166.
18. Taussig, *Mimesis and Alterity*, 25.
19. Merleau-Ponty, *Phenomenology of Perception*, 167, 114.
20. Hansen, *Bodies in Code*, 48.
21. Merleau-Ponty, *Phenomenology of Perception*, 165–66.
22. Hansen, *Bodies in Code*, 29. It was Hansen's book that first alerted me to the possibilities of this aspect of Merleau-Ponty's thinking. I will discuss *Bodies in Code* more fully in chapter 1.
23. Altieri, "Inner Sensuousness," 293.
24. Merleau-Ponty, *The Structure of Behavior*, 210.
25. Simpson, *Merleau-Ponty and Theology*, 13.
26. Merleau-Ponty, *Institution and Passivity*, 25–27, cited in Simpson, *Merleau-Ponty and Theology*, 18.
27. Simpson, *Merleau-Ponty and Theology*, 16.
28. Merleau-Ponty, *Institution and Passivity*, 210.
29. Simpson, *Merleau-Ponty and Theology*, 47.

30. P, 13:446–52 (citations are from the 1805 version unless otherwise noted).
31. Haekel, *The Soul in British Romanticism*, 202, 200.
32. For another important exploration of the role of the soul in Romanticism see Wolfson, "Gendering the Soul."
33. For more on the meaning of this phrase and the larger critical approach it entails see Lakoff and Johnson's *Metaphors We Live By* (1980) and *Philosophy in the Flesh* (1999).
34. Haekel, *The Soul in British Romanticism*, 31.
35. Ficino, *Platonic Theology*, 1:233.
36. Darwin, *Zoonomia*, 1:10.
37. Engell, "The Soul," 5.
38. Engell, "Coleridge (and His Mariner) on the Soul," 128.
39. Reames, *Seeming and Being in Plato's Rhetorical Theory*, xii.
40. Porter, *Flesh in the Age of Reason*, 3.
41. Haekel, *The Soul in British Romanticism*, 178.
42. Here Haekel draws upon Roman Jakobson's theory of the poetic function of literature. See Jakobson, "Linguistics and Poetics," 32–57.
43. Haekel, *The Soul in British Romanticism*, 15.
44. Havelock, *Preface to Plato*, 197. It is worth noting that Richard Seaford argues that it was money rather than textuality that enabled this externalization of contents. See Seaford's chapter on "Money and Inner Self in Greece" in his *The Origins of Philosophy in Ancient Greece and Ancient India: A Historical Comparison*, 253–70.
45. Haekel, *The Soul in British Romanticism*, 199.
46. It is worth nothing here how Havelock became a decisive influence on Marshall McLuhan's work on mass media in the 1960s and 1970s, as well as upon McLuhan's student Walter Ong's work in *Orality and Literacy* (1982). For more on this relationship see Reames, *Seeming and Being in Plato's Rhetorical Theory*, 4. Although these pioneers of media studies have subsequently been critiqued for not fully anticipating or taking into account the rise of digital, as opposed to "electronic," media, there is still much to learn from the forms of media studies that emerged out of their efforts. I return to this scholarly terrain in the next chapter, where I suggest that Romanticism emerges at least in part out of a second orality. For work that both surveys and complicates these issues see Erik Simpson's "Orality and Improvisation."
47. Hansen, *Bodies in Code*, 29.
48. Bergson, *The Two Sources of Morality and Religion*, 103.
49. Williams, *Marxism and Literature*, 134.

50. See Budge, *Romantic Empiricism*; Lindstrom, "Hume in Coleridge's Imagination"; Milnes, *The Testimony of Sense*; and Schey, "After Skepticism."
51. Abrams, *Natural Supernaturalism*, 13.
52. Haekel, *The Soul in British Romanticism*, 202, 200.
53. Posteraro, "Nothing but Habits," 98–99.
54. Deleuze, *Difference and Repetition*, 75.
55. Deleuze and Guattari, *What Is Philosophy?*, 169.
56. The logic here again recalls Wordsworth's suggestion at the end of *The Prelude* that the task of the "Prophets of Nature" is to teach others how to take the "frame of things" upon which we dwell and to (cinematographically) project a mind above it "Of substance and of fabric more divine" (*P*, 13:448, 452).
57. Abrams, "Structure and Style in the Greater Romantic Lyric," 218.
58. De Man, "The Rhetoric of Temporality," 207.
59. Deleuze, *The Fold*, 24.
60. Deleuze, *Difference and Repetition*, 74.
61. Panagia, *Impressions of Hume*, 35.
62. Silverman, *The Threshold of the Visible World*, 17.
63. A good discussion of these competing etymologies can be found in Mark C. Taylor's *After God*. "The etymology of religion compounds rather than clarifies the difficulties. According to the Oxford English Dictionary, religion is 'of doubtful etymology.' It appears to derive from at least two Latin terms. The first and more widely acknowledged is *religare*, which means 'to bind back' (*re-*, 'back,' plus *ligare*, 'to bind'). *Leig* is also the stem of 'ligament,' 'ligature,' and 'obligation.' Cicero, by contrast, maintains that 'religion' derives from *relegere* (to read over again), whose stem, *leg*, means 'thought through again'" (5).
64. Taylor, *After God*, xviii.
65. Durkheim, *Elementary Forms of the Religious Life*, 227.
66. O'Keeffe, "Deleuze on Habit," 74.
67. Mauss, "Techniques of the Body," 85. It is also worth noting Mauss's suggestion that "at the bottom of all our mystical states there are techniques of the body which we have not studied, but which were perfectly studied by China and India, even in very remote periods. This socio-psycho-biological study should be made. I think that there are necessarily biological means of entering into 'communication with God'" (87).
68. Grosz, "Habit Today: Ravaisson, Bergson, Deleuze and Us," 219.
69. Chandler, *An Archaeology of Sympathy*, 180.

70. Although my current reading of this poem may now swerve from Marjorie Levinson's, in ways that I hope to elaborate upon at another time, her Spinozistic interpretation is still a strong precursor and stimulant to my thinking. See "A Motion and a Spirit."
71. Given that Wordsworth composed this poem in Germany it is worth considering whether the line "A slumber did my spirit seal" contains a pun on the German word for soul—"Seele."
72. Hansen, "The Primacy of Sensation," 220.
73. Schiller, "On Naïve and Sentimental Poetry," 204. Emphasis in original.
74. Chandler, *An Archaeology of Sympathy*, 153.
75. Jackson, "The Senses," 269.
76. Schelling and Žižek, *The Abyss of Freedom / Ages of the World*, 114. Although I will not develop this connection here, William Hazlitt's philosophic work may connect in clarifying ways to this notion of the folded self when he talks about personal identity containing a "radical disjunction between the (present) self which acts and the (future) self which enjoys the fruit of that action." Natarajan, "Introduction," 2.
77. Chandler, *An Archaeology of Sympathy*, 190.
78. Chandler, "The Politics of Sentiment," 575.
79. Chandler, *An Archaeology of Sympathy*, 4.
80. Ahmed, "Happy Objects," 29.
81. Ahmed, *The Promise of Happiness*, 230.
82. Although, as Marjorie Levinson notes, an "affect historicist studies" had already been "challenging the seemingly transparent but in fact historically specific distinction between feeling and knowing." See Levinson, "What Is New Formalism," 561–62.
83. Collings, "Troping Mood," 373. For recent overviews of the relationship between Romanticism and affect studies see Reno, "Romanticism and Affect Studies"; Faflack and Sha, *Romanticism and the Emotions;* and Favret, "The Study of Affect and Romanticism."
84. Ahmed, *The Promise of Happiness*, 230–31.
85. Bennett, "Systems and Things," 234.
86. Bennett, *Vibrant Matter*, xi.
87. Gumbrecht, *Atmosphere, Mood, Stimmung*, 3.
88. Hirshkind, "Is There a Secular Body?," 636.
89. Mahmood, "Religious Reason and Secular Affect," 843.
90. Connolly, "Refashioning the Secular," 167.
91. Jakobsen and Pellegrini. *Secularisms*, 22.

92. Badiou, *Ethics*, 69. Some of the texts I have in mind include Burkett, *Romantic Mediations*; Louise Economides, *The Ecology of Wonder in Romantic and Postmodern Literature*; Faflack and Sha, *Romanticism and the Emotions*; Gurton-Wachter, *Watchwords*; Haekel, *The Soul in British Romanticism*; Igarashi, *The Connected Condition*; Jager, *Unquiet Things*; Kareem, *Eighteenth-Century Fiction and the Reinvention of Wonder*; King, *Imagined Spiritual Communities*; McCarthy, *Awful Parenthesis*; Milnes, *The Testimony of Sense*; Savarese, *Romanticism's Other Minds*; Singer, *Romantic Vacancy*; Tomko, *Beyond the Willing Suspension of Disbelief*; and Woodman and Faflak, *Revelation and Knowledge*. For a recent work that shares some of the same interests I do in theology, religious studies, and phenomenology see Burrows, Ward, and Gregorgzewska, *Poetic Revelations*.
93. Felski, *The Limits of Critique*, 32.
94. Levinson, "What Is New Formalism," 560.
95. Felski, *The Limits of Critique*, 34.
96. Gumbrecht, *Atmosphere, Mood, Stimmung*, 3–4.
97. Novalis, *Notes for a Romantic Encyclopaedia*, 186.
98. Gumbrecht, *Atmosphere, Mood, Stimmung*, 18.
99. Benjamin, "The Concept of Criticism in German Romanticism," 159.
100. De Bolla, *Art Matters*, 12.
101. McGann, *The Romantic Ideology*, 2.
102. Panagia, *The Poetics of Political Thinking*, 5.
103. Goodman, introduction to *The Weight of All Flesh*, 13.
104. Taylor, *Sources of the Self*, 381.
105. Eliot, *Collected Poems*, 189.
106. Bachelard, *The Poetics of Space*, 216.
107. Although I started using the phrase "speculative formalism" as a way of differentiating my approach from new formalism, there is a recent book with that title that seems to share some of the same sympathies: Eyers, *Speculative Formalism*.
108. Jager, "This Detail, This History," 179.
109. For two recent overviews of this field see Felch, *The Cambridge Companion to Literature and Religion*, and Knight, *The Routledge Companion to Literature and Religion*.
110. Bell, *Ritual Theory, Ritual Practice*, 84; Schaefer, *Religious Affects*.
111. Tweed, *Crossing and Dwelling*, 54; Schaefer, *Religious Affects*, 33.
112. Taylor, *After God*, 12.
113. Nikkel, "A Theory of the Embodied Nature of Religion," 171.
114. Schaefer, "Beautiful Facts," 79.

115. Schaefer, *Religious Affects*, 3.
116. Tracy, "Writing," 392.
117. Schaefer, *Religious Affects*, 5.
118. Benjamin, *The Arcades Project*, 483.
119. Brooke-Smith, "Remediating Romanticism," 344.
120. Kittler, *Literature, Media, Information Systems*, 39.
121. Jackson, *Science and Sensation in Romantic Poetry*, 126; Miall, "The Body in Literature," 202, cited by Jackson.
122. Kaufman, "Everybody Hates Kant," 222.
123. A posture of attention is a mode of embodiment. Attention comes from the "Latin *attendere*, meaning stretching toward. Its primary meaning is to direct one's faculties toward something or some one." See Marno, *Death Be Not Proud*, 8.
124. As Santner notes, "These impasses and conflicts pertain to shifts in the fundamental matrix of the individual's relation to social and institutional authority, to the ways he or she is addressed by and responds to the calls of 'official' power and authority. . . . These calls are largely calls to order, rites and procedures of symbolic investiture whereby an individual is endowed with a new social status, is filled with a symbolic mandate that henceforth informs his or her identity in the community." Santner, *My Own Private Germany*, xi–xii.
125. Santner, *On the Psychotheology of Everyday Life*, 11.
126. Grossman, *True-Love*, 8.
127. Jager, *Unquiet Things*, 240.
128. As I will discuss in chapter 5, Shelley uses these terms in a note to "An Essay on the Punishment of Death," the implications of which are developed by Robert Mitchell in *Sympathy and the State*.
129. Chandler, *An Archaeology of Sympathy*, 180.

1. THEORIZING THE POSTSECULAR

1. Santner, *On the Psychotheology of Everyday Life*, 38–39.
2. Wallace Stevens, "Notes toward a Supreme Fiction."
3. Certeau, *The Mystic Fable*, 20. Emphasis in original. As Certeau notices, this can be seen in the development of mysticism as mystics deployed their own corporeal phenomena as a way of saying the "unsayable." They thus proceeded to a "description that ran the gamut of 'sensations,' allowing us to measure the distance between the common usage of these words and the truth that the mystics, led by their experience, gave to them. . . . The

'emotions' of affectivity and the alterations of the body thus became the clearest indicators of the movement produced before or after the stability of intellectual formulations. . . . Mysticism found its modern social language in the body" (Certeau, "Mysticism," 15).
4. See Lloyd and Thomas, *Culture and the State*, 7.
5. Ferris, "Aesthetic Violence and the Legitimacy of Reading Romanticism," 10.
6. Hunt and Rudolf, "Introduction," 26.
7. Taylor, *A Secular Age*, 22.
8. Abrams, *Natural Supernaturalism*, 13.
9. Jager, *The Book of God*, 1.
10. See Casanova, *Public Religions in the Modern World*. Casanova specifically spells out these distinctions in a post on "The Immanent Frame," a scholarly blog devoted to the debates surrounding secularism, religion, and the public sphere (https://tif.ssrc.org/2007/10/25/secular-secularizations-secularisms/). As Mark C. Taylor notes in *After God*, "The current sense of these words can be traced to the Treaty of Westphalia (1648), in which 'secularity' was used to designate 'the conversion of an ecclesiastical or religious institution or its property to sovereigns, princes or lay people.' By extension, *secular* came to mean 'belonging to this world or its affairs as distinguished from the church and religion; civil, with the meaning of non-ecclesiastical, non-religious or non-sacred'" (131).
11. Benavides, "Modernity," 196.
12. Asad, *Formations of the Secular*, 25.
13. Scherer, "Landmarks in the Critical Study of Secularism."
14. Mahmood, "Religious Reason and Secular Affect," 837.
15. Stout, *Democracy and Tradition*, 97.
16. Jager, *The Book of God*, 169.
17. Jager, *Unquiet Things*, 35.
18. Jager, "Shelley after Atheism," 625.
19. Connolly, *Why I Am Not a Secularist*, 27.
20. Foucault, "Technologies of the Self," 18.
21. Partridge, *High Culture*, 11.
22. Connolly, *Why I Am Not a Secularist*, 27.
23. Martin, "Sexualities without Genders and Other Queer Utopias," 110.
24. Schaefer, *Religious Affects*, 125.
25. Gregg and Seigworth, "An Inventory of Shimmers," 1.
26. Johnston and Malabou, *Self and Emotional Life*, 5.

27. "On Two Strains of Affect Theory" (n.d.), *Theoretical Living* (blog), October 11, 2013, https://theoreticalliving.tumblr.com/post/63718644621/on-two-strains-of-affect-theory.
28. Shouse, "Feeling, Emotion, Affect."
29. Johnston and Malabou, *Self and Emotional Life*, 52.
30. Spinoza, *Complete Works*, 278.
31. Johnston and Malabou, *Self and Emotional Life*, 37.
32. Johnston and Malabou, *Self and Emotional Life*, 39. The notion of subjectivity operative in this Aeolian logic resembles the one Johnston and Malabou argue for in *Self and Emotional Life*, wherein "affirmative or negative affects are not affects of a subject, but modifications of an ontological structure, which implies that it is not an 'I' that is passive or active, but the conatus that, like a musical instrument, is played with more or less intensity" (39).
33. S, 511. In his essay "On Christianity," Shelley argues that "there is a Power by which we are surrounded, like the atmosphere in which some motionless lyre is suspended, which visits with its breath our silent chords at will" (*Shelley's Prose*, 202).
34. Shelley, *Shelley's Prose*, 277.
35. Morton, "An Object-Oriented Defense of Poetry," 205. Although the string theory of subjectivity associated with the Aeolian harp is registered in a variety of ways throughout Romanticism in general, and Coleridge in particular, the philosophy of David Hume provides another key source. In the *Treatise*, he writes that "if we consider the human mind, we shall find, that with regard to the passions, 'tis not of the nature of a wind-instrument of music, which in running over all the notes immediately loses the sound after the breath ceases; but rather resembles a string-instrument, where after each stroke the vibrations still retain some sound, which gradually and insensibly decays" (*T*, 2.3.9.12). The passions reverberate over time, and how we are ultimately affected is dependent on resonance or a "relation of difference where one note resounds at the same time as another, and the over-layering of sound waves juxtaposes aspects of one upon the other" (Panagia, *Impressions of Hume*, 58).
36. Rzepka, "Re-collecting Spontaneous Overflows," paragraph 46.
37. Sha, "The Turn to Affect," 260.
38. Leys, "The Turn to Affect," 443.
39. Ahmed, *The Cultural Politics of Emotion*, 40. Also see Faflack and Sha, *Romanticism and the Emotions*.

40. Schaefer, *Religious Affects*, 39.
41. Schaefer, "Beautiful Facts," 78.
42. Schaefer, *Religious Affects*, 32.
43. Ahmed, *The Cultural Politics of Emotion*, 46.
44. Johnston and Malabou, *Self and Emotional Life*, 30.
45. Schaefer, *Religious Affects*, 40–41, 58. A similar emphasis on elasticity and the potential for reconfigurability will be important to the reading of Austen's *Persuasion* in the last chapter.
46. Schaefer, *Religious Affects*, 39. Schaefer is detailing an exchange he witnessed between Massumi and Grusin during a conference in Milwaukee in 2012.
47. Schaefer, *Religious Affects*, 40.
48. Schaefer, *Religious Affects*, 42; Burke, *Reflections on the Revolution in France*, 66.
49. Bergson, *The Two Sources of Morality and Religion*, 103.
50. Asad, *Formations of the Secular*, 4. In Asad's view, "secularism is not simply an intellectual answer to a question about enduring peace and toleration. It is an enactment by which a *political medium* (representation of citizenship) redefines and transcends particular and differentiating practices of the self that are articulated through class, gender, and religion" (5).
51. Siskin and Warner, *This Is Enlightenment*, 1. Here I am alluding to Clifford Siskin and William Warner's insightful argument that the Enlightenment should be identified as an "'event'—one that conventionally occupies roughly a half century between the 1730s–1740s and the 1780s"—and one that emerged as an effect of new and proliferating forms of mediation (11).
52. McLuhan and Fiore, *The Medium Is the Massage*, 41.
53. Williams, *Culture and Materialism*, 60.
54. Brooke-Smith, "Remediating Romanticism," 344.
55. Brooke-Smith, "Remediating Romanticism," 344.
56. Langan and McLane, "The Medium of Romantic Poetry," 247.
57. Ong, *Rhetoric, Romance, and Technology*, 277–78.
58. Langan and McLane, "The Medium of Romantic Poetry," 248.
59. Ong, *Rhetoric, Romance, and Technology*, 271.
60. Havelock, *Preface to Plato*, 197.
61. Earlier media theorists, like McLuhan and Ong, have been critiqued for not fully taking in account or anticipating the rise of digital, as opposed to merely electriconic, media. One reason to turn to more recent figures in media studies like Mark Hansen and, in a different way, to Davide Panagia's reading of Hume, is because these thinkers enable us to think of the digital

in ways that can supplement this earlier work. Fortunately, Langan and McLane, as well as Alan Liu, have all recognized the significance of the digital to our understanding of Romanticism, thus providing a useful bridge between these various approaches.

62. Massumi, *Parables for the Virtual*, 135.
63. Hansen, "Media Theory," 305.
64. *OED*, "digital."
65. Hansen, *Bodies in Code*, 20.
66. Hansen, "Media Theory," 304.
67. Kittler, *Gramophone, Film, Typewriter*, 10.
68. My interest in the intersection of religion and mediation in nineteenth century studies is shared by Joshua King, who has sought to explore how within the course of the nineteenth century "a British print network transformed into a medium for imagining national Christian community" by "adapting to the matrix of print," a method of participation "in a divinely illumined community" (*Imagined Spiritual Communities*, 8). In terms of a longer *durée*, I have also been influenced by the efforts of Mark C. Taylor and others to show how both "Reformation theology and print technology" place an emphasis on linear prospective in a way that "contributes to the constitution of a new subject, which is isomorphic with the individual self in Luther's theology." In different ways, the arguments of both King and Taylor suggest how "print actually contributed to the transformation of the way people see and, by extension, interpret the world" (Taylor, *After God*, 82).
69. Liu, "Imagining the New Media Encounter," 19–20.
70. Langan and McLane, "The Medium of Romantic Poetry," 242.
71. Langan, "Understanding Media in 1805," 49–70.
72. Langan and McLane, "The Medium of Romantic Poetry," 251.
73. See Hansen, *Bodies in Code*.
74. Langan, "Understanding Media in 1805," 53.
75. Langan, "Understanding Media in 1805," 55. She cites McLuhan, *Understanding Media*, 289.
76. Kittler, *Literature, Media, Information Systems*, 39.
77. For more on this idea see Gabriele, *The Emergence of Pre-Cinema*.
78. Trotter, "T. S. Eliot and Cinema," 240.
79. Kittler, *Gramophone, Film, Typewriter*, 10.
80. Scott, *The Complete Poetical Works of Walter Scott*, 41, cited by Langan, "Understanding Media in 1805," 59.
81. Agamben, *The Time That Remains*, 79.

82. *OED*, "cinematagraphic."
83. Hansen, "Media Theory," 303. For a related discussion on the doctrine of inner sense in Kant see Green, *The Aporia of Inner Sense*.
84. Clough, "The Affective Turn," 212; Hansen, "Media Theory," 304.
85. Within the context of eighteenth-century literature, Chandler is particularly interested in the work of Sterne and how he built upon the ideas of writers like Shaftesbury, Samuel Richardson, and Adam Smith, developing new techniques for representing spectatorial networks while also laying bare his devices as he went. Later, in the sentimental style of cinematic pioneers like D. W. Griffith and his disciple Frank Capra, we can see how "their practices of shooting, editing, and *mise-en-scene*—are deeply informed by the manner in which spectators are disposed in a sentimentally ordered world" (Chandler, *An Archaeology of Sympathy*, xv).
86. Locke, *An Essay Concerning Human Understanding*, 227.
87. Koehler, *Poetry of Attention in the Eighteenth Century*, 26.
88. Keith, "Poetry, Sentiment, and Sensibility," 131.
89. Keith, "Poetry, Sentiment, and Sensibility," 131, Citing Lord Kames, *Elements of Criticism*, 7th ed., 1788, 1:91–93.
90. For a helpful discussion of the relationship between Romanticism and virtual reality see Peter Otto's *Multiplying Worlds*.
91. Frye, "Towards Defining an Age of Sensibility," 148.
92. Keith, "Poetry, Sentiment, and Sensibility," 132.
93. Chandler, *An Archaeology of Sympathy*, 12.
94. Chambers, *Cyclopaedia; or, An Universal Dictionary of Arts and Sciences*, vol. 4, s.v. "Sentiments," cited in Brewer, "Sentiment and Sensibility," 21.
95. Chandler, *An Archaeology of Sympathy*, 2.
96. *Monthly Magazine* 2:706 (October 1796), cited in Brewer, "Sentiment and Sensibility," 22.
97. Hansen, "The Primacy of Sensation," 220.
98. Chandler, *An Archaeology of Sympathy*, 180.
99. Sha, "The Turn to Affect," 262.
100. Fisher, *The Vehement Passions*, 40.
101. Ibid., overview.
102. Ibid., 174, 46.
103. Chandler, *An Archaeology of Sympathy*, 12.
104. Fisher, *The Vehement Passions*, 44.
105. Chandler, *An Archaeology of Sympathy*, 12.
106. Chandler, "The Affection-Image and the Movement-Image," 236.
107. Savarese, "Social Minds in Romanticism," 1.

108. Chandler, *An Archaeology of Sympathy*, 12.
109. Mullan, "Sensibility and Literary Criticism," 428.
110. Chandler, *An Archaeology of Sympathy*, xvii. For earlier work on the relationship between Romanticism and sympathy see Marshall, *The Surprising Effects of Sympathy*, and Soni, *Mourning Happiness: Narrative and the Politics of Modernity*.
111. Greiner, *Sympathetic Realism in Nineteenth-Century British Fiction*, 1.
112. Keith, "Poetry, Sentiment, and Sensibility," 128.
113. Smith, *The Theory of Moral Sentiments*, 87, 89.
114. Frazer, *The Enlightenment of Sympathy*, 8.
115. Smith, *The Theory of Moral Sentiments*, 12. At the beginning of *The Theory of Moral Sentiments*, Adam Smith highlights this point: "Though our brother is upon the rack, as long as we ourselves are at our ease, our senses will never inform us of what he suffers. They never did, and never can, carry us beyond our own person, and it is by the imagination only that we can form any conception of what are his sensations. . . . By the imagination we place ourselves in his situation, we conceive ourselves enduring all the same torments, we enter as it were into his body, and become in some measure the same person with him" (11–12).
116. Frazer, *The Enlightenment of Sympathy*, 12.
117. Burgess, "On Being Moved," 304.
118. Chandler, *An Archaeology of Sympathy*, 271–72.
119. Mitchell, *Sympathy and the State*, 89.
120. Chandler, *An Archaeology of Sympathy*, 172.
121. Smith, *The Theory of Moral Sentiments*, 131.
122. Burgess, "On Being Moved," 307.
123. Milbank, "A Closer Walk on the Wild Side," 75.
124. Pfau, *Minding the Modern*, 350.
125. Sha, "The Turn to Affect," 267.
126. Hume, *An Enquiry Concerning the Principles of Morals*, 61.
127. Gibbs, "Contagious Feelings," 1.
128. Ahmed, *The Promise of Happiness*, 39.
129. Burgess, "On Being Moved," 303.
130. Pinch, *Strange Fits of Passion*, 33.
131. Nandrea, "Desiring Difference," 115.
132. Ibid., 114.
133. Chandler, *An Archaeology of Sympathy*, 170.
134. Ibid., 270.
135. Ibid., 281.

136. Panagia, *Impressions of Hume*, 55.
137. Ibid., 55.
138. McLuhan, *The Gutenberg Galaxy*, 153.
139. O'Keeffe, "Deleuze on Habit," 74.
140. Panagia, *Impressions of Hume*, 119.
141. O'Keeffe, "Deleuze on Habit," 74.
142. "David Hume's account of perception as an intrinsically temporal phenomenon—the source for the very notion of temporality, as Locke had argued—informed a number of efforts in the medical literature of this period to define the work of sensation as the marking of time" (Jackson, *Science and Sensation*, 76).
143. O'Keeffe, "Deleuze on Habit," 84.
144. Chandler, "Sensibility, Sympathy and Sentiment," 167.
145. Panagia, *Impressions of Hume*, 2.
146. Chandler, *An Archaeology of Sympathy*, 2.
147. Schiller, "On Naïve and Sentimental Poetry," 204 (Schiller's emphasis).
148. Pfau, *Wordsworth's Profession*, 151.
149. As Chandler notes, "Tintern Abbey" has previously been called protocinematic by at least one commentator (*An Archaeology of Sympathy*, 153). See McConnell, *The Spoken Seen*, 112–14.
150. Wordsworth, *The Borderers*, IV.ii, 143–45.
151. Collings, "The Force of Indirection," 412.
152. Levinson, *Wordsworth's Great Period Poems*, 45.
153. Jackson, *Science and Sensation*, 32.
154. Ibid., 26, 27.
155. Deleuze, *Difference and Repetition*, 74. This seems akin to Wordsworth's use of the concept "under soul" (*P*, 3:540). Herbert Lindenberger notes some other related concepts: "Like Wordsworth's other word coinages in The Prelude—under-powers (1, 163), under-countenance (vi, 236, a reference to the powers latent within a single human soul, in fact, his bride-to-be), under-thirst (vi, 489), and underpresence (xiii, 71)—the 'under soul,' whatever its origins in the mystic tradition, is essentially a symbol of the life within: as a metaphor of direction under can work more powerfully than inner" (*On Wordsworth's Prelude*, 168).
156. Deleuze, *Empiricism and Subjectivity*, x.
157. O'Keeffe, "Deleuze on Habit," 74.
158. Posteraro, "Habits, Nothing but Habits," 95.
159. Deleuze, *Difference and Repetition*, 70.
160. O'Keeffe, "Deleuze on Habit," 75.

161. Panagia, *Impressions of Hume*, 4.
162. Murray and Schuler, "Disappearing Act," 487, cited in Shey, "After Skepticism," 105.
163. Panagia, *Impressions of Hume*, 49.
164. Collings, "The Force of Indirection," 413.
165. Panagia, *Impressions of Hume*, 49.
166. Panagia, *Impressions of Hume*, 64.
167. For a related conception of the self see Santner's discussion of "the Ego and the Ibid" in *On the Psychotheology of Everyday Life*, 51.
168. Panagia, *Impressions of Hume*, 68.
169. Ibid., 3.
170. Connor, "Literature, Technology, and the Sense," 177, citing Locke, *An Essay Concerning Human Understanding*, 109.
171. Locke, *Essay*, 2.11.17.
172. Locke, *Essay*, 2.19.1.
173. Addison, "Pleasures of Imagination."
174. Panagia, *Impressions of Hume*, 67.
175. Ibid., 79.
176. Broglio, "Romantic," 32. "Elemental space" is a phrase used by Keats in his "vale of Soul-making" letter.
177. Panagia, *Impressions of Hume*, 33, 37.
178. Panagia, *Impressions of Hume*, 67. "This fiction of the imagination almost universally takes place; and 'tis by means of it, that a single object, plac'd before us, and survey'd for any time without our discovering in it any interruption or variation, is able to give us a notion of identity" (*T*, 1.4.2.29).
179. Hume, *An Enquiry Concerning Human Understanding*, 129. "Custom, then, is the great guide of human life. It is that principle alone, which renders our experience useful to us, and makes us expect, for the future, a similar train of events with those which have appeared in the past" (122).
180. Cited in Christensen, *Practicing Enlightenment*, 8. See also Christensen, *Coleridge's Blessed Machine of Language*, 163–67.
181. Coleridge, *Notebooks*, 2370.
182. Coleridge to John Prior Estlin (February 13, 1798), CL I 385–86.
183. McGann, "The Ancient Mariner."
184. Lindstrom, "Between Cant and Anguish," 125.
185. Coleridge, *Marginalia*, 3:720.
186. King, *Imagined Spiritual Communities*, 26.
187. Schey, "After Skepticism," 72.
188. Burke, *Reflections on the Revolution in France*, 66.

189. Schey, "After Skepticism," 15.
190. Panagia, *The Political Life of Sensation*, 6.
191. Burke, *Reflections on the Revolution in France*, 66.
192. Sapiro, *A Vindication of Political Virtue*, 192.
193. Burke, *Reflections on the Revolution in France*, 74–75.
194. Although we may ultimately decide that a given element of tradition does not fit our needs, there does seem to be value in at least provisionally entertaining Burke's suggestion that "many of our men of speculation, instead of exploding general prejudices, employ their sagacity to discover the latent wisdom which prevails in them. If they find what they seek, and they seldom fail, they think it more wise to continue the prejudice, with the reason involved, than to cast away the coat of prejudice, and to leave nothing but the naked reason; because prejudice, with its reason, has a motive to give action to that reason, and an affection which will give it permanence" (Burke, *Reflections on the Revolution in France*, 74). Regardless of whether one ultimately wishes to adopt the affections of any given "coat of prejudice," understanding how a given religion or worldview fashions a second nature for its adherents is worthwhile, even if only because it is by understanding how religion and worldviews are formed that one can gain a better vantage point from which to critique or even begin to alter its fabrications.
195. Paine, *Rights of Man, Common Sense, and Other Political Writings*, 115.
196. Hume, "Of the Standard of Taste," 151.
197. Mary Wollstonecraft, of course, in contrast to Burke, declared that "romance destroys all simplicity" and was more concerned with how "deceptive costumes and masks and manipulative prose masquerading as 'natural feelings and common sense'" can cover over man's true nature (Sapiro, *A Vindication of Political Virtue*, 197). For her, a community's natural goodness would only be revealed once these layers of false ideology are stripped away.
198. Although by taking a non-Kantian trajectory out of Hume the speculative realist and object-oriented emphasis on the critique of correlationalism becomes much less compelling.
199. Morton, "An Object-Oriented Defense of Poetry," 205.
200. O'Keeffe, "Deleuze on Habit," 87.
201. Chandler, *England in 1819*, 539.
202. Ankersmit, *Sublime Historical Experience*, 326.
203. Latour, *Facing Gaia*, 140. Emphasis in original.
204. Silverman, *The Threshold of the Visible World*, 37.
205. Merleau-Ponty, *The Visible and the Invisible*, 139.

206. Goodman, introduction to *The Weight of All Flesh*, 8.
207. Merleau-Ponty, *The Visible and the Invisible*, 88–89.
208. Simpson, *Merleau-Ponty and Theology*, 39.
209. Merleau-Ponty, *The Primacy of Perception*, 373.
210. Hansen, *Bodies in Code*, 5.
211. Merleau-Ponty, *The Visible and the Invisible*, 28.
212. Flusser, *Towards a Philosophy of Photography*, 7.
213. Merleau-Ponty, *The Primacy of Perception*, 25.
214. Kearney, *Anatheism*, 89.
215. Merleau-Ponty, *Phenomenology of Perception*, 246.
216. Ibid., 248. In both cases, the "sensory encounter with the strangeness of the world is an invitation to a 'natal pact' where, through sympathy, the human self and the strange world give birth to one another" (Kearney, *Anatheism*, 89).
217. Kearney, *Anatheism*, 89.
218. Ibid., 89, 91.
219. Simpson, *Merleau-Ponty and Theology*, 8.
220. Johnston and Malabou, *Self and Emotional Life*, 10.
221. See Merleau-Ponty, *The Visible and the Invisible*, 151.
222. Parsons, "A Philosophy of Wonder," 85.
223. Malpas, "Beginning in Wonder," 296.
224. Miller, *The Linguistic Moment*, xiv. This is one reason why I often find myself saying in class: "If you don't know what a poem is about, pretend it is about poetry." For an interesting discussion of parabasis see Paul Hamilton's *Metaromanticism*.
225. Malpas, "Beginning in Wonder," 285.
226. Miller, *The Corporeal Imagination*, 63.
227. Mitchell, *Experimental Life*, 73.
228. Morton, *Ecology without Nature*, 44.
229. Panagia, *The Political Life of Sensation*, 10.
230. Faflak, "Speaking of Godwin's Caleb Williams," 121, cited by Rajan, *Romantic Narrative*, 83.
231. Panagia, *The Political Life of Sensation*, 3.
232. Kristeva, *Time and Sense*, 247.
233. Burke, *Reflections on the Revolution in France*, 66.
234. King, *Imagined Spiritual Communities*, 27.
235. Donne, *John Donne and the Theology of Language*, 127–28.
236. Ibid., 128.
237. Goodman, introduction to *The Weight of All Flesh*, 7.

238. Santner, *The Royal Remains*, xiii.
239. Ibid., 100.
240. Ibid., 100.
241. Santner, *The Weight of All Flesh*, 46.
242. Žižek, *For They Know Not What They Do*, 256.
243. Santner, *The Weight of All Flesh*, 69.
244. Santner, *On Creaturely Life*, 81
245. Santner, *The Royal Remains*, 89.
246. Ibid., xvi–xvii.
247. Esposito, "The Person and Human Life," 207.
248. Jager, *Unquiet Things*, 236.
249. Foucault, *Discipline and Punish*, 25–26. Talal Asad similarly argues that secular modernity stems from a shift in an underlying grammar of concepts about what it means to be human. This shift seemed to occur all at once in revolutionary France and more gradually in Britain, but in either case the extension of universal suffrage and participation in representational government produces "new methods of government based on new styles of classification and calculation, and new forms of subjecthood" (*Formations of the Secular*, 24). The principles of government become secular in the sense that "they deal solely with a worldly disposition," unlike the "medieval conception of a social body of Christian souls each of whom is endowed with equal dignity—members at once of the City of God and of divinely created human society" (24). The decisive shift of the nineteenth century is a move away "from thinking of a fixed 'human nature' to regarding humans in terms of a constituted 'normality,'" which "facilitated the secular idea of moral progress defined and directed by autonomous human agency" (24). This move from a view of fixed human nature to one of normality and deviance highlights the role of error in the construction of identity. One's deviance from the norm becomes the distinctive signature of one's self.
250. Jager, *Unquiet Things*, 236.
251. An emphasis on the centrality of bodily experience within modernity is found in figures such as Henri Bergson, Maurice Merleau-Ponty, Gilles Deleuze, and Michel Foucault, who despite their various differences all share in the assumption that human experience should be thought, "not in the transcendental prism of the individual consciousness, but in the indivisible density of life." For all of them, "what we call the subject, or person, is nothing but the result, always provisory, of a process of individuation or subjectification, quite irreducible to the individual and his

masks" (Esposito, "The Person and Human Life," 217). Nevertheless, as the Italian philosopher Roberto Esposito has argued, "To identify this process with the first or second of these terms, individuation or subjection, is not a matter of indifference for the direction that the discourse intends to assume" (217). And thus within criticism a Deleuzean investment in the side of individuation and the philosophical affirmation of life often squares off against a Foucaultian focus on the disciplinary mechanisms of subjection. Suggestively, Esposito's hope is that "an affirmative biopolitics" can be constructed through some conjunction of these two trajectories. See also Esposito, *Bíos: Biopolitics and Philosophy*, 10.

2. POETIC FAITH

1. Useful starting places for considering Coleridge's relationship to the concept of the soul include Engell's "Coleridge (and His Mariner) on the Soul" and "The Soul, Highest Cast of Consciousness," and Hedley, *Coleridge, Philosophy and Religion*.
2. Herder, "Treatise on the Origin of Language," 87
3. Asad, *Formations of the Secular*, 37–38.
4. Donne, *John Donne's Sermons on the Psalms and Gospels*, 104.
5. Ward, *True Religion*, 21–22.
6. Milbank, *Theology and Social Theory*, 9.
7. Asad, *Formations of the Secular*, 38.
8. Lessing, *Lessings Werke*, 23:47.
9. Shaffer, "Ideologies in Readings of the Late Coleridge."
10. Coleridge, *Shorter Works and Fragments*, 1129, 1123.
11. Shaffer, "Religion and Literature," 142–43.
12. Lloyd, *Reclaiming Wonder*, 46–47.
13. Lowth, *Lectures on the Sacred Poetry of the Hebrews*, 25, 39.
14. Jager, "The Entangled Spirituality of 'The Thorn,'" 467.
15. Canuel, "Coleridge's Polemic Divinity," 955.
16. Canuel, "Coleridge's Polemic Divinity," 954, citing Coleridge, *Collected Works*, 4.1:440.
17. Žižek, *The Sublime Object of Ideology*, 34.
18. Ibid., 43.
19. Vigus, "The Philosophy of Samuel Taylor Coleridge," 524.
20. Savarese, "Lyric Mindedness and the 'Automaton Poet,'" para. 4.
21. Coleridge to Robert Southey (December 11, 1794), CL 1:137.
22. Canuel, "Coleridge's Polemic Divinity," 956.

23. As God says to Job out of the whirlwind, "Where were you when I laid the foundation of the earth? Tell me, if you have understanding" (Job 38:4).
24. Shaffer, "Metaphysics of Culture," 210–11.
25. Kant, *Critique of Judgement*, 119.
26. Žižek, *The Sublime Object of Ideology*, 203.
27. Although it came to my attention too late to be incorporated into this argument, Peter Cheyne's *Coleridge's Contemplative Philosophy* (2020) argues that in the late stages of his career Coleridge advocates for a form of contemplation that would be functionally "equivalent to what Plato called noesis: a direct, intuitive beholding of timeless moral values and the constitutive powers that shape reality and frame its rational space" (16). Cheyne's book is an important intervention in the field and helps articulate how Coleridge ultimately aims to move beyond reflection, mediation, and the "sea of ideas" and into the "ocean of philosophical theology" and the direct contemplation of the divine ideas (4).
28. Dante, *The Divine Comedy*.
29. Kordela, "It Looks Down upon Us (Allegorical Fields and Repetitive Errors)," 99–129.
30. In this conception of an "absent cause" that can only be perceived "through its effects," I have in mind Frederick Jameson's appropriation of the term from Althusser and Spinoza in *The Political Unconscious*: "History is what hurts, it is what refuses desire and sets inexorable limits to individual as well as collective praxis, which its 'ruses' turn into grisly and ironic reversals of their overt intention. But this History can be apprehended only through its effects, and never directly as some reified force. This is indeed the ultimate sense in which History as ground and untranscendable horizon needs no particular theoretical justification: we may be sure that its alienating necessities will not forget us, however much we might prefer to ignore them" (88).
31. Coleridge, *Collected Lectures*, 91.
32. Shaffer, "Metaphysics of Culture," 201.
33. Beer, "Coleridge and Wordsworth on Reflection," 21.
34. Locke, *An Essay Concerning Human Understanding*, 2.1.4.
35. Beer, "Coleridge and Wordsworth on Reflection," 22, citing Locke, *An Essay Concerning Human Understanding*, 2.7.10.
36. Taylor, *The Language Animal*, 14.
37. T, "Abstract," 417.
38. Taylor, *The Language Animal*, 15.
39. Taylor, *After God*, 106.

40. See Gopnik, *The Philosophical Baby*.
41. Vigus, "The Philosophy of Samuel Taylor Coleridge," 526.
42. Taylor, *The Language Animal*, 16.
43. Vigus, "The Philosophy of Samuel Taylor Coleridge," 526.
44. Kant, *Critique of the Power of Judgment*, §49, cited by Vigus, "The Philosophy of Samuel Taylor Coleridge," 530,
45. Shaffer, "Metaphysics of Culture," 207.
46. Coleridge, *Opus Maximum*, lxv.
47. Frye, *The Educated Imagination*, 143.
48. Quoted in McFarland, "Prolegomena," in Coleridge, *Opus Maximum*, lxiii.
49. Quoted in ibid., lxix.
50. Schelling, *Ages of the World*, 117–18.
51. Brown, *The Later Philosophy of Schelling*, 201.
52. Vigus, "The Philosophy of Samuel Taylor Coleridge," 528.
53. Beer, "Coleridge and Wordsworth on Reflection," 24.
54. As Wordsworth puts it in the Immortality Ode, l. 157.
55. One source of inspiration for the way Coleridge conceived of reflection was his encounters with mystics such as Jacob Boehme, George Fox, and William Law, writers who helped him, after his "wanderings through the wilderness of doubt," keep "alive the heart in the head," and enabled him "to skirt, without crossing, the sandy deserts of utter unbelief" (*BL*, 1:152; cf. 200, cited by Vigus, "The Philosophy of Samuel Taylor Coleridge," 525).
56. Benjamin, "The Concept of Criticism in German Romanticism," 129.
57. Ibid., 138, citing Charlotte Pingoud, *Grundlinien der iisthetisclaen Doletrin Fr. Schlegels* [Outline of Friedrich Schlegel's Aesthetic Doctrine] (Stuttgart, 1914), 32ff.
58. Taylor, *The Language Animal*, 12.
59. Burwick, "Coleridge's Conversation Poems," 179.
60. Taylor, *The Language Animal*, 5.
61. Taylor, *Philosophical Arguments*, 84.
62. Taylor, *The Language Animal*, 9.
63. Rzepka, "Re-collecting Spontaneous Overflows," paragraph 46.
64. Herder, "Treatise on the Origin of Language," 87.
65. Taylor, *The Language Animal*, 12.
66. Beer, "Coleridge and Wordsworth on Reflection," 24.

3. COLERIDGE'S PARABLE OF MODERNITY

1. Benjamin, *Illuminations*, 87. It is worth noting that this chapter's focus on the "Ancient Mariner" pairs nicely with one of the two typical types of storytellers Benjamin highlights: the "trading seaman" and the "resident tiller of the soil." The latter is the form of storyteller that tends to attract Wordsworth's attention.
2. Santner, *The Royal Remains*, 118.
3. Fisher, *Vehement Passions*, 246.
4. Warner, VanAntwerpen, and Calhoun, "Editors' Introduction," *Varieties of Secularism in a Secular Age*, 18.
5. Santner, *My Own Private Germany*, xii. The work of symbolic investiture is so important because it names "the performative act that endows an individual with a new social status within a shared space of representation—one that, when matters progress smoothly, he [or she] can, in turn, invest [his or her] energies in or 'cathect.'" Goodman, introduction to *The Weight of All Flesh*, 3.
6. Faflak, *Romantic Psychoanalysis*, 8.
7. Santner argues that the crisis in investiture experienced in modernity involves the application of what psychoanalysis calls "transference." Transference, the "central feature of psychic life and therapeutic efficacy, ultimately revolves around the enigmatic processes and procedures whereby a human life becomes authorized, placed in a relation to the resources of value and legitimacy that constitute the very 'stuff' of sovereignty. The transference is 'where and how what Lacan referred to as the 'discourse of the Master' gets under our skin" (Santner, *On the Psychotheology of Everyday Life*, 26–27). It is through the processes of transference that the unconscious transmission of cultural patterns and values is performed. More specifically, Santner defines transference as "the condition of finding oneself obsessively engaged in the effort to interpret, to translate into the language of reason, valuational speech acts whose ultimate authority remains grounded in the performative force of their enunciation" (Santner, *My Own Private Germany*, 123).
8. Goodman, "introduction to *The Weight of All Flesh*," 2.
9. Santner, *The Royal Remains*, xii.
10. Ibid., xiv.
11. See *CPP*, 64n4.
12. Burwick, "Coleridge's Conversation Poems," 179.
13. Pfau, *Minding the Modern*, 462.
14. Ibid., 463.

15. See Coleridge's marginal gloss of lines 97–102. *CPP*, 67.
16. The failure to attend to this "orienting a priori" of the body can be pernicious, and Robert Penn Warren suggestively noted that because the crew "judge the moral content of an act by its consequence . . . they would make good disciples of Bishop Paley, who, according to Coleridge, in *Aids to Reflection*, was no moralist because he would judge the morality of an act by consequence and not 'contemplate the same in its original spiritual source,' the state of the will" ("A Poem of Pure Imagination," 401). Warren's characterization of the mariner's shipmates as potential disciples of William Paley is suggestive because it raises the possibility of reading into their spectral life aboard the ship a critique of the rhetoric of design's iterative machinery. Unlike the mariner, who is somehow singled out and alone survives the ordeal, the rest of the "ghastly crew" (340) raise "their limbs like lifeless tools" (339), becoming embodiments of a controlling yet lifeless agency. These "dead men" (334) are without wills of their own but are instead compelled by outside forces to act as they do. The discourse of design has been an influential form of religiosity within secularity from William Paley's clockmaker God to present-day advocates of intelligent design. As Colin Jager has argued, the rhetoric of design attempts to generate a "religious humility" through a "repetitive pedagogy" in "nontransformative poetics" that builds up "a certain kind of pious subject through the adoption and inculcation of a set of habits, dispositions, and bodily postures" (*Book of God*, 100).
17. Mitchell, *Experimental Life*, 60.
18. Coleridge, *Lectures*, 124, cited by Mitchell, *Experimental Life*, 60.
19. Burgess, "On Being Moved," from *Emotions: On the Affective Turn* panel at MLA 2008.
20. Rzepka, *The Self as Mind*, 119.
21. Iser, "Representation," 232.
22. Žižek, *The Indivisible Remainder*, 14.
23. McGann, "The Ancient Mariner," 152.
24. Eliot, *Collected Poems*, 431. The underlying epistemological model of this logic can already be seen in the trinitarian thinking of Jacob Boehme, who is a sometimes underappreciated influence on both Schelling and Coleridge. This model can be schematized as the interaction of three interlocking aspects or conditions. In the initial stage (A_1), all is one and in a condition of complete similarity, repetition, and identity. This is the situation prior to the beginning, before temporality and language exist. Time (A_2) begins abruptly when the Word is (finally) spoken to express the

eternal similarity, but (un)fortunately this expression falls short and introduces an awareness of difference instead. Other words are subsequently spoken in an attempt to recover this difference, and strata of time are filled with these attempts to recall eternity's silent eloquence. Each temporal moment is posited in the present as an answer to the troubling desire for closure but is deposited in the past when some new solution attracts the attention. The movement to the third stage (A_3) occurs when the void that language has been hoping to recover is seen within the fabric of language itself, within the stratified history of missed occasions, and through this fissure a figure of eternity may be glimpsed—at least momentarily.

25. McGann, "The Ancient Mariner," 151.
26. Like Coleridge, I would be inclined to argue that "Christianity is not a Theory, or a Speculation; but a Life. Not a Philosophy of Life, but a Life and a living Process" (AR, 202).
27. Santner, draft version of preface to *The Royal Remains*, 8.
28. Santner, *On Creaturely Life*, 206. Thus the role of the critic is seen as being akin to Apollonius's role in Keats's "Lamia."
29. McGann, "The Ancient Mariner," 158.
30. McGann, *The Romantic Ideology*, 2.
31. Certeau, *The Mystic Fable*, 77.
32. The reinterpretation of tradition signaled by mystic fables is "characterized by a set of procedures allowing a new treatment of language—of all contemporary language, not only the area delimited by theological knowledge or the corpus of patristic and scriptural works" (Certeau, *Heterologies*, 81). Although Certeau recognizes precursors to this new formality going back to at least Meister Eckhart (1260–1327), he is most interested in observing the new mystics at "the moment of its greatest formalization and its end—from Teresa of Ávila to Angelus Silesius" (Certeau, *The Mystic Fable*, 16–17).
33. Certeau, "Mysticism," 15.
34. Certeau, *The Mystic Fable*, 163–64.
35. As Walter Pahnke noted in his influential doctoral dissertation, written under the supervision of Timothy Leary, "Set is defined as expectation, mood, mental attitude and past experience of the subject; setting is the external environment and atmosphere and includes the expectations of the investigator." Cited in Partridge, *High Culture*, 19.
36. Pfau, *Minding the Modern*, 454.
37. Pfau's sole reference to the water snakes comes in a footnote discussing David Watkins's reading of the "Rime" as being "expressive of a 'demonic'

energy that manifests itself repeatedly, such as in the mariner's apparently heretical blessing of the water snakes, which he does 'in the same way he shot the Albatross, unthinkingly and impulsively. What is more, the objects of his blessing, the water snakes, have obvious connections to the biblical serpent, and to bless them is to abandon the system of belief to which he had previously adhered, not to submit to it" (*Minding the Modern*, 493).

38. Pfau, "The Philosophy of Shipwreck," 983.
39. Pfau, *Minding the Modern*, 465.
40. Ibid., 491, 488.
41. Shaffer, "Metaphysics of Culture," 209.
42. Pfau, "The Philosophy of Shipwreck," 988.
43. Shaffer, "Metaphysics of Culture," 210.
44. Pfau, *Minding the Modern*, 491.
45. Eliot, *Collected Poems*, 419.
46. Coleridge, *Shorter Works and Fragments*, 517.
47. McSweeney, *The Language of the Senses*, 84.
48. Burwick, "Coleridge's Conversation Poems," 168.
49. Shelley, "On Christianity," 246–71.
50. Derrida, *The Animal That Therefore I Am*, 17.
51. Grossman, *True-Love*, 8.
52. Panagia, *The Political Life of Sensation*, 10.
53. Grossman, *True-Love*, 7.
54. Kant, "What Does It Mean to Orient Oneself in Thinking?," 8, cited in Grossman, *True-Love*, 7.
55. Grossman, *True-Love*, 7.
56. Jackson, *Science and Sensation in Romantic Poetry*, 122.
57. Grossman, *True-Love*, 15.
58. Schmitt, *Political Theology*, 15.
59. Egerton MS 2801, © The British Library, cited in Berkeley, *Coleridge and the Crisis of Reason*, 56. With respect to his influence on Coleridge, Berkeley's book convincingly explores how an engagement with Spinoza lies at the heart of Coleridge's intellectual life. Coleridge claimed that Spinoza's "System is to mine just what a Skeleton is to a Body, fearful because it is only the Skeleton" (*CL*, 4:775), but understanding just how Coleridge attempted to put flesh on these bones is challenging. Coleridge's specific critiques of Spinoza, as with Hume, centered around the problem of infinity and focused on issues surrounding God's nature, causality, human free will, and the problem of evil.

60. Kant, *Prolegemona to Any Future Metaphysics*, 34.
61. Of course it is worth remembering that although Hume would deny such a map is actually available, he steers clear of his own doubts simply by changing his affective disposition. Right after the experience of "shipwreck" at the conclusion of book 1, when Hume is once again writing and thinking in an "easy disposition," Hume himself is able to proceed with his philosophy and encourages his reader who "finds himself in the same easy disposition, let him follow me in my future speculations. If not, let him follow his inclination, and wait the returns of application and good humour." Ultimately, anyone who can follow "in this careless manner, is more truly sceptical than that of one, who feeling in himself an inclination to it, is yet so over-whelm'd with doubts and scruples, as totally to reject it" (*T*, 1.4.7.14). The importance of "good humour" to the way we pilot our vehicular consciousness is a key issue that will return in the last chapter's discussion of Jane Austen.
62. I borrow the concept of itinerary from Certeau's *The Practice of Everyday Life* (1984), where a distinction is made between "itineraries" and "maps" that can help suggest the difference between Kant's and Coleridge's approaches. A map is "a totalizing stage on which elements of diverse origin are brought together to form the tableau of a 'state' of geographical knowledge" (121). Modernity gives rise to mapping because its move toward universality is accompanied by a geometric rationality that privileges the utility of mapping space on a grid.
63. Certeau, *The Practice of Everyday Life*, 121.
64. Cavanaugh, *Theopolitical Imagination*, 100.
65. Goodrich, "The Judge's Two Bodies," 118.
66. Langan, "Pathologies of Communication from Coleridge to Schreber," 118.
67. Freud, *Standard Edition*, 1:207.
68. Reinhard, "Toward a Political Theology of the Neighbor," 33.
69. Freud, *Standard Edition*, 1:212; cited in Reinhard, "Toward a Political Theology of the Neighbor," 28.
70. Johnston and Malabou, *Self and Emotional Life*, 25.
71. Santner, *The Royal Remains*, xiv.
72. Santner, *On the Psychotheology of Everyday Life*, 48.
73. Ibid., 48. Emphasis in original.
74. Connor, "Scilicet," 118. Conner is summarizing Kittler's position.
75. Ibid., 128. "Similarly systematic delusions were set out in 1838 by John Perceval (1838, 1961) and from 1852 onwards by Friedrich Krauß (1967), both of which depend upon contemporary and proleptic ideas of media machinery" (Connor, "Scilicet," 128).

76. Khalip and Mitchell, introduction, to *Releasing the Image*, 10.
77. Mesmer, *Mesmerism*, 67.
78. Faflak, *Romantic Psychoanalysis*, 50.
79. Darnton, *Mesmerism and the End of the Enlightenment in France*, 3.
80. Santner, *The Royal Remains*, 98.
81. Bloch, *The Royal Touch*, 4. The phrases "flashing eyes" and "floating hair" are from Coleridge's "Kubla Khan."
82. Schelling, *Ages of the World*, 114.
83. Deleuze, *The Fold*, 24.
84. Friedrich Schelling provides one explication of the soul that is a helpful first step in answering this question: "Drawn from the source of things and akin to it, what is eternal of the soul is a co-science/ con-sciousness [*Mitt-Wissenschaft*] of creation. Because this essence holds time enveloped, it serves as a link that enables man to make an immediate connection with the most ancient past as well as with the most distant future" (Schelling, *Ages of the World*, 114).
85. William James would say "stream of consciousness."
86. Chandler, *An Archaeology of Sympathy*, 180.
87. Plotinus, *Enneads*, 4.3.21. Pfau references this quote but comes to different conclusions, claiming that for Plotinus, "the breakdown of the nautical trope exposes body and soul as fundamentally incommensurable categories" (*Minding the Modern*, 485). Compare to Descartes's claim in his Sixth Meditation: "I am not merely present in my body as a sailor is present in a ship, but . . . am very closely joined and, as it were, intermingled with it, so that I and the body form a unit" (Descartes, *The Passions of the Soul*, 56).
88. Plotinus, *Enneads*, 4.3.21.
89. Eliot, *Collected Poems*, 419.
90. Jaspers, *Reason and Existenz*, 31.
91. Santner, *On the Psychotheology of Everyday Life*, 48.
92. Coleridge to Thomas Poole (October 16, 1797). Emphasis in original. "From my early reading of Faery Tales, & Genii &c &c—my mind had been habituated to the Vast—& I never regarded my senses in any way as the criteria of my belief. I regulated all my creeds by my conceptions not by my sight—even at that age. Should children be permitted to read Romances, & Relations of Giants & Magicians, & Genii?—I know all that has been said against it; but I have formed my faith in the affirmative.—I know no other way of giving the mind a love of 'the Great,' & 'the Whole.'—Those who have been led by the same truths step by step thro' the constant testimony of their senses, seem to me to want a sense which I possess—They

contemplate nothing but parts—and as parts are necessarily little—and the Universe to them is but a mass of little things" (*CL*, 1:354).
93. Reinhard, "Toward a Political Theology of the Neighbor," 35. Emphasis in original.
94. Kordela, "Marx's Update of Cultural Theory," 53.
95. Lowes, *The Road to Xanadu*, 42.
96. McKusick, *Green Writing*, 46.
97. Grossman, *True-Love*, 15.
98. Santner, *On the Psychotheology of Everyday Life*, 136.
99. Havelock, *Preface to Plato*, 197.
100. Johnston and Malabou, *Self and Emotional Life*, 17.
101. Barth, "'A Spring of Love,'" 77.
102. Descartes, *The Passions of the Soul*, §§51–148, 75.
103. Johnston and Malabou, *Self and Emotional Life*, 18.
104. Freud, *Standard Edition*, 1:331 (translation modified by Reinhard), cited in Reinhard, "Toward a Political Theology of the Neighbor," 30.
105. Freud, *Standard Edition*, 1:212
106. Reinhard, "Toward a Political Theology of the Neighbor," 27.
107. Santner, *On the Psychotheology of Everyday Life*, 44.
108. Kordela, *Surplus*, 137.
109. Bergson, *Matter and Memory*, 228.
110. Crary, *Suspensions of Perception*, 317.
111. Kordela, *Surplus*, 137.
112. Poulet, "Phenomenology of Reading," 54.

4. "TO SEE AS A GOD SEES"

1. Santner, *The Weight of All Flesh*, 46.
2. *LJK*, 2:101–2. In the "vale of Soul-making" letter, Keats writes that soul should be "distinguished from an Intelligence. There may be intelligences or sparks of the divinity in millions, but they are not Souls till they acquire identities, till each one is personally itself. Intelligences are atoms of perception; they know and they see and they are pure, in short they are God. How then are Souls to be made? How then are these sparks which are God to have identity given them so as ever to possess a bliss peculiar to each one's individual existence? How, but by the medium of a world like this? This point I sincerely wish to consider because I think it a grander system of salvation than the chrystain religion, or rather it is a system of Spirit-creation" (*LJK*, 2:101–2).

3. Engell, "The Soul, Highest Cast of Consciousness," 7.
4. Bate, *John Keats*, 473.
5. Chandler, *England in 1819*, 413.
6. Chandler, *England in 1819*, 417.
7. Altieri, "Inner Sensuousness," 281.
8. Perkins, "Sympathy with Nature," 80.
9. Lacan, *Écrits*, 166.
10. Perkins, "Sympathy with Nature," 80.
11. Altieri, "Inner Sensuousness," 291.
12. Crary, *Suspensions of Perception*, 155.
13. Crary, *Techniques of the Observer*, 24.
14. During, *Modern Enchantments*, 285.
15. Kittler, *Optical Media*, 78. Also see Keats's "Eve of St. Agnes."
16. Gane and Hansen-Magnusson, "Materiality Is the Message?," 319.
17. Chandler, *England in 1819*, 421.
18. Deleuze, *The Fold*, 24.
19. William Hazlitt's philosophic work could help clarify what this might mean when he talks about how our personal identity contains a "radical disjunction between the (present) self which acts and the (future) self which enjoys the fruit of that action" (Natarajan, "Introduction," 2).
20. O'Keeffe, "Deleuze on Habit," 87.
21. Bruno, "Pleats of Matter, Folds of the Soul," 114.
22. See the preceding chapter's discussion of the epigraph to the 1817 version of the "Rime."
23. Hazlitt, *The Plain Speaker*, 1:155. A useful discussion of Hazlitt's essay can be found in Pfau, *Romantic Moods*, 354–56.
24. According to Georg Simmel in "The Metropolis and Mental Life" (1903) the experience of the city is one in which life is fragmented, experiences juxtaposed. He speaks of "the intensification of nervous stimulation that results from the swift and uninterrupted change of outer and inner stimuli" (Simmel, 175). For more on the role of the city in Romanticism see Chandler and Gilmartin, *Romantic Metropolis*.
25. Hazlitt, *The Plain Speaker*, 1:177.
26. See Gill, *William Wordsworth*, 146.
27. Hertz, "The Notion of Blockage in the Literature of the Sublime," 84.
28. Gabriele, "Visions of the City of London," 369.
29. Chandler and Gilmartin, *Romantic Metropolis*, 5.
30. Gabriele, *Reading Popular Culture in Victorian Print*, 7.
31. Eisenstein, *The Film Sense*, 17.

32. Deleuze, *Cinema 1*, 109.
33. Benjamin, *Illuminations*, 236.
34. Shaya, "The Flâneur, the Badaud, and the Making of a Mass Public," 46.
35. Jackson, "The Time of Beauty."
36. Oerlemans, *Romanticism and the Materiality of Nature*, 21.
37. Hazlitt, *The Plain Speaker*, 1:156.
38. *LJK*, 1:193–94.
39. Terada, *Looking Away*, 18.
40. Baudelaire, *The Painter of Modern Life*, 9.
41. Shaya, "The Flâneur, the Badaud, and the Making of a Mass Public," 49.
42. Benjamin, *Selected Writings*, 41.
43. Like the Cockney, negative associations are often attached to the badaud, and the badaud may be looked down upon in a manner not unlike that of Keats in W. B. Yeats's "Ego Dominus Tuus": "With face and nose pressed to a sweet-shop window, . . . Shut out from all the luxury of the world."
44. Benjamin, *Selected Writings*, 69. Benjamin quotes Fournel from *Ce qu'on voit dans les rues de Paris* (Paris, 1858), 263.
45. Webster's *Revised Unabridged Dictionary* (C. G. Merriam, 1913), s.v. "badaud." One indication of the continuing importance of the figure of the badaud in the internet age can be found in the fact that at one time a popular gossip and media site was named *Gawker.com*.
46. Hazlitt, *The Plain Speaker*, 1:155–56.
47. For more on anonymity and Romanticism see Khalip, *Anonymous Life*.
48. Newey, "*Hyperion, The Fall of Hyperion*, and Keats's Epic Ambitions," 79.
49. A phrase used by Walter Pater in his influential conclusion to *The Renaissance*, 153.
50. Bennett, *Vibrant Matter*, xii.
51. Gunning, "From the Kaleidoscope to the X-Ray," 31.
52. Cited in Groth, "Kaleidoscopic Vision," 221.
53. Gunning, "From the Kaleidoscope to the X-Ray," 33.
54. Wang, "Coming Attractions," 500. Here, Keats is found to be "the English poet of mediated cultural experience par excellence," and Wang argues that the precinema may be the key to unlocking new ways of understanding a wide range of Keats's canonical works (475).
55. Fulford, *Landscape, Liberty, and Authority*. For more on loco-descriptive poetry see Barrell, *The Idea of Landscape and the Sense of Place*; Pfau, *Wordsworth's Profession*; Broglio, *Technologies of the Picturesque*; and Potkay, "Eye and Ear."
56. Abrams, "Structure and Style in the Greater Romantic Lyric," 201.

57. In this way the "cathedral cavern" functions much like a playhouse in Keats's day. As Christopher Baugh has argued, whereas in 1740 the typical stage "would display the formal qualities of a scenically neutral theatrical place," by 1840 "the physical presence of scenic techniques and effects would underpin almost all aspects of production" ("Scenography and Technology," 43). Larger theaters, the separation of the audience from the action by a decorated proscenium frame, and the use of gaslight and a variety of lighting effects all helped to transform the nature of spectatorship. In 1740 "The act of becoming engaged in performance involved balancing a social sense of self alongside admiration of the performer's skill in taking them over the threshold of belief into the world of the play," but by 1840 the audience was encouraged to lose their sense of separateness as "every possible aspect of architecture, scenography and its associated technologies was being used in order to transport the spectator's imagination into the 'other worlds' which the theatre sought to (re)create" (43).
58. A similar unspooling occurs in the pantomime dioramas popular at Drury Lane, the Covent Garden, and other venues in the 1820s and 1830s. As Baugh notes, "Like a film running across the back of a camera, the diorama/panorama back-cloth rolled from one vertical roller at the side of the stage to another on the opposite side.... With this technique, spectacular transitions became the order of the day" (Baugh, "Scenography and Technology," 54).
59. Woodhouse records this belief in his own annotated copy of *Endymion* (1818).
60. Eisenstein, *The Film Sense*, 1.
61. Ibid., 57.
62. Cited in Calè, *Fuseli's Milton Gallery*, 3.
63. Eisenstein, *The Film Sense*, 61.
64. Calè, *Fuseli's Milton Gallery*, 3. Similarly, in William Hazlitt's *Lectures on the English Poets*, which Keats attended, Hazlitt finds Milton's genius to be "essentially undramatic," but he nevertheless celebrates the musicality and visuality of Milton's verse, claiming, "He makes words tell as pictures." As Beth Lau notes, in this same lecture Hazlitt describes the central characters of *Paradise Lost* in a manner that recalls Keats's own observation of Milton's gift for "stationing or statu[a]ry": "The persons of Adam and Eve, of Satan, &c. are always accompanied, in our imagination, with the grandeur of the naked figure; they convey to us the ideas of sculpture." See Lau, *Keats's Paradise Lost*, 44–45.
65. Newey, "Hyperion, The Fall of Hyperion, and Keats's Epic Ambitions," 75.

66. Leigh Hunt wrote that "Keats had read Dante in Mr. Cary's translation, for which he had a great respect. He began to read him afterwards in Italian, which language he was mastering with surprising quickness." For details about the history of the scholarly debate about how much Keats may have read of Dante in translation and in the original see Vassallo, "Keats's 'Dying into Life,'" and Braida, *Dante and the Romantics*. The starting point of much of this discussion was Saly, "Keats's Answer to Dante."
67. Dante uses the phrase "visibile parlare" in canto X of *Purgatorio*, which is translated by Cary as "visible speaking." The avant-garde filmmaker Stan Brakhage pushes the logic of visible speech in interesting ways in his 1987 short *The Dante Quartet*, a film whose imagery draws upon the tangled motifs of modernist artists such as Jackson Pollock and Mark Rothko to create "a 'painterly' dynamism that moves the eye materially to different, interior rhythms." Using an idiom that Brakhage calls "moving visual thinking," his film produces a paradoxically "mobilized stasis of light and colour" that links Dante to Deleuze in interesting ways. See Testa, "Dante and Cinema."
68. Franke, *Secular Scriptures*, 5.
69. Pite, *The Circle of Our Vision*, 129.
70. Franke, *Secular Scriptures*, 32. "Dante finds that he can express his mystical vision and passion for what transcends the world perhaps best in ways turned toward the world. With the Incarnation of God that constitutes the central proclamation and the shattering novelty of Christian revelation, the body and specifically the flesh become the crucial site of revelation. This revelation in the flesh is crucial in Christian tradition right from John the Evangelist's declaration that the divine Word 'was made flesh and dwelt among us, and we beheld his glory, the glory as of the only begotten of the father, full of grace and truth' (Gospel According to John 1:14)" (32).
71. Baudelaire, *The Painter of Modern Life*, 9.
72. Bennett, *Vibrant Matter*, xi.
73. Bennett, *The Enchantment of Modern Life*, 5.
74. Fisher, *Wonder, the Rainbow, and the Aesthetics of Rare Experiences*, 131.
75. For a helpful discussion of the "motionless wonder" Catherine Morland experiences in *Northanger Abbey* see Hofkosh, "The Illusionist." Related issues are discussed in Mitchell, "Suspended Animation, Slow Time, and the Poetics of Trance."
76. Rubenstein, *Strange Wonder*, 3. Also see Malpas, "Beginning in Wonder."
77. Rubenstein, "A Certain Disavowal," 11.
78. Plato, *Theaetetus*, 155d.

79. During, *Modern Enchantments*, 37.
80. Rubenstein, "A Certain Disavowal," 15.
81. *LJK*, 1:386.
82. An experience Keats will realize even more fully in "To Autumn."
83. Deleuze, *Cinema 2*, 81.
84. Santner, *On the Psychotheology of Everyday Life*, 137. Santner's conception of beauty is more fully described in chapter 4's discussion of the Ancient Mariner's blessing of the sea snakes.
85. Blake, *Milton*, 35:42–45.
86. Grossman, *True-Love*, 8. Grossman's argument was also invoked in the last chapter.
87. Benjamin, *Walter Benjamin*, 4:328.
88. I will not open this debate here, but it is worth considering to what extent the difference between the movement-image and the time-image coordinates with the difference between allegory and symbol within Romantic discourse. See Coleridge's *The Statesman's Manual*: "Now an allegory is but a translation of abstract notions into picture-language which is itself but an abstraction from objects of the senses; the principle being more worthless even than its phantom proxy, both alike insubstantial, and the form shapeless to boot. On the other hand, a symbol is characterized by translucence of the Special in the individual or the General in the Especial or of the Universal in the General. Above all by the translucence of the eternal through and in the temporal. It always partakes of the Reality which it renders intelligible; and while it enunciates the whole, abides itself as a living part in that unity, of which it is the representative. The other are but empty echoes which the fancy arbitrarily associates with apparitions of matter, less beautiful but not less shadowy than the sloping orchard or hill-side pasture field seen in the transparent lake below" (*CW*, 6:30).
89. Deleuze, *Cinema 2*, 39.
90. For a suggestive reading of William Blake along these lines see Leonard, "'Without Contraries There Is No Progression.'"
91. Deleuze, *Cinema 2*, 40–41.
92. Although I will not develop this line of thinking here, and despite the fact that earlier in this chapter I was emphasizing the aspects of Wordsworth's poetry that coordinate most closely with the posture of the flâneur, it is worth noting that much of his poetry—including the "spots of time," "Tintern Abbey," "I wandered lonely as a cloud," and many others examples—does in fact tap into the dynamics of the time-image. This is why Herbert Samuel Lindenberger suggested long ago that "*The Prelude*

had to wait until the twentieth century, the great age of the time-book, to achieve its major acclaim" (*On Wordsworth's Prelude*, 204).
93. Terada, "Looking at the Stars Forever," 278.
94. Ibid., 299.
95. Ibid., 286, citing Deleuze, *Cinema 2*, 55.
96. Santner points to Deleuze's work on the twentieth-century painter Francis Bacon to indicate why this might be so as well as to help clarify what Deleuze means by a "logic of sensation." For Deleuze, the aim of Bacon's work is toward "the facilitation of the body's escape from the confines of its organic composition, from what renders it all too visible and recognizable within a space of representation." In this reading of Deleuze's project, great art is kenotic because it functions as a ritual of divestiture, which attempts to "undo or render inoperative the subject's libidinal implication in the space of signifying representations" by separating out "something like a purely vital pressure from the pressures that enter life by way of subjection to normative authority" (Santner, *Royal Remains*, 132).
97. Santner, *Royal Remains*, 134.
98. Hallward, *Out of This World*, 114–15.
99. Santner, *The Royal Remains*, 138.
100. Connolly, *A World of Becoming*, 61.
101. Santner, *The Weight of All Flesh*, 46.
102. See Gallagher and Cole, "Body Schema and Body Image in a Deafferented Subject," 371.
103. Bennett, *Vibrant Matter*, 3.
104. Silverman, *The Threshold of the Visible World*, 86.
105. Merleau-Ponty attributes this to Cézanne in "Cézanne's Doubt." The idea of a world spectator is taken from Kaja Silverman's book *World Spectators*. She argues that ultimately what the world of creatures and things wants is not our desire in the abstract but rather our unique touch, the texture of our flesh, "that very particular passion of the signifier through which we have individuated what is common to all subjects." The phenomenal forms of the world invite us to make them part of our singular language of desire—to make them components of the rhetoric through which we "care" for the unique touch by which we each weave and unweave sense and understanding. But in order to care, the perceiving subject must be "open" to the perceptual object and "answer the appeal which comes to us from the world to find our memories in its forms." Although "we cannot confer Being upon the world without appropriating it, carrying it away from itself, conferring upon it a supplemental value," the world "knows" this, and

5. "AWFUL DOUBT"

1. S, *Prometheus Unbound*, IV, 158, 111–13, 153–55.
2. Hazlitt, *The Complete Works*, 12:246.
3. As I will discuss shortly, Shelley uses this term in a note to "An Essay on the Punishment of Death," the implications of which are developed by Robert Mitchell in *Sympathy and the State*.
4. Shelley claims, "This is the source of the erroneous excesses of Remorse and Revenge; the one extending itself over the future, and the other over the past; provinces in which their suggestions can only be the sources of evil. The purpose of a resolution to act more wisely and virtuously in future, and the sense of a necessity of caution in repressing an enemy, are the sources from which the enormous superstitions implied in the words cited have arisen" (*Shelley's Prose*, 157).
5. Sullivan, *Secular Assemblages*, 58.
6. Ibid., 32.
7. Kahn, "Happy Tears," 110.
8. Sullivan, *Secular Assemblages*, 66.
9. Descartes, "The Passions of the Soul," 387.
10. Cottingham, Cartesian *Reflections*, 238.
11. Williams, *The Tragic Imagination*, 13.
12. Kahn, "Happy Tears," 110.
13. Langan and McLane, "The Medium of Romantic Poetry," 256.
14. Ibid., 257.
15. Hazlitt, *The Complete Works*, 12:245–46.
16. Hazlitt, review of Shelley's Posthumous Poems, 342.
17. Jager, *Unquiet Things*, 227.
18. Havelock, *Preface to Plato*, 197.
19. Shelley, "On Christianity," 262.
20. Shelley, *Shelley's Prose*, 188.
21. Mitchell, *Sympathy and the State*, 157.
22. Ibid., 157.
23. Altieri, "Wordsworth's Poetics of Eloquence," 401.
24. Mahmood, "Religious Reason and Secular Affect," 845. Although Mahmood is discussing the example of the Prophet Muhammed, her argument is also applicable to the forms of poetic eloquence often practiced by

Wordsworth: "These mimetic ways of realizing the Prophet's behavior are lived not as commandments but as virtues; one wants to ingest, as it were, the Prophet's persona" (846–47).
25. Mitchell, *Sympathy and the State*, 158.
26. Ibid., 188.
27. Ibid., 186.
28. Ibid., 24, 202.
29. Shelley, *Shelley's Prose*, 157.
30. Mitchell, *Sympathy and the State*, 24.
31. Ibid., 172. As Taylor Schey notes, "when Shelley explains his understanding of power in his 'Speculations on Metaphysics,' he lifts his discussion almost verbatim from Hume's text" ("Skeptical Ignorance," 72). For additional readings that address Hume's influence on "Mont Blanc," Schey points to Isomaki, "Interpretation and Value in 'Mont Blanc' and 'Hymn to Intellectual Beauty,'" and William Keach, *Shelley's Style*, 200.
32. Mitchell, *Sympathy and the State*, 202.
33. Ibid., 171.
34. Deleuze, *Cinema 2*, 81.
35. Silverman, *The Threshold of the Visible World*, 86.
36. Mitchell, *Sympathy and the State*, 173.
37. Rajan, *Romantic Narrative*, 142. The "glorious phantom" is referred to in the last lines of Shelley's "England in 1819."
38. Ibid., 27.
39. Havelock, *Preface to Plato*, 197.
40. Shelley, *Shelley's Prose*, 188.
41. Shelley, *Shelley's Prose*, 173–74.
42. Panagia, *Impressions of Hume*, 49.
43. Bennett, *Vibrant Matter*, 37–38.
44. Panagia, *Impressions of Hume*, 59.
45. One way this can be accomplished is by introducing vacancies or forms of caesura, moments of nonlinear "broken" time or what Walter Benjamin called "messianic time."
46. Notice how Prometheus's refusal to do so inverts the dynamic found at the end of the "Rime": "To walk together to the kirk / And all together pray, / While each to his great Father bends" (605–7).
47. De Quincey, *"Confessions of an English Opium-Eater" and Other Writings*, 130.
48. As critics such as Roger Blood have argued, it "is precisely this anagnorisis that does not take place, is not represented, in *The Cenci*" (382). See Blood's "Allegory and Dramatic Representation in *The Cenci*."

49. For an exemplary discussion of the role of casuistry in Romantic writing see Chandler, *England in 1819*.
50. Schille, "Orsino's 'Solemn Comedy,'" 64.
51. Ibid., 76.
52. Kohler, "Shelley in Chancery," 584.
53. Cox, *In the Shadows of Romance*, 412.
54. Ibid.
55. Ibid.
56. Reading Shelley in the light of Benjamin's analysis is less anachronistic than it might at first appear, because as Robert Kaufman has demonstrated in a series of insightful articles, Shelley was himself a decisive influence on the thinking of both Benjamin and Bertolt Brecht in the summer of 1938, as well as upon the charged debates surrounding the Frankfurt School. See Kaufman, "Intervention and Commitment Forever! Shelley in 1819, Shelley in Brecht, Shelley in Adorno, Shelley in Benjamin."
57. Schmitt, *Political Theology*, 49.
58. See Weber, "Taking Exception to Decision."
59. Benjamin, *The Origin of German Tragic Drama*, trans. John Osborne (New York: Verso, 2003), 69.
60. Ibid., 71.
61. Ibid., 85.
62. Reinhard, "Toward a Political Theology of the Neighbor," 56.
63. Ibid., 56. Nevertheless, it is important to note that since Count Cenci must pay to have his sins forgiven, he is clearly already enmeshed in social networks that would complicate any claim to a totalizing sovereignty.
64. Lupton, "Creature Caliban," 1. Lupton's essay usefully explicates some of the genealogy of the word "creature" as well as its role in the thinking of Benjamin and in William Shakespeare.
65. Benjamin, *The Origin of German Tragic Drama*, 85.
66. Lupton, "Creature Caliban," 5.
67. Shelley, "Philosophical View of Reform," in *Shelley's Prose*, 235.
68. Ibid., 236.
69. Scarry, *The Body in Pain*, 125.
70. Santner, *My Own Private Germany*, 10.
71. Ibid., 43.
72. For more on the political implications of these passionate attachments see Kahn, Saccamano, and Coli, *Politics and the Passions, 1500–1850*; Connolly, *Neuropolitics*; and Leys, "The Turn to Affect."
73. Roberts, "Between the Lines," 710.

74. Žižek, *The Puppet and the Dwarf*, 69–70.
75. Benjamin, *The Origin of German Tragic Drama*, 71.
76. Santner, *My Own Private Germany*, 43.
77. Ibid., 43.
78. This translation by Simon Sparks is drawn from Walter Benjamin, *Gesammelte Schriften*, 1:294. A different translation can be found in John Osbourne's translation of *The Origin of German Tragic Drama*, 115.
79. Sparks: "Fatalities: Freedom and the Question of Language in Walter Benjamin's Reading of Tragedy," 197.
80. Cox, *In the Shadows of Romance*, 141.
81. Williams, *The Tragic Imagination*, 57.
82. Erin Manning contrasts the "minor gesture" with the grand. History tends to be sought in terms of the grand gesture because it is easier to see, but it is the "the nuanced rhythms of the minor" that can begin to pattern new forms of being. These minor gestures help "make felt the intervals, the openings and captures within a process that is on its way to becoming a practice." In this way, the minor gesture resists "formation long enough to allow us to see the potential of worlds in the making" (*The Minor Gesture*, 1, 14, 15). By emphasizing minor gestures like Hope's laying "down in the street, / Right before the horses feet" in the "Masque of Anarchy" and Marzio's final smile in *The Cenci*, Shelley's poetic tendency is not to stage eloquent personas worthy of emulation but to instead draw attention toward how minor gestures can produce a "punctual reorienting of the event" (8).
83. Dickinson, *Poems*, 327.

6. "OPEN-HEARTED"

1. Williams, *The Tragic Imagination*, 157.
2. Brown, "The Feminist Depreciation of Austen," 307.
3. Zupančič, *The Odd One In*, 140.
4. Baier, *A Progress of Sentiments*.
5. Astell, "Anne Elliot's Education," 2, emphasis added.
6. Galperin, *The Historical Austen*, 5.
7. Butler, *Jane Austen and the War of Ideas*, 277.
8. Pinch, "Lost in a Book," 108.
9. Richardson, *British Romanticism and the Science of the Mind*, 102.
10. Wiltshire, *Jane Austen and the Body*, 177.
11. Litz, "Persuasion," 228.

12. Harris, *Revolution Almost beyond Expression*, 144.
13. Heydt-Stevenson, "'Slipping into the Ha-Ha,'" 312.
14. Austen, *Pride and Prejudice*, 51.
15. Austen, *Mansfield Park*, 116.
16. Heydt-Stevenson, "'Slipping into the Ha-Ha,'" 311.
17. Heydt-Stevenson, *Austen's Unbecoming Conjunctions*, 27.
18. Ibid., 25.
19. Connolly, *A World of Becoming*, 61.
20. Bergson, *Laughter*, 38.
21. Zupančič, *Odd One In*, 49–50.
22. Ibid., 181.
23. Panagia, *The Political Life of Sensation*, 10.
24. Kant, *Critique of Judgement*, 162.
25. Pinch argues that "as the novel progresses, Anne's moments of shock and inundation increasingly take a typically sublime turn" ("Lost in a Book," 109). There certainly seems to be a sublime element to Anne's experiences, and the applicability of the sublime has an added resonance when we recall that for Edmund Burke, "The efficient cause of the 'delight' occasioned by the experience of the Sublime is the power of terrible objects to 'clear the parts' of the nervous system of dangerous and debilitating blockages arising from mental lassitude" (Rzepka, "Re-collecting Spontaneous Overflows," para. 11). In the Burkean model, the sublime helps clear out the blockages that inhibit us from being good subjects. Both Anne, who becomes "hardened" by the daily affronts she suffered in her own household, and Wentworth, who is affected by the "madness of resentment," could certainly benefit from some of the sublime's delightful agitation (*P*, 263). Nevertheless, Austen swerves from the Burkean model in important ways, and I propose that the comic rather than the sublime is the better basis for an understanding of what Austen is up to in *Persuasion*.
26. Kant, *Critique of Judgement*, 161.
27. Schopenhauer, *The World as Will and Representation*, 1:59.
28. Atkinson, "Humour in Philosophy," 17.
29. Kant, *Critique of Judgement*, 162.
30. Rubenstein, "A Certain Disavowal," 12. As discussed earlier in chapter 5, in the Platonic dialogues, Socratic wonder (*thaumazein*) "arises when the understanding cannot master that which lies closest—when surrounded by utterly ordinary concepts and things, the philosopher suddenly finds himself surrounded on all sides by aporia." Wonder is what strikes Theaetetus in the Platonic dialogue that bears his name, when "he loses his

grasp on notions that had seemed utterly self-evident, sending him reeling, his head spinning" (Plato, *Theaetetus*, 155d).

31. Zupančič, *Odd One In*, 34.
32. Zupančič, *Odd One In*, 180.
33. Panagia, *The Political Life of Sensation*, 42.
34. Austen, *Northanger Abbey*, 167.
35. For more on this critique see Levinson, *Keats's Life of Allegory*.
36. Austen, *Emma*, 251.
37. Stevens, "The Snow Man," in *Collected Poems*, 9–10.
38. Bennett, *The Enchantment of Modern Life*, 5. See also Fisher, *Wonder, the Rainbow, and the Aesthetics of Rare Experiences*; Mitchell, "Suspended Animation, Slow Time, and the Poetics of Trance"; and Clune, *Writing against Time*. For a helpful discussion of the role of wonder in Austen, see Hofkosh, "The Illusionist."
39. Soni, "Committing Freedom," 380.
40. Panagia, *Impressions of Hume*, 35, 2.
41. Silverman, *The Threshold of the Visible World*, 17.
42. Finch and Bowen, "'The Tittle-Tattle of Highbury.'"
43. Canuel, "Jane Austen and the Importance of Being Wrong," 128.
44. Austen, *Emma*, 143.
45. Austen, *Mansfield Park*, 310. This is the fate Fanny Price anxiously imagines awaits her at an upcoming ball.
46. Southward, "Jane Austen and the Riches of Embarrassment," 764–65.
47. See Elias, *The History of Manners*, vol. 1.
48. Bourdieu, *Outline of a Theory of Practice*, 94.
49. Grossman, "Labor of the Leisured in *Emma*," 153.
50. Paster, *Humoring the Body*, 19.
51. Ibid., 13.
52. Ibid., 14.
53. Ibid., 19.
54. Freud, *Civilization and Its Discontents*, 11.
55. Chandler, *An Archaeology of Sympathy*, 203.
56. Pinch, "Lost in a Book," 106.
57. Lacan, *Écrits*, 166.
58. For a suggestive Lacanian approach to the role of the comic in Austen see Rothenberg's "Jane Austen's Wit-Craft."
59. Faflak, "Jane Austen and the Persuasion of Happiness," 116.
60. Johnson, "*Persuasion*: The Unfeudal Tone of the Present Day," 303.
61. Panagia, *Impressions of Hume*, 7.

62. Chandler, *Archaeology of Sympathy*, 203.
63. Pfau, "Art and Ethics of Attention," 38.
64. Eliot, *Collected Poems*, 420.
65. Pfau, "Art and Ethics of Attention," 37.
66. Keller and Boesel, *Apophatic Bodies*, 10.
67. Ibid., 146.
68. Vermeule, "Machiavellian Narratives," 214.
69. Machiavelli, *The Discourses*, 459.
70. Bennett, "Jane Bennett."

CODA

1. Hirshkind, "Is There a Secular Body?," 636.
2. Lloyd and Thomas, *Culture and the State*, 15.
3. Mahmood, "Religious Reason and Secular Affect," 847.
4. Bourdieu, *The Logic of Practice*, 53.
5. Pfau, "On Attention," 148.
6. Hirschkind, "Is There a Secular Body?," 635.
7. Bergson, *The Two Sources of Morality and Religion*, 93.
8. Jager, "After the Secular," 304.
9. Latour, *Facing Gaia: A New Enquiry into Natural Religion* (lecture 2, 18:30).

* BIBLIOGRAPHY *

Abrams, M. H. *Natural Supernaturalism: Tradition and Revolution in Romantic Literature.* New York: Norton, 1971.
———. "Structure and Style in the Greater Romantic Lyric." In *Romanticism and Consciousness: Essays in Criticism,* edited by Harold Bloom, 201–29. New York: Norton, 1970.
Addison, Joseph. "Pleasures of Imagination." *Spectator* 411 (June 21, 1712).
Agamben, Giorgio. *The Time That Remains: A Commentary on the Letter to the Romans.* Stanford. CA: Stanford University Press, 2005.
Ahmed, Sara. "Happy Objects." In *The Affect Theory Reader,* edited by Melissa Gregg and Gregory J. Seigworth, 29–51. Durham, NC: Duke University Press, 2010.
———. *The Cultural Politics of Emotion.* New York: Routledge, 2014.
———. *The Promise of Happiness.* Durham, NC: Duke University Press, 2010.
Alighieri, Dante. *The Divine Comedy of Dante Alighieri: Hell, Purgatory, Paradise.* Translated by Henry Francis Cary. New York: P. F. Collier and Son, 1909.
Altieri, Charles. "Are There States of Mind Which We Can Call 'Inner Sensuousness'?" In *The Palgrave Handbook of Affect Studies and Textual Criticism,* edited by Donald R. Wehrs and Thomas Blake, 279–98. New York: Springer, 2017.
———. "Taking Lyrics Literally: Teaching Poetry in a Prose Culture." *New Literary History* 32 (2001): 259–81.
———. "Wordsworth's Poetics of Eloquence: A Challenge to Contemporary Theory." In *Romantic Revolutions: Criticism and Theory,* edited by Kenneth R. Johnston, Gilbert Chaitin, Karen Hanson, and Herbert Marks. Bloomington: Indiana University Press, 1990.
Ankersmit, F. R. *Sublime Historical Experience.* Stanford, CA: Stanford University Press, 2005.

Asad, Talal. *Formations of the Secular: Christianity, Islam, Modernity*. Stanford: Stanford University Press, 2003.
Astell, Ann W. "Anne Elliot's Education: The Learning of Romance in Persuasion." *Renascence* 40 (1987): 2–14.
Atkinson, Ronald. "Humour in Philosophy." In *Humour and History*, edited by Keith Cameron. Oxford: Intellect, 1993.
Austen, Jane. *Emma*. Edited by Richard Cronin and Dorothy McMillan, in *The Cambridge Edition of the Works of Jane Austen*. Cambridge: Cambridge University Press, 2005.
———. *Mansfield Park*. Edited by John Wiltshire, in *The Cambridge Edition of the Works of Jane Austen*. Cambridge: Cambridge University Press, 2005.
———. *Northanger Abbey*. Edited by Barbara M. Benedict and Deirdre Le Faye, in *The Cambridge Edition of the Works of Jane Austen*. Cambridge: Cambridge University Press, 2006.
———. *Persuasion*. Edited by Janet M. Todd and Antje Blank, in *The Cambridge Edition of the Works of Jane Austen*. Cambridge: Cambridge University Press, 2006.
———. *Pride and Prejudice*. Edited by Pat Rogers, in *The Cambridge Edition of the Works of Jane Austen*. Cambridge: Cambridge University Press, 2006.
Bachelard, Gaston. *The Poetics of Space*. Translated by Maria Jolos. Boston: Beacon, 1994.
Badiou, Alain. *Ethics: An Essay on the Understanding of Evil*. London: Verso, 2001.
Baier, Annette. *A Progress of Sentiments: Reflections on Hume's Treatise*. Cambridge, MA: Harvard University Press, 1991.
Barrell, John. *The Idea of Landscape and the Sense of Place, 1730–1840: An Approach to the Poetry of John Clare*. Cambridge: Cambridge University Press, 1972.
Barth, J. Robert. "'A Spring of Love': Prayer and Blessing in Coleridge's 'Rime of the Ancient Mariner.'" *Wordsworth Circle* 30 (1999): 75–80.
Bate, Walter Jackson. *John Keats*. Cambridge, MA: Belknap Press of Harvard University Press, 1963.
Baudelaire, Charles. *The Painter of Modern Life and Other Essays*. London: Phaidon, 1995.
Baugh, Christopher. "Scenography and Technology." In *The Cambridge Companion to British Theatre, 1730–1830*, edited by Jane Moody and Daniel O'Quinn, 43–56. Cambridge: Cambridge University Press, 2007.
Beer, John. "Coleridge and Wordsworth on Reflection." *Wordsworth Circle* 20 (1989): 20–29.

Bell, Catherine. *Ritual Theory, Ritual Practice*. New York: Oxford University Press, 1992.
Benavides, Gustavo. "Modernity." In *Critical Terms for Religious Studies*, edited by Mark C. Taylor, 186–204. Chicago: University of Chicago Press, 1998.
Benjamin, Walter. *The Arcades Project*. Translated by Howard Eiland and Kevin McLaughlin. Cambridge, MA: Belknap, 1999.
———. "The Concept of Criticism in German Romanticism." In *Selected Writings, 1913–1926*, edited by Marcus Bullock and Michael W. Jennings, 116–200. Cambridge, MA: Belknap, 1996.
———. *Gesammelte Schriften*, vol. 1.3. Edited by Rolf Tiedemann and Herman Schweppenhäuser. Frankfurt am Main; Suhrkamp, 1980.
———. *Illuminations*. Edited by Hannah Arendt. Translated by Harry Zohn. New York: Schocken Books, 1986.
———. *The Origin of German Tragic Drama*. Translated by John Osborne. Cambridge: Cambridge University Press, 2003.
———. *Selected Writings, 1913–1926*. Edited by Marcus Bullock and Michael Jennings. Cambridge, MA: Harvard University Press, 1996.
Bennett, Jane. *The Enchantment of Modern Life: Attachments, Crossings, and Ethics*. Princeton, NJ: Princeton University Press, 2001.
———. "Jane Bennett: The Interview." Conducted by Peter Gratton. "Philosophy in a Time of Error," https://philosophyinatimeoferror.wordpress.com/2010/05/25/jane-bennett-the-interview/.
———. "Systems and Things: On Vital Materialism and Object-Oriented Philosophy." In *The Nonhuman Turn*, edited by Richard Grusin, 223–40. Minneapolis: University of Minnesota Press, 2015.
———. *Vibrant Matter: A Political Ecology of Things*. Durham, NC: Duke University Press, 2010.
Bergson, Henri. *Laughter: An Essay on the Meaning of the Comic*. Translated by Cloudesley Brereton and Fred Rothwell. New York: Macmillan, 1914.
———. *Matter and Memory*. New York: Zone Books, 1991.
———. *The Two Sources of Morality and Religion*. Notre Dame, IN: University of Notre Dame Press, 1977.
Berkeley, Richard. *Coleridge and the Crisis of Reason*. New York: Palgrave, 2007.
Bernstein, J. M. *Against Voluptuous Bodies: Late Modernism and the Meaning of Painting*. Stanford, CA: Stanford University Press, 2006.
Blair, Hugh. *Lectures on Rhetoric and Belles Lettres*. Edited by Harold Harding. Carbondale: Southern Illinois University Press, 1965.
Blake, William. *Milton, a Poem, and the Final Illuminated Works: The Ghost of Abel, on Homers Poetry, [and] on Virgil, Laocoön*. Edited by Robert N. Essick

and Joseph Viscomi. Princeton, NJ: William Blake Trust / Princeton University Press, 1993.

Bloch, Marc. *The Royal Touch: Monarchy and Miracles in France and England.* Translated by J. E. Anderson. New York: Dorset, 1989.

Blood, Roger. "Allegory and Dramatic Representation in *The Cenci.*" *Studies in Romanticism* 33 (1994): 355–89.

Bloom, Harold. *Natural Supernaturalism: Tradition and Revolution in Romantic Literature.* New York: Norton, 1971.

Bourdieu, Pierre. *The Logic of Practice.* Stanford, CA: Stanford University Press, 1990.

———. *Outline of a Theory of Practice.* Translated by Richard Nice. Cambridge: Cambridge University Press, 1997.

Braida, Antonella. *Dante and the Romantics.* Basingstoke: Palgrave Macmillan, 2004.

Branch, Lori. "Postsecular Studies." In *The Routledge Companion to Literature and Religion,* edited by Mark Knight, 91–101. New York: Routledge, 2016.

Brewer, John. "Sentiment and Sensibility." In *The Cambridge History of English Romantic Literature.* Edited by James Chandler, 19–44. Cambridge: Cambridge University Press, 2009.

Broglio, Ron. "Romantic." In *The Cambridge Companion to Literature and the Posthuman,* edited by Bruce Clarke and Manuela Rossini, 29–40. New York: Cambridge University Press, 2017.

———. *Technologies of the Picturesque: British Art, Poetry, and Instruments, 1750–1830.* Lewisburg, PA: Bucknell University Press, 2008.

Brooke-Smith, James. "Remediating Romanticism." *Literature Compass* 10, no. 4 (2013): 343–52.

Brown, Julia Prewitt. "The Feminist Depreciation of Austen: A Polemical Reading." *Novel: A Forum on Fiction* 23 (Spring 1990): 303–13.

Brown, R. F. *The Later Philosophy of Schelling: The Influence of Boehme on the Works of 1809–1815.* Lewisburg, PA: Bucknell University Press, 1977.

Bruno, Giuliana. "Pleats of Matter, Folds of the Soul." *Log* 1 (2003): 113–22.

Budge, Gavin, ed. *Romantic Empiricism: Poetics and the Philosophy of Common Sense, 1780–1830.* Lewisburg, PA: Bucknell University Press, 2007.

Burgess, Miranda. "On Being Moved," from *Emotions: On the Affective Turn* panel at MLA 2008.

———. "On Being Moved: Sympathy, Mobility, and Narrative Form." *Poetics Today* 32 (2011): 289–321.

Burke, Edmund. *Reflections on the Revolution in France.* Edited by Frank M. Turner and Darrin M. McMahon. New Haven, CT: Yale University Press, 2003.

Burke, Kenneth. "Literature as Equipment for Living." In *The Philosophy of Literary Form*, 293–304. Berkeley: University of California Press, 1973.

Burkett, Andrew, and James Brooke-Smith, eds. "Multi-Media Romanticism." *Romantic Praxis* (November 2016). Online publication at https://romantic-circles.org/praxis/multi-media.

———. "William Blake and the Emergence of Romantic Media Studies." *Literature Compass* 12 (2015): 439–47.

Burkett, Andrew. *Romantic Mediations: Media Theory and British Romanticism*. Albany: State University of New York Press, 2016.

Burroughs, Mark, Jean Ward, and Malgorzata Gregorgzewska, eds. *Poetic Revelations: Word Made Flesh Made Word (The Power of the Word III)*. New York: Routledge, 2017.

Burwick, Frederick. "Coleridge's Conversation Poems: Thinking the Thinker." *Romanticism* 14 (2008): 168–82.

Butler, Marilyn. *Jane Austen and the War of Ideas*. New York: Oxford University Press, 1987.

Calè, Luisa. *Fuseli's Milton Gallery: Turning Readers into Spectators*. New York: Oxford University Press, 2006.

Canuel, Mark. "Coleridge's Polemic Divinity." *English Literary History (ELH)* 68 (2001): 929–63.

———. "Jane Austen and the Importance of Being Wrong." *Studies in Romanticism* 44, no. 2 (Summer 2005): 123–50.

Casanova, José. *Public Religions in the Modern World*. Chicago: University of Chicago Press, 1994.

Cavanaugh, William. *Theopolitical Imagination: Christian Practices of Space and Time*. Edinburgh: T. and T. Clark International, 2003.

Certeau, Michel de. *Heterologies: Discourse on the Other*. Minneapolis: University of Minnesota Press, 1986.

———. *The Mystic Fable: The Sixteenth and Seventeenth Centuries*. Chicago: University of Chicago Press, 1992.

———. "Mysticism." *Diacritics* 22 (1992): 11–25.

———. *The Practice of Everyday Life*. Berkeley: University of California Press, 1988.

Chandler, James. "The Affection-Image and the Movement-Image." In *Afterimages of Gilles Deleuze's Film Philosophy*, edited by David Norman Rodowick. Minneapolis: University of Minnesota Press, 2010.

———. *An Archaeology of Sympathy: The Sentimental Mode in Literature and Cinema*. Chicago: University of Chicago Press, 2013.

———. *England in 1819: The Politics of Literary Culture and the Case of Romantic Historicism*. Chicago: University of Chicago Press, 1998.

———. "Sensibility, Sympathy and Sentiment." In *William Wordsworth in Context*, edited by Andrew Bennett. Cambridge: Cambridge University Press, 2015.

———. "The Politics of Sentiment: Notes toward a New Account." *Studies in Romanticism* 4 (Winter 2010): 553–76.

———. *Wordsworth's Second Nature: A Study of the Poetry and Politics*. Chicago: University of Chicago Press, 1984.

Chandler, James, and Kevin Gilmartin, eds. *Romantic Metropolis: The Urban Scene of British Culture, 1780–1840*. Cambridge: Cambridge University Press, 2005.

Cheyne, Peter. *Coleridge's Contemplative Philosophy*. Oxford: Oxford University Press, 2020.

Christensen, Jerome. *Coleridge's Blessed Machine of Language*. Ithaca, NY: Cornell University Press, 1981.

———. *Practicing Enlightenment: Hume and the Formation of a Literary Career*. Madison: University of Wisconsin Press, 1987.

Clough, Patrica. "The Affect Turn: Political Economy, Biomedia, and Bodies." In *The Affect Theory Reader*, edited by Melissa Gregg and Gregory J. Seigworth, 206–25. Durham, NC: Duke University Press, 2010.

Clune, Michael W. *Writing against Time*. Stanford, CA: Stanford University Press, 2013.

Coleridge, Samuel Taylor. *Aids to Reflection*. Edited by John B. Beer. Princeton, NJ: Princeton University Press, 1993.

———. *Biographia Literaria, or, Biographical Sketches of My Literary Life and Opinions*. Edited by James Engell and Walter Jackson Bate. Princeton, NJ: Princeton University Press, 1983.

———. *Lectures, 1795: On Politics and Religion*. CW 1. Edited by Lewis Patton and Peter Mann. Princeton, NJ: Princeton University Press, 1971.

———. *Coleridge's Poetry and Prose: Authoritative Texts, Criticism*. Edited by Nicholas. Halmi, Paul Magnuson, and Raimonda Modiano. New York: Norton, 2004.

———. *Collected Letters*. Edited by Earl Leslie Griggs. Oxford: Clarendon, 1956.

———. *The Collected Works of Samuel Taylor Coleridge*. Princeton, NJ: Princeton University Press, 1969.

———. "Confessions of an Inquiring Spirit." In Coleridge, *Shorter Works and Fragments*. Edited by H. J. Jackson and J. R. de J. Jackson. Princeton, NJ: Princeton University Press, 1995.

———. *The Notebooks of Samuel Taylor Coleridge*. Vol. 2, 1804–1808. Edited by Kathleen Coburn. London: Routledge and Kegan Paul, 1961.

———. *Opus Maximum*. Edited by Thomas McFarland. Princeton, NJ: Princeton University Press, 2002.

———. *Shorter Works and Fragments*. Edited by H. T. Jackson and J. R. de J. Jackson, 2 vols. Princeton, NJ: Princeton University Press, 1995.

Collings, David. "The Force of Indirection: 'Tintern Abbey' in the History of Mood." In *British Romanticism: Criticism and Debates*, edited by Mark Canuel, 409–17. New York: Routledge, 2015.

———. "Troping Mood: Pfau, Wordsworth, and Hegel." *Literature Compass* 6, no. 2 (2009): 373–83.

Connolly, William E. *Neuropolitics: Thinking, Culture, Speed*. Minneapolis: University of Minnesota Press, 2002.

———. "Refashioning the Secular." In *What's Left of Theory? New Work on the Politics of Literary Theory*, edited by Judith Butler, John Guillory, and Kendall Thomas. New York: Routledge, 2000.

———. *Why I Am Not a Secularist*. Minneapolis: University of Minnesota Press, 1999.

———. *A World of Becoming*. Durham, NC: Duke University Press, 2010.

Connor, Steven. "Literature, Technology, and the Sense." In *The Cambridge Companion to the Body in Literature*, edited by David Hillman and Ulrika Maude. New York: Cambridge University Press, 2015.

———. "Scilicet: Kittler, Media and Madness." In *Kittler Now: Current Perspectives in Kittler Studies*, edited by Stephen Sale and Laura Salisbury. Malden, MA: Polity, 2015.

Conway, Alison, and Corrinne Harol. "Toward a Postsecular Eighteenth Century." *Literature Compass* 12 (2015): 565–74.

Cottingham, John. *Cartesian Reflections: Essays on Descartes's Philosophy*. Oxford: Oxford University Press, 2008.

Cowper, William. "The Casteaway." In *The Norton Anthology of Poetry*, edited by Margaret Ferguson, Mary Jo Salter, and Jon Stallworthy. New York: Norton, 2005.

Cox, Jeffery. *In the Shadows of Romance: Romantic Tragic Drama in Germany, England, and France*. Athens: Ohio University Press, 1987.

Crabbe, James, ed. *From Soul to Self*. New York: Routledge, 1999.

Crary, Jonathan. *Suspensions of Perception: Attention, Spectacle, and Modern Culture*. Cambridge, MA: MIT Press, 1999.

———. *Techniques of the Observer: On Vision and Modernity in the Nineteenth Century*. Cambridge, MA: MIT Press, 1990.

Culler, Jonathan. "Why Lyric?" *PMLA* 123, no. 1 (2008): 201–6.

Darnton, Robert. *Mesmerism and the End of the Enlightenment in France*. Cambridge: Harvard University Press, 1968.
Darwin, Erasmus. *Zoonomia, or the Laws of Organic Life*. London, 1794.
De Bolla, Peter. *Art Matters*. Cambridge, Mass.: Harvard University Press, 2001.
Deleuze, Gilles. *Cinema 1: The Movement-Image*. Minneapolis: University of Minnesota Press, 1986.
———. *Cinema 2: The Time-Image*. Minneapolis: University of Minnesota Press, 1989.
———. *Difference and Repetition*. Translated by Paul Patton. New York: Columbia University Press, 1994.
———. *Empiricism and Subjectivity: An Essay on Hume's Theory of Human Nature*. New York: Columbia University Press, 1991.
———. *The Fold: Leibniz and the Baroque*. Minneapolis: University of Minnesota Press, 1993.
Deleuze, Gilles, and Félix Guattari. *What Is Philosophy?* New York: Columbia University Press, 1994.
De Man, Paul. "The Rhetoric of Temporality." In *Blindness and Insight: Essays in the Rhetoric of Contemporary Criticism*. 2nd ed., 187–228. Minneapolis: University of Minnesota Press, 1983.
———. *The Rhetoric of Romanticism*. New York: Columbia University Press, 1984.
De Quincey, Thomas. *"Confessions of an English Opium-Eater" and Other Writings*. Oxford: Oxford World's Classics, 1998.
Derrida, Jacques. *The Animal That Therefore I Am*. Edited by Marie-Louise Mallet. New York: Fordham University Press, 2008.
———. "Structure, Sign and Play in the Discourse of the Human Sciences." In *Writing and Difference*, 278–94. Chicago: University of Chicago Press, 1978.
Descartes, René. "The Passions of the Soul." In *The Philosophical Writings of Descartes*. Vol. 1, translated by John Cottingham, Robert Stoothof, and Dugald Murdoch. Cambridge: Cambridge University Press, 1985.
Dickinson, Emily. *Emily Dickinson's Poems: As She Preserved Them*. Edited by Cristanne Miller. Cambridge, MA: Belknap Press of Harvard University Press, 2016.
Dieleman, Karen. *Religious Imaginaries: The Liturgical and Poetic Practices of Elizabeth Barrett Browning, Christina Rossetti, and Adelaide Procter*. Athens: Ohio University Press, 2012.
Donne, John. *Donne: The Complete Poems of John Donne*. Edited by Robin Robbins. New York: Longman, 2010.

———. *John Donne and the Theology of Language*. Edited by P. G. Stanwood and Heather Ross Asals. Columbia: University of Missouri Press, 1986.

———. *John Donne's Sermons on the Psalms and Gospels*. Edited by Evelyn Simpson. Los Angeles: University of California Press, 1963.

During, Simon. *Modern Enchantments: The Cultural Power of Secular Magic*. Cambridge, MA: Harvard University Press, 2002.

Durkheim, Émile. *Elementary Forms of the Religious Life*. New York: Free Press, 1995.

Eisenstein, Sergi. *The Film Sense*. Translated by Jay Leyda. Harcourt, 1986.

Elias, Norbert. *The Civilizing Process*, vol. 1, *The History of Manners*, translated by Edmund Jephcott. New York: Pantheon, 1978.

Eliot, T. S. *Collected Poems: 1909–1962*. New York: Harcourt Brace, 1991.

———. *Selected Essays*. London: Faber and Faber, 1999.

Engell, James. "Coleridge (and His Mariner) on the Soul: 'As an Exile in a Far Distant Land.'" In *The Fountain Light: Studies in Romanticism and Religion: In Honor of John L. Mahoney*, edited by J. Robert Barth and John L. Mahoney, 128–51. New York: Fordham University Press, 2002.

———. "The Soul, Highest Cast of Consciousness." In *The Cast of Consciousness: Concepts of the Mind in British and American Romanticism*, edited by Beverly Taylor and Robert Bain, 3–19. New York: Greenwood, 1987.

Esposito, Roberto. *Bíos: Biopolitics and Philosophy*. Minneapolis: University of Minnesota Press, 2008.

———. "The Person and Human Life." In *Theory After "Theory,"* edited by Jane Elliott and Derek Attridge, 205–20. New York: Routledge, 2011.

Eyers, Tom. *Speculative Formalism: Literature, Theory, and the Critical Present*. Evanston, IL: Northwestern University Press, 2017.

Faflak, Joel. "Jane Austen and the Persuasion of Happiness." In *Romanticism and the Emotions*, edited by Joel Faflak and Richard C. Sha, 98–123. Cambridge: Cambridge University Press, 2014.

———. *Romantic Psychoanalysis: The Burden of the Mystery*. Albany: State University of New York Press, 2008.

———. "Speaking of Godwin's Caleb Williams: The Talking Cure and the Psychopathology of Enlightenment." *English Studies in Canada* 21 (2003): 99–122.

Faflak, Joel, and Richard Sha, eds. *Romanticism and the Emotions*. New York: Cambridge University Press, 2014.

Favret, Mary. "The Study of Affect and Romanticism." *Literature Compass* 6 (2009): 1159–66.

Felch, Susan, ed. *The Cambridge Companion to Literature and Religion*. New York: Cambridge University Press, 2016.
Felski, Rita. *The Limits of Critique*. Chicago: University of Chicago Press, 2015.
Ferris, David. "Aesthetic Violence and the Legitimacy of Reading Romanticism." *Romantic Circles* (April 2005), http://www.rc.umd.edu/praxis/aesthetic/ferris/ferris.html.
Ficino, Marsilio. *Platonic Theology: English and Latin*. Translated by Michael J. B. Allen with John Warden. Edited by James Hankins with William Bowen. 6 vols. Cambridge, MA: Harvard University Press, 2001.
Finch, Casey, and Peter Bowen. "'The Tittle-Tattle of Highbury': Gossip and the Free Indirect Style in *Emma*." *Representations* 31 (Summer 1990): 1–18.
Fisher, Philip. *The Vehement Passions*. Princeton, NJ: Princeton University Press, 2002.
———. *Wonder, the Rainbow, and the Aesthetics of Rare Experiences*. Cambridge, MA: Harvard University Press, 1998.
Flusser, Vilem. *Towards a Philosophy of Photography*. Gottingen, Germany: European Photography, 1984.
Foucault, Michel. *Discipline and Punish: The Birth of the Prison*. New York: Pantheon Books, 1977.
———. "Technologies of the Self." In *Technologies of the Self: A Seminar with Michel Foucault*, edited by Luther Martin, Huck Gutman, and Patrick Hutton, 16–49. Amherst: University of Massachusetts Press, 1988.
Fournel, Victor. *Ce qu'on voit dans les rues de Paris*. Paris, 1858.
Franke, William. *Secular Scriptures: Modern Theological Poetics in the Wake of Dante*. Columbus: Ohio State University Press, 2016.
Frazer, Michael. *The Enlightenment of Sympathy: Justice and the Moral Sentiments in the Eighteenth Century and Today*. New York: Oxford University Press, 2010.
Freud, Sigmund. *Civilization and Its Discontents*. Edited by James Strachey. New York: Norton, 1989.
———. *The Standard Edition of the Complete Psychological Works of Sigmund Freud*. London: Hogarth, 1958.
Frye, Northrop. *The Educated Imagination and Other Writings on Critical Theory, 1933–1963*. Edited by Germaine Warkentin. Toronto: University of Toronto Press, 2006.
———. "Towards Defining an Age of Sensibility." *ELH* 23 (1956): 144–52.
Fulford, Tim. *Landscape, Liberty, and Authority: Poetry, Criticism, and Politics from Thomson to Wordsworth*. New York: Cambridge University Press, 2006.

Gabriele, Alberto. *The Emergence of Pre-Cinema: Print Culture and the Optical Toy of the Literary Imagination*. New York: Palgrave Macmillan, 2016.
———. *Reading Popular Culture in Victorian Print: Belgravia and Sensationalism*. New York: Palgrave Macmillan, 2009.
———. "Visions of the City of London: Mechanical Eye and Poetic Transcendence in Wordsworth's Prelude, Book 7." *European Romantic Review* 19 (2008): 365–84.
Gallagher, Shaun, and Jonathan Cole. "Body Schema and Body Image in a Deafferented Subject." *Journal of Mind and Behavior* 16 (1995): 369–90.
Galperin, William. *The Historical Austen*. Philadelphia: University of Pennsylvania Press, 2003.
Gane, Nicholas, and Hannes Hansen-Magnusson. "Materiality Is the Message?" *Theory, Culture & Society* 23 (2006): 315–28.
Gibbs, Anna. "Contagious Feelings: Pauline Hanson and the Epidemiology of Affect." *Australian Humanities Review* 24 (2001), http://australianhumanities review.org/2001/12/01/contagious-feelings-pauline-hanson-and-the-epidemiology-of-affect/.
Gill, Stephen. *William Wordsworth: A Life*. Oxford: Oxford University Press, 1990.
Ginsberg, Allen. "Howl." In *The Norton Anthology of Poetry*, edited by Margaret Ferguson, Mary Jo Salter, and Jon Stallworthy. New York: Norton, 2005.
Goodman, Kevis. *Georgic Modernity and British Romanticism: Poetry and the Mediation of History*. Cambridge: Cambridge University Press, 2004.
———. Introduction. to *The Weight of All Flesh: On the Subject-Matter of Political Economy*, by Eric L. Santner. Edited by Kevis Goodman. Oxford: Oxford University Press, 2016.
Goodrich, Peter. "The Judge's Two Bodies: The Case of Daniel Paul Schreber." *Law Critique* 26 (2015): 117–33.
Gopnik, Alison. *The Philosophical Baby: What Children's Minds Tell Us about Truth, Love, and the Meaning of Life*. New York: Farrar, Straus and Giroux, 2009.
Green, Garth. *The Aporia of Inner Sense: The Self-Knowledge of Reason and the Critique of Metaphysics in Kant*. New York: Brill, 2010.
Gregg, Melissa, and Gregory J. Seigworth. "An Inventory of Shimmers." In *The Affect Theory Reader*, edited by Melissa Gregg and Gregory J. Seigworth, 1–28. Durham, NC: Duke University Press, 2010.
Greiner, Rae. *Sympathetic Realism in Nineteenth-Century British Fiction*. Baltimore: Johns Hopkins University Press, 2012.

Grossman, Allen. *True-Love: Essays on Poetry and Valuing.* Chicago: University of Chicago Press, 2009.

Grossman, Jonathan. "The Labor of the Leisured in *Emma*: Class, Manners, and Austen." *Nineteenth-Century Literature* 54, no. 2 (Fall 1999): 143–64.

Grosz, Elizabeth. "Habit Today: Ravaisson, Bergson, Deleuze and Us." *Body & Society* 19 (2013): 217–39.

Groth, Helen. "Kaleidoscopic Vision and Literary Invention in an 'Age of Things': David Brewster, Don Juan, and 'A Lady's Kaleidoscope.'" *ELH* 74 (2007): 217–37.

Gumbrecht, Hans Ulrich. *Atmosphere, Mood, Stimmung: On a Hidden Potential of Literature.* Translated by Erik Butler. Stanford, CA: Stanford University Press, 2012.

Gunning, Tom. "From the Kaleidoscope to the X-Ray: Urban Spectatorship, Poe, Benjamin, and *Traffic in Souls* (1913)." *Wide Angle* 19 (1997): 25–61.

Habermas, Jürgen. "What Is Meant by a 'Post-Secular Society'? A Discussion on Islam in Europe." In *Europe: A Faltering Project.* Translated by Ciaran Cronin, 59–77. Malden, MA: Polity, 2009.

Haekel, Ralf. *The Soul in British Romanticism: Negotiating Human Nature in Philosophy, Science and Poetry.* Trier, Germany: Wissenschaftlicher Verlag Trier, 2014.

Hallward, Peter. *Out of This World: Deleuze and the Philosophy of Creation.* London: Verso, 2006.

Hamilton, Paul. *Metaromanticism: Aesthetics, Literature, Theory.* Chicago: The University of Chicago Press, 2003.

Hansen, Mark B. N. *Bodies in Code: Interfaces with Digital Media.* New York: Routledge, 2006.

———. "Media Theory," *Theory, Culture & Society* 23 (2006): 297–306.

———. "The Primacy of Sensation: Psychophysics, Phenomenology, Whitehead." In *Theory Aside,* edited by Daniel Stout and Jason Potts, 218–36. Durham, NC: Duke, 2014.

Harris, Jocelyn. *Revolution Almost beyond Expression: Jane Austen's Persuasion.* Newark: University of Delaware Press, 2007.

Havelock, Eric Alfred. *Preface to Plato.* Cambridge, MA: Belknap Press of Harvard University Press, 1963.

Hazlitt, William. *The Complete Works of William Hazlitt.* Edited by P. P. Howe. 21 vols. London: Dent and Sons, 1931.

———. *The Plain Speaker: Opinions on Books, Men, and Things.* London: Henry Colburn, 1826.

———. Review of Shelley's *Posthumous Poems*. In *Shelley: The Critical Heritage*, edited by James E. Barcus, 335–45. London: Routledge & Kegan Paul, 1975.

Hedley, Douglas. *Coleridge, Philosophy and Religion: Aids to Reflection and the Mirror of the Spirit*. New York: Cambridge University Press, 2000.

Herder, Johann Gottfried. "Treatise on the Origin of Language." In *Herder: Philosophical Writings*, translated by Michael N. Forster. Cambridge: Cambridge University Press, 2004.

Hertz, Neil. "The Notion of Blockage in the Literature of the Sublime." In *Psychoanalysis and the Question of the Text*, edited by Geoffrey H. Hartman. Baltimore: Johns Hopkins University Press, 1978.

Heydt-Stevenson, Jillian. *Austen's Unbecoming Conjunctions: Subversive Laughter, Embodied History*. New York: Palgrave Macmillan, 2005.

———. "'Slipping into the Ha-Ha': Bawdy Humor and Body Politics in Jane Austen's Novels." *Nineteenth-Century Literature* 55. 3 (December 2000): 309–39.

Hirschkind, Charles. "Is There a Secular Body?" *Cultural Anthropology* 26 (2011): 633–47.

Hofkosh, Sonia. "The Illusionist: *Northanger Abbey* and Austen's Uses of Enchantment." In *A Companion to Jane Austen*, edited by Claudia L. Johnson and Clara Tuite, 101–11. Chichister: Wiley-Blackwell, 2009.

Hopkins, Gerard Manley. *Poems and Prose of Gerard Manley Hopkins*. Edited by and W. H. Gardner. New York: Penguin Books, 1967.

Hume, David. *An Enquiry Concerning Human Understanding*. Edited by Tom L. Beauchamp. Oxford: Oxford University Press, 1999.

———. *An Enquiry Concerning the Principles of Morals*. Edited by J. B. Schneewind. Indianapolis: Hackett, 1983.

———. "Of the Standard of Taste." In *Selected Essays*, edited by Stephen Copley and Andrew Edgar, 133–54. Oxford: Oxford University Press, 1993.

———. *A Treatise of Human Nature*. Edited by David Fate Norton and Mary J. Norton. New York: Oxford University Press, 2007.

Hunt, Alastair, and Matthias Rudolf. "Introduction: The Romantic Rhetoric of Life." Romantic Circles, *Romanticism and Biopolitics* (December 2012), 26, https://romantic-circles.org/praxis/biopolitics/HTML/praxis.2012.hunt-rudolf.

Iser, Wolfgang. "Representation: A Performative Act." In *The Aims of Representation: Subject, Text, History*, edited by Murray Krieger, 217–34. New York: Columbia University Press, 1987.

Isomaki, Richard. "Interpretation and Value in 'Mont Blanc' and 'Hymn to Intellectual Beauty.'" *Studies in Romanticism* 30, no. 1 (1991): 57–69.

Jackson, Noel. *Science and Sensation in Romantic Poetry.* Cambridge: Cambridge University Press, 2008.

———. "The Senses." In *William Wordsworth in Context,* edited by Andrew Bennett, 267–74. Cambridge: Cambridge University Press, 2015.

———. "The Time of Beauty." *Studies in Romanticism* 50, no. 2 (2011): 309–32.

Jager, Colin. "After the Secular: The Subject of Romanticism." *Public Culture* 18, no. 2 (2006).

———. *The Book of God: Secularization and Design in the Romantic Era.* Philadelphia: University of Pennsylvania Press, 2007.

———. "The Entangled Spirituality of 'The Thorn.'" In *British Romanticism: Criticism and Debates,* edited by Mark Canuel, 264–72. New York: Routledge, 2015.

———. "Shelley after Atheism." *Studies in Romanticism* 49 (Winter 2010): 611–31.

———. "This Detail, This History: Charles Taylor's Romanticism." In *Varieties of Secularism in a Secular Age,* edited by Michel Warner, Jonathan VanAntwerpen, and Craig J. Calhoun, 166–92. Cambridge, MA: Harvard University Press, 2010.

———. *Unquiet Things: Secularism in the Romantic Age.* Philadelphia: University of Pennsylvania Press, 2015.

Jakobsen, Janet, and Ann Pellegrini. *Secularisms.* Durham, NC: Duke University Press, 2008.

Jameson, Fredric. *The Political Unconscious: Narrative as a Socially Symbolic Act.* Ithaca, NY: Cornell University Press, 1981.

Jaspers, Karl. *Reason and Existenz: Five Lectures.* New York: Noonday, 1955.

Jakobson, Roman. "Linguistics and Poetics." In *Modern Criticism and Theory: A Reader.* Edited by David Lodge, 32–57. London and New York: Longman, 1988.

Johnson, Claudia. "*Persuasion:* The Unfeudal Tone of the Present Day." In *Persuasion,* by Jane Austen, edited by Patricia Meyer Spacks (Norton Critical Editions), 286–306. New York: Norton, 1994.

Johnston, Adrian, and Catherine Malabou. *Self and Emotional Life: Philosophy, Psychoanalysis, and Neuroscience.* New York: Columbia University Press, 2013.

Kahn, Victoria. "Happy Tears: Baroque Politics in Descartes' *Passions de l'Âme.*" In *Politics and the Passions, 1500–1850,* edited by Victoria Kahn, Neil Saccamano, and Daniela Coli, 93–110. Princeton, NJ: Princeton University Press.

Kant, Immanuel. *Critique of Judgement.* Translated by Nicholas Walker. Oxford: Oxford University Press, 2007.

———. *Critique of the Power of Judgment.* Translated by Paul Guyer and Eric Matthews. Cambridge: Cambridge University Press, 2000.

———. *Immanuel Kant's Prolegomena to Any Future Metaphysics.* Edited by Beryl Logan. London: Routledge, 1996.

———. "What Does It Mean to Orient Oneself in Thinking?" In *Religion and Rational Theology,* edited by Allen W. Wood and George di Giovanni, translated by Allen W. Wood, 1–18. Cambridge: Cambridge University Press, 1996.

Kaufman, Robert. "Everybody Hates Kant: Blakean Formalism and the Symmetries of Laura Moriarty." In *Reading for Form,* edited by Susan Wolfson and Marshall Brown, 203–30. Seattle: University of Washington Press, 2006.

———. "Intervention and Commitment Forever! Shelley in 1819, Shelley in Brecht, Shelley in Adorno, Shelley in Benjamin." In "Reading Shelley's Interventionist Poetry, 1819–1820," *Romantic Circles Praxis Series,* edited by Orrin Wang and John Morillo, https://www.rc.umd.edu/praxis/interventionist/kaufman/kaufman.html.

Keach, William. *Shelley's Style.* New York: Methuen, 1984.

Kearney, Richard. *Anatheism: Returning to God after God.* New York: Columbia University Press, 2010.

Keats, John. *John Keats: Complete Poems.* Edited by Jack Stillinger. Cambridge: Belknap Press of Harvard University Press, 1991.

———. *The Letters of John Keats, 1814–1821.* Edited by Hyder Edward Rollins. 2 vols. Cambridge: Harvard University Press, 1958.

Keith, Jennifer. "Poetry, Sentiment, and Sensibility." In *A Companion to Eighteenth-Century Poetry,* edited by Christine Gerrard, 127–41. Oxford: Blackwell, 2006.

Keller, Catherine, and Chris Boesel. *Apophatic Bodies: Negative Theology, Incarnation, and Relationality.* New York: Fordham University Press, 2009.

Khalip, Jacques. *Anonymous Life: Romanticism and Dispossession.* Stanford, CA: Stanford University Press, 2008.

Khalip, Jacques, and Robert Mitchell. Introduction to *Releasing the Image: From Literature to New Media.* Stanford, CA: Stanford University Press, 2011.

Kierkegaard, Søren. *Either/Or.* Edited by Howard V. Hong and Edna H. Hong. Princeton, NJ: Princeton University Press, 1987.

King, Joshua. *Imagined Spiritual Communities in Britain's Age of Print.* Columbus: Ohio State University Press, 2015.

Kittler, Friedrich. *Gramophone, Film, Typewriter.* Stanford, CA: Stanford University Press, 1999.

———. *Literature, Media, Information Systems: Essays*. Edited by John Johnston. Amsterdam: GB Arts International, 1997.

———. *Optical Media: Berlin Lectures 1999*. Cambridge: Polity, 2010.

Knight, Mark, ed. *The Routledge Companion to Literature and Religion*. New York: Routledge, 2016.

Koehler, Margaret. *Poetry of Attention in the Eighteenth Century*. New York: Palgrave Macmillan, 2012.

Kohler, Michael. "Shelley in Chancery: The Reimagination of the Paternalist State in *The Cenci*." *Studies in Romanticism* 37 (1998): 545–89.

Kordela, A. Kiarina. "It Looks Down upon Us (Allegorical Fields and Repetitive Errors)." *Modern Language Studies* 31 (2001): 99–129.

———. "Marx's Update of Cultural Theory." *Cultural Critique* 65 (2007): 43–66.

———. *Surplus: Spinoza, Lacan*. Albany: State University of New York Press, 2007.

Kristeva, Julia. *Time and Sense: Proust and the Experience of Literature*. New York: Columbia University Press, 1996.

Lacan, Jacques. *Écrits: A Selection*. New York: Norton, 1977.

Lakoff, George, and Mark Johnson. *Metaphors We Live By*. Chicago: University of Chicago Press, 1980.

———. *Philosophy in the Flesh: The Embodied Mind and Its Challenge to Western Thought*. New York: Basic Books, 1999.

Langan, Celeste. "Pathologies of Communication from Coleridge to Schreber." *South Atlantic Quarterly* 102 (2003): 117–52.

———. "Understanding Media in 1805: Audiovisual Hallucination in 'The Lay of the Last Minstrel.'" *Studies in Romanticism*, 40 (Spring 2001): 49–70.

Langan, Celeste, and Maureen McLane. "The Medium of Romantic Poetry." In *The Cambridge Companion to British Romantic Poetry*, edited by James Chandler and Maureen McLane, 239–62. Cambridge: Cambridge University Press, 2008.

Latour, Bruno. *Facing Gaia: Eight Lectures on the New Climatic Regime*. Translated by Catherine Porter. Cambridge: Polity, 2017.

———. *Facing Gaia: A New Enquiry into Natural Religion*. Gifford Lectures, https://www.giffordlectures.org/lectures/facing-gaia-new-enquiry-natural-religion.

Lau, Beth. *Keats's Paradise Lost*. Gainesville: University Press of Florida, 1998.

Lessing, Gotthold Ephraim. *Lessings Werke*. Edited by J. Pedersen and W. von Olshausen. Berlin-Leipzig, 1924.

Leonard, Gary. "'Without Contraries There is No Progression': Cinematic Montage and the Relationship of Illustration to Text in William Blake's The [First] Book of Urizen." *University of Toronto Quarterly* 80, no. 4 (October 2011): 918–34.

Levinson, Marjorie. "A Motion and a Spirit: Romancing Spinoza." *Studies in Romanticism* 46.4 (2007): 367–408.
———. *Keats's Life of Allegory*. Oxford: Blackwell, 1988.
———. "What Is New Formalism?" *PMLA* 122 (March 2007): 558–69.
———. *Wordsworth's Great Period Poems: Four Essays*. Cambridge: Cambridge University Press, 1986.
Leys, Ruth. "The Turn to Affect: A Critique." *Critical Inquiry* 37 (2011): 434–72.
Lindenberger, Herbert. *On Wordsworth's Prelude*. Westport, CT: Greenwood, 1976.
Lindstrom, Eric. "Between Cant and Anguish: Hume in Coleridge's Imagination." In *Romantic Fiat: Demystification and Enchantment in Lyric Poetry*, 115–38. New York: Palgrave, 2011.
Litz, A. Walton. "*Persuasion*: Forms of Estrangement." In *Jane Austen: Bicentenary Essays*. Edited by John Halperin. Cambridge: Cambridge University Press, 1975.
Liu, Alan. "Imagining the New Media Encounter." In *A Companion to Digital Literary Studies*, edited by Raymond Siemens and Susan Schreibman. Malden, MA: Blackwell, 2007.
Lloyd, David, and Paul Thomas. *Culture and the State*. New York: Routledge, 1998.
Lloyd, Genevieve. *Reclaiming Wonder: After the Sublime*. Edinburgh: Edinburgh University Press, 2018.
Locke, John. *An Essay Concerning Human Understanding*. Edited by Peter H. Nidditch. Oxford: Clarendon, 1975.
Lowes, John Livingston. *The Road to Xanadu: A Study in the Ways of the Imagination*. Boston: Houghton Mifflin, 1930.
Lowth, Robert. *Lectures on the Sacred Poetry of the Hebrews*. Translated by G. Gregory, 4th ed. London, 1839.
Lupton, Julia Reinhard. "Creature Caliban." *Shakespeare Quarterly* 51 (2000): 1–23.
MacDonald, Paul S. *History of the Concept of Mind*. Burlington, VT: Ashgate, 2003.
Machiavelli, Niccolò. *The Discourses of Niccolò Machiavelli*. Edited by Leslie J. Walker. London: Routledge and Paul, 1975.
Mahmood, Saba. "Religious Reason and Secular Affect: An Incommensurable Divide?" *Critical Inquiry* 35 (2009): 836–62.
Malpas, Jeff. "Beginning in Wonder: Placing the Origin of Thinking." In *Philosophical Romanticism*, edited by Nikolas Kompridis, 282–98. New York: Routledge, 2006.
Manning, Erin. *The Minor Gesture*. Durham, NC: Duke University Press, 2016.

Marno, David. *Death Be Not Proud: The Art of Holy Attention*. Chicago: University of Chicago Press, 2016.

Marshall, David. *The Surprising Effects of Sympathy: Marivaux, Diderot, Rousseau, and Mary Shelley*. Chicago: University of Chicago Press, 1988.

Martin, Biddy. "Sexualities without Genders and Other Queer Utopias." *Diacritics* 24 (Summer–Autumn 1994): 104–21.

Martin, Raymond, and John Barresi. *The Rise and Fall of Soul and Self: An Intellectual History of Personal Identity*. New York: Columbia University Press, 2006.

Mason, Emma. "Romanticism and Religion." *Literature Compass* 1 (2004): 1–4.

Massumi, Brian. "The Autonomy of Affect." *Cultural Critique* 31 (1995): 83–109.

———. *Parables for the Virtual: Movement, Affect, Sensation*. Durham, NC: Duke University Press, 2002.

Mauss, Marcel. "Techniques of the Body." *Economy and Society* 2, no. 1 (1973): 70–88.

McConnell, Frank. *The Spoken Seen: Film and the Romantic Imagination*. Baltimore: Johns Hopkins University Press, 1975.

McGann, Jerome. "The Ancient Mariner: The Meaning of Meanings." In *The Beauty of Inflections: Literary Investigations in Historical Method and Theory*. Oxford: Oxford University Press, 1985.

———. *The Romantic Ideology: A Critical Investigation*. Chicago: University of Chicago Press, 1983.

McKusick, James. *Green Writing: Romanticism and Ecology*. New York: Palgrave, 2000.

McLuhan, Marshall. *The Gutenberg Galaxy: The Making of Typological Man*. Toronto: University of Toronto Press, 1962.

———. *Understanding Media: The Extensions of Man*. Cambridge, MA: MIT Press, 1994.

McLuhan, Marshall, and Quentin Fiore. *The Medium Is the Massage*. New York: Random House, 1967.

McSweeney, Kerry. *The Language of the Senses: Sensory-Perceptual Dynamics in Wordsworth, Coleridge, Thoreau, Whitman, and Dickinson*. Montreal: McGill-Queen's University Press, 1998.

Merleau-Ponty, Maurice. *Institution and Passivity: Course Notes from the Collège de France (1954–1955)*. Translated by Leonard Lawlor and Heath Massey. Evanston, IL: Northwestern University Press, 2010.

———. *Phenomenology of Perception*. Translated by Colin Smith. London: Routledge, 2002.

———. *The Primacy of Perception, and Other Essays on Phenomenological, Psychology, the Philosophy of Art, History, and Politics*. Edited by James M. Edie. Evanston, IL: Northwestern University Press, 1964.

———. *The Structure of Behavior*. Translated by Alden L. Fisher. Boston: Beacon, 1963.

———. *The Visible and the Invisible*. Translated by Claude Lefort. Evanston, IL: Northwestern University Press, 1968.

Mesmer, Franz Anton. *Mesmerism: A Translation of the Original Scientific and Medical Writings of F. A. Mesmer*. Translated by by George Bloch. Los Altos, CA: William Kaufmann, 1980.

Miall, David S. "The Body in Literature: Mark Johnson, Metaphor, and Feeling," *Journal of Literary Semantics* 26, no. 3 (October 1997): 191–210.

Milbank, John. "A Closer Walk on the Wild Side." In *Varieties of Secularism in a Secular Age*, edited by Michel Warner, Jonathan VanAntwerpen, and Craig J. Calhoun, 54–82. Cambridge, MA: Harvard University Press, 2010, 54–82.

———. *Theology and Social Theory: Beyond Secular Reason*. Cambridge, MA: Basil Blackwell, 1990.

Miller, Joseph Hillis. *The Linguistic Moment*. Princeton, NJ: Princeton University Press, 1985.

———. *Poets of Reality: Six Twentieth-Century Writers*. Cambridge: Belknap Press, 1965.

Miller, Patricia Cox. *The Corporeal Imagination: Signifying the Holy in Late Ancient Christianity*. Philadelphia: University of Pennsylvania Press, 2012.

Milnes, Timothy. *The Testimony of Sense: Empiricism and the Essay from Hume to Hazlitt*. Oxford: Oxford University Press, 2019.

Mitchell, Robert. *Experimental Life: Vitalism in Romantic Science and Literature*. Baltimore: Johns Hopkins University Press, 2013.

———. "Suspended Animation, Slow Time, and the Poetics of Trance." *PMLA* 126 (2011): 107–22.

———. *Sympathy and the State in the Romantic Era: Systems, State Finance, and the Shadows of Futurity*. New York: Routledge, 2007.

Mondzain, Marie-José. *Image, Icon, Economy: Byzantine Origins of the Contemporary Image*. Translated by Rico Franses. Stanford, CA: Stanford University Press, 2005.

Morton, Timothy. *Ecology without Nature*. Cambridge, MA: Harvard University Press, 2007.

———. "An Object-Oriented Defense of Poetry." *New Literary History* 43 (2012): 205–24.

Mullan, John. "Sensibility and Literary Criticism." In *The Cambridge History of Literary Criticism*, vol. 4, *The Eighteenth Century*, edited by H. B. Nisbet and Claude Rawson, 419–33. Cambridge: Cambridge University Press, 1997.

Murray, Patrick and Jeanne Schuler. "Disappearing Act: The Trick Philosophy of Woody Allen." In *A Companion to Woody Allen*, edited by Peter Bailey and Sam Girgus, 481–503. New York: Wiley-Blackwell, 2013.

Nandrea, Lorri. "Desiring Difference: Sympathy and Sensibility in Jane Eyre." *Novel* 37 (2004): 112–34.

Natarajan, Uttara. "Introduction: Hazlitt's Essay on the Principles of Human Action, 1805–2005." In *Metaphysical Hazlitt: Bicentenary Essays*, edited by Uttara Natarajan, Tom Paulin, and Duncan Wu, 1–14. New York: Routledge, 2005.

Newey, Vincent. "*Hyperion*, *The Fall of Hyperion*, and Keats's Epic Ambitions." In *The Cambridge Companion to Keats*, edited by Susan Wolfson, 69–85. Cambridge: Cambridge University Press, 2001.

Nikkel, David. "A Theory of the Embodied Nature of Religion." *Journal of Religion* 99, no. 2 (April 2019): 137–72.

Novalis. *Notes for a Romantic Encyclopaedia: Das Allgemeine Brouillon*. Edited by David W. Wood. Albany: State University of New York Press, 2007.

Oerlemans, Onno. *Romanticism and the Materiality of Nature*. Toronto: University of Toronto, 2002.

O'Keeffe, Brian. "Deleuze on Habit." *Comparatist* 40 (2016): 71–93.

Ong, Walter. *Orality and Literacy*. New York: Metheun, 1982.

———. *Rhetoric, Romance, and Technology: Studies in the Interaction of Expression and Culture*. Ithaca, NY: Cornell University Press, 1971.

Otto, Peter. *Multiplying Worlds: Romanticism, Modernity, and the Emergence of Virtual Reality*. New York: Oxford University Press, 2011.

Paine, Thomas. *Rights of Man, Common Sense, and Other Political Writings*. Edited by Mark Philp. Oxford: Oxford University Press, 1995.

Panagia, Davide. *Impressions of Hume: Cinematic Thinking and the Politics of Discontinuity*. Lanham, MD: Rowman and Littlefield, 2013.

———. *The Poetics of Political Thinking*. Durham, NC: Duke University Press, 2006.

———. *The Political Life of Sensation*. Durham, NC: Duke University Press, 2009.

Parsons, Howard L. "A Philosophy of Wonder." *Philosophy and Phenomenological Research* 30 (1969–70): 84–101.

Partridge, Christopher. *High Culture: Drugs, Mysticism, and the Pursuit of Transcendence in the Modern World*. New York: Oxford University Press, 2018.

Paster, Gail Kern. *Humoring the Body: Emotions and the Shakespearean Stage.* Chicago: University of Chicago Press, 2004.
Pater, Walter. *The Renaissance: Studies in Art and Poetry.* Oxford: Oxford University Press, 1998.
Perkins, David. "Sympathy with Nature: Our Romantic Dilemma." *Harvard Review* 9 (Fall 1995): 69–82.
Pfau, Thomas. "The Art and Ethics of Attention." *Hedgehog Review* 16, no. 2 (Summer 2014): 34–42.
———. *Minding the Modern: Human Agency, Intellectual Traditions, and Responsible Knowledge.* Notre Dame, IN: University of Notre Dame Press, 2013.
———. "On Attention." *Salmagundi* 194 (Spring 2017): 145–63.
———. "The Philosophy of Shipwreck: Gnosticism, Skepticism, and Coleridge's Catastrophic." *MLN* 122 (2007): 949–1004.
———. *Romantic Moods: Paranoia, Trauma, and Melancholy, 1790–1840.* Baltimore: Johns Hopkins University Press, 2005.
———. *Wordsworth's Profession: Form, Class, and the Logic of Early Romantic Cultural Production.* Stanford, CA: Stanford University Press, 1997.
Pinch, Adela. "Lost in a Book: Jane Austen's *Persuasion*." *Studies in Romanticism* 32, no. 1 (Spring 1993): 97–117.
———. *Strange Fits of Passion: Epistemologies of Emotion, Hume to Austen.* Stanford, CA: Stanford University Press, 1997.
Pite, Ralph. *The Circle of Our Vision: Dante's Presence in English Romantic Poetry.* Oxford: Clarendon, 1994.
Plato. *Euthyphro. Apology. Crito. Phaedo. Phaedrus.* Translated by Harold North Fowler. Loeb Classical Library 36. Cambridge, MA: Harvard University Press, 1914.
———. *Theaetetus. Sophist.* Translated by Harold North Fowler. Loeb Classical Library 123. Cambridge, MA: Harvard University Press, 1921.
Plotinus. *Enneads.* Translated by A. H. Armstrong. Cambridge, MA: Harvard University Press, 1995.
Porter, Roy. *Flesh in the Age of Reason.* New York: Norton, 2004.
Posteraro, Tano. "Nothing but Habits: Biological Time in Deleuze." *Comparatist* 40 (2016): 94–110.
Potkay, Adam. "Eye and Ear: Counteracting Senses in Locodescriptive Poetry." In *The Blackwell Companion to Romantic Poetry*, edited by Charles Mahoney, 176–94. Malden, MA: Wiley-Blackwell, 2010.
Poulet, Georges. "Phenomenology of Reading." *New Literary History* 1 (1969): 53–68.

Rajan, Tilottama. *Romantic Narrative: Shelley, Hays, Godwin, Wollstonecraft*. Baltimore: John Hopkins University Press, 2010.

Reames, Robin. *Seeming and Being in Plato's Rhetorical Theory*. Chicago: University of Chicago Press, 2018.

Reinhard, Kenneth, "Toward a Political Theology of the Neighbor." In *The Neighbor: Three Inquiries in Political Theology*, co-authored by Slavoj Žižek, Eric Santer, and Kenneth Reinhard, 11–75. Chicago: University of Chicago Press, 2005.

Reno, Seth, ed. "Introduction: Romanticism and Affect Studies." *Romantic Circles Praxis Series* (May 2018), https://romantic-circles.org/praxis/affect.

Richardson, Alan. *British Romanticism and the Science of the Mind*. Cambridge: Cambridge University Press, 2001.

Roberts, Tyler. "Between the Lines: Exceeding Historicism in the Study of Religion." *Journal of the American Academy of Religion* 74 (2006): 697–719.

Rothenberg, Molly Anne. "Jane Austen's Wit-Craft." In *Lacan, Psychoanalysis, and Comedy*, edited by Patricia Gherovici and Manya Steinkoler, 184–205. New York: Cambridge University Press, 2016.

Rubenstein, Mary-Jane. "A Certain Disavowal: The Pathos and Politics of Wonder." *Princeton Theological Review* (Autumn 2006): 11–17.

———. *Strange Wonder: The Closure of Metaphysics and the Opening of Awe*. New York: Columbia University Press, 2008.

Rzepka, Charles. "Re-collecting Spontaneous Overflows: Romantic Passions, the Sublime, and Mesmerism." *Romantic Circles Praxis Series* (Winter 1998), https://romantic-circles.org/praxis/passions/rzepka/rzp.html.

———. *The Self as Mind: Vision and Identity in Wordsworth, Coleridge, and Keats*. Cambridge, MA: Harvard University Press, 1986.

Saly, John. "Keats's Answer to Dante: *The Fall of Hyperion*." *Keats-Shelley Journal* 14 (1965): 65–78.

Santner, Eric. *My Own Private Germany: Daniel Paul Schreber's Secret History of Modernity*. Princeton, NJ: Princeton University Press, 1996.

———. *On Creaturely Life: Rilke, Benjamin, Sebald*. Chicago: University of Chicago Press, 2006.

———. *On the Psychotheology of Everyday Life: Reflections on Freud and Rosenzweig*. Chicago: University of Chicago Press, 2001.

———. *The Royal Remains: The People's Two Bodies and the Endgames of Sovereignty*. Chicago: University of Chicago Press, 2011.

———. *The Weight of All Flesh: On the Subject-Matter of Political Economy*. Edited by Kevis Goodman. Oxford: Oxford University Press, 2016.

Sapiro, Virginia. *A Vindication of Political Virtue: The Political Theory of Mary Wollstonecraft*. Chicago: University of Chicago Press, 1992.
Savarese, John. "Lyric Mindedness and the 'Automaton Poet.'" In *Romantic Numbers*, edited by Maureen N. McLane. *Romantic Circles Praxis Series* (April 2013), https://romantic-circles.org/praxis/numbers/HTML/praxis.2013.savarese.
———. *Romanticism's Other Minds: Poetry, Cognition, and the Science of Sociability*. Columbus: Ohio State University Press, 2020.
———. "Social Minds in Romanticism." *Literature Compass* 14, no. 2 (2017): 1–8.
Scarry, Elaine. *The Body in Pain: The Making and Unmaking of the World*. New York: Oxford University Press, 1985.
Schaefer, Donovan O. "Beautiful Facts: Science, Secularism, and Affect." In *Feeling Religion*, edited by John Corrigan, 69–92. Durham, NC: Duke University Press, 2017.
———. *Religious Affects: Animality, Evolution, and Power*. Durham, NC: Duke University Press, 2015.
Schelling, Friedrich Wilhelm Joseph von, and Slavoj Žižek. *The Abyss of Freedom / Ages of the World*. Ann Arbor, MI: University of Michigan Press, 1997.
Scherer, Matthew. "Landmarks in the Critical Study of Secularism." *Cultural Anthropology*, 26, no. 4 (2011): 621–32.
Schey, Taylor. "After Skepticism: Hume and the Political Aesthetics of Romanticism." PhD diss., Emory University, 2015.
———. "Skeptical Ignorance: Hume, Shelley, and the Mystery of 'Mont Blanc.'" *Modern Language Quarterly* 79 (2018): 53–80.
Schille, Candy. "Orsino's 'Solemn Comedy' and Shelley's 'Tragedy' *The Cenci*." *Restoration and 18th Century Theatre Research* 20 (2005): 64–79.
Schiller, Friedrich. "On Naïve and Sentimental Poetry." In *Essays*, edited by Walter Hinderer and Daniel O. Dahlstrom. New York: Continuum, 1993.
Schmitt, Carl. *Political Theology: Four Chapters on the Concept of Sovereignty*. Chicago: University of Chicago Press, 2005.
Schopenhauer, Arthur. *The World as Will and Representation*. Trans. E. F. J. Payne. New York: Dover, 1966.
Schwartz, Regina. *Sacramental Poetics at the Dawn of Secularism: When God Left the World*. Stanford, CA: Stanford University Press, 2008.
Scott, Walter. *The Complete Poetical Works of Walter Scott*. Edited by Horace E. Scudder. Boston: Houghton Mifflin, 1900.
Seaford, Richard. *The Origins of Philosophy in Ancient Greece and Ancient India: A Historical Comparison*. New York: Cambridge University Press, 2019.

Sedgwick, Eve Kosofsky, and Adam Frank. "Shame in the Cybernetic Fold: Reading Silvan Tomkins." *Critical Inquiry* 21, no. 2 (1995): 496–522.

Sha, Richard. "The Turn to Affect: Emotions without Subjects, Causality without Demonstrable Cause." In *The Palgrave Handbook of Affect Studies and Textual Criticism*, edited by Donald R. Wehrs and Thomas Blake, 259–78. New York: Springer, 2017.

Shaffer, Elaine. "Ideologies in Readings of the Late Coleridge: Confessions of an Inquiring Spirit." *Romanticism on the Net* 17 (February 2000), https://www.erudit.org/en/journals/ron/1900-v1-n1-ron429/005894ar/.

———. "Metaphysics of Culture: Kant and Coleridge's *Aids to Reflection*." *Journal of the History of Ideas* 31 (1970): 199–218.

———. "Religion and Literature." In *The Cambridge History of Literary Criticism*, vol. 5, *Romanticism*, edited by Marshall Brown. New York: Cambridge University Press, 2007.

Shaya, Gregory. "The Flâneur, the Badaud, and the Making of a Mass Public in France, circa 1860–1910." *American Historical Review* 109 (2004): 41–77.

Shelley, Percy Bysshe. "On Christianity." In *The Prose Works of Percy Bysshe Shelley*, edited by E. B. Murray, 246–71. Oxford: Clarendon, 1993.

———. *Shelley's Poetry and Prose: Authoritative Texts, Criticism*. Edited by Donald H. Reiman and Neil Fraistat. New York: Norton, 2002.

———. *Shelley's Prose, or, The Trumpet of a Prophecy*. Edited by D. L. Clark. New York: New Amsterdam Books, 1988.

Shouse, Eric. "Feeling, Emotion, Affect." *M/C Journal* 8.6 (2005), http://journal.media-culture.org.au/0512/03-shouse.php.

Silverman, Kaja. *The Threshold of the Visible World*. London: Routledge, 1996.

———. *World Spectators*. Stanford, CA: Stanford University Press, 2000.

Simpson, Christopher Ben. *Merleau-Ponty and Theology*. New York: Bloomsbury, 2013.

Simpson, Erik. "Orality and Improvisation." In *The Oxford Handbook of British Romanticism*, edited by David Duff, 373–87. Oxford: Oxford University Press, 2018.

Siskin, Clifford, and William Warner, eds. *This Is Enlightenment*. Chicago: University of Chicago Press, 2010.

Smith, Adam. *The Theory of Moral Sentiments*. Edited by Knud Haakonssen. New York: Cambridge University Press, 2002.

Soni, Vivasvan. "Committing Freedom: The Cultivation of Judgment in Rousseau's *Emile* and Austen's *Pride and Prejudice*." *Eighteenth Century: Theory & Interpretation* 51, no. 3 (Fall 2010): 364–87.

———. *Mourning Happiness: Narrative and the Politics of Modernity.* Ithaca, NY: Cornell University Press, 2010.

Southward, David. "Jane Austen and the Riches of Embarrassment." *Studies in English Literature, 1500–1900* 36, no. 4 (Autumn 1996): 763–84.

Sparks, Simon. "Fatalities: Freedom and the Question of Language in Walter Benjamin's Reading of Tragedy." In *Philosophy and Tragedy,* edited by Miguel de Beistegui and Simon Sparks, 193–218. New York: Routledge, 2000.

Spinoza, Benedictus de. *Complete Works.* Translated by Samuel Shirley. Indianapolis: Hackett, 2002.

Stevens, Wallace. *The Collected Poems of Wallace Stevens.* New York: Alfred A Knopf, 1971.

Stout, Jeffrey. *Democracy and Tradition.* Princeton, NJ: Princeton University Press, 2005.

Strawson, Galen. "Hume on Personal Identity." In *The Oxford Handbook of Hume,* edited by Paul Russell, 269–92. New York: Oxford University Press, 2016.

Sullivan, Marek. *Secular Assemblages: Affect, Orientalism and Power in the French Enlightenment.* New York: Bloomsbury, 2020.

Taussig, Michael. *Mimesis and Alterity: A Particular History of the Senses.* New York: Routledge, 1993.

Taylor, Charles. *The Language Animal.* Cambridge: Harvard University Press, 2016.

———. *Philosophical Arguments.* Cambridge, MA: Harvard University Press, 1995.

———. *A Secular Age.* Cambridge, MA: Harvard University Press, 2007.

———. *Sources of the Self: The Making of the Modern Identity.* Cambridge, MA: Harvard University Press, 1989.

Taylor, Mark C. *After God.* Chicago: University of Chicago Press, 2007.

Terada, Rei. "Looking at the Stars Forever." *Studies in Romanticism* 50 (2011): 275–309.

———. *Looking Away: Phenomenality and Dissatisfaction, Kant to Adorno.* Cambridge, MA: Harvard University Press, 2009.

Testa, Bart. "Dante and Cinema: Film across a Chasm." In *Dante, Cinema, and Television,* edited by Amilcare A. Iannucci, 189–212. Toronto: University of Toronto Press, 2004.

Tomko, Michael. *Beyond the Willing Suspension of Disbelief: Poetic Faith from Coleridge to Tolkien.* London: Bloomsbury, 2016.

Tracy, David. "Writing." In *Critical Terms for Religious Studies,* edited by Mark C. Taylor, 383–94. Chicago: University of Chicago Press, 1998.

Trotter, David. "T. S. Eliot and Cinema." *Modernism/Modernity* 13 (2006): 237–65.
Tweed, Thomas. *Crossing and Dwelling: A Theory of Religion.* Cambridge, MA: Harvard University Press, 2006.
Vassallo, Peter. "Keats's 'Dying into Life': *The Fall of Hyperion* and Dante's *Purgatorio*." In *The Challenge of Keats: Bicentenary Essays, 1795–1995,* edited by Allan C. Christensen et al., 209–18. Amsterdam: Rodopi, 2000.
Vermeule, Blakey. "Machiavellian Narratives." In *Introduction to Cognitive Cultural Studies,* edited by Lisa Zunshine, 214–30. Baltimore: John Hopkins University Press, 2010.
Vigus, James. "The Philosophy of Samuel Taylor Coleridge." In *The Oxford Handbook of British Philosophy in the Nineteenth Century,* edited by W. J. Mander, 520–40. Oxford: Oxford University Press, 2014.
Wang, Orrin N. C. "Coming Attractions: 'Lamia' and Cinematic Sensation." *Studies in Romanticism* 42 (2003): 461–500.
Ward, Graham. *True Religion.* Oxford: Blackwell, 2003.
Warner, Michael, Jonathan VanAntwerpen, and Craig J. Calhoun. "Editor's Introduction." In *Varieties of Secularism in a Secular Age,* 1–31. Cambridge: Harvard University Press, 2010.
Warren, Robert Penn. "A Poem of Pure Imagination (Reconsiderations VI)." *Kenyon Review* 8 (1946): 391–427.
Weber, Samuel. "Taking Exception to Decision: Walter Benjamin and Carl Schmitt." *Diacritics* 22, no. 3/4 (1992): 5–18.
Williams, Raymond. *Culture and Materialism: Selected Essays.* New York: Verso, 2005.
———. *Marxism and Literature.* Oxford: Oxford University Press, 1977.
Williams, Rowan. *The Tragic Imagination.* Oxford: Oxford University Press, 2016.
Wiltshire, John. *Jane Austen and the Body: "The Picture of Health."* Cambridge: Cambridge University Press, 1992.
Wolfson, Susan. "Gendering the Soul." In *Romantic Women Writers: Voices and Countervoices,* edited by Paula R. Feldman and Theresa M. Kelley. Hanover, NH: University Press of New England, 1995.
Woodman, Ross, and Joel Faflak. *Revelation and Knowledge: Romanticism and Religious Faith.* Toronto: University of Toronto Press, 2011.
Wordsworth, William. *The Borderers.* Edited by Robert Osborn. Ithaca, NY: Cornell University Press, 1982.
———. *The Prelude, 1799, 1805, 1850.* Edited by Jonathan Wordsworth, M. H. Abrams, and Stephen Gill. New York: Norton, 1979.

———. *Wordsworth's Poetry and Prose: Authoritative Texts, Criticism*. Edited by Nicholas Halmi. New York: Norton, 2014.
Yolton, John W. *Thinking Matter: Materialism in Eighteenth-Century Britain*. Minneapolis: University of Minnesota Press, 1983.
Žižek, Slavoj. *For They Know Not What They Do: Enjoyment as a Political Factor*. London: Verso, 1991.
———. *The Indivisible Remainder: An Essay on Schelling and Related Matters*. New York: Verso, 1996.
———. *The Puppet and the Dwarf: The Perverse Core of Christianity*. Cambridge, MA: MIT Press, 2003.
———. *The Sublime Object of Ideology*. New York: Verso, 1989.
Žižek, Slavoj, Eric Santer, and Kenneth Reinhard, *The Neighbor: Three Inquiries in Political Theology*. Chicago: University of Chicago Press, 2005.
Zupančič, Alenka. *The Odd One In: On Comedy*. Cambridge, MA: MIT Press, 2008.

* INDEX *

Abrams, M. H., 14, 16, 161; *Natural Supernaturalism*, 38, 41
absolution, 79, 156, 176; rituals of, 181
actuality (*entelecheia*), 10
Adorno, Theodor, 171
Aeolian string theory, 43–44, 49, 108, 251n35
aesthetic education, 35–36, 47, 237; literature as a form of, 139; new forms of, 40. *See also* aesthetics; Arnold, Matthew; *Bildung;* interpellation; investiture
aesthetics, 21, 24; culture and, 36; Deleuzean, 175. *See also* aesthetic education; art; beauty; sublime
affect: affirmative or negative, 251n32; economies of, 26; ethical relevance of, 168; and feeling, 42–43; joyful, 43; ontological and culture models of, 75; political implications of, 279n72; release of, 137; sorrowful, 43; tragedy and, 213–14. *See also* affect theory; emotion; feeling; sensibility; sentiment; sympathy; wonder
affect theory, 15, 20–21, 27, 36; cultural, 45, 79; ontological, 44–45, 78–79, 176; and representation, 42; Romanticism and, 247n83; two branches of, 42–47. *See also* affect; Massumi, Brian

affirmative biopolitics, 83, 193. *See also* biopolitics; Esposito, Roberto
Agamben, Giorgio, 51, 191
agency, 183–84; laughter associated with, 220
Ahmed, Sara, 20–21, 44–45, 58
allegory, 116; "filmy" allegories of Shelley, 181, 185; and symbol in Romantic discourse, 275n88
Althusser, Louis, 262n30
Altieri, Charles, 146
anagnorisis, 195–97, 204, 209, 211, 278n48; affective, 213; in the space of the audience's soul, 216
anamnesis, 9
Ankersmit, Frank: *Sublime Historical Experience*, 74
anorthoscope, 148
Apuleius, 144
Aquinas. *See* Thomas Aquinas, Saint
Arendt, Hannah, 129–30
Aristotle, 9–10, 105, 168; on anagnorisis, 195; *De Anima*, 130; on schesis, 236; on unity of action, 200
Arnold, Matthew, 36. *See also* aesthetic education
art: Benjamin on, 106; contemplation of, 118; encounters with, 74; as kenotic, 177, 276n96; synesthetic works of, 78; value of, 2–3. *See also* aesthetics

Asad, Talal, 47, 88, 90, 243n2, 252n50, 260n249
atheism, 40, 70
attention, 108, 146–47, 249n123; good-humored posture of, 231
Austen, Jane, 4, 27, 59; "civilizing process" in, 226; comic vision of, 227, 281n25, 282n58; *Emma*, 227; *Mansfield Park*, 220, 224–26; *Northanger Abbey*, 274n75; *Persuasion*, 32, 217–33, 252n45, 281n25; *Pride and Prejudice*, 220; Romanticism of, 225; wonder in, 282n38

Bachelard, Gaston, 24
Bacon, Francis, 276n96
badaud, 31, 142, 155–60, 170, 272n43; in the internet age, 272n45
Barresi, John: *The Rise and Fall of Soul and Self*, 9
Baudelaire, Charles, 157, 168
Baugh, Christopher, 273n57
beauty: exalted, 8; natural, 136; new beauty in what is vanishing, 110; self-interrupting, 137. *See also* aesthetics; sublime
Bell, Catherine, 25
Benjamin, Walter, 23, 27, 155, 157; analysis of the representation of sovereignty in Baroque drama of, 198–201, 204; "The Concept of Criticism in German Romanticism," 106; "Critique of Violence," 207; film as a concise model of technology and modernity for, 171; on "messianic time," 278n45; *The Origin of German Tragic Drama*, 199, 214–15; on the political anthropology of the *Trauerspiel*, 200, 209, 214–15; on the rule of law, 207; Shelley as an influence on, 279n56; "The Storyteller," 110; two typical types of storytellers according to, 264n1

Bennett, Jane, 21, 193; *The Enchantment of Modern Life*, 168; *Vibrant Matter*, 168
Bergson, Henri, 14, 47, 221, 237, 260n251
Berkeley, Richard: *Coleridge and the Crisis of Reason*, 267n59
Berlant, Lauren, 44
Bible, 70, 87–95, 97–98; commandment to "love your neighbor as you love yourself" in the, 139; as a fetishized object, 92–93, 98; God speaks to Job out of the whirlwind in the, 262n23; higher criticism of the, 91, 117; literal view of the, 93–94; literary approach to the, 91–92; true meaning of the, 91, 99. *See also* bibliolatry; Christianity; Scripture
bibliolatry, 29, 87, 92–96, 98, 122; media environment of, 94; reversal of the view of, 100
Bildung, 38. *See also* aesthetic education; mesmerism
biopolitics, 60, 81–83, 198. *See also* affirmative biopolitics
Blake, William, 59, 233; "Moment in Each Day That Satan Cannot Find," 170; prophetic books of, 60; *Songs of Innocence and of Experience*, 59
Blood, Roger, 197, 278n48
Blumenberg, Hans, 243n2
body, 75–83; Coleridge on, 124; early modern understanding of the humoral, 227; humoring the, 226–31; and language, 11, 120; mysticism and techniques of the, 246n67; "orienting a priori" of the, 265n16; phenomenological, 174, 176; and soul, 182
Boehme, Jacob, 263n55, 265n24
Book of Common Prayer (1549), 90
books, 28
Bourdieu, Pierre, 226, 236
Bowen, Peter: "The Tittle-Tattle of Highbury," 226

Brakhage, Stan: *The Dante Quartet* (film), 274n67
Brawne, Fanny, 162
Brecht, Bertolt, 279n56
Brennan, Teresa, 44
Brewster, David, 159
British empiricism, 10, 14–15, 28. *See also* empiricism; Hume, David; Locke, John
British Romanticism, 4, 14, 27. *See also* Romanticism
Bruno, Giuliana, 149
Burch, Noël, 160
Burgess, Miranda, 56, 115
Burke, Edmund, 46, 74; on prejudice, 71–72, 258n194; *Reflections on the Revolution in France*, 70–72, 258n194; on second nature, 71, 74–75, 258n194; wardrobe of a moral imagination of, 46, 71, 74
Burnet, Thomas: *Archaeologiae Philosophicae*, 134
Butler, Marilyn, 218
Byron, George Gordon (Lord Byron), 224

Cambridge Platonists, 10, 20, 54, 57. *See also* latitudinarians
camera obscura, 68, 101, 103, 115, 132, 147–49, 152. *See also* empiricism; Locke, John
Canuel, Mark, 93, 226
Capra, Frank, 254n85
Cary, Henry Francis, 165
Casanova, José, 243n2, 250n10; *Public Religions in the Modern World*, 39
casuistry, 196; in Romantic writing, 279n49
catharsis, 195–96, 204, 206
causality: absent, 100–101, 262n30; appearance of, 66; linear, 171–72; models of, 95; as ontologically "in front" of objects, 73; sense of causality as only a habit for Hume, 65–66, 69, 188–89, 225; vicarious, 73. *See also* Hume, David
Certeau, Michel de, 35–36; *Heterologies*, 266n32; *The Mystic Fable*, 119, 128, 249n3; *The Practice of Everyday Life*, 268n62
Cézanne, Paul, 177, 276n105
Chandler, James, *An Archaeology of Sympathy*, 11, 20, 51–54, 56, 59–62, 74, 254n85; *England in 1819*, 144; on "Ode to Psyche," 144; on sentiment, 53–54
Cheyne, Peter: *Coleridge's Contemplative Philosophy*, 262n27
Christianity, 20, 118–21; authority of, 91–92; blind faith of, 144; doctrine of the immortality of the soul in, 144; doctrine of the Incarnation in, 274n70; as a living faith for Coleridge, 97–100, 266n26; medieval conception of a social body of souls of, 260n249; purpose of, 87, 95; theology and practice of, 142; tradition of, 79–80; Unitarian, 95–96. *See also* Bible; religion; Scripture
Cicero, 246n63
cinema. *See* film
cinematic empiricism, 13–22; of Hume, 36, 61–75; Keats's notion of the soul and, 142–77, 185; of Shelley, 182, 185, 192. *See also* empiricism
cinematic form, 60–75. *See also* film; sensibility
cinematic subjectivity, 15, 61–75, 142–77. *See also* film; sensibility; soul; subjectivity
Clough, Patricia, 42
cognition, 44
Coleridge, Samuel Taylor, 4, 10, 27–30, 43, 47–48, 79, 156, 265n24; *Aids to Reflection*, 29–30, 87–109, 121, 265n16; approach to the Bible of, 91–95, 97, 99; *Biographia Literaria*, 69–70, 95–96,

Coleridge, Samuel Taylor (*continued*) 102, 114; "Christabel," 129; "Confessions of an Inquiring Spirit," 29, 87–109; contemplation of the divine ideas for, 262n27; critique of bibliolatry, 92–96, 98, 122, 187, 192; critique of necessitarianism, 95–96, 102, 122, 192; distinction between reason and understanding of, 104–5; on free will, 102; "Frost at Midnight," 122, 126–27; on history, 70; Hume's philosophy as stimulant for, 70, 102, 267n59; Kant's philosophy as stimulant for, 104; "Kubla Khan," 60; lectures on religion (1795), 101; poetic and intellectual development, 116; reflection in the thought of, 101–9, 263n55; "The Rime of the Ancient Mariner," 29–31, 60, 70, 108, 112–41, 176, 218, 265n16, 266n37, 278n46; on the senses, 269n92; Spinoza's philosophy as stimulant for, 267n59; *The Statesman's Manual*, 70, 92–93; on the Will, 96–99; work on church and state of, 124

Collings, David, 21, 64

comedy: biological-mythical roots of, 217; essence of, 217; as genre of misrecognition, 184; incongruity theory of, 222; Kant on, 222–23; in modernity, 182; and pleasure, 221–23; Schopenhauer on, 222; solemn, 210; as well suited to navigating a postsecular age, 218–19. *See also* good humor; laughter

Condillac, Étienne Bonnot de, 106–7

Connolly, William, 6, 21–22, 40–42, 72; *Why I Am Not a Secularist*, 41; *A World of Becoming*, 175

consciousness: affects and dispositions operating below the threshold of, 236; buffered, 112, 117–18; as an emotional reaction to the intrusion of the outside, 45; experience and structure in early modernity of, 182; and knowledge, 182; savage necessity as a form of false, 191; savage time, 189; and unconscious thoughts and feelings, 219. *See also* soul; vehicular consciousness

contemplation: Cheyne on Coleridge's advocacy of, 262n27; secondary act of, 63; of the self, 15–19

countermodernity, 31

Counter-Reformation, 148

Cowper, William: "The Castaway," 53

Cox, Jeffery, 197, 215

Crabbe, James: *From Soul to Self*, 9

Crary, Jonathan: *Techniques of the Observer*, 147–48

creature, 203–4

Cvetkovich, Ann, 44

Dante, 31, 133, 142, 157, 165, 170; Divine Comedy, 99, 165, 274n67; Keats's reading of, 274n66

Darnton, Robert, 131

Darwin, Erasmus, 10–11

death, 18, 114, 213, 216; and immortality, 46; loss of one's very sense of self for Wordsworth a form of, 153; in the sermons of Donne, 79–80; of the sons of the tyrant, 201

deconstructionism, 20, 23

Deleuze, Gilles, 15–16, 31, 41–42, 52, 60, 132, 157, 169–77, 260n251; *Cinema*, 151, 171; distinction between the movement-image and the time-image of, 151, 170–77, 189; *Empiricism and Subjectivity*, 65; modernity understood through film for, 171–72, 174; perception of creative time for, 174; on the "sensory-motor schema," 171; work on the twentieth-century painter Francis Bacon of, 276n96. *See also* movement-image; time-image

de Man, Paul, 16

Denham, John: "Cooper Hill," 161

De Quincey, Thomas: *Suspiria de Profundis*, 195
Derrida, Jacques: *The Animal That Therefore I Am*, 125
Descartes, René, 19, 182–83; cogito of, 229; *The Passions of the Soul*, 183–84, 269n87
de Vries, Hent, 176
Dickens, Charles, 52
Dickinson, Emily, 216
digital, 49–51, 245n46, 252n61. *See also* media
dissensus, 223
divine providence, 198
documentary film, 50
Donne, John, 79–80; "Anatomy of the World," 88; preacher as tailor of man's soul, 89; sermon (1625) preached by, 88–89
Doolittle, Hilda (H. D.): *Trilogy*, 126
During, Simon: *Modern Enchantments*, 148
Durkheim, Émile, 17, 139

Earl of Shaftesbury, 20
Eckhart, Meister, 119, 266n32
Eichhorn, Johann Gottfried: *Einleitung in das Alte Testament*, 91
Eisenstein, Sergei, 154, 163; *The Film Sense*, 163–64
Eliade, Mircea, 26
Elias, Norbert, 226
Eliot, T. S., 243n5, 244n12; *The Waste Land*, 126, 133
emotion, 20–21, 64; analytic distinction between affect and, 44; and cognition, 44. *See also* affect; feeling; passions
empiricism: atomism of experience of, 103; cinematic, 36, 61–75, 142–77; skeptical, 30, 66, 120, 127–28, 134, 218. *See also* British empiricism; camera obscura; cinematic empiricism
enchantment: glimpses of an enchanted world for Wordsworth, 1; of literature, 150–51; as a "moment of pure presence," 168. *See also* wonder
Engell, James, 11, 144
English latitudinarians. *See* latitudinarians
enjambment, 163, 191; poetics and politics of, 191
Enlightenment, 3, 11, 13, 26, 47, 252n51; epistemologies of the, 147; rationality of the, 126; secularized worldview of the, 199; skepticism of the, 144; soul and body in the, 149
epistemology, 61–75, 147. *See also* knowledge; philosophy
Esposito, Roberto, 82–83, 261n251. *See also* affirmative biopolitics
ethics, 21, 74; of wonder, 31. *See also* philosophy
experience: aesthetic, 120; affective, 4; cinematic transformation of, 67–68; Hume's view of, 257n179; Locke's model of subjective, 101; sensible, 98

Faflack, Joel, 79, 111, 229
faith, 91. *See also* religion
fantasy, 35. *See also* imagination
feeling: affect and, 42–43; of excitement and vitality in the experience of film, 171; of loss, 74. *See also* affect; emotion; sensibility; sentiment
Felski, Rita, 23
fetishism, 94
Fichte, Johann Gottlieb, 14
Ficino, Marsilio: *Platonic Theology*, 10
film: archaeology of, 163; emergence of, 159–60; fantasy of neorealist, 173; history of, 31; narrative-driven, 160; philosophy of, 171; response of the mind to the discontinuity of, 69; rhythm in, 50–51; time-image in, 60–61. *See also* cinematic form; cinematic subjectivity; media; montage

Finch, Casey: "The Tittle-Tattle of Highbury," 226
Fisher, Philip, 2, 168; *The Vehement Passions,* 54
flâneur, 31, 142, 154–60, 168, 170, 275n92
Fleiss, Wilhelm, 129
formalism, 24, 27; speculative, 248n107
Foucault, Michel, 40, 83, 148, 226, 243n2, 260n251
Fournel, Victor, 157
Fox, George, 263n55
Frank, Adam: "Shame in the Cybernetic Fold," 42, 44
Franke, William, 165
Frankenstein, Victor, 121
Frankfurt School, 279n56
Frazer, James George: *The Golden Bough,* 58
free will, 121–24, 216
French Revolution, 20, 46, 70–72, 74, 82, 95, 131, 206–7
Freud, Sigmund, 30, 112, 128–29, 138–39, 141, 151; *Civilization and Its Discontents,* 228; myth of the primal horde of, 201
Fry, Paul, 155–56
Fulford, Tim, 161

Gabriele, Alberto, 154–55
German Idealism, 14, 38–39. *See also* idealism
German Romanticism, 23. *See also* Romanticism
Germany, 91, 247n70
Gibbs, Anna, 58
Ginsberg, Allen: "Howl," 172
Gnosticism, 122
God: and the absolute, 176; becoming a, 77; and creation, 11, 123; Derrida on, 125; direct contact with, 129; eternal language of, 122–23; the father, 125; Keats on, 142–43; presence in the world of, 5; real presence of, 77; Shelley on, 125, 215; sovereignty and, 205; word of, 67
Godwin, William, 185, 190–91
Goethe, Johann Wolfgang von, 147
good humor, 32; cultivation in Austen's *Persuasion* of, 217–33; importance to Hume of, 268n61; politics of, 232–33; posture of attention of, 231; vehicular consciousness and, 32, 268n61. *See also* comedy; vehicular consciousness
Goodman, Kevis, 24, 75, 79
Gopnik, Allison, 103
Gregg, Melissa: *The Affect Theory Reader,* 42
Greiner, Rae, 55
Griffith, D. W., 254n85
Grossman, Allen, 125–26, 170
Grossman, Jonathan H., 226–27
Grusin, Richard, 45–46
Gumbrecht, Hans, 23
Gunning, Tom, 159–60

Habermas, Jürgen, 3, 243n2
habit, 6–7, 17, 62; accumulation of, 66; in the cultivation of virtue, 183; of mind, 63–65, 69; religion formulated by and articulated in the relationships that bind the practitioner in a set of, 236; of self, 65; traditional, 70. *See also* Hume, David; sentiment
Haekel, Ralf: *The Soul in British Romanticism,* 9–12, 14–15
Hansen, Mark, 7, 13, 19, 51, 252n61; *Bodies in Code,* 49, 244n22
Harman, Graham, 73
Hartley, David, 95–96, 102, 122
Havelock, Eric: Preface to Plato, 12–13, 48; and selfhood, 12–13; separation of knower from known for, 12–13, 48
Haydon, Benjamin Robert, 162

Hazlitt, William, 185, 247n76, 271n19; *Lectures on the English Poets,* 273n64; "On Londoners and Country People," 152–53, 155–59

Hegel, Georg Wilhelm Friedrich, 14, 139; definition of wonder, 173

Heidegger, Martin, 169

Herder, Johann Gottfried, 30, 88, 116; conception of reflection (*Besonnenheit*), 30, 87, 106–8; feeling (*Einfuhlung*) one's way for, 92; ocean of sensations for, 88, 108–9, 116; *The Spirit of Hebrew Poetry,* 92

hermeneutics: of restoration, 23; of suspicion, 23

Hertz, Neil, 153

Heydt-Stevenson, Jill, 220–21

Hobbes, Thomas, 19, 106; *Leviathan,* 81. *See also* political theology

Hopkins, Gerard Manley, 96; "Pied Beauty," 125

Horkheimer, Max, 171

human rights, 37

Hume, David, 15–16, 20, 28, 57, 72, 268n61; account of perception of, 256n142; appearances as "broken appearances" for, 225; cinematic subjectivity for, 61–75; picture of Being itself of, 69; political implications of the model of ontology and epistemology of, 70; reception history of, 218; skepticism of, 95, 102–3, 128, 218; as a stimulant to the thinking of Coleridge, 70; as a stimulant to the thinking of Shelley, 188–89; as a stimulant to the thinking of Wordsworth, 62, 63; *A Treatise of Human Nature,* 32, 52–54, 57–58, 60–62, 67, 69–70, 127, 218, 251n35. *See also* British empiricism; causality; habit

humor. *See* good humor

Husserl, Edmund, 76

Hutcheson, Francis, 20, 222

idealism: Fichtean, 3; perennial philosophy of, 38. *See also* German Idealism

identity: contemporary Western secular sense of, 11, 16; deconstruction of, 15; personal, 247n76; philosophic work of Hazlitt and, 271n19; poetry of Keats and, 181; symbolic, 29

ideology, 3, 74; false, 258n197; as taking pleasure in a particular tautology, 213, 216

imagination, 11, 15–16, 35, 52; Coleridge's definition of the primary, 124; control of the flow of the, 87; empiricism as a philosophy of the, 61–75, 102; fictions of the, 69, 73, 257n178; Hume on the, 225, 257n178; Kant on the, 103–4; in literature, 114; and mind for Coleridge, 134; moral, 46, 75, 79; Pfau's account of the active role of the secondary, 124; poetry and the circumference of the, 192; power of the, 193; projective, 54; Romantic psychology of the, 65; Shelley on the, 215; and sympathy, 55–56, 255n115; tragic, 215. *See also* fantasy; soul

immanence: Baroque refusal of any limitation of, 199–200; representations in the nineteenth century of, 199; world of, 200

interpellation, 36. *See also* aesthetic education

interpretation. *See* hermeneutics

investiture, 29; crisis in, 6, 21, 29, 71, 111–12, 117, 140, 264n7; processes of, 236; symbolic, 249n124, 264n5. *See also* aesthetic education

Iser, Wolfgang, 116

Jackson, Noel, 19, 28, 65, 127, 155

Jager, Colin, 2, 24, 31, 38, 40, 185, 237, 265n16

James, William, 26

Jameson, Frederick: *The Political Unconscious*, 262n30
Jaspers, Karl, 133
Jesuits, 148
justice, 37; apocalyptic arrival of, 214; political, 191

Kafka, Franz, 120
Kahn, Victoria, 183, 185
kaleidoscope, 159–60
Kames, Lord: *Elements of Criticism*, 52
Kant, Immanuel, 14, 16, 41, 51, 98–99, 102–5, 126, 139; on comic response, 222–23; distinction between understanding and reason of, 104; limits of our knowledge for, 105; *Prolegomena*, 128; view of freedom of, 104; "What Does It Mean to Orient Oneself in Thinking," 126
Kantorowicz, Ernst: *The King's Two Bodies*, 75. *See also* political theology
Kaufman, Robert, 279n56
Kearney, Richard, 76–77
Keats, John, 4, 27–28, 156, 235; "To Autumn," 31, 169, 177, 181, 275n82; and cinematic subjectivity, 142–77; definition of the "egotistical sublime" by, 169; "elemental space" in the works of, 257n176; *Endymion*, 162–63; "The Fall of Hyperion," 60, 150–51, 155–58, 164–70, 173, 176, 181; "Hyperion," 31, 157–58, 161–62, 164, 170, 173; Hyperion project of, 158–70, 173, 176–77; mediated cultural experience in the poetry of, 272n54; model of contemplative soul in, 177; model of "Mansion of Many Apartments" of, 235; "Ode to a Nightingale," 45–46; "Ode to Psyche," 31, 144–47, 149–50, 177, 181; philosophical form of time consciousness for, 190; physical poetry of, 149; protocinematic poetry of, 142–77; resistance to enlightenment and to Christianity of, 145; theater in the time of, 273n57; "vale of Soulmaking" in the works of, 17–18, 31, 142–51, 257n176, 270n2;
Keats, Tom, 162
Keith, Jennifer, 52
Keller, Catherine, 231
Kern Paster, Gail: *Humoring the Body*, 227
Kierkegaard, Søren, 139
King, Joshua: *Imagined Spiritual Communities*, 70, 253n68
Kittler, Friedrich, 28, 47–50, 130–31, 148
knowledge: consciousness and, 182; in the Kantian model, 102, 105; Kant on truth and, 126; limitations of, 38, 105; paranoiac, 135; poetic, 126; representation corresponding with reality and, 107; revelatory rush of positive, 213. *See also* epistemology
Kohler, Michael, 197
Kristeva, Julia, 79
Kubrick, Stanley: *2001* (film), 60, 171

Lacan, Jacques, 94, 100, 135, 139; "discourse of the Master" for, 264n7; logic of the signifier for, 174; version of the cogito of, 146, 229
Langan, Celeste, 48, 129, 185, 253n61; "Understanding Media in 1805," 50
language: body and, 11, 120; constitutive theory of, 107; designative or "enframing" approach to, 106–7; of desire, 276n105; materiality of, 120; of nature, 123; of poetry, 123; of the private self, 226; religious ideas reformulated into secular and philosophical, 39; and ritual, 36; scriptural, 92; silence of the tragic hero as the most originary and proper sense of, 215; temporality and, 265n24; as a transparent medium of meaning, 78

latitudinarians, 19–20. *See also* Cambridge Platonists
Latour, Bruno, 74, 237
Lau, Beth, 273n64
laughter, 220; Bergson on, 221; Schopenhauer on, 222; surprise and, 220. *See also* comedy
Law, William, 263n55
Leary, Timothy, 266n35
Lessing, Gotthold Ephraim, 91
Levinas, Emmanuel, 139
Levinson, Marjorie, 64–65, 247n70, 247n82
Leys, Ruth, 44
Lindenberger, Herbert, 256n155, 275n92
literary criticism, 119. *See also* literature
literature: eighteenth-century, 254n85; formal dimensions of Romantic, 24; imaginative, 49; Machiavellian reasoning in, 232; as a media technology, 28–29; objectivity and subjectivity joined in, 151; religion and, 7, 25, 29, 119; representation and, 21; Romantic, 24, 38; Scripture and, 29, 113, 140; of sensibility, 52–55; sentimental, 53. *See also* literary criticism; novel; poetry; Romanticism
Liu, Alan, 49, 253n61
Locke, John, 28, 101, 106; "camera obscura" model of, 132, 147; *An Essay Concerning Human Understanding*, 68, 101. *See also* British empiricism; camera obscura
London, 152–54, 158, 160
love, 137–41; of neighbor, 138–41
Löwith, Karl, 243n2
Lowth, Robert: *Lectures on the Sacred Poetry of the Hebrews*, 92
Lumière Cinematographe, 160
Lupton, Julia Reinhard, 204, 279n64

MacDonald, Paul: *History of the Concept of Mind*, 9

Machiavelli, Niccolò: *The Discourses*, 232; *The Prince*, 232
magic, 148
Mahmood, Saba, 3, 21, 243n2, 277n24
Malabou, Catherine, 77, 137
Malick, Terrence: *The Tree of Life* (film), 60, 171, 189–90
Manning, Erin, 42, 280n82
marriage, 217
Martin, Raymond: *The Rise and Fall of Soul and Self*, 9
martyr, 194, 196, 198–205, 209, 214–15
Marx, Karl, 94, 100
mass culture, 157
Massumi, Brian, 45–46; "The Autonomy of Affect," 42, 45–46. *See also* affect theory
materialism, 10; critique of the immortality of the soul of, 20; mechanistic, 20
Mauss, Marcel, 17, 246n67
McGann, Jerome, 116–19; *Romantic Ideology*, 24, 30, 70
McLane, Maureen, 48, 185, 253n61
McLuhan, Marshall, 47, 50, 61, 245n46, 252n61
media: as alternative modes, 47; digital, 49–51, 245n46, 252n61; forms of, 47, 131; mass, 115, 245n46; ontologies of transcription and inscription in, 66. *See also* digital; film; media theory; mediation; print culture; technology
media theory, 15, 28, 47–48, 245n46, 252n61. *See also* media
mediation, 47–51, 65, 115, 140; of the experience of Wordsworth, 64–65; history of, 36, 52, 130–31; of outward scenes for Shelley, 181, 185–91; political control of the forms of, 183; printing press as a form of, 67; religion and, 253n68; Romanticism in the history of, 83; shifts in, 130–32, 134; theorization of, 36. *See also* media; subjectivity

meditation: Donne's meditations of the heart, 88; habits of, 62, 237; Wordsworth's characteristic structural devices for his lyrics and, 146

memory: dual process of judgment and, 139; registration of ideas in the, 68. *See also* mind

Merleau-Ponty, Maurice, 6–10, 28, 41, 75–79, 244n22, 260n251; "Cézanne's Doubt," 276n105; *Phenomenology of Perception*, 76–77; version of flesh of, 176; *The Visible and the Invisible*, 75–76

Mesmer, Franz Anton, 131

mesmerism, 131–32, 134; beneficient, 186; torture and, 211. See also *Bildung*

Milbank, John, 57, 90, 243n2

Miller, J. Hillis, 78, 244n12

Miller, Patricia Cox, 78

Milton, John, 31, 142, 157, 165, 170, 273n64; *Paradise Lost*, 163–65

Miltonic style, 163–64

mimesis, 48

mind: as a blank slate for Locke, 68; continuity of an object conceived as a habit of, 69; and imagination for Coleridge, 134; as a space that holds memories, 69; as a web of memories for Hume, 66. *See also* imagination; memory; self; soul

minor gesture, 211–16

Mitchell, Robert, 115, 186–88; *Sympathy and the State in the Romantic Era*, 187–88, 277n3

mobility, 55

modernity, 2–3, 6, 29, 37–38, 60–61; advent of, 119; buffered subjects of, 52; capitalist, 55, 161; centrality of bodily experience within, 260n251; dissociation in sensibility of, 111, 243n5; and forms of sovereignty, 81; intensifications of the body felt in, 80; mapping and, 268n62; new, 88; normative understandings of, 183; parable of, 120; 133; political and cultural industries of, 51; postsecular neighborliness within, 214; Romanticism and, 72, 125–26; secular, 74, 260n249; strong poems of the post-Enlightenment, 127, 170; tragedy in, 182, 197. *See also* secularity

montage, 154–55, 163, 189; of tableaux, 164. *See also* film

More, Henry, 10, 20, 54

Morton, Timothy, 78; "Object-Oriented Defense of Poetry," 72–73

movement-image, 60, 151, 170–77, 275n88; film running on the principles of the, 189–90; temporality of the, 171. *See also* Deleuze, Gilles; sensibility; time-image

mysticism, 38, 246n67, 249n3, 263n55; fables of, 266n32

mythology, 145

mythopoetic epic, 162, 194–95. See also poetry

Nandrea, Lorri, 58–59
natural law, 182
Neoplatonism, 10, 38
Newey, Vincent, 158
new historicism, 20, 23, 26, 41
New York, 160
Nietzsche, Friedrich, 139
Nikkel, David, 25
Novalis, 23
novel, 51–52. *See also* literature

Oedipus, 195
O'Keeffe, Brian, 61, 73
Ong, Walter, 47–48, 50, 252n61; *Orality and Literacy*, 245n46
optics, 147–49. *See also* technology
Otto, Rudolf, 26

Pahnke, Walter, 266n35
Paine, Thomas, 46–47, 72

Paley, William, 265n16
Panagia, Davide, 66, 71, 78–79, 193, 223, 252n61
paranoia, 128–31, 134–35, 138, 203. See also Schreber, Daniel
Paris, 160
passions, 54. See also emotion
Paul, Saint, 75
Pecora, Vincent, 243n2
pedagogy, 237; repetitive, 265n16
perception: and the emergence of physiological optics, 147; new order of, 158; paranoiac immersion in "blank," 116; primacy of, 76; psychological perception involved in the montage effect, 154; sensibility as an expanded model of, 54; of a time and space released from their human coordinates, 174; the time-image as focused on, 60; virtual monopoly of writing on, 49. See also sensation; sensibility
Peterloo Massacre, 198
Pfau, Thomas: on attention, 231; on Plotinus, 269n87; reading of "The Rime of the Ancient Mariner" of, 30, 112, 114, 116, 120–25, 127–28, 266n37; reading of "Tintern Abbey" of, 64; on secularization, 243n2; on sympathy, 57
phenakistoscope, 148
phenomenology, 26, 76; *epoché* of, 102; of the kaleidoscope, 159; Merleau-Ponty, 8, 77–78. See also philosophy
philosophy: analytic, 156; cinematic, 66; of the flesh, 75–83; Greek, 11–13; idealist, 244n12; perennial, 41. See also epistemology; ethics; phenomenology
physiological optics, 147
Pinch, Adela, 281n25
Pitt, Brad, 189
Plato, 38, 48, 105, 144, 168, 262n27; *Phaedo*, 9; *Phaedrus*, 9–10; *Republic*, 12; *Theaetetus*, 168, 281n30

Platonic order of things, 182
Plotinus, 105, 132–33, 269n87
poetry: cinematographic, 51; ethics of, 21; loco-descriptive, 60, 161–62, 168–69, 171, 272n55; physical, 149; protocinematic, 28, 51–61, 142–77, 256n149; rhythm in, 50–51; Romantic, 20–21, 36, 48–51, 60–65, 125–26, 142–77, 244n12; sentimental, 63–64; tradition of spoken, 48; value of, 126. See also literature; mythopoetic epic; Romanticism
poiesis, 13, 28, 36, 49
point of view, 55
political reform, 208
political theology, 72, 81–83, 130–32, 195, 198–202; medieval, 200; postsecular, 60; shifts in, 134, 199–200; utopian vision and, 175. See also Hobbes, Thomas; Kantorowicz, Ernst; sovereignty
Pollock, Jackson, 274n67
Pope, Alexander: "Windsor Forest," 161
popular culture, 60
Porter, Roy, 11
postsecular: anthropology of the, 182–84; politics of the, 216; religion in the age of the, 116, 236; subjectivity as, 6, 25; terminology of the, 243n8; understanding of the, 4, 21–22. See also secularity
Poulet, Georges, 141
print culture, 48–50, 155, 253n68; and the printing press, 66–67. See also media
Protevi, John, 42
psychoanalysis, 81, 94, 100, 264n7
psychology, 10; child, 103

Rancière, Jacques, 71; moment of dissensus for, 223
rationalism, 71

reading: attentive, 13–14; mesmeric quality of the experience of, 115; pleasures of, 218; projective method of, 30; redemptive mode of, 24; scriptural, 29
reality: imagined, 66; as a natural weave of constraint and possibility, 25; physical, 21, 119; purely virtual, 174; reflection and, 106; representation and, 107; technological, 28
reason: Coleridge on, 104–5; Descartes on, 182–83; Kant on, 103–4; Locke on, 104
reflection (*Besonnenheit*), 101–9, 133; Herder's understanding of, 30, 87, 106–8; and reality, 106; as serious thought in the eighteenth century, 105; sympathy and, 112
Reinhard, Kenneth, 129, 139; *The Neighbor*, 201
religion: as a check to the mind, 202–3; critics of, 35; disciplines and spiritual exercises of the praxis of, 88, 90; etymology of, 246n63; intuition of religion that is beyond the limits of reason alone, 87, 98; and literature, 7, 25, 29, 119; and mediation, 253n68; in a postsecular age, 116, 124; practices of, 36, 39; rational, 3, 37; Romanticism and, 243n8; and secularity, 17, 21–22; the supernatural in, 98; superstitious and ornamental decadence in, 89–90; true, 30. *See also* Christianity; faith; religious studies; spirituality
religious studies, 25–26; affect theory and, 42; linguistic turn in, 26. *See also* religion
representation: aesthetic, 199; affect theory and, 42; crisis of, 140; and literature, 21; readers' powers of, 187; reading texts within a paradigm of, 23; and reality, 107; signification and, 174; of sovereignty in Baroque drama, 198
resentment, 175

Resnais, Alain: *L'Année dernière à Marienbad* (film), 60, 171
Richardson, Alan, 219
Richardson, Samuel, 254n85
Rimbaud, Arthur, 133
Romanticism, 3, 9–16, 21, 25–26, 41, 47–51, 59–61, 73–79; and affect studies, 247n83; crucial questions for, 112; definition of, 72; model of a mediated soul in, 4; and modernity, 72, 125–26; poetics of, 27, 41, 78–79, 108, 170; poets and thinkers of, 72; political debates and the emergence of, 46; protocinematic technologies and, 51–61; reading of, 15; and religion, 243n8; "reordered sensorium" of, 40; role of the city in, 271n24; role of the soul in, 245n32; second orality of, 245n46; shifts in mediation in the time of, 131; skeptical enabling of, 181–216; study of, 38; "subtler language" of, 28; and sympathy, 255n110; and virtual reality, 254n90; writing of, 4, 22, 41. *See also* British Romanticism; German Romanticism; literature; poetry
Romantic string theory. *See* Aeolian string theory
Rome, 144
Rosenzweig, Franz, 139
Rothko, Mark, 274n67
Rousseau, Jean-Jacques, 188
Rubenstein, Mary-Jane, 168
Rzepka, Charles, 44

sacramentality, 2
Santner, Eric, 2, 28, 79–82, 130–33, 139; on beauty, 275n84; on the crisis in investiture, 111–12, 264n7; critique of Deleuzean aesthetics of, 175, 276n96; critique of time-image, 174–75; on flesh, 174–75, 194; *On the Psychotheology of Everyday Life*, 35, 137; on

rule of law, 207–8; on torture, 211; on transference, 264n7; "unplugging" in the social theory of, 208; *The Weight of All Flesh*, 75

Savarese, John, 54–55

Schaefer, Donovan, 25–26; *Religious Affects*, 42, 45

Schelling, Friedrich, 14, 265n24; *Die Weltalter* (*Ages of the World*), 118, 269n84

Schey, Taylor, 278n31

Schille, Candy, 197

Schiller, Friedrich, 18, 19, 36, 53; "On Naïve and Sentimental Poetry," 244n10

Schmitt, Carl: *Political Theology*, 199, 201

Schopenhauer, Arnold: *The World as Will and Representation*, 222

Schreber, Daniel, 30, 112, 128–32. *See also* paranoia

Schwärmerei, 126–27

Scott, Walter, 51

Scripture: as an "aid to reflection," 98–99; appreciation of, 92; as the blueprint and pattern for all meaning, 89–90; Christ as inscribed into, 80; form of, 174; and literature, 29, 113, 140; performance of the meaning of, 100; process of interpreting, 89; reading of, 29–30, 88, 97–100; understanding of flesh in, 79–80. *See also* Bible

Seaford, Richard, 245n44

secularity, 2–3, 35, 37–41; accounts of, 40; blind spots of, 21; buffered subjectivity in, 61; definition of, 4, 39; investiture crisis experienced in, 6, 21, 29, 71, 111–12, 117, 140; modern, 90, 117; and a political medium, 252n50; productive forces of history and, 110; religion and, 21–22; rise of, 83; terminology of, 250n10; universal, 37; varieties of, 24. *See also* modernity; postsecular; secularization; Taylor, Charles

secularization: account of, 38–40; the affective turn in Romanticism and, 26; Benjamin's notion of, 199; as a functional problem, 5; narratives of, 3; processes in England of, 89; readings of, 3, 37; seminal thinkers of, 243n2. *See also* secularity; secularization thesis

secularization thesis, 36. *See also* secularization

Sedgwick, Eve: "Shame in the Cybernetic Fold," 42, 44

Seigworth, Gregory: *The Affect Theory Reader*, 42

self: buffered, 4–6, 15, 28, 45, 65, 120, 123; cinematic, 67–69; contemplative, 15, 177; fundamental misrecognition of the, 217; Humean, 66–69, 225; loosening off of the, 177; perception of, 67; porous sense of, 4–6; quilted, 73; reflection as the faculty of the mind that operates at a deeper level of the, 70; technologies of the, 40. *See also* mind; subjectivity

self-consciousness, 127

self-knowledge, 101, 106, 204

sensation, 16, 35; empiricist account of, 63–75, 133; external and internal, 68; habits of, 65; Keats and cinematic, 160; materialist philosophers of, 44; ocean of, 88, 116, 125, 133; representation in poetry of experiences of, 65. *See also* perception

sensibility: and the affective alteration of perception, 150; definition of, 53–54; discourses surrounding, 54; dissociation of, 2; and dynamic repetition, 59; forms of, 4, 6; of good humor, 231; literature of, 52–55, 72; modern, 131; organic, 62; protocinematic technologies and, 51; sense and, 226. *See also* affect; cinematic form; cinematic subjectivity; feeling; movement-image; perception; sensorium

sensorium, 20, 32, 36; felt presence of, 218; impoverished models of the, 95; pious, 236–37; points of view as the most marked index of an embedded, 53, 55; political shaping of the popular, 183; reordered, 40; urbanized, 155; vital, 228. *See also* sensibility; soul; vehicular consciousness

sentiment, 20, 52–57; moral, 56–57; poetics of, 52; as something felt, 63; structure of society as, 56–57; in the style of cinematic pioneers, 254n85. *See also* affect; feeling; habit

sentimentality, 59

Shaffer, Elaine, 91, 98, 104

Shaftesbury, Third Earl of (Anthony Ashley Cooper), 57, 254n85

Shakespeare, William, 217, 279n64

Shaviro, Steven, 42

Shaya, Gregory, 157

Shelley, Percy, 4, 27, 43–44, 47, 151, 159; Anarchy of, 207; articulation of God of, 125; *The Cenci*, 32, 182, 195–216, 278n48, 280n82; communal impulse in the poetry of, 181; *A Defense of Poetry*, 7, 43, 187; "England in 1819," 191, 278n37; "An Essay on the Punishment of Death," 187, 277n3; "imageless images" of, 151, 170–71, 181–82, 187–88; on the imagination, 215; "Julian and Maddalo," 163; "The Mask of Anarchy," 187–88; mental revolution for, 185–86; "Mont Blanc," 126, 191–92, 278n31; "On Christianity," 186, 251n33; "On Life," 216; "A Philosophical View of Reform," 187, 206–7; "philosophic" necessity of, 181, 187–88, 191–92; poetics of, 60, 175; *Prometheus Unbound*, 31–32, 44, 60, 125, 185, 187, 194–95; "Queen Mab," 190; radical logic of the law of reflection in, 206; redemptive mode of sympathy for, 190; "savage" necessity of, 151, 171, 181, 187–89, 191–93, 213; "Speculations on Metaphysics," 278n31; "Speculations on Morals," 192; tragic imagination of, 185; tragic skepticism of, 181–216; "The Triumph of Life," 60, 165, 185, 188; utopian vision of, 175; on vacancy in political and ethical questions for, 190

Silesius, Angelus, 119

Silverman, Kaja, 177, 276n105

Simmel, Georg: "The Metropolis and Mental Life," 271n24

Siskin, Clifford, 252n51

skepticism: avoiding the shipwreck of, 127–33; divestment from passionate attachment of, 207; empiricist, 101–2, 112; enabling, 191, 208; Humean, 95, 102–3, 127

Smith, Adam, 20, 254n85; "impartial spectator" of, 60; on sympathy, 55–58, 255n115; *The Theory of Moral Sentiments*, 255n115

Smith, Charlotte, 161; "Beachy Head," 60, 170

Smith, Jonathan Z., 26

society: commercial civil, 56; modern industrial, 1; postsecular, 3; sentimental structure of, 56–57; traditional habits and practices as foundational to a just, 70

Socrates, 168

soul: affective fabric of the, 149; as the basis for personal identity, 13; body and, 182; concept of the, 142; contemplative, 16–19, 132, 142; death of the, 11; Greek term (*psychê*) for, 11; immortality of the, 20; Latin terms (*animus, anima*) for, 11; mechanics of the body and the, 149; mediated, 12–22, 31, 87, 132, 142; as a medium for reflection, 10; in Romanticism, 12–13, 245n32, 270n2; as a sensorium or spirit of animation, 11. *See also* cinematic subjectivity; consciousness; imagination; mind; sensorium; vehicular consciousness

Southward, David, 226
sovereignty, 81; and God, 205; logic of, 216; shift in the basis of, 199–200, 209; structural position of "father" within the system of, 202; transcendence of Baroque, 199–201. *See also* political theology
speech acts, 130, 133
Spinoza, Baruch, 19, 42–43, 91, 127, 262n30
spirituality, 121. *See also* religion
Stengers, Isabelle, 42
Sterne, Laurence, 11, 53, 254n85
Stewart, Kathleen, 44
Stimmung, 23–24
subjectivity: in Aeolian logic, 43, 251n32, 251n35; buffered, 15–16, 26, 36, 61, 128, 219, 228; cinematic, 15, 61–75, 142–77; Copernican Revolution in, 99; cradle of, 45; and cultural identity, 44; ecological view of, 227; Keats's lyric, 181; Locke's camera obscura model of, 132, 147; modern, 5, 38; new form of mediation and new form of, 67; phenomenological experience of, 4; role of reflectivity in, 122; Romantic writers on, 112, 251n35; secular, 29, 38–39; understandings of, 59, 251n32; unyielding hostility of the cosmos to human, 214. *See also* cinematic subjectivity; mediation; self; Taylor, Charles
sublime: the Bible as, 98–99; Burkean model of the, 222, 281n25; consolation of the, 172; in the experience of Austen's characters, 281n25; Keats's critique of Wordsworthian or egotistical, 169; "sense sublime" of Wordsworth, 19, 36, 63, 77. *See also* aesthetics
Sullivan, Lawrence, 25–26
Sullivan, Marek, 183
surplus value, 82
sympathy, 55–59; enabling of, 186; imagination and, 55–56, 255n115; moral, 57; natural, 58; personal and political implications of, 192–93; as a potentially disruptive force for Hume, 69; as a redemptive mode for Shelley, 190; and reflection, 56, 112; Romanticism and, 255n110. *See also* affect

Tausk, Victor, 131
Taylor, Charles: on buffered subjectivity, 5–6, 16, 26, 36–37, 61, 112, 117–23, 182–83; *The Language Animal*, 102, 106; *A Secular Age*, 4–6, 24, 36–38; on secularity, 61, 183; on secularization, 243n2
Taylor, Mark C.: *After God*, 17, 25, 102–3, 246n63, 250n10, 253n68
technology, 7, 130–31; broadcasting, 131; cinematographic, 154–55; digital, 49, 131; early empiricist, 147; print, 48, 67, 131, 253n68; protocinematic, 157–58; recording, 131; Romantic poetry as protocinematic, 50. *See also* media; optics
Terada, Rei: critique of Deleuze's notion of the time-image of, 173–75; critique of Keats of, 173; drawing on Hegel's definition of wonder of, 173; "Looking at the Stars Forever," 172–73; *Looking Away*, 156; view of "The Fall of Hyperion" of, 173
Teresa of Ávila, Saint, 119
theogony: epic, 169; mythopoetic, 162; psychologized, 158
Thomas Aquinas, Saint, 236
Thomson, James: *The Seasons*, 161
time, 51, 61; evolutionary, 190; messianic, 278n45; moments of nonlinear "broken," 278n45; narrative, 190; nonchronological, 169; philosophic form of consciousness of, 195; Proustian dimension of, 171–72; "savage" consciousness of, 182; unspooling of, 166, 273n58

time-image, 60, 151, 170–77, 187–90, 275n88; as engine of wonder, 175; experience of the image in itself of the, 171–72; poetics of the, 170–72; political value of the, 174; pure optical and sound situations of the, 172; Shelley on the power of the, 170, 187–89; therapeutic dimension to the forms of experience of the, 175. *See also* Deleuze, Gilles; movement-image; sensibility

torture, 211–13; and mesmerism, 211

tragedy, 31; and affect, 213–14; Aristotelian theory of, 209; characters of, 206; classical, 197; essence of, 217; as genre of misrecognition, 184; Greek, 195, 214; in modernity, 182, 197; traditional model of, 195, 197; Williams on, 213. *See also* tragic hero

tragic hero, 195–96; hubris of the, 214–15. *See also* tragedy

transcendence: immanent, 217; medieval worldview of theological, 199; of the sovereign in the seventeenth and the eighteenth centuries, 199–200

Trauerspiel, 200, 209, 214–15

Trotter, David, 50

truth, 186; subversion by tragic characters of, 214

tyrant, 201–5, 209, 214–15

vehicular consciousness, 19–20, 123, 132–33, 139, 149; and good humor, 32, 268n61; ideal, 230–31; navigation of, 60, 87; overall mobility of, 56; technologic modifications of, 50. *See also* consciousness; good humor; sensibility; sensorium; soul; sympathy

Vermule, Blakey, 232

Vertov, Dzinga: *Man with the Movie Camera* (film), 154

via negativa, 99

virtuality, 55

virtue, 183–84

Voltaire: *Philosophical Dictionary*, 144

Wang, Orrin, 160, 272n54
Ward, Graham, 243n2; *True Religion*, 90
Warner, William, 252n51
Warren, Robert Penn, 265n16
Watkins, David, 266n37
Weber, Max, 139
Williams, Raymond, 14, 47
Williams, Rowan: *The Tragic Imagination*, 184, 213
Wiltshire, John, 220
Wollstonecraft, Mary, 46–47, 72, 258n197
wonder: apophatic experiences of, 224; ethics and politics of, 31, 168; in the experience of textual encounter, 23; good humor enables a moment of, 223; of the human face, 167; intense moments of dislocation or, 219; in joyful affects, 43; motionless, 224, 274n75; political efficacy of, 168; potential of moments of, 175; of pure perception, 165; Socratic, 168–69, 281n30. *See also* affect; enchantment
Woodhouse, Richard, 162
Wordsworth, William, 48, 52, 60–65, 74–78, 111–13, 161, 175–76, 235–36; characteristic structural devices of, 146; concept "under soul" of, 256n155; contemplative mode of vision of the poetry of, 154; *The Excursion* (preface), 152; "I Wandered Lonely as a Cloud," 146–47, 275n92; *Lyrical Ballads* (preface), 62; "Michael," 187; model of poetic eloquence of, 186, 277n24; "Ode: Intimations of Immortality," 9; "The Old Cumberland Beggar," 71, 226–27; physical poetry of, 149; posture of the flâneur and poetry of, 275n92; *The Prelude*, 8, 73, 129, 153–55,

186–87, 246n56; "A Slumber Did My Spirit Seal," 18, 247n71; "spots of time" of, 170, 275n92; "Tintern Abbey," 19, 36, 63–65, 77, 256n149, 275n92; "The World Is Too Much with Us," 1–2

writing: Hume on, 67; literary, 28; paranoid schizophrenic, 131; Romantic, 73, 279n49; scriptural, 28

Yeats, W. B.: "Byzantium," 116, 123
Yolton, John: *Thinking Matter,* 9

Žižek, Slavoj, 81, 94; *The Neighbor,* 139
zoetrope, 148
Zupančič, Alenka: *The Odd One In,* 221–22

Recent books in the series
STUDIES IN RELIGION AND CULTURE

A Language of Things: Emanuel Swedenborg and the American Environmental Imagination
Devin P. Zuber

The Pragmatist Turn: Religion, the Enlightenment, and the Formation of American Literature
Giles Gunn

Rethinking Sincerity and Authenticity: The Ethics of Theatricality in Kant, Kierkegaard, and Levinas
Howard Pickett

The Newark Earthworks: Enduring Monuments, Contested Meanings
Lindsay Jones and Richard D. Shiels, editors

Ideas to Live For: Toward a Global Ethics
Giles Gunn

The Pagan Writes Back: When World Religion Meets World Literature
Zhange Ni

Freud and Augustine in Dialogue: Psychoanalysis, Mysticism, and the Culture of Modern Spirituality
William B. Parsons

Vigilant Faith: Passionate Agnosticism in a Secular World
Daniel Boscaljon

Postmodernism and the Revolution in Religious Theory: Toward a Semiotics of the Event
Carl Raschke

Textual Intimacy: Autobiography and Religious Identities
Wesley A. Kort

When the Sun Danced: Myth, Miracles, and Modernity in Early Twentieth-Century Portugal
Jeffrey S. Bennett

Encountering the Secular: Philosophical Endeavors in Religion and Culture
J. Heath Atchley

Religion after Postmodernism: Retheorizing Myth and Literature
Victor E. Taylor

Mourning Religion
William B. Parsons, Diane Jonte-Pace, and Susan E. Henking, editors

Praise of the Secular
Gabriel Vahanian

Doing Justice to Mercy: Religion, Law, and Criminal Justice
Jonathan Rothchild, Matthew Myer Boulton, and Kevin Jung, editors

Bewildered Travel: The Sacred Quest for Confusion
Frederick J. Ruf

Sacred Claims: Repatriation and Living Tradition
Greg Johnson

Religion and Violence in a Secular World: Toward a New Political Theology
Clayton Crockett, editor

John Ruskin and the Ethics of Consumption
David M. Craig

Pontius Pilate
Roger Caillois

The Value of Solitude: The Ethics and Spirituality of Aloneness in Autobiography
John D. Barbour

Meditation and the Martial Arts
Michael L. Raposa

Between Faith and Thought: An Essay on the Ontotheological Condition
Jeffrey W. Robbins

Exhibiting Religion: Colonialism and Spectacle at International Expositions, 1851–1893
John P. Burris

Taking Responsibility: Comparative Perspectives
Winston Davis, editor

www.ingramcontent.com/pod-product-compliance
Lightning Source LLC
Chambersburg PA
CBHW021943240426
43668CB00037B/525